The Life of The CROW FARM COOKBOOK

That you are now reading **The CROW FARM COOKBOOK** gives us great pleasure. This book began life as a self-publishing venture in 1998 with copies sent to family and friends, and the remainder sold by word-of-mouth. Frankly, after carrying nearly every book to the post office ourselves, we were relieved to be out of the retail business the following year. Our 800 cookbooks had been launched into the world.

With our focus on the production and distribution of the book, we were unprepared for the enthusiasm with which the cookbook was received, used and appreciated. The eight-inch pile of love letters still amazes us. We also received countless telephone calls, faxes and e-mails from near and far. (For a sampling of our fan mail, see the next two pages.)

More than 11 years later, **The CROW FARM COOKBOOK** seems to have acquired a new life of its own. We still get book requests and hear stories about how often it has been used and enjoyed and how important it is to people as "good reading" as well as a guide to cooking and entertaining. One reader told of reading it whenever she needed a "lift." Another was glued to the Appendix, his first foray into a cookbook EVER, according to his wife. Nancy's mother put up photocopies of favorite recipes in her kitchen.

The CROW FARM COOKBOOK has everything from soup to nuts. The brownies are legendary. Paella is dissected. Rice has an afterlife. Celery root gets its due. Meatloaf and mashed potatoes hold onto tradition. Manners get suitable attention, not to mention difficult guests, bad roosters and a wedding cow.

There were many requests for re-printing the cookbook or putting it online. We dragged our feet, still in "recovery" from our truckload of books. Finally, our friend Joey Blum persuaded us that "on demand" publication is possible, and he became our guide. Joey gets credit for this second edition.

The second edition of **The CROW FARM COOKBOOK**
has new recipes for Catalan pasta paella, seviche, steamed cranberry pudding,
two salads plus a food test and the story of Bathtub Barbie.

Royalties from sales of The Crow Farm Cookbook will support scholarships in the humanities, arts & sciences.

You have added so much easy JOY with your book.
— Emmy Smith (1998)

FEEDBACK on The Crow Farm Cookbook

Let me tell you about your book. When Julia was alive, I loved to sit in our kitchen rocking chair and read the paper while she practiced piano in the living room. This grew to be one of my most favorite marital pastimes of all. Well, I couldn't sit happily in that chair after her death until your book! Without realizing it, I found myself back in the rocker, in glee reading your book. Now it's a very pleasant ritual again, sitting in that chair and reading with great delight your anecdotes, observations, recipes and comments, which are very companionable. —Johnny from New York

I've never seen anything like it before and wish I'd had it years ago. I have put so many bookmarks in the book that it is a forest of bookmarks, which rather misses the point of bookmarks, I guess. —Pat from Colorado

I've gotten NOTHING done since your cookbook's arrival 2 days ago. Read read read and feel all the new names are old friends of mine & each animal is one I've fed & petted. —Stuey from Rhode Island

I have read the book cover to cover, sharing it with Trish, in lieu of the "spiritual" texts on Buddhism I also brought. Your book is a very "Zen" book: it is all about savoring each moment – friends, food, work, play, joy, sorrow. The celebratory spirit, the appreciation of each person and place. —Shelley from California

Already this summer I have been late more than once due to standing by the microwave reading the quotes and stories. It will be our Christmas gift of choice this year for all. —Mitzi from California

What a fabulous book! It arrived today and I can't stay away from it. You've come up with a new form of social history here, besides the cornucopia of great recipes. —Jimmy from California

I am reading it from cover to cover. Some of your stories take me back to my young years. I remember the first cake Mother let me make at age 10. —Edna from Kentucky

All the way up to Vermont, I was chuckling over the chocolate cake vs brown rice story. —Mary from New York

The first thing I looked for was Emmy's chocolate sauce. It's there. Of course it's there, it's all there. Ten glorious pages on paella mean this book has profound culinary value. —Don from Kentucky

I know I will be spending a lot of time in many years to come seeking inspiration in the cookbook. —Lisa from Oregon

Our Crow Farm Cookbook keeps wandering off with others who wish to look at it – so I guess if we ever hope to finish looking through it or trying any of the many interesting recipes we'll just have to have another. —Your neighbors from up the hill

Your book is a hit in Spain. Everyone wants one, including Ariadna who thinks she could cook better with your book. —Anuncia from Catalonia

In a few indulgent glances, I have discovered recipes seasoned with unforgettable love stories and gems of everyday wisdom that have brought tears to my eyes and caused me to laugh out loud, surprising my pets. —Caroline from Oregon

I am having to hide the cookbook from myself so I can get my chores done. —Joan from Oregon

Regarding the brownies, Madeline remarked, "I could live on these." We agree. I am laughing out loud over some of the stories, like Comb Boy. —Kate from California

Your book is keeping me awake nights! I'm reading it cover to cover; each page has sooooo much more than recipes. —Renata from California

My marvelous cookbook already has been indoctrinated with spills of coffee and thumb prints. I read it on the way to Canada where my friend Sheila ordered the banana bread – recipe delicious. —Lu from Washington

Going through the Crow Farm Cookbook is like a trip through "Memory Lane." Recipes are like digging through the family attic – you never know what you'll find but surely surprises and delights are there. —Sam & Zi from New York

I just can't put your cookbook down. I've just reached the olivada recipe and am starting on my second page of ingredients I need from the market. —Barbara from California

So I have yet to really read through any of the recipes. We sat up the other night reading stories from your book & LAUGHING. —Amy from Colorado

I haven't seen anything so very stunning and charming and heartfelt in so long, it is truly a breath of fresh air! It's got genuine spark. —Lin from Oregon

Have read and re-read the account of your garden. In 1947 we bought 100 baby chicks & they thrived & the pen was moved for fresh territory. What we didn't know was that wild garlic was rampant next to the fence. Those chickens ate so many garlic tops that we could not sell them as fryers. —Elizabeth from Kentucky

Your cookbook is definitely coming to Germany with us, and I look forward to sharing the recipes with new friends and reading your stories. —Judy & Tim from Oregon

We are wild about your cookbook! —Barry from Kentucky

Dedication

We dedicate this book to those who create home cooked meals
& preserve this tradition by passing along recipes
from one household to another & one generation to another.
Without this spirited work our daily lives would be poorer indeed.

IN MEMORIAM

*We honor these remarkable people who have been important
to our appreciation of food & life:*

Louisa Starks & Winthrop Allen, Mary San & Warrick Anderson,
Bessie Taylor Bankerd, Lois Bankerd, Ann Monks Barry, Gladys Biram Belden,
Betty Higgins Benton, Rachel Macauley & Alfred Anson Bigelow,
Barry Bingham, Jr., Harper Grover Brown,
Frances Rowins & Willard Charles Bruce, Julia Child, Clifton Clay,
Norton Clay, Lu Connolly, Pat Davidson, Myrtle Franklin,
Howard & Edith French, Evagelia Galson, Lee Ella Tipping Garrison,
Eleanor Groves, Sally Harper, Louise Hickman,
Susan Elswick Howell, William Weber & Elizabeth Johnson, Roy & True Kellogg,
Ruth Kammerer Lord, Franklin Allen & Marjorie Rowins Manz,
Mae Neal & Franklin P. Manz, Henrietta Griffin McNeilly,
Ann Smith & John Peabody Monks, Elida Griffin & Owen Ogden,
Emma Ellis Owens, Elizabeth Strong Cowles Partridge,
Ilse Strauch Rothschild & Hans Albert "Henry" Raff, Marian Reed,
Lucille Stookesberry & Edward Holton Rowins,
Marian Bertina Loberg & Howard Holton Rowins, Macauley Letchworth Smith,
Mary Macauley & Letchworth Smith, Margot Stewart,
Christina Davidson & Dakota Stookesberry, Bill Strong,
Eliza McCreery & John Henry Strong, Maria & William P. Tate,
Linnie Doyle Savage Trumble, Robert Waters, Elizabeth & Duquet Waters,
Mary Lucille McCormick Weber, Elizabeth Woolsey
& Alexandra's grandmother
(December 2009)

Table of Contents

Where you are is who you are.
The further inside you the place moves,
the more your identity is intertwined with it.

—Frances Mayes

From her book, *Under the Tuscan Sun*

Max's Poem

SPRING AT CROW FARM

As we pull up in the drive
to borrow the truck
Catherine and John
look up rosy from the garden
where they're turning the earth,
the barnyard aqueous
rising in this new heat
where words swim slowly to the surface.

Perhaps they've been wordless for hours,
their lifting a mantra,
the same peace
I've felt in the candled light
of their table deep in winter,
what falls away
when we join them here
caught in a drift of blossoms,
heady with the scent of ancient lilac
climbing the house.

—Maxine Scates

In addition to her exceptional gifts as a poet, Max is a great teacher and an enthusiastic gardener. She and her husband, Bill, are major animal people, sharing their home with Skip the Magnificent, the follow-up golden retriever to the sainted Stella and the abidingly sweet Sorella. Their family cats include the impressively large Zeus and his smaller, but large-in-personality sister, Lily, successors to the shy, beautiful Lila named for Max's great-grandmother, and the indomitable Hawk.

Introduction

> *To be happy at home is the ultimate result of all ambition,*
> *the end to which every enterprise and labor tends . . .*
>
> —Samuel Johnson
>
> The Rambler (November 10, 1750)

About Crow Farm

Do we find special places, or do they find us?

I was lost while searching for a piece of Oregon property that I could call home. Unsuccessfully trailing classified ads through rural counties, I stopped to ask the way back to town from a man who had just returned from church. "Take the slow route," the man said, "turn here and follow that lane." I followed his advice and 20 minutes later I spotted a yellow farmhouse through the winter trees. Going to investigate, I found a ten-acre farm with a For Sale sign leaning against the mailbox. My passenger that day was a young friend named Eli. As I looked over the property, he fell asleep under a tree — a good omen.

I bought the farm the next day. It was only then that I realized that I had been this way once before, when the trees were full. I was traveling faster and I recalled a strong pull — literally a tug — toward this small valley. I had turned my head, but could see only a blur among the trees as I passed by. I was unable to find that valley again until the day before I bought it. The farm had been for sale only five days. Was this destiny, I wondered?

A house, a barn and eight out-buildings. How did I know it was the right place? There was a gentle feeling that seemed to emanate from the property like a warm glow. I used to wonder if that quality somehow came with the land itself, or if good people had lived here and left some of their goodness with the property when they moved on. As time passed, we came to believe that the people made the difference.

As we dig in the garden, we are still finding artifacts from years past. An arrowhead, pieces of china, a spoon, a deep blue marble, rusted tools and pieces of harness. Lorna Staveland, one of the farm's previous owners, told us that she burned a thicket of blackberries to clear an area on the south side of the house. Too late she discovered a buggy, concealed in the tangle of vines, had been consumed by the flames.

I called the place Crow Farm, but it was a farm in name only. It was going to take a lot more than two words on the mailbox and a man with a gimpy back to turn the property into something worthy of its name. I was going to need help. How does the universe locate exactly the people you need and deliver them when you need them most? It has got to be more than blind luck, of that I am certain.

Dean and Lisa Livelybrooks were the answer. They soon moved into the farm's converted chicken house. They had been married just over a year. He was a Brooks from Michigan, she a Lively from Texas. Dean, Lisa and I became co-farmers and we raised bees, chickens, ducks, pigs, calves, hay and a huge garden. We shared the cooking, cleaning, tilling, planting and harvesting. Eventually they left to pursue their academic and teaching careers.

In 1984 Jim Ottaway, my college roommate, visited the farm and must have detected some essential element missing in my life. He signed the two of us up for a trek to Mt. Everest and off we flew to Nepal. Jim guided me into the Mala Hotel in Kathmandu and there in the lobby we met Catherine who was also on our trek. On the long walks and high passes of the Khumbu, we fell in love and she returned with me to the farm and marriage. Catherine was everything and more that the farm and I needed. Crow Farm before Catherine was, well, certainly livable, but stark. But with Catherine aboard, the place blossomed. Flower beds were resurrected, the garden was expanded, the kitchen graduated from basic to bountiful and the farmhouse from bare to cozy. Catherine's energies, which previously benefited high-echelon corporate America, were at last directed toward more meaningful achievements.

Ten years later Dean and Lisa came back to their chicken house at the farm, helping with this cookbook as they prepared to travel to Scotland for three years of teaching and post-doctoral research. From Edinburgh they moved to Montreal. Finally, late in the summer of 1996, they returned to the farm with their daughter, Zoë, and moved into the double-wide next door as Barbara's roommates. In 1997 they decided to build a house here, making our dream and theirs come true. In 1998 they completed their three-story farmhouse designed in three whirlwind days by Dean's brother Chris. And five year old Zoë worked side-by-side with her dad to install the switch plates for the light fixtures and electrical outlets with her own screwdriver, making her debut as our kind of "cover girl."

We believe in big dreams and we are so fortunate that Crow Farm is a place where so many dreams have come true.

—John Smith

The tides are in our veins,
we still mirror the stars,
life is your child,
but there is in me older and harder than life
and more impartial,
the eye that watched before there was an ocean.

—Robinson Jeffers (1887-1962)

Inscription on an impressive bronze sculpture of a compass at Lookout Beach in Summerland, California, home of the late Claire Chichester

---

About This Book

This book began as an effort to organize our favorite recipes and assemble them in a book for our family and friends, a dream that I've had for more than 20 years. It was laborious work getting started but we did it with the help of our graphic designer friend, Ron Rick, and our computer mentors, Dean and Lisa Livelybrooks. The project inched along for some years, sometimes energetically and often not at all. Somehow we managed to get most of the recipes written down and into our home computer. We even carried a disk to Edinburgh so that Dean and Lisa could instruct us in the art of making an index. We were getting serious.

Shortly after that, Bruce and Faith came to visit and changed everything. Faith is an outstanding photographer with numerous cookbooks to her credit as well as many other books and articles. She got excited about our project and the possibility of having it published. With a mind always working on new ideas, Faith looked at our cookbook and envisioned something more than just a collection of recipes. She came up with the concept of a *Manual of Food, Hospitality and Dancing* and suggested that we write about our favorite tools, our pantry, garden and kitchen. We liked this idea and began a firestorm of production that culminated in the first draft of this book that Faith presented to her publisher along with a plate of assorted cookies from our recipes. Our Crow Farm Cookbook was received kindly, but it was no go. We were unknown in the food world.

So, we sent the book to our friend Liz Johnson who had expressed an interest in the project. Liz had been a highly successful cookbook agent for many years, including shepherding Diana Kennedy's first cookbook. She offered her advice, support, encouragement and an introduction to a New York agent. The agent explained that while our book was "interesting" it did not have the "spectacular" quality required for publication. We agreed with her assessment and mailed her a copy of our *After Dinner Tail* that we had previously removed from the book for reasons of taste. (See our appendix, pages 324-25.) In the meantime, we had enjoyed 15 minutes worrying about how fame might erode our treasured privacy. No, we did not want to do the talk shows but perhaps an interview on NPR. It was fun.

The book drifted to the bottom of our pile until our friend Jim Ottaway asked about it. He then offered to give it to a friend who has a small publishing house in Vermont. This publisher and his staff were enthusiastic but felt that it was not a book that would ever make money for them. He wrote us a marvelous letter explaining the economics of cookbook publishing.

And so, thankfully, we returned to our original idea of publishing this book ourselves for our family and friends. Thanks to Faith and the process she initiated, we have a real book for you and not just a collection of recipes.

Writing this book has given us great pleasure, the chance to look back on our lives and think about important people and places as well as food and recipes. We have come a long way.

Our cookbook includes more than the 200 recipes. We've also written about the farm and our kitchen, cooking and shopping, our family and friends. We give you our household hints and assorted food trivia, our opinions about secret ingredients, fast food, hospitality, manners, party giving, tables and flowers. We tell you more than you ever wanted to know about washing dishes, peeling tomatoes and chopping onions. We discuss our home-grown band and kitchen museum. If you thought you'd heard everything, prepare yourselves for our dog stories, cow stories, chicken stories, fish stories and even wooden boat stories. You'll find a guide to the assorted tall tales under two captions in the Index, Quotes and Stories. We hope that you'll use the Index. We've tried to create a complete and interesting one. Where else could we gleefully bring together Mae West, Fidel Castro and Maximilian I?

—Catherine Smith

IN CONTEXT

No one who cooks cooks alone.
Even at their most solitary,
a cook in the kitchen is surrounded
by generations of cooks past,
the advice and menus of cooks present,
the wisdom of cookbook writers.

—Laurie Colwin
From the forward to her book *Home Cooking*

Joey's Poem

AT JOHN & CATHERINE'S

A nuclear nudist* greets your eyes turning into the drive
The pasture tall and thick
glistening in the scant rays of late afternoon sunshine
John firmly offers his hand
Catherine smiles a smile warmer than the finest sip of brandy
You feel welcome

Gathered around the kitchen island
Anuncia tells of Florida
Maxine about poetry and finding a place to live in Portland
the offer of room sharing with a man of questionable character
and dedication to a not so uncommon epileptic dog

A simple dinner
A gathering of friends
Conversations mix over mouthfuls
Concerns diffuse into a soft glass of red wine
Distractions, secondary to the confederacy of good will

Ruby, clinging to me like a simian
gazes in wonderment from a perch above her unfinished potato
The forgotten obstacle
She settles asparagus into her belly
on the way to a whisper
"Yes, dad, I guess I'll have a little ice cream with my cake"
Later she reports with shining eyes to Nancy
"The asparagus was not from the garden
Tavi read two Pooh stories
Paul had colorful fish on some shorts made of silk
There were eight candles on the cake
We put rubber stamps on the wrapping paper
I wore my pretty shoes
Catherine held me when I petted Ivy
I helped her pick greens for the salad"

Life is comfortable looking across the table out the window
into the receding glow of May light on the hillside
at John and Catherine's

—Joseph Emil Blum

*The "nuclear nudist" is a 10-foot tall image of the well-baked Coppertone girl with a sign
"Don't get burned by nuclear power." Paul Semonin carried this sign in a parade in San Francisco
before retiring it to our barn. • For more about Joey, see page 124.

Crow Farm

RETREAT

*When the world wearies
and society ceases to satisfy,
there is always the Garden.*

—Minnie Aumônier

The Mystique of Place

Like people, places have character. They anchor us and become part of who we are. The mystique of special places can be powerful, formed by a combination of our experience and memory, shaped by people and events.

The formative place in John's early years was a run-down farm called Locust Grove which was rich in history and offered him a rough and ready escape from the conventions of suburban life in Kentucky. The old farmhouse had been a stately Georgian plantation house when it was built about 1790 on a hill overlooking the Ohio River. Visited by Presidents James Monroe and Andrew Jackson, General George Rogers Clark, a frontier hero who won the Illinois Territory for the United States, spent his last days there. Then the farm had come on hard times. Locust Grove was owned by brothers Robert and Duquet Waters, and Duquet's remarkable wife, Elizabeth. The three of them somehow farmed the 200 acres by themselves, one step away from bank foreclosure and the tax collector.

The Waters were custodians of a hundred skills that had kept the pioneers and their successors, the farmers, self-sufficient and independent down through the generations. The family produced its own milk, eggs and meat, grew its own vegetables and fruit, churned butter, made preserves, soap, sauerkraut and sausage. They had their own vineyard and blacksmith shop. In their world, no commodity could be wasted and no resource neglected. To them a hole in a feed sack was the same as a hole in the pocket and required a quick application of needle and twine.

As a child, John played in the hayloft at Locust Grove and looked for spearheads in the newly plowed fields. As he grew older, he drove the tractor, helped harvest the grain and put up hay during the summer months. There was a wonderful rough sort of freedom to life on that farm. John described the kitchen as "a small, busy place. On one wall was a pair of deep sinks where we would plunge our arms and dunk our heads into cool water after coming in from the fields. There were two stoves, one for cooking and one for heat in winter. A cream separator with its stainless steel buckets was also in the room along with an icebox and a cupboard. A partitioned area contained sacks of flour and sugar, shelves of preserves and other provisions. Strung across the kitchen were clotheslines hung with feed sack dishcloths as well as bills and mail to be answered, all attached with clothespins. Along one wall was a small tenement of wooden boxes. This was Elizabeth's animal hospital. She had the touch of God with small creatures. With care, warmth and cautious feeding, she would breathe life back into tiny piglets, chicks and goslings that would normally have been given up for lost. After John grew up, Locust Grove was rescued by the county who purchased the farm and restored it as an historic home.

More than a century after Locust Grove was built and 2,000 miles to the west, Roy and True Kellogg built their beachfront cottage on the shore of the Pacific Ocean in 1910, the year they married. They called their vacation home *The Music Box* that was a long but manageable distance from their main residence in Pasadena. A red clapboard cottage facing the ocean, *The Music Box* looked out over a broad expanse of pure white sand to the water. It seemed like another world, this magic place where my (Catherine's) family loved to spend time as guests of our neighbors.

Crow Farm

The Kelloggs were in their 70's by the time my family moved next door to them. Their five children were long gone but their house was still abuzz with people, visiting family, friends, neighbors and their student boarders. A natural entertainer and a spellbinding storyteller, Roy was retired from a career in advertising and a past president of the Pasadena Historical Society. We loved his stories of the Hahamog-na Indians, the original settlers in the San Gabriel Valley, and the old family movies that he would run backwards for our delight. True, a former Pasadena Tournament of Roses' Princess that counted as a kind of local royalty, loved to shop with coupons and visit with everyone. At *The Music Box*, she always kept us busy with activities, beach combing, walks, games and helping in the kitchen. The house was filled with the Kelloggs' music as they played duets on the piano and sang with fine, strong voices. Their rendition of *True Love* made you believe in it.

The Music Box itself was charmingly funky, with old washbasins in every conceivable corner, two postage stamp-sized bedrooms, a big, square mildewy shower room and enough old couches to sleep an army. Old photographs covered the walls, including one of the Balboa beach front in 1910, just a long open strand, sparsely inhabited. There were piles of magazines and books, shells, assorted kitsch and clutter which spoke of busy people and curious minds. The guest book, illustrated with drawings and filled with anecdotes, told the story of the house, its family and visitors for more than half a century. An old upright piano dominated one wall of the living-room which looked west to the ocean. True kept her fishing pole by the front door, ready for an early morning walk to the nearby pier.

After Roy died, True moved to *The Music Box* full-time because it was her real home. Years later when she died, their children could not afford taxes on that priceless piece of property and it was sold, the house razed and the ugliest possible apartment building constructed in its place. Yet the *Music Box* lives on in my memory with a permanence beyond bulldozers. It was the most enchanting place of my childhood.

About Crows

Not long ago, the local newspaper ran a letter to the editor that went something like this: "Every afternoon about 5:30 I notice the sky is full of crows winging their way toward the hills from all directions. Where are they going and where do they spend the night?" In an astonishing reply from a profession normally dedicated to answers, an enlightened editor wrote: "Some great mysteries of the universe should remain intact."

That's sort of the way it is with crows. On the one hand, they are a very common bird, familiar to all. On the other, crows are ciphers that pique the curiosity. They have been the subject of myth and cosmic speculation since people began scratching their heads about the world around them.

It's no wonder. Simple observation tells us that crows have something else on their minds besides business-as-usual. One day we watched for an hour as a crow walked closer and closer to a new calf until the curious little critter took notice and begin to follow the bird. When the calf moved too close, the crow would take flight, frightening the calf. Then it would start all over. Finally the calf, worn out and bewildered by following his new acquaintance all over the field without being able to get close enough for a sniff, gave up and went back to his mother. We gave up our perch by the window and chalked up another win for the crows.

Crow antics provide unsurpassed entertainment for those fortunate enough to witness them. Lisa's mother, Norma Lively in Texas, wrote us the following anecdote several years ago:

"Last Friday I heard a ruckus outside. I looked out and under the hack-berry tree there was a big gopher snake all coiled up. It was occasionally striking at a crow that was dancing all around it. The crow was making all the moves of a bull. It was scratching the ground with its beak, then pawing the earth with its feet and throwing grass all around. The crow would hop up in the air, then strut around, then paw again. The snake kept its eyes on the crow, striking at times but always missing the dancing bird. After about 20 minutes, the crow got tired and flew away. The snake, which I could now see was 5 feet long, slithered off. It was quite a drama."

From the book *Crows, An Old Rhyme*, illustrated and with notes by Heidi Holder, we uncovered the truth about where crows fly in the evening. "Crows treasure the privacy of their nests and hide them extremely well," she reports. Although we don't hide our nest, we treasure our privacy also, and we honor the crow with the name of our farm.

Eat crow but call it pigeon.

—An Ethiopian proverb

From Michael Hodd's *East Africa Handbook* (page 665)

Crow Farm

The Spring

The main water supply for Crow Farm comes from a spring high on the hill behind the house. That land once was part of the farm, but was split off and deeded to the widow of one of the Hollands, the family who originally settled this farm. Her name was Eva and she had a reputation as one of the best steelhead fishers in the county.

Whenever it rains, it is possible for the collecting pool at the intake to silt up and cut off the supply of water to the farm. For that reason, it is important to make regular trips up the hill to be sure that water is flowing into the holding tank that feeds water to the farmhouse. It was always a treat to make that trip into the woods, especially in the heat of summer. The spring seeps from the bottom of a deep ravine that was blanketed in ferns growing out of a thick carpet of moss and rich loam from the decomposing forest. Even at high noon on a summer's day, it was always dim, damp and cool down there, protected from the sun by a high canopy of alders, oaks and Douglas fir trees. I would shovel out the small pool where the water collects and clean the screen that prevents leaves and twigs from entering the intake. Then I would sit, listen to the sound of the water as it dropped into the pool and soak up the peacefulness of that cool, primeval spot and feel the power and silence of the surrounding forest.

One day heavy machinery moved in. Eva had sold out to a logging outfit and she was gone overnight. In a week most of the trees were down, by the end of the month only limbs, stumps and splinters were left on the ground. By the end of summer, the property had been sold again to a fellow who cut up most of the remaining small trees for firewood and fence posts. He added his own touch to the land by scattering a dozen car bodies and parts around the property.

The spring is no longer the cool, green spot that it once was. Most of the overhanging trees are gone and the moist soil has dried up and snuffed out the ferns. Things can change quickly in this region. Fortunately, our reckless neighbor sold the property to a couple that replanted the hillside and built a beautiful log home, restoring peace to our neighborhood. In another 50 years, the spring may once again be the cool refuge that it once was.

> *When a wise man is foolish it's a big matter.*
>
> —An Ethiopian proverb

The Barn

In this rainy region, things that are out in winter weather tend to rust or rot. That's why covered space is at a premium. That is also why covered bridges were built before the age of steel and concrete — to protect the planks and their supporting wooden beams from the effects of rain. The largest covered space we have on the farm is the barn. It is 60 feet long by 50 feet wide and roofed over with galvanized sheets of corrugated metal. The supporting poles reach 40 feet to the ridge-line. The sides and one end of the barn were closed in with Douglas fir boards by Jack Ledgerwood, a millwright, and his wife Estelle, who sold us the farm. The cost of this lumber today would be prohibitive, which is why wooden barns are seldom built anymore. Today rural areas are dotted with pre-fabricated, colored metal structures that are quick to assemble, cheaper and longer lasting than their wooden predecessors. Those new metal barns have everything but character. For looks, there is really nothing to beat the old-style weathered wooden barns that lend texture and history to the landscape.

There was once an even older barn on this property. It had hand-hewn timbers held together with wooden pegs and old fashioned square nails. Our neighbors George and Lorna lived in this house then. George said that during the famous Columbus Day storm of 1962, which was actually a hurricane, the old barn simply collapsed in on itself under the imploding vacuum. The four walls folded in and the roof split into two parts. All of these pieces miraculously stacked into a neat pile just like playing cards. George torched the pile to clear the barnyard and rich grass now grows where that beautiful old barn once stood.

Our existing barn used to house cows in one corner and chickens in another. Hay bales are still stored in the center and so is wood for winter fires. The barn is a catchall for assorted lumber, piping for the water system, old windows and doors, sheets of plywood and metal siding, and everything else under the sun. The barn also houses the tractor and two inflatable boats, maintenance-free substitutes for two wooden sailboats that used to keep John out of mischief.

One August morning, John was upstairs in the room that looks toward the closed-in, weathered end of the barn. He was on the telephone. He suddenly stopped talking mid-sentence and he blinked in disbelief. There on the end of the barn hung a huge circular disk, eight feet in diameter, with the image of a wild iris painted in purple, white, green and gold. It had been stealthily created by Dean and Lisa during the previous weeks and hung on the barn like a permanent full moon during the night before his birthday. Admired by everyone, this wild iris has become an icon for the farm. You can see it on the cover of the cookbook.

The Garden

Getting kitchen waste out of the house is the crucial first step in making compost. As Faith said, "Compost isn't compost until it leaves the kitchen. Until then, it's fermenting garbage."

We compost almost all food waste in a plastic bucket (for easy rinsing) with a loose-fitting metal garbage can lid (for easy covering). The bucket sits two steps from the kitchen sink in its own recycling drawer under the butcher block-topped island. When we had chickens, we kept a small covered stainless steel bucket for them next to the sink to receive green vegetable waste, stale bread, potato peelings, old rice and cereal. We do not compost any meat or bones. We feed leftover meat scraps and some bones to the dogs and burn the remainder, including fat, in our wood stove, fireplace or outside in a 50-gallon burn barrel. Also, we do not compost onion skins from store-bought onions with black spots, evidence of a virus which could spread to our garden.

We carry our bucket of kitchen waste to the compost pile, a corral formed by a circle of five or six wooden pallets, located under an aged apple tree just outside our vegetable garden. This first step in compost-making involves the collection and initial decomposition of food waste as well as grass clippings and most weeds. We are always amazed by the volume of material that goes into the corral, countless buckets and wheelbarrow loads that condense to less than one-quarter of the original volume. Months later in a second corral we combine this partially decomposed material with layers of straw, chicken manure, a sprinkling of blood meal and water. (The front-end loader on the tractor comes in handy for this step.) This mixture literally cooks. John once covered a dead peacock with grass clippings and the next week he uncovered a fully roasted bird. (We did not have it for dinner.) In about six weeks of warm weather, the compost finishes cooking and is ready to be dug into the garden beds.

We have an herb garden half-a-dozen steps from the back door. It's close enough for easy gathering as well as attractive to look at with its mix of bulbs and other flowers. We grow parsley, rosemary, tarragon, mint, several varieties of thyme, sage, oregano and lavender. In the vegetable garden itself, we grow chives, basil and marjoram as annuals as well as sorrel and freely sown borage. We grow garlic in its own large bed next to the vegetable garden and, in a separate bed, corn.

Our vegetable garden is a 40-foot fenced square about 20 steps from the back door. The ten-foot deer fence (also suitable for giraffes) was a construction of last resort. We finally had to fence in the vegetables, protecting them from deer, which joined local peacocks as our most persistent local predators.

The Porch

A porch is a spare room. It can be the most important spare room in the house if you live in a hot climate and the porch is properly placed to collect any breeze or in a rainy climate where covered space is priceless.

At 327 South Holliston in Pasadena where Catherine grew up in Southern California, the front porch was an important gathering place in summer. Marj, Frank and the girls would sit there on hot summer evenings, perched on the swing and Gramp's old canvas stools. We would drink lemonade and visit with the neighbors, playing croquet on the front lawn and trying to beat True Kellogg, our 80-year old neighborhood ace.

At 711 Fountain where John's mother lived in Kentucky, the screen porch saves her life in the hot, humid late spring and summer months. It became a seasonal living and dining room, a perfect space to make life tolerable. With a ceiling fan creating a breeze even when the air is still and heavy, Emmy was outside breathing fresh air when others are prisoners inside. She joked that she was the only person in town without air conditioning and proud of it. Emmy also used her porch as auxiliary cool storage for food in winter.

The porch at Crow Farm is our most versatile spare room. It runs along the north and east sides of the house with a short cousin on the south side, just outside the kitchen door. It is an old fashioned covered porch, a verandah. It is no accident that the word *verandah* comes to us from India where the pre-monsoon heat and still air demand places that may catch any breeze.

We sometimes sleep on the east porch in summer, setting up a summer nest with a foam pad, feather mattress, real sheets, a blanket and light comforter for cool summer nights. (At night temperatures are usually in the 50°s and 60°s with days in the 70°s, 80°s and sometimes 90°s.) Over the top of our summer bed is an old sail to protect it from pet feet during the day.

Falling asleep becomes major entertainment with two dogs and a cat who believe the point of this is their amusement and comfort. Best of all is the wake-up call of the summer sun's bright first rays on our faces as it comes up over the hills to the east of the farm.

The porch is our summer dining room and sitting room, too. We keep a decrepit rocker, two Adirondack chairs and a table in the northeast corner to catch the breeze. It's a cool spot for lunch on a hot day and a gentle place for dinner with its views across the hay field and toward the barn. By the middle of July, we can usually catch sight of a deer or two feeding in the pasture.

On the south side of the house we have a small deck, opening off the sun room/ green house. On it sits an old style picnic table with crossed 2x4's for legs. This is where we dine on fine nights, looking up at the stars.

Often John grills vegetables, chicken, beef or fish over an open fire about 10-feet away. His first outdoor sculpture began with firebricks buried in sand, around which he gathered a dozen big rocks from around the farm and positioned them in a half-circle with the help of our faithful tractor and its front-end-loader. Then John slipped in the Tuscan grill, a useful gift from Bruce LeFavour, and we were in the business of camp cooking, smelling the fruit wood fire and listening to the sounds of night.

Years later we decided to graduate from bending over that ground level fire and began talking about a "standing barbecue." John scratched his head and looked around the farm for inspiration. What about that old bathtub that had served as a cattle trough in the hayfield? Enter Don Canavan, our weekly helper for farm chores. More head-scratching followed. A small concrete slab was poured. John and Don used the muscle of the tractor and the physics of a big chain to position the bathtub on top of cinder blocks on the slab. Then they filled it with gravel and topped it with firebricks. "Hmm, what about a wind break?" the creative team mused. Soon they perched a section of galvanized metal culvert from Pacific Pipe at the back of the tub. Catherine added more cinder blocks on each side to create two areas for food preparation. Voilá, Bathtub Barbie, the barbecue balm for senior backs. And, yes, form does follow function. (Read how Bathtub Barbie got her name on page 178.)

PORCHING

Bruce LeFavour introduced us to "porching" as an activity. Our definition:

[A verb from the Latin *porticus*]

1. The art of sitting quietly on a porch in a comfortable chair.

2. The opportunity to look around and admire nature without interacting with it directly.

3. A form of relaxation with optional social interaction that allows the participant to enjoy silence, a good book, a good dog or a good conversation.

4. Food and drink are not required but may enhance the experience of porching.

Cool Pool, Hot Springs

During most of the year, the small stream that runs through Crow Farm lives up to its unofficial name "Lively Brook." But during the hottest and driest part of the summer, usually the end of August and most of September, the flow is reduced to a trickle. And it is during these hot, dry months that one most wishes for something akin to the old swimming hole, yet the most water we have would barely cover an ankle.

We explained this to our friend Ryan Collay, a master of rural hydraulics. Ryan found an old wooden tub that needed a home, and he built a base for it down in the streambed. One spring afternoon, we rolled the tub out of the pickup truck, down the hill and onto its new resting place. We then built a small deck around the tub and piped cool water into it from the stream. We finally had our cool pool and, once again, we realized that the best additions to the farm have come from the ingenuity of our friends.

When Paul, Anuncia and their son Tavi lived next door, they used to visit the cool pool every day after work on hot summer evenings. They called it "the beach" and Tavi would float there in his Mickey Mouse inner tube.

And the hot springs? The Turtle, a 1950 International bread truck, has leaned against a tree in the upper pasture since John bought the farm in 1980. In the Turtle is a wood stove, donated by Barry Bingham, a Kentucky sharpshooter. The truck also has a kerosene lamp and cedar benches, built one Christmas Day by our friend Bill White. When visitors wish to purge themselves of noxious poisons accumulated from modern living or if they just want to get overheated, the stove is lit. As the temperature in the bread truck rises, the occupants as well as the Turtle's springs get hotter and hotter. Fortunately cool relief is just a plunge away.

The great things in this world are not necessarily practical.

—John Smith

Former owner of two wooden boats.

Crow Farm

The Farm Year

The farm always hands us our next assignment. If the cows get out, the fences need repair. When a storm goes through, there may be days of chain saw work removing downed trees and branches. A big freeze and we scramble to keep the water running and the wood stove hot. When a geyser appears in the front yard, the underground water pipes need to be dug up and repaired. In spite of these unexpected demands, there are some events that identify our seasons.

About the size of a knuckle, colored parrot green, trimmed in neon yellow with black highlights, our local designer frogs remind us that spring is on its way. They live in the wetland zones of our hayfield. Occasionally we'll find one sitting on a rhododendron leaf or even perched on an apple in mid-August. But mostly we know them for their amazing sounds in winter.

It begins with one barely audible croak just as you are drifting off to sleep on a December or January night. The next night you hear two or three and, by the end of the week, there's no mistaking it. The frogs are up! The noise builds frog by frog until at the height of their passionate mating we are engulfed by a thundering night-time chorus of croaks. Cold weather silences them temporarily and mild weather encourages them until their mating season finally wanes with the beginning of spring. According to local tradition, we should plant peas as soon as "the frogs begin to sing" or by Lincoln's birthday, February 12. For potatoes, the planting date is St. Patrick's Day, March 17.

We identify the beginning of spring with the bloom of the first daffodils, usually in mid-February. If we haven't done so already, that's when we get out our seed catalogs and start planning our summer garden. We also turn over the first beds in the garden to plant peas, greens and hardy lettuce. We gear up the sun room, too, with its two heated sand boxes and overhead grow lights, providing a cozy atmosphere to start our tomatoes, peppers and other plants.

We have had surprise snows in February, including the Siberian Express storm which plunged us close to zero degrees Fahrenheit for about two weeks one year. We also had snow on Valentine's Day in 1995. Most years we look forward to the week of false spring in February, the sort of gorgeous, clear 60° weather that gets everyone outdoors and dreaming of fresh corn. That's when we eat our first lunch outside.

We also know it is spring because the grass starts shooting up, challenging John to keep it mowed between rain showers. Its color — that intense blue green — fills the countryside with a lush softness, the perfect backdrop for the new lambs and calves that fill our neighbors' pastures. In nearby Eugene we admire the telltale pink litter of cherry blossoms on certain streets and the canopy of our own blooming fruit trees, cherry, pear, plum and apple.

Summer begins for us after the danger of frost has passed in early June when we transplant our tomatoes and peppers into the garden. By then the tomato plants, started from seeds in the sunroom in late February, are several feet tall and, if we're lucky, the early varieties have produced a few tomatoes.

One morning, usually in late June, we'll notice that the goldfinches have arrived. There they are, perched by the hundreds on the swaying heads of nearly ripe pasture grass in our hayfield. If you move too close, they'll startle, fly off and then settle on the overhead wires like a long row of golden acrobats. They flutter over our field for several weeks while feeding on the ripening grain. We marvel at their stunt flying and celebrate the arrival of summer.

At the end of August, we begin to notice a change in the air, a cool nip on some mornings and evenings that call for a sweater. Sometime between mid-September and mid-October we know it's officially fall when we rush out late one afternoon to rescue the last tomatoes and basil from the first frost. In good years, like 1995, 1996 and 1997, we fill every available basket with ripe or ripening tomatoes and one or two five-gallon buckets with the uprooted basil plants. Then we set to work. We can feel the change of season in the air and see it as the canning jars and freezer bags pile up in the kitchen.

We know for sure that it's winter when Eve, our cat, barely moves from her inside napping spots — the living-room couch, the kitchen chair and the upstairs bed. She, like us, retreats inside for more of each shortening day. We also know that it's very cold weather — maybe 20° outside — when we see Eve cozying up to the wood stove, napping as close as she can get to its steady warmth.

The winter of 1995-96 was memorable: windy, wet, frozen and snowy. We had record winds of over 100 miles an hour off the coast in December and record rainfall in November, December and January. Then the big February storm hit during which we had 5 inches of rain in 30 hours resulting in the worst flooding in decades. Our normally placid Coyote Creek jumped its banks by more than the length of a football field. We were grateful to be in a house well situated on high ground. Then there was an ice storm followed by an unexpectedly heavy snowstorm. Although the record-breaking 76° on Easter Sunday was welcome indeed, the rains were far from over. We wound up 1996 with an all time high of 101.93 inches of rain, more than a fathom as our local newspaper pointed out and enough to overwhelm the new fangled rain measuring system installed at our airport weather station. Sometimes when it rains it just pours.

Farm Spirits

A friendly black and white mongrel greeted John in the driveway the day he came to look at the farm. His name was Dog and it turned out he was part of a package deal that included the farm and a cat. He proved to be such an important creature that his name was upgraded to Doggus. We'll never forget how he cared for the sick pigs, tried to talk when he got excited and loved swimming in the Russian River on a trip to California.

Doggus was but one of many spirits who have shared Crow Farm with us. Lil' Bit, also called Bits, picked up John on the Oregon coast one day, hitchhiking with style. A blond Pomeranian-cocker mix, John told people she was a miniature golden retriever. A Shelley Winters look-a-like, as our daughter Emily described her, was perhaps the most popular dog of all time.

The gray Manx named Momma Kitty came with the farm. Her headquarters was the barn and her mission was overseeing everything. Then Fort Rock, nearly dead from starvation and exposure, found us at dusk one wintry January afternoon at an extinct volcano in Eastern Oregon that provided her name. This sweet natured cat would walk with us down the road for a mile or two, always perfectly attired in her black and white fur tuxedo.

Named for a favorite neighbor, Snyder found us one summer morning outside the local cafe. A calico kitten with ferociously independent ways, she taught the new puppy, Lively, the ways and wiles of inter-species play. After Snyder disappeared, Spike, Harper and Polly passed through. Beautiful Eve is the queen now and we think she may be Fort Rock re-incarnated in gray and white.

Lively succeeded Bits as our farm dog and a more comic, sweet and nutty creature you can't imagine. He was a border collie with a black and white coat of punkish fur and wild amber eyes. Over-sensitive to sounds, he went nuts over sawing, violin playing and peeling scotch tape. His little sister Ivy, also a border collie, found us while cruising the side of the interstate. It was love at first sight. She was as beautiful and compliant as her brother is unruly and stubborn. Their games were our major form of entertainment.

We pay tribute to these great spirits for their companionship and inspiration. They have enriched our lives.

WISHFUL THINKING

I know it wouldn't work out, but I wish I could marry Ivy.

—Zoë Livelybrooks (Age 5)
Expressing love for her best friend, our border collie.

Plastic Owls & Gum Balls:
Battling the Pervasive Predators

Karen suggested something that would catch the breezes and flutter. I shredded fuchsia-colored rip-stop nylon to make a dozen streamers that I hung from the porch roof with thumbtacks. My sister recommended a fake owl. I bought two at the hardware store and hung them in strategic locations on our front porch. I hoped for the best. Secretly I was counting on our cat to do the trick. But, no luck. The swallows arrived and began to case the house like real estate experts. At the sight of them, I dashed out the back door to find something more substantial than streamers and owls. I scoured the shop for scrap pieces of 2x4 lumber and the woodshed for suitable kindling. I covered the lintels of our windows and doors with precarious piles.

On the front porch they built one nest attached to my jury-rigged wood pile inches from the glassy-eyed gaze of the fake owl. At the other end of that porch, behind my beautifully rippling fuchsia streamers, they built not only a second nest but also a structure that looked like a retaining wall. It seems to serve no purpose other than to remind me who is in charge here.

And so I ceded victory to the swallows on the front porch, abandoning my futile hope of protecting our newly painted house from these annual visitors. They graciously ceded me the back porch. Then Barbara explained that these creatures eat their weight in mosquitoes each day. Thanks to them our porch is a mosquito-free zone.

In another battle, I bought a lot of Juicy Fruit chewing gum — enough for a football team for a whole season. I carried my gum outside one Saturday morning, donned heavy leather garden gloves, kneeled down and set to work with Dean's grandmother's instructions in mind. My gloved hands struggled to remove more than 100 paper wrappers with not-quite-operating-room efficiency. After assembling a truly impressive pile of gum sticks, I wadded them into walnut-sized balls. Then, hoping against hope that no one would drive up and ask me to explain what I was doing, I crawled around on my hands and knees, stuffing a gum ball down each of our plentiful gopher holes. And then I waited . . . . and waited . . . . and waited for the miracle of no more gophers. I'm still waiting and it's been more than a decade.

After that failure, Lisa gave us a deadly looking gopher trap, the same model her father had used successfully in his Texas garden. What Lisa forgot to explain was that we needed an engineering degree from Texas A & M to operate this contraption safely. I stared at the deadly looking spikes and finally concluded that ten fingers can do more in the garden than even our gopher population can undo. So, we retired the trap.

I once asked Nicholas to drill holes in Life Buoy soap and hang the bars with baling twine from our apple trees in order to keep the deer away. That did not work any better than the gum balls, but at least it added to my reputation as a clean gardener and Nicholas' reputation as a dutiful son.

And then there was the bat that took control of our bedroom one summer night, driving us to sanctuary under the sheets. We finally overcame our primal fears and captured the bat — rather cleverly, we thought — in a basket which John then carried downstairs to release into the summer night. After talking with Karen and Tenold, we learned of the great benefits of bats that quickly clean one's house of mosquitoes on their nocturnal visits. We now avoid bat alerts and sleep through their welcome house cleaning chores.

I once scared our dog Lil' Bit nearly to death by swatting flies so aggressively that pieces of our bedroom ceiling began raining down on us. We also cooked a marauding peacock in homemade plum wine.

THINGS TO CROW ABOUT

Crows are moving uptown by the tens of thousands, taking up residence around shopping malls, city parks, golf courses and other metropolitan sites. Apparently the all-night lights at places such as shopping malls allow the crows to spot predators more easily. As a result, they are flourishing in very un-rural settings.

Researchers also report on the complex language patterns of crows as well as their cooperative breeding patterns that are highly unusual among birds. Crow families of as many as 15 birds live together with young crows helping their parents and siblings to raise the new hatchlings.

Crows play games, too, including tug of war, swinging from tree branches like monkeys and a kind of fetch with dropped sticks. There was also a report of a crow rolling down a grass slope on a plastic cup, a sort of avian log-rolling. And then there's the crow child who lived about three quarters of a mile from her parents and dropped in on the family nest every Friday afternoon for a visit.

—From an article by Jane E. Brody

Sent by Jim Ottaway (*The New York Times*, May 27, 1997)

More about Crow Farm

They drove up in an RV, parked and knocked on the door. He introduced himself, Hugh Holland and his wife, Alice. He explained that he had grown up here, the youngest of four sons whose parents had built our house in 1905 on their 100-acre hops farm. Hugh and Alice had just attended the Crow Old-timers Grange picnic and stopped by because they had heard through the grapevine that we were interested in learning about the house and their family.

It turned out that the grapevine involved our friend Myrtle Franklin who then lived in southern Oregon where she had met a relative of the Hollands at a meeting in Grant's Pass. They got talking and the subject turned to Crow Farm where Myrt had visited several times. She reported our interest in the Holland family that was then transmitted to a nephew here in Lane County who passed it along to his Uncle Hugh in Portland. And so Hugh brought his wife to see where he had grown up and to show us the album of family photos.

We ate breakfast together the next morning and then Hugh led us on a tour of the farm, telling us of his mother's garden located in what was now our hayfield, the outhouse sited on the hillside adjacent to our vegetable garden, his parents' bedroom downstairs in what was then John's office and the squeaky step on the stairs that the boys avoided assiduously when sneaking in late at night. Mr. and Mrs. Holland, schoolteachers who met in this area, were a handsome couple and just the kind of people that we imagined had lived here. Hugh confirmed that the family had indeed been a happy one and, for more than 40 years, their happiness filled this house, a legacy of which we are the beneficiaries.

CHILD PRODIGY

Lively was the most eccentric, stubborn and lovable dog of all time. We took him to obedience school and he obeyed perfectly when the teacher was watching him, otherwise not at all. He's an expressive character, trying to talk and overwhelming those he loves with his curmudgeonly affection.

Lively showed an early aptitude for piano playing in water. He would stand with his back half firmly planted on shore, beating out a syncopated tune with his front paws in gently lapping water. His aquatic enchantment did not include swimming.

The Kitchen

Eve, looking like Kilroy the cat, hangs from her front claws peering in the window of the back door. Lively hurls himself against the door with an unmistakable thud while Ivy stands politely nearby. John is seated at the table, shoes under it, papers spread in front of him, writing letters and postcards. He opens the door, mopping muddy paws as the "bumbies" come racing in and head for their favorite spots, Lively on the rug in front of the door, Ivy under the windows and Eve in the easy chair. Catherine is chopping red peppers and considering how to cook chicken tonight. It's dinner-time and everyone wants to be in the kitchen.

Kitchen Keeping

Our old kitchen was jury-rigged. It had evolved over 85 years in response to the needs of half a dozen different families. It had one electrical outlet. The window over the sink was painted shut. The metal modular sink unit was rusting, the rust covered with contact paper. The fan over the cook top had shut down in a previous life. In order to keep from bumping our heads, we had taken off the cupboard doors making the shelves look like a jungle gym. When we finally removed the cook top, the plywood base was charcoal. Two people were hazards to each other in the small central workspace, a square that was four-and-a-half feet on each side. There was only our wood stove for heat and two bulbs for light. Our chest freezer was outside in the carport. Things were crowded and poorly organized. The old kitchen was cozily eccentric, and its ad-libbed design functioned on a basic level. There was room for improvement, but we did not want to lose the feeling of the room.

We slowly began planning a new kitchen. We got out pencils and graph paper, we made wish lists of desired features, we studied other kitchens as well as books on kitchen design. We talked to everyone we knew and solicited their advice. Over several years we synthesized what we had heard and seen, clarified our ideas in writing and drew up our own preliminary design.

Our wish list included more space, good light and heat, multiple electrical outlets, new plumbing, more storage, including drawers and a pantry, larger work areas, gas for cooking, good ventilation, a place inside for the freezer and an area for compost and recycling. Our friends insisted that we use all the space available to us, dismissing our worry about the kitchen becoming too large. They also urged us to get a dishwasher and make sure someone could walk past while it was being loaded. They counseled us on the height of countertops and made us consider potential views from our eating area.

We found professional help, people we liked right away because they listened to us carefully. Heidi Sachet, our architect and designer, urged us to use our imagination and so we got a laundry room in place of our old carport. Ray Preston, our contractor, seemed to like tearing into our old house with its daily technical demands and surprises. Our old friend Ryan Collay came up with excellent plans for the plumbing and electrical, providing enough outlets and lights plus new plumbing with convenient shut-off valves. Our friend John Jones doubled our natural light with windows identical to their 1905 counterparts. Dwayne Schaffner built Douglas fir cabinets, the same wood used throughout the house.

We ended up with an 18-foot square kitchen and double the work surfaces, including the butcher-block topped island in the center with drawers, bookshelves and a recycling center. We selected a Gaggenau double oven with conventional and convection units and a versatile cook top with two gas burners, two electric burners and a grill. We have a hood with excellent lighting and a powerful fan. We quadrupled the number of drawers, added a pantry with pull-out shelves and made a place for the chest freezer in the new laundry room. The high ceilings combined with the new windows and Ryan's generous lighting make the room light and airy even on the grayest winter day. And bless every one of the seven new electrical outlets and the double stainless steel sink that holds our biggest pots and pans. Ryan soundproofed our dishwasher so successfully that we can turn it on during dinner and barely notice it. We still have our small round table that seats from four to eight. It's warm in that corner now thanks to two new baseboard heaters and a furnace vent. There's even room for a reading lamp and my grandfather's old chair which doubles as a cat bed.

We have baskets for storing everything throughout the house. The kitchen baskets hold current magazines, garden catalogs and other reading material, old towels for wiping muddy paws, old newspapers waiting to be recycled and paper trash. We have a box of envelopes, pens, pencils and scissors sitting on one windowsill. The barometer hangs nearby. Our television sits on top of the refrigerator. We don't use it much except during football season when we watch the San Francisco 49ers while canning, baking, making pots of chili or, John's favorite, culling papers. Our yellow walls are covered with masks, photos, old toys and even a small cupboard with artifacts unearthed from around the farm. Our kitchen is always comfortable, usually untidy and very cozy.

Lisa once told us that her dream house would have our kitchen with a bedroom above it, plus a bathroom and utility room. Lisa now has her dream kitchen in their new farmhouse, a neighborly version of our own.

> *You cannot build a kitchen for last winter.*
>
> —Adapted from an Ethiopian proverb.

Pantry Essentials

Our nearest grocery store is eight miles away and our favorite one twice that distance. This influences how we shop (usually once a week) as well as how we stock our pantry and freezer. We stock supplies that we might not if we lived in town because we want to be able to make dinner for company on the spur of the moment. We buy multiple loaves of bread, for example, and freeze it. We also often eat fish on the night we've done our grocery shopping. • This is an actual list of the contents of our pantry one day. Those items that we consider essential are in *italics* and favorite brand names are in parentheses.

OIL
Olive
Wesson
Pam spray

VINEGAR
Balsamic (Trader Joe's)
Red & white wine
Champagne
Rice

DRINKS
Cocoa
Lemonade
Iced tea
Tea
Coffee beans (in freezer)

PASTA, etc.
Assorted dried (De Cecco)
Couscous
Chinese noodles
Polenta
Masa

CEREAL
Oatmeal
9 Grain
Cream of wheat
Irish oats
Granola
Assorted cold cereals
Grits

BEANS
Black
Pinto
Lentils
Split peas

FLOUR
White
Wheat
Pastry
Buckwheat
Cornmeal

SUGAR
Brown
White
Powdered
Honey
Corn syrup
Golden syrup
Molasses
Maple syrup
Sorghum

CHOCOLATE
Cocoa powder
Baking
Chips

FRUIT	**VEGGIES**	**MEATS**
Applesauce	*"Ready-cut" tomatoes*	*Tuna*
Rhubarb	*Tomato purée*	Clams
Pineapple	*Tomato paste*	
Raisins	*Anaheim chiles*	
Currants		
Prunes		
Cranberries		

SOUP	**SAUCES**	**MISCELLANEOUS**
Assorted (Trader Joe's)	*Mushroom soy*	*Crackers*
Miso cup	Worcestershire	Cookies
Instant broth packets (MBT)	Tabasco	*Pectin*
Scotch broth mix	*Thai sweet chile*	Gelatin
	Pickapeppa	*Bran*
	Mayonnaise	*Assorted herbs & spices*
	Mustard	*Dog biscuits*
	Assorted jams & jellies	*Vanilla, almond, orange &*
	Pickle relish	*lemon flavoring*
	Chutney	*Assorted nuts* (in freezer)

It's no secret that good food begins with good ingredients. And that means shopping in grocery stores and specialty stores, visiting the butcher, the baker and the fishmonger. We are fortunate to have great grocery shopping in our largest nearby city. The best was a locally owned store called Oasis that lived up to its name in every way until it was gobbled up by an out-of-state chain. We have fond memories of the original place with a papier-mâché camel crowning the frozen food department.

FOOD SINS

In Eva's family, Lisa reported, they are called "food sins," those errors of taste that usually draw comment and sometimes fire. Not cleaning your plate is one. Feeding the dog from the table is another. Failing to refill the ice trays. Picking grapes from the fruit bowl one-by-one off the stem. Digging out the inside of a soft cheese and leaving the rind. Leaving dishes and glasses in the sink instead of putting them in the dishwasher. Tidying up the edges of brownies and cakes. Well, actually, we cultivate this sin in our family.

Tools of Choice

Our favorite tools bring us pleasure from their design, origins and reliable service day after day.

KNIVES, STEEL & SHARPENING STONE

Our knives are an assortment, both carbon steel and stainless, hand-me-downs, gifts and purchases. Catherine's favorite is a small, perfectly shaped carbon steel paring knife made by Chicago Cutlery. It is a indispensable. We have two because one disappeared in the compost and had to be replaced immediately. It was recovered six months later in perfect condition. A serrated knife is essential for bread but also useful for slicing tomatoes and oranges, a medium-sized chef's knife for chopping; and a boning knife for slicing meat and poultry. Sharp knives make all the difference in the world between smooth, safe chopping and slicing and dangerous clawing. Spend the few minutes it takes to learn how to sharpen your knives. Invest in a good steel and sharpening stone. You can't do anything in the kitchen without these tools.

COOKWARE

Our cookware is a mixture of cast iron, enameled cast iron, stainless steel with layered bottoms, old Revereware and copper. What they have in common is their heavy bottoms which conduct heat efficiently and distribute it evenly, an essential feature. In addition, heavy metal is more forgiving of cook's error, so when food does get cooked on (even burned on) it is much easier to remove. We are fond of our old cast iron frying pans, muffin tin and griddle that contribute to our diet by leaving traces of iron in the food cooked in them. They must be properly cleaned — **never with soap** — and dried thoroughly to avoid rust. Set them to dry in an oven with a pilot light or on a warm spot on the wood stove. Wipe occasionally with cooking oil to season

WOODEN SPOONS

Wooden spoons are beautiful, an enduring design which feels good in the hand. We have an assortment of sizes and shapes, large-headed, long handled ones for soup pots and short, small ones for a quick stir of melting chocolate.

FOOD PROCESSOR

Ours dates from the mid-1970's. It has had one minor repair, a remarkable record for a tool that has logged countless hours of service. We use it to chop nuts, grate vegetables, purée soups and sauces, and make breadcrumbs. We prefer to chop vegetables by hand.

STEAMER

Emmy gave us an aluminum double-walled Mexican steamer that works wonders on all vegetables, but especially beets, potatoes, asparagus and onions. The cavity between the double walls is filled with water and then steam can be directed inside the pan or out. We've never seen another one.

BAKING PANS

Catherine bought her favorite heavy coated metal cake pans many years ago. They are worth their weight in gold for their even distribution of heat and easy release of cakes. They work much better than lightweight aluminum pans. Our Gaggenau ovens have excellent heavy enameled metal baking tray/cookie sheets that work nicely. Catherine treasures her mother's unmistakably well-used cupcake tins that now hold generous muffins.

GRATER

We searched long and hard for an easy grater for Parmesan cheese, trying and discarding a half dozen different designs as well as burying several Mouli hand graters which collapsed under stress. We reverted to an old upright box grater that produced about equal quantities of grated knuckle and cheese until Karen and Tenold introduced us to their new Swedish stainless steel box grater that grated Parmesan almost like butter. Recently Connie discovered a small hand grater made by Zyliss, a Swiss company. It's works smoothly and comes apart for easy cleaning. (These graters get dull and must be replaced occasionally.)

WOK SPATULA & MEAT HOOK

One of John's favorite outdoor cooking utensils is a Chinese wok spatula. Its head is a multi-purpose scraper/spoon/ turner/server with a long hollow handle in which he inserts a stick to keep a comfortable distance from his fire. He is also fond of a hand-forged meat hook, a barbecue tool that Lisa gave him years ago and we in turn have given to many others.

KITCHEN SCISSORS

There is no substitute for good kitchen scissors. Catherine's mother gave her a handsome pair of heavy Italian steel scissors as a bridal shower gift in 1973, the same design Marjorie was given as a bride in 1939. Then Edie gave us a lightweight, sturdy pair of kitchen scissors that come apart for easy washing. Surprisingly they don't have a brand name on them.

RUBBER SPOON & POTATO PEELER

Sometimes someone does invent a better mousetrap. We think this is the case with Rubbermaid's new spatula, a rubber spoon that stirs as well as scrapes mixing bowls. We have several of these essential tools for baking and other cooking. In the same good design category is the new Good Grips peeler with a large, soft rubber handle perfectly shaped for the human hand. It's a great leap forward.

PANCAKE TURNER & EGG SLICER

Another essential tool is our pancake turner with its flexible stainless steel head which slips smoothly under the most delicate piece of fish or a sturdy buckwheat cake, lifting easily because its thin but substantial head has some spring to it. Finally, we celebrate the design and utility of our German egg-slicer that Catherine remembers from childhood potato-salad-making. Its tightly strung metal cutting wires close over the tin "bed" where the egg sits tight.

SOUP SKIMMER

Last but not least is the soup skimmer, a perforated scoop shaped like a small hand, which belonged to Catherine's grandmother. It is indispensable for skimming the foam from pots of soup or stock.

Other favorite tools are discussed elsewhere in the cookbook:
KITCHEN AID MIXER on page 83.
VICTORIO STRAINER on page 83.
GRAVY CUP on page 68.
FOLEY FOOD MILL on pages 65 & 247,
TUSCAN GRILL on page 280,
DUTCH OVEN on pages 280-4.

THE ALL OF IT

The nicest thing about love is that you can have it without merit.

—Gertrude Bell (1868-1926)
From *The Letters of Gertrude Bell.*

The Kitchen Gallery

Friends gather around our refrigerator, not to look in it — although some do — but to look over its surface, to spot new photographs among the layers of old ones, to identify mutual friends or put a face to someone we've talked about. This is our kitchen gallery with its more than 200 photographs covering every available surface in a free-form collage secured by a massive assortment of magnets. This gallery is the heart of the kitchen.

We display all new babies, new puppies, brides and grooms, our pets, past and present and famous emotional moments, such as the one in the newspaper clipping of Jim Ottaway smiling, next to a bearded Fidel Castro in a designer suit. We perform introductions with the refrigerator as inter-mediary. (We know of one love affair that began with questions about each other's photographs.)

Ryan once stood studying the gallery and then asked why he wasn't there. "All we need is a good picture," we explained. Shortly after that, he arrived with a snapshot of himself with a characteristic coffee cup in hand. Up he went.

Although photographs dominate the haphazard composition of the gallery, there are other artifacts as well. A reminder from the vet for the dogs to have their shots, illustrated thank you notes from Melissa and Emily Shankman, a patch from the Clingman Dairy uniform, a color xerox photo collage of AnnaDay and David's wedding, Faith's brown envelope with its x-rated contents, Day Rose's cut-paper American flag, Lizzy B's list of recommended movies, Natty's pink and purple valentine heart, Zoë's drawing of a chair, one of Ruby's landscapes and our current grocery list. This is domestic art at its best.

SAVED BY THE TOOL

Sofia removed the cake and ice cream dome from the freezer, covered it with meringue and baked it briefly at 350° until it was nicely browned. We sang and John blew out the candles on his beautiful baked Alaska.

Then Sofia reached for the knife and we watched intently. Again and again she attempted to cut the baked Alaska but it was a losing battle. The brick-like dome of chocolate and strawberry ice cream remained impenetrable as it teetered on its angel food mooring.

Devin raced to the kitchen and returned carrying the new electric knife. He plugged it in and handed it to his mother. With the dexterity of a logger handling a chain saw, Sofia pierced the frozen mass and served her masterpiece with a flourish. We savored every mouthful.

Bill's Poem

LOVING A WOMAN IN THE WORLD

Outside,
sixty million starts of
grass inside crisp frost huts.
The horses' hooves mash the new
green shoots into the molds of ancient prints
remembered by the Earth
in dried river beds.
Inside,
the man sees the orange light
from the wood stove,
feels the warmth left by the woman
who rose before him.
The baking mold warm and full,
He finally sits down to eat the bread
she baked, loving her slowly, deeply
in quiet forgotten ways.

—Bill White

Bill is a man of many talents, an innovative designer of houses and cabins, the creator of a classic restaurant, an excellent cook, a fine letter writer, an artist and a poet. He is also a master of the art of conversation and political commentary. His wife, Sue, a special education teacher, was the inspiration for this poem as she is for many things in Bill's life.

Our Cookbook

The soul of cooking lies in nurturance,
sharing and simple kindness.

—Julia Child

From the introduction to Robert Clark's biography of
James Beard, *The Solace of Food*.

Cooking & Recipes

I like cooking. It's concrete and finite. It has a beginning, an end, a product and presentation. It's performance, home theater with stars, script, supporting cast, audience and even critics. It feeds us in many ways, both literally and figuratively. It's also restful, the absorbing tasks of peeling, chopping and stirring. It's creative, too. On the farm, it ties us to the land and the seasons through our garden. It ties us to the outside world through the grocery store. And, of course, it ties us together through the fellowship of food. We remember great meals and celebrations around a table, the shared stories, the plans, the laughter, the exchange of ideas, the support and friendships that enrich our lives. These sustain us.

The most important relationships in my life have been cemented at the dinner table, then prospered over food, recipes and a few other gritty topics. It wasn't a beau who sent me my first extravagant long-stemmed roses but rather an out-of-town colleague grateful for a home-cooked meal. Food works wonders.

My earliest memory of food is watching, perched on the kitchen stool, as my mother magically filled the bowl of her Sunbeam Mixmaster to its very top with egg whites. For years, I thought she started with an empty bowl because those raw egg whites were invisible to my four-year-old eyes. I still feel that same amazement about cooking. You start with something and, most often, end up with something else. Dried beans are pretty tame until they're transformed into soup, raw poultry is ugly at best and eggplants are gorgeous but impossible, although not so impossible as coconuts. Even chocolate seems hopeless in those unsweetened small bricks. And then the magic.

My mother, Marjorie, was an excellent cook and a great collector of recipes. We grew up eating delicious food at the family table that was literally the center of our house. I started cooking in a toy kitchen soon after I could walk and moved on to elaborate tea parties for my dolls and then into the family kitchen. Mama and Pop — he cooked, too — encouraged me and endured more than enough sweets before I branched out into quiche and moussaka. There were infamous cherries jubilee, laced with sufficient booze to reward my father.

My sister provided essential help, too. She and I have a pact dating back more than 30 years — I cook, she cleans up. For all those years, Connie left the cooking to me until recently when she got bitten by the bug. Now she calls with questions and reports on results. I feel like framing in gold the first recipe that she gave me, a delicious casserole with chicken and couscous that won the Pillsbury Bake-Off.

This cookbook began with a great collage of worn paper scraps, food-stained file cards, blotched pages, well-thumbed notebooks, old letters, wrinkled postcards, napkins with blurred writing, scrawl-covered envelopes and an occasional page of neatly typed text, all shoved in drawers for safe-keeping. It represented a lifetime of collecting recipes and making notes about food preparation.

The oldest recipe is this cookbook comes from my grandmother and dates back more than 90 years. We like to imagine all the occasions when her oatmeal cookies have been enjoyed. That recipe is part of my heritage just as the Kentucky chocolate sauce is part of John's.

We give you our favorite recipes and related stories. This cookbook celebrates all of you who are part of it through your recipes, the food you've prepared for us and the times we've shared together in kitchens and dining-rooms. You will meet our family and friends. Many names will be mentioned, including four Bills and one Billy, three Emilys and one Emilie called Emmy, three Pats, two Andys, two Bruces, two Maxes and two Sallys. All are important. Unlike Russian novels, however, you won't have to learn the names in order to follow the plot.

Our lives have been greatly enriched by the communication that these recipes represent. As our friend, the late, great Harper Brown used to say, "Give thanks and expect more." We give great thanks and expect more great meals, more recipes, more friends and more good times together.

—Catherine Smith

KEEP YOUR EYE ON THE BALL

More than a pound of Italian Perugina bittersweet chocolate went into Anuncia's Queen of Sheba cake for her fiftieth birthday. The three layers were perched on the pedestal cake plate with chocolate butter cream between each layer. The saucepan with soft chocolate icing was cooling in an ice water bath in the sink.

I started to cut up potatoes for dinner and then toss them with olive oil. John came into the kitchen to ask me a question and we got talking. I walked over to the sink and washed my hands thoroughly with soap. Then I looked down at the rich, dark frosting in the sink below, now covered with a film of soapy residue. Time to start over.

A Word from Emmy

John's mother, Emmy, wrote the following letter to Mary Stewart Anderson, a young bride-to-be in 1970. We think it is timeless advice.

Dear Mary,

Cooking is either an A-1 therapy or a traumatic pain in the neck. What quality of the individual it is that decides how it will be for her, I cannot figure.

If you are one of the former, and I am so blessed, to start stirring at the stove will rest you when you were dead on your feet from a day "in the salt mine."

I quarrel with all cookbooks. Even before I begin, I'm arguing with the writer. And the only value in new books is as light pick-up reading. Every-thing we need to know is in any good solid classic book.

My best results seem never to be the effortful productions for company, but the surprise meal I seemingly made out of nothing — leftovers and this and that from the shelf.

There is no substitute for leftovers. They are priceless — as they start the imagination moving. And I am convinced all new ideas come from a substitution, necessary because an ingredient was not on hand, or a leftover that made the dish enough for two unexpected mouths to feed.

Conservation in the kitchen enriches many a dull dish, and boiling up those bones is an effort that pays off tenfold.

So I wish you happy adventures at the stove. I for one can thank my cooking for a very good marriage of near forty years.

May you have the same good fortune.

With love from Emmy Smith

There's no beauty greater than the beauty of the human character.

—Eliza McCreary Strong

Emmy's mother

Before You Start

We use the following standard abbreviations, terms and approximate sizes in the recipes in this cookbook:

c. = cup T. = tablespoon t. = teaspoon lb. = pound oz. = ounce qt. = quart pkg. = package	sugar = white granulated sugar powdered sugar = confectioner's sugar bread flour = white flour with more gluten medium onion = about 2 inches in diameter large onion = about 3 inches in diameter

Writing clear directions is a challenge. We've tried to be clear without being tedious and concise without being too abbreviated. We hope that a phrase like "until it disappears" with respect to incorporating flour is more descriptive than mysterious. There will be puzzles but, hopefully, nothing too head-rattling.

Measuring makes all the difference in the world when you are learning to cook. It's best to begin by measuring everything accurately. On the other hand, much "real cooking" depends on what's on hand when you get started. You use two carrots, three potatoes and a can of chilis in your soup because that's what you have in your refrigerator and pantry. Salt, pepper, herbs and spices all depend on taste. Although you can generally please yourself, "perfect" combinations can be elusive. We encourage you to experiment.

Oven temperatures are tricky because each oven has its own personality. For example, our convection oven bakes cakes and pies more rapidly than a conventional oven. In our recipes, we usually give a range of time — such as 20 to 30 minutes — to emphasize that cooking times are variable.

Every cookbook ought to have a good index. Often they don't which is frustrating in a reference book. Because we want you to use this cookbook, we have tried to make the index as useful as possible with clear categories and complete cross-references. We have omitted the whimsical titles of the recipes and used conventional descriptions. We have also indexed the most important stories by topic or name as well as all the poems and quotes.

We are pleased that you have joined us for this cooking adventure. Please make this cookbook your own by writing in it, making notes, corrections, annotations and comments.

The Perfect Party

There's no recipe for a perfect party. Yes, the guests are all important, the food must be good, too, and the location can make or break it. But the secret ingredient is a kind of magic that is as illusive as it is powerful.

For my fortieth birthday on Christmas Eve, we planned to be with my family in Pasadena. It turned out to be impossible to put together a big party because of everyone's traditional holiday plans. So we decided to keep it simple, a dinner with my mother, sister, aunt, uncle and Mama's best friend, Henrietta.

The stew was in the oven, a kind of *carbonada criolla* (like the one on page 145), and the table was set for seven. The doorbell rang and it was Bruce Klepinger and his wife, then living in Los Angeles, who dropped by unexpectedly with a bouquet of yellow roses. We got to talking and having such a good time that we invited them to stay for dinner. They accepted.

Then we got involved removing ticks from our dog Lil' Bit using the clear nail polish technique. (It doesn't work.) Uncle Ed, Aunt Lucille and Henrietta arrived, and laughter filled the house.

We set two more places at the table and got out the champagne. I'll never forget sitting next to Aunt Lucille. "Oh, my," she said as John refilled her champagne glass and offered her a little more paté and another cornichon, "this is a far cry from our usual low fat, no salt fare."

As we ate our stew, Bruce regaled us with his best stories of high altitude rescues. I don't think that he ever had a more attentive or appreciative audience. Of course, the good cabernet sauvignon helped our spirits, too. Uncle Ed asked for seconds on the chocolate mousse pie. I never did change into my party clothes.

Memory now confers a kind of gilt edge on that evening. Aunt Lucille died a year later and that was one of the last times we saw her. It was also my last Christmas Eve in our family home. It was the perfect party.

PEARLS OF WISDOM

*There is something to be gotten from every person
if you are just clever enough.*

—Emmy Smith

From her *BrainScan*, a collection of thoughts and observations written down at the request of her grandson, Nicholas Smith, during train trips in 1988 and 1990.

Our Cookbook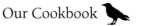

Before Everything Else:
Ubiquitous Chocolate

SKIP THE BROWN RICE

When she was 91, our friend Elda informed her son that she was baking a chocolate cake as part of a new dietary regime. "What diet is that?" he asked. Elda explained that she had recently learned that she should be eating more brown food. In her analysis, nothing could top chocolate cake in the brown food department.

The Secret Kentucky Chocolate Sauce

Because of its great richness and high potency, this sauce has been a favorite for three generations of Kentucky Smiths and family dentists alike. Until this very moment the recipe has been closely guarded, coveted in fact, and known cryptically as "The Secret Recipe for You Know What." • John's mother Emmy kept a special container filled with this sauce in her refrigerator at all times and a spoon for easy sampling day or night. • The secret ingredient is coffee. Emmy said "the stronger the coffee, the better." • When our cousin Olga came to visit, we pulled weeds and reminisced about favorite childhood desserts. Hers was peppermint ice cream with chocolate sauce. The chocolate sauce was easy, but we had to drive all over town to find real "pepp-o-mint," as John's father called it, ice cream. It was worth the effort.

Serves 6

4 oz. unsweetened baking chocolate
1 c. strong coffee
½ to 1 c. sugar

2 t. vanilla
1 pinch salt

In a small saucepan, combine chocolate, coffee and sugar. Stir gently as chocolate melts over low heat. When sauce bubbles, reduce heat to lowest setting and simmer until it reaches a sauce-like consistency, at least 10 minutes. (We usually get the sauce started and then ignore it for awhile.) Add vanilla and salt and stir well. Serve warm or cold. Pour liberally over anything or just use a finger for dipping.

Emmy's original recipe calls for 1 cup of sugar, but we make it with ½ cup. Emmy tried it with less sugar but found that the reduced-sugar sauce did not keep as well in Louisville's hot, moist summer climate. (Even in our climate, this sauce never keeps well for other reasons.) It should be stored in the refrigerator.

To make **HEDGEHOGS**, put half of a canned or fresh poached pear on each plate, core-side down. Spoon chocolate sauce carefully over the bottom ¾ of the pear to form the hedgehog's body. Stick toasted, slivered almonds into the chocolate body for fur. Make two small incisions in the small end of the pear and insert 2 currants for eyes. Serve with whipped cream.

AND SPEAKING OF ART . . . .

We have photos to prove that Lisa once encouraged or aided or abetted our Australian nieces, Belinda and Suzanne, in their now infamous Chocolate Face Painting Contest using this very sauce. All were declared winners. Of course, we do not recommend this.

Years later, Suzanne requested this recipe by fax, the first request on our new fax machine.

Laura's Unforgettable Chocolate Brownies

Yes, we talk about these brownies, the ones that put everyone to sleep on an enchanted afternoon, high on a hillside overlooking the Pacific Ocean. No one knows quite what happened. The only substance involved was chocolate, but, oh, the magic of these brownies and the charmed company of that memorable picnic.
• We searched long and hard for the perfect brownie recipe and it finally came to us from Laura, our goddaughter Day Rose's grandmother. • Brownies are a staple in our freezer to provide sustenance and rewards to friends and workers alike, another of Emmy's valued practices. (The county tax assessor is the only person to have turned one down as a likely bribe.) • Our friend John Jones has a history of arriving just as we are taking a batch of these brownies from the oven. We like the idea of preparing certain foods to produce visits from important friends.

Makes 2 dozen

6 oz. unsweetened baking chocolate
1-½ c. butter (3 cubes)
3-½ c. sugar

6 eggs
1-½ c. all-purpose white flour
2 c. chocolate chips (12 oz. pkg.)

Pre-heat oven to 325°. Grease generously a 9x13-inch baking pan. Melt chocolate and butter slowly in a small saucepan with a good bottom over low heat or in the top of a double boiler over gently simmering water. Remove from heat and stir in sugar immediately.

In a medium-mixing bowl, beat eggs thoroughly and then gradually stir in the chocolate mixture. Add flour and mix gently **by hand** until flour disappears. (Too much beating makes brownies tough.) Stir in chocolate chips and pour into prepared pan. For **diet brownies**, omit chocolate chips.

Bake until brownies are beginning to pull away from the sides of the pan and the center feels spongy when pressed gently, about 45 minutes. Do not over-bake. These are fudgy brownies, best moist.

Remove from oven and cool pan on a rack. Cut into squares while warm. These brownies freeze well wrapped individually in wax paper and stored in a shoebox or tin.

AN EDITORIAL ON FAT-FREE BROWNIES

Fat-free brownies are a contradiction in terms. If you want fat-free, eat an orange. Never pretend that you can eat a brownie without fat. A brownie is a brownie because it is made from butter, chocolate and sugar.

It is sort of like the Seven Wonders of the World. You can't substitute Disneyland for the Hanging Gardens of Babylon because you don't like Saddam Hussein's politics.

More Brownies for Serious People

These delicious graham cracker brownies are filled with chocolate chips and orange peel. Catherine still remembers taking a tin of these on vacation as a child, no doubt influencing the direction of her life. • *Someone once said that these brownies were almost too rich to eat. Almost, but not quite.*

Makes 2 dozen

1-½ c. graham cracker crumbs
  (9 double crackers)
1 c. chocolate chips (6 oz. pkg.)

14 oz. can sweetened condensed milk
Grated peel from 1 or 2 oranges
1 c. chopped nuts

Pre-heat oven to 325°. Grease a 9x9-inch baking pan. To make graham cracker crumbs, break graham crackers in half and process gently in a food processor or blender. Or place crackers in a plastic bag and crush by rolling gently with a rolling pin.

In a medium-mixing bowl, combine all ingredients and mix thoroughly. Batter is very thick. Spread batter into prepared baking pan and press into place with a rubber scraper or your hands.

Bake until lightly browned, 20 to 30 minutes. Remove from oven and cool pan on a rack. Cut into squares while still warm. Cool thoroughly and store in a tin. These brownies freeze well.

THE DOOR MOUSE

Occasionally something happens which is not part of this world but the pure magic of fairies and fairy tales.

One October evening we had a group of friends for dinner, three families with children, Geneva, Devin and Nicholas. We seated the children at their own table in the front hall.

Midway through the meal, we walked into the hall and found the children transfixed, staring at a small mouse sitting up on his haunches, bright-eyed, gazing directly at the kids. We watched in wonder for several minutes as the Door Mouse worked his magic. Then he scampered off, back home through the heating vent, and we've not seen him since.

Crow Cookies: Chips Galore & More

We sometimes take visiting children to talk to the local trolls who inhabit our nearby covered bridge. After dinner when it is dark, Dean, John or Nicholas leaves the group and sneaks off to hide in the rafters of the bridge. The rest of us take our time walking down the road. Standing under the darkened bridge, one of us calls out, "Are there any trolls here tonight?" There is silence except for the sound of running water in Coyote Creek. Suddenly out of the darkness comes the voice of an old geezer demanding, "Who's walking on my bridge?" "It's just us, Mr. Troll. We wanted to pay you and your wife, Gertrude, a visit." Long pause. "Do you have any of those cookies?," the troll always asks. • Not only do trolls like these cookies but also our children and grandchildren, the folks at the tractor store, service station, post office, hardware store, our veterinarian and neighbors. They love 'em. We make a quadruple batch at Christmas for the important people in our life. • These are great "freezer cookies" that you can pull out for any occasion, including simple hunger pangs.

Makes 5-6 dozen

1 c. butter (2 cubes), at room
   temperature
1 c. brown sugar
1 t. vanilla
1 egg, lightly beaten
1 c. unflavored cooking oil
3-½ c. all-purpose white flour
1 t. baking soda

1 t. salt
1-½ c. rolled oats
1 c. currants (about 4-¼ oz.)
1 c. shredded coconut, sweetened or
   unsweetened (about 2-½ oz.)
1 c. corn flakes or Special K cereal
1 c. walnuts or toasted filberts (4 oz.),
   chopped
2 c. chocolate chips (12 oz. pkg.)

Pre-heat oven to 325°. In a large mixing bowl, cream butter and sugar together until light and fluffy. Add vanilla, egg and cooking oil and mix well. Then add flour, soda and salt. Mix until flour disappears. Stir in remaining ingredients and combine gently but thoroughly.

Form into walnut-sized balls, place about 1 inch apart on un-greased cookie sheets and flatten slightly. Bake until very lightly browned, about 15 to 18 minutes. Remove cookies from oven. Let sit on cookie sheets for five minutes before removing to cool on racks. Store in tins. These cookies freeze well.

Too much of a good thing is wonderful.

—Mae West

Nancy's Oscar-Winning Nanaimo Bars

Nancy made these unforgettable cookies for the Lorane Film Society, the inspired creation of her husband, Joey. On Film Society nights, everyone gathers in a rural Grange Hall to see old film classics such as **North by Northwest, The Thief of Baghdad, Broadway Danny Rose, The Night of the Iguana** *and* **Carmen.** *• Even Humphrey Bogart and Mae West look better after you've eaten one or two or more of these splendid cookies. • Nancy herself has the same effect on plants. Plants love her and they try to do better to keep her happy. We know people with green thumbs but Nancy has green hands. • Although the origin of these cookies is obscure, the Vancouver Island city of Nanaimo has celebrated them for more than 50 years.*

Makes 3 dozen

Bottom layer:
¾ c. butter (1-½ cubes)
⅓ c. sugar
½ c. unsweetened cocoa powder
1-½ t. vanilla
1 egg & 1 yolk, beaten lightly
1-½ c. finely shredded coconut, unsweetened (about 3-¾ oz.)
3 c. graham cracker crumbs (18 double crackers; see page 42.)
¾ c. walnuts (3 oz.), chopped

Filling:
6 T. butter (¾ cube), at room temperature
About 3 T. milk
3 T. vanilla custard powder (Bird's), instant pudding powder or cornstarch
3 c. powdered sugar (about 14 oz.), sifted

Top Layer:
3 oz. unsweetened baking chocolate
1-½ T. butter

Grease a 9x13-inch baking pan. If shredded coconut seems too coarse, process it in a blender or food processor for a few seconds.

Melt butter in a small saucepan over low heat. Add sugar, cocoa, vanilla, whole egg and egg yolk. Cook briefly, less than a minute, until mixture thickens slightly, stirring constantly.

Remove from heat and stir in coconut, graham cracker crumbs and walnuts. Scrape into prepared pan and press firmly with a spatula or your hands to cover the bottom of the pan evenly. Refrigerate at least 1 hour or freeze while you do the next step.

To make filling, cream butter. Beat in milk, custard powder and powdered sugar. If this mixture is too thick to spread easily, then add another teaspoon of milk. Spread filling evenly over the first layer and refrigerate until firm, about ½ hour.

For top layer, melt chocolate and butter in a small saucepan with a heavy bottom over low heat or in the top of a double boiler over gently simmering water. Spread melted chocolate evenly over filling. Nancy explained that this unsweetened top layer sets off the sweetness of the bottom layer and filling. Before the chocolate hardens, mark out squares. Refrigerate or freeze for at least 1 hour. Cut into squares and serve. Store in tins in the refrigerator or freezer.

Ubiquitous Chocolate

Mum's-the-Word Chocolate Peanut Bickies

First, the translation: A bickie or biscuit is a cookie in Australia. Mum is Lorna Kumnick of Melbourne, Australia. Her family, including her husband Jack, son John and daughter Mary Jean took Catherine, age 16, into their home and family as an American Field Service exchange student in 1964. That experience changed Catherine's life and created an extraordinary family bond. • Jack was the manager of the National Bank of Australasia in the Melbourne suburb of Elsternwick, and the Kumnick family lived behind and on top of the bank on Glenhuntly Road. Catherine loved to tell people that the bedroom she shared with Mary Jean was over the vault. • Mum's the word about how many of these melt-in-your-mouth cookies . . . uh . . . biscuits Catherine actually ate that year. Fortunately, both Big Brother John and Mary Jean also had their hands in the cookie tin. • The original recipe calls for self-rising flour that eliminates the need for baking powder.

Makes 5 dozen

¼ lb. butter (1 cube), at room
  temperature
1 c. sugar
1 egg, beaten
½ t. vanilla

1 c. all-purpose white flour
½ t. baking powder
2 T. unsweetened cocoa powder
1 c. peanuts (4 oz.)

Pre-heat oven to 350°. In a mixing bowl, cream butter and sugar until light and fluffy. Add beaten egg and vanilla. Mix thoroughly. Sift together flour, baking powder and cocoa and add to butter mixture. Mix gently until flour disappears. Stir in peanuts.

Form dough into walnut-sized balls and arrange on un-greased cookie sheets about 1 inch apart. Bake until lightly browned, 10 to 12 minutes. Remove from oven and cool on racks. Store in a covered tin. These freeze well.

CALCULATING AN ELEGANT SUFFICIENCY

Mum prepared a beautiful lamb curry for "tea," as dinner was called, on the day Catherine arrived in Melbourne. At the end of that enjoyable first meal, Catherine announced that she was "stuffed." That brought shocked looks to the faces of Mum, Dad, John and Mary Jean, quickly followed by laughter.

When everyone got their breath again, the family explained to the puzzled Catherine that "stuffed" was not a suitable phrase to express delight at the end of a delicious meal. "Stuffed" meant "pregnant."

Big brother John, always the wordsmith, offered a more polite and now immortal alternative. Catherine's first sentence in Australian was "I have reached a glorious state of elegant sufficiency."

Alexandra's Queenly Grandmother's
Very Chocolate Cake & Frosting

Russian hospitality was an order of magnitude beyond anything Catherine had known when she entered Alexandra's family home for the first time. She was swept into the arms of Alexandra's mother and grandmother, engulfed by spellbinding warmth, generosity and kindness. Alex's family made guests feel like royalty as they offered Sacher torte, Perugina chocolates, homemade cakes and tea in fine china cups. The perfect food was abundant, beautifully prepared and served with a style that epitomizes hospitality. Conversation was always lively and interesting and laughter was plentiful. • Catherine's mother, Marjorie, also an honored guest in Alex's family home, loved to tell about the most remarkable egg of her life, fresh from the Tolstoy farm down the road, cooked to perfection and served on an exquisite plate. • The recipe for this classic chocolate cake comes from Alexandra's grandmother who looked like a duchess and cooked like a queen. She cooked until she was 90, a role model in that and many other ways.

Serves 8-10

Cake:
4 oz. unsweetened baking chocolate
½ c. butter (1 cube)
1 c. boiling water
2 c. sugar
2 c. all-purpose white flour
½ t. salt
1-½ t. baking powder
½ c. buttermilk
2 eggs, beaten

Frosting:
4 oz. unsweetened baking chocolate
1 T. butter
1-½ T. cornstarch
½ c. sugar
1 c. milk
1 t. vanilla

Pre-heat oven to 350°. Grease generously two 8 or 9-inch round cake pans. In a small saucepan with a heavy bottom over low heat or in the top of a double boiler over gently simmering water, cover chocolate, butter and sugar with boiling water. Stir gently while chocolate melts. Beat lightly to combine thoroughly and pour into a mixing bowl.

Sift flour, salt and baking powder four times into a second mixing bowl. (If you don't have a flour sifter, shake through a wire mesh strainer.)

Add buttermilk and eggs to chocolate-butter mixture and combine well. Then add sifted flour mixture. Beat batter until very liquid. Pour into prepared pans. Bake until cake tests done, 25 to 30 minutes. (See next page.) Remove from oven and cool for 10 minutes on racks before removing from the pans. Cool thoroughly.

For frosting, melt chocolate and butter slowly in a small saucepan with a heavy bottom over low heat or in the top of a double boiler over gently simmering water. Stir in cornstarch and sugar. Then add milk and increase heat to medium. Stir constantly for several minutes until mixture thickens. Remove from heat and add vanilla. Mix well. Stir frequently while cooling to room temperature and then frost cake.

Ubiquitous Chocolate

TESTING DONE

Cake or tea bread is done when it pulls away from the sides of the pan, the center springs back when touched lightly or a toothpick, knife blade or cake tester inserted in the center comes out clean.

REMOVING CAKE FROM PAN

After removing from the oven, cool cake or tea bread for 10 minutes in the pan on a rack. Run a spatula or knife around the circumference of the pan. Place the rack on top of the pan and invert quickly. Tap the bottom of the pan to release the cake or tea bread. Lift off the pan carefully.

WAX PAPER TRICK

To keep the cake plate tidy while frosting a cake, place 3 or 4 strips of wax paper under the bottom layer of the cake, enough to cover the plate's exposed rim. After cake is frosted, pull out wax paper gently and discard.

Where ARE the fellas?
—*Marjorie Manz*

A question asked by Catherine's mother more than half a dozen times during a weekend visit in March 1998. Was she expecting her deceased husband or older brother? Her absent son-in-law? Or remembering the excitement at her sorority house before a dance many years ago? Or simply missing the regular presence of men in her cloistered life at a home for elderly ladies? We would like to know where this line of thought began, in what long ago memory or current longing. Marjorie died on June 28, 1999.

Ilse's Feather-Light German Torte
with Carrots, Cocoa & History

Carol's German mother-in-law Ilse Raff gave her this recipe for Gelbe Rüben torte, and Carol shared it with Catherine. (In German a carrot is a "yellow root.") Cocoa is the secret ingredient in this elegant confection that should get a prize for combining unlikely ingredients, carrots and chocolate. • Ilse and her husband Hans immigrated to Los Angeles from Goeppingen in 1937 because the squeeze of social and economic conditions for Jews in the Third Reich had made their future untenable there. • The "culinary arts" studied by Ilse at a Swiss boarding school came in handy when she and her mother had to bake and sell cakes to help make ends meet for the family, including their young son. • About 20 years later, Ilse, perfectly turned out like a kitchen nurse in her starched white apron, meticulously lined up and measured ingredients in the kitchen of her beautiful home in the Hollywood Hills with her new daughter-in-law Carol at her side.

Serves 8

3 T. crumbs (Zwieback, vanilla wafers, graham or wheat meal crackers) (Method for crumbs on page 42.)
7 eggs, separated
1-¼ c. sugar
2 large or 4 medium carrots, grated (about ½ lb. or 2 c.)
1 T. unsweetened cocoa powder

Grated rind & juice of 1 lemon
1 t. vanilla
1 t. almond extract
1 lb. almonds or other nuts, ground finely (4 c.)

½ pt. heavy cream, whipped

Pre-heat oven to 350°. Grease two 8 or 9-inch round cake pans. (This cake is not suitable for bundt or tube-type pans.) Line pans with wax paper, then grease wax paper.

In a large mixing bowl, beat egg yolks and 1 cup of sugar until thick and pale yellow. Continue beating slowly while adding grated carrots, crumbs, cocoa, lemon rind and juice, vanilla and almond extracts, and half of the ground nuts (2 cups).

In a second bowl, beat egg whites at medium speed until they foam, increase speed to high and beat until soft peaks form. Add remaining ¼ cup of sugar tablespoon-by-tablespoon and beat until peaks are stiff and glossy. Gently fold in remaining 2 cups of ground nuts with a whisk. Fold about ⅓ of egg white mixture into carrot mixture, and then fold the carrot mixture into remaining egg white mixture. Combine gently until the egg whites disappear. Pour into prepared pans.

Bake until puffy and lightly browned, 25 to 30 minutes. Remove from oven and cool in pans on racks for 5 minutes. Remove from pans. (See previous page.) Cool thoroughly. Place one layer of torte on a serving plate and cover with half of whipped cream. (See wax paper trick on previous page.) Top with second layer and remaining whipped cream.

For serious chocolate eaters, serve with chocolate sauce on page 40, or substitute chocolate frosting on page 46 for whipped cream.

Ubiquitous Chocolate

Aunt Betsy's Charismatic
Khumbu Mousse au Chocolate

Everyone loved John's Aunt Betsy, and she loved everyone in return. She also loved mountains and became a great mountaineer. • Invited to go on the first American expedition to Mt. Everest in 1950, she wrote home to her family about celebrating Thanksgiving in Nepal at the end of the expedition: "Tomorrow is Thanksgiving. While you are all sitting down to you-know-what with stuffing and cranberry sauce, we too shall have a gala dinner and our feelings of thankfulness will equal anyone's, anywhere, I know. Want to hear what we're going to have to eat? Chicken and ham with rice, a touch of cheese in the sauce. Little tiny tomatoes grown around here, and Gyaljen cooks them marvelously. Think I'll use a few layers of mosquito netting for a white tablecloth and see what wild flowers I can find to decorate. Bill is going to bake a cake (just fixed a date and nut mixture for him) and we'll have chocolate pudding to end up with. Think it sounds good? So do I." • Mt. Everest, called Sagarmatha in Nepali and Chomolungma in Tibetan, is located in the Khumbu region of Nepal.

Serves 6-8

3 oz. bittersweet chocolate
2-½ t. unflavored gelatin
½ c. hot coffee
6 eggs, separated
¾ c. sugar

1 t. vanilla
Pinch of salt

Optional:
½ pt. heavy cream, whipped

In the top of a double boiler over gently simmering water or in a small saucepan with a heavy bottom over low heat, melt chocolate. Remove from heat and cool. In a measuring cup or small bowl, dissolve gelatin in hot coffee. Stir well.

In a mixing bowl, beat egg whites at medium speed until they foam. Increase speed to high and beat until soft peaks form. Add ¼ cup of sugar, 1 tablespoon at a time, and continue beating until the peaks are stiff and glossy.

In a second bowl, beat egg yolks until thick and pale yellow, adding remaining ½ cup of sugar, 1 tablespoon at a time. (See note about raw eggs on page 266.)

Add gelatin-coffee mixture to cooled chocolate and beat well. Stir in vanilla and salt. Combine with egg yolks, mixing thoroughly.

Gently fold ⅓ of egg whites into chocolate mixture. Then scrape into remaining egg whites and fold together gently until egg whites disappear. Scrape into a serving bowl and smooth top with a spatula. Cover, chill several hours and serve with whipped cream.

UNDER-STANDING

Freudian Slip $203.42

—Message on a scrap of paper, handwriting not identified.

Hearty Hot Fudge Pudding

There's something wonderful about a hot dessert, especially one that makes its own fudge sauce while cooking. Catherine and Karen enjoyed reminiscing about how much they liked pudding cakes when they were growing up. This is Emmy's recipe.

Serves 6

Cake:
2 T. butter
2 T. unsweetened cocoa powder
1 c. all-purpose white flour
2 t. baking powder
½ t. salt
¾ c. sugar
½ c. milk
1 t. vanilla
⅓ c. chopped nuts (about 1-⅓ oz.)

Fudge Sauce:
¼ c. unsweetened cocoa powder
¾ c. brown sugar
1-¾ c. boiling water (Part coffee
   is very good.)

Optional:
½ pt. heavy cream, whipped

Pre-heat oven to 350°. Grease an 8x8-inch baking pan or a 2-quart casserole. In a small saucepan, melt the butter over low heat.

Sift together cocoa, flour, baking powder, salt and sugar into a medium-mixing bowl. Add melted butter, milk and vanilla. Stir well. Add chopped nuts and mix. Pour into the prepared pan.

SAUCE • Combine brown sugar and cocoa in a small bowl and sprinkle over top of batter. Then gently pour boiling water over it. Bake until cake has risen and set somewhat, and the sauce is bubbly, 20 to 30 minutes. Remove from oven and cool slightly before serving. Serve warm with whipped cream.

THE SECRET INGREDIENT

Some years ago, we saw "Good Fellas," a gangster film with a memorable scene in which the bad guy explained that a pinch of cloves was the secret ingredient in his family's recipe for spaghetti sauce.

The secret ingredient makes the difference. Taste goes from ordinary to interesting, from unremarkable to special. You may not identify it right away — after all, it is a secret — but you'll know when it is there. It's the extra spark in good food.

A hint of cinnamon, a teaspoon of almond flavoring, juice from half a lemon, a tablespoon of left-over bacon grease, a little rye flour, half a cup of oats, a splash of balsamic vinegar, a few crushed mint leaves or a spoonful of Dijon mustard.

Beginning with Breakfast

When one is served, all may eat.

—Emmy Smith

All-You-Can-Eat Bran Muffins

These muffins are a staple at Crow Farm, and the original recipe comes from Lisa. (Emmy introduced us to Joy Bennett's bran muffins, a satisfying variation with a nice texture from grated carrots. See Joy's recipe at the bottom of the next page.)

Makes 18-24 muffins

3 c. unprocessed bran
1 c. boiling water
½ c. unflavored cooking oil
2 eggs
3 c. all-purpose white flour

1 T. baking soda
2 c. buttermilk
1 c. dark molasses
1 c. currants or raisins
1 c. nuts, chopped

This batter keeps well in a tightly covered container in the refrigerator for several weeks, allowing you to make a few muffins at a time.

Pre-heat oven to 400°. Grease muffin tins. Measure bran into a large mixing bowl, pour boiling water over it and stir well. Mix in cooking oil and eggs, then add flour, soda, buttermilk and molasses. Stir briefly until flour disappears. Stir in currants and nuts. Fill prepared muffin cups about ¾ full.

Bake until muffins test done, about 20 minutes. Muffin is done when the center is pressed gently and the top springs back. Remove from oven and cool briefly on racks. Loosen muffins with a knife and lift out. Serve warm. These also freeze well when thoroughly cooled.

ABOUT BIRTHDAYS

We have a photo of John on the porch where he learned to walk shortly before his first birthday. It was the porch of a cottage at Christmas Cove, Maine, where his mother had also spent summers as a child.

John was a solemn, wide-eyed child as he sat in a high chair wearing a crown of flowers, his cake with one candle off to the side. There were no presents, Emmy explained, because there was no place to shop, but it was also 1934, the bottom of the Depression. Wearing the crown of fresh nasturtiums singled you out as the birthday person.

Emmy's granddaughter and namesake Emily continued this tradition for Emmy's 90th birthday, spending the afternoon of July 4, 1998 with her young son Macauley while making a crown of daisies. Emmy wore her floral tribute with delight at her birthday dinner that evening.

Slugabed Blueberry Muffins

When we have company, we often make muffins the night before and leave them out for a self-serve breakfast. This is an easy way to deal with early birds or slugabeds who — through choice or genetics — tend to sleep late.

Makes 8-10 muffins

1-⅓ c. all-purpose white flour
1 c. rolled oats
½ to ¾ c. brown sugar
1 t. cinnamon
1 T. baking powder

1 t. baking soda
1 c. buttermilk
1 egg, lightly beaten
¼ c. unflavored vegetable oil
1 c. blueberries, fresh or frozen

Pre-heat oven to 400°. Grease muffin tins, or use paper liners. (Paper liners prevent blueberries from sticking to the muffin tin.) In a medium-sized mixing bowl, combine dry ingredients. Add buttermilk, egg and oil. Stir briefly until flour disappears. Fold in blueberries gently. Fill prepared muffin cups about ¾ full.

Bake until lightly browned and muffins test done, 15 to 20 minutes. Muffin is done when the center is pressed gently and the top springs back. Remove from oven and cool briefly on racks. Loosen muffins with a knife and lift out. Serve warm. These also freeze well when thoroughly cooled.

JOY BENNETT'S BRAN MUFFINS

Makes 10-12

1 c. white flour
½ c. wheat flour
⅔ c. sugar
1-½ t. baking soda
1 t. cinnamon
½ t. salt
1-½ c. unprocessed bran
1 egg

1 c. milk
½ c. oil
1-½ mashed bananas (about ¾ cup)
1 c. grated carrots (about 2 medium)
½ c. nuts, chopped

Pre-heat oven to 425°. Grease muffin tins. Combine dry ingredients in a mixing bowl and stir together. In a small bowl, beat the egg lightly and add milk, oil and mashed bananas. Mix thoroughly. Add to flour mixture. Mix together gently until flour disappears. Add carrots and nuts. Mix briefly. Fill prepared muffin cups about ¾ full. Bake until the muffins test done, 15 to 18 minutes. Remove from oven and cool briefly. Serve warm. These freeze well.

Ruth Lord's Kentucky Corncakes

A traditional family breakfast in Kentucky, corncakes are much heartier than pancakes. There's often debate about the type of cornmeal, white versus yellow. We use yellow.

Serves 4

2 c. yellow cornmeal
2 t. baking powder
1 t. baking soda
2 t. sugar
1 t. salt

2 eggs
1 c. buttermilk
Approximately 1 c. boiling water
Bacon grease or unflavored vegetable oil

Pre-heat a griddle or large, heavy frying pan gradually to medium-high. Combine dry ingredients in a large mixing bowl. In a small bowl, beat eggs gently. Add buttermilk to eggs and mix together thoroughly. Pour into dry ingredients, mixing briefly until flour disappears. Add boiling water a little at a time, using enough to make a fairly thin batter.

Grease the griddle with bacon grease or an unflavored vegetable oil. Pour a sample pancake onto hot, greased griddle. If batter is the right consistency, the edges of the corncakes will be lacy. Adjust consistency of batter by adding more water as needed. Corncakes are ready to turn when their edges are lightly browned. Serve immediately with butter and warm maple or berry syrup.

ORGANIZATIONAL GENIUS

Aunt Lucille's fascinating Aunt Pat was born in Arizona in the 1880's, one of the four Davidson sisters, Christina, Pat, Ida and Ina. She had a long career with the YMCA, working for many years in South America. Then in "retirement" in the 1950's she went to work for the Curry family who at that time still ran the small operation on the valley floor of Yosemite that was called Camp Curry. Her second retirement job was working as a housemother at Stanford in the early 1960's, shepherding a house full of brainy young women. Pat was always one step ahead.

Pat said that she wasn't a natural cook, but she loved to entertain. Because she wanted to do it well, she applied her considerable organizational talents to the task. She would work up a menu for dinner and then invite her friends, keeping tabs on the menu and guests on cards in a small file box. When she exhausted the first menu, she would work up a second one and so on, always recording the details so she wouldn't serve anyone the same dinner twice. How I would love to have taken a peek into that file box!

Beginning with Breakfast

Beat-the-Bears Buckwheat Cakes

We've heard that mountain men in the old west used buckwheat flour because it would give them a jump-start when running from grizzly bears.

Serves 4

1-¼ c. buckwheat flour
1-¼ c. all-purpose white flour
2 t. sugar
2 t. baking powder

1 t. salt
½ t. baking soda
2 eggs, separated
1-½ c. buttermilk

Pre-heat a griddle or large, heavy frying pan gradually to medium-high. Combine dry ingredients in a large mixing bowl. In a small bowl, beat egg yolks lightly. Add buttermilk and mix together thoroughly. In a third bowl, beat egg whites until stiff but not dry. Pour egg yolk mixture into dry ingredients, and stir together briefly until flour disappears. Fold in egg whites gently until partially incorporated. (Some egg white "lumps" are fine.)

Grease griddle with bacon grease or unflavored vegetable oil. Pour pancakes onto hot, greased griddle. Buckwheat cakes are ready to turn when bubbles form and break around each one. Serve immediately with butter and warm maple or berry syrup.

ENOUGH IS ENOUGH

The cat said, "Hiss." I've had enough of this balderdash.

—Zoë Livelybrooks (Age 3)

Zoë's mother, Lisa, wrote of the events leading up to Zoë's low opinion of feline behavior: *This morning Zoë and I were invited to visit with a neighbor for coffee and muffins, along with six of her friends and as many of mine. Sometimes at these things there are scuffles and a lack of cooperation but this morning all the children were on the same team. On the opposite side was a hotly pursued black cat named Fluffy. The majority of the visit focused around a cat chase, "Finding the Lost Cat." Lucky for the cat, it was used to hiding and had already scoped out several very well concealed spots. Finally when she was found for the umpteenth time and cornered, she let out a great, "Hisssssssssss!" Zoë announced, "That means leave me alone!" With great seriousness the kids all arrived to tell of the hiss and its meaning.*

Tested-by-Grandchildren Scones

These scones have passed a test more discriminating than the Good Housekeeping Seal of Approval. Carol's eight grandchildren — Kevin, Madeline, Collin, Nick, Derek, Aaron, Scott and Julia — perch on stools looking into her kitchen or lounge on comfortable old chairs in the flower be-decked patio of her heritage bungalow on Balboa Island, a haven of warmth and tenderness for all who walk through her door. The fragrance of baking eventually brings even the late sleepers out from under their covers to gobble up these scones. This is the only test that counts.

Makes 6

2 c. flour, a combination of	**1 egg**
all-purpose white & wheat	**½ c. milk**
1 T. baking powder	**Handful of raisins or currants**
3 T. brown sugar	
1 t. cinnamon	**Milk**
½ c. butter or Crisco	**Cinnamon & sugar**

Pre-heat oven to 425°. In a mixing bowl, combine flour and baking powder with brown sugar and cinnamon. Cut in butter with a fork or pastry blender until mixture resembles coarse corn meal. (Or use a food processor cautiously for this step.)

In a small bowl or measuring cup, beat egg lightly. Add egg, milk and raisins to flour mixture. Stir briefly until flour disappears.

On a floured board, roll out dough into an 8-inch circle, about ¾ inch thick. Divide into 6 pie-shaped wedges and cut apart. Lift scones onto an un-greased cookie sheet with a pancake turner, leaving about 1 inch between them. Although the wedge shape is traditional, scones may be cut like biscuits with a cookie cutter or water glass. Brush scones with milk, and sprinkle with cinnamon and sugar.

Bake until lightly browned, 10 to 15 minutes. Remove from oven and serve immediately.

ANOTHER DEFINITION OF HOMELAND SECURITY

In later years, Henry Raff, the great-grandfather of Carol's grandchildren, laughed about becoming an "Air Raid Warden" in Los Angeles during World War II in spite of having been an "Enemy Alien" and a citizen of Nazi Germany at the time. This civic assignment allowed Henry to circumvent wartime curfews and spend long hours managing the family market.

Fifteen years after Henry and his wife Ilse immigrated to the U.S. with their toddler Bill, they were able to measure success by their son's acceptance to Stanford University where he met Carol.

Emmy's Essential Irish Bread

This easy-to-make bread has been a staple in Irish homes for generations. It is perfect for breakfast and other times of day.

Makes 1 loaf

3 c. wheat flour or substitute
   wheat germ for 1 cup
1 c. all-purpose white flour
2 t. baking soda

¾ t. baking powder
1 t. salt
2 c. buttermilk

Pre-heat oven to 350°. Grease and flour a standard loaf pan and a piece of aluminum foil large enough to cover it, about 12x18 inches. (A standard loaf pan measures about 10x5x3 inches.)

In a medium-sized mixing bowl, combine dry ingredients thoroughly. Stir in buttermilk and mix until flour disappears.

Scrape dough into prepared pan and smooth top. Make a cross in it with your finger or the handle of a wooden spoon. "To make it Irish," said Emmy. Seal greased foil in a hump over the top of the pan.

Bake until lightly browned, 50 to 60 minutes. Bread is done when a knife blade or toothpick inserted in the center comes out clean. Serve warm or at room temperature.

A SCHOLARLY NOTE

Bill Cadbury makes Irish bread regularly. This activity may be related to the fact that he is a scholar of James Joyce who analyzed and catalogued the intricacies of Finnegan's Wake word by word. In retirement, he has graduated to playing a hot piano with Flat Stanley, a local jazz band.

Based on his extensive research in the kitchen, Bill has determined that the secret ingredient of Irish bread is baking powder and the definitive amount is ¾ teaspoon.

BALANCING ACT

Try to do one less thing each day.

—Mary Hyde Ottaway
Advice to her ever-busy executive husband

Barb's Top-Ranked Pecan Rolls

Cinnamon rolls are so important that John has delivered them to friends on Sunday mornings. It's a ritual that may be genetic. Until shortly before his death at age 89, John's father made weekly rounds to deliver mushrooms. • We rank cinnamon rolls on a scale of 1-10 for overall quality, including texture (not too doughy), quantity of cinnamon (abundant) and sweetness (not too). We think Barb's are tops.

Makes 18-24 rolls

Dough:
1 c. milk
½ c. butter (1 cube), cut in small
    pieces
½ c. sugar
1 t. salt
2-¼ t. yeast (¼ oz. pkg.)
¼ c. warm water
1 egg, lightly beaten
4 c. bread flour
    (See notes on pages 91 & 215.)

Glaze:
1 c. well-packed brown sugar
¼ c. hot water
6 T. cold butter (¾ cube), cut in
    small pieces
1-½ c. pecans (5-¼ oz.), chopped

Filling:
About 6 T. butter (¾ cube),
    at room temperature
About 3 T. cinnamon
About ¾ c. brown sugar

Make dough for cinnamon rolls up to 2 days ahead and refrigerate until needed. In a small saucepan, warm milk almost to a boil over medium heat (scald) and skim skin from surface. Remove from heat, add butter, sugar, and salt. Stir until butter melts, pour into a mixing bowl and cool to lukewarm. In a measuring cup or small bowl, dissolve yeast in warm water and then add to cooled milk mixture. Add beaten egg, 2 cups of flour and mix until smooth. Add remaining 2 cups of flour and stir until flour disappears. Cover and refrigerate for 2 hours or up to 2 days.

When ready to continue, make glaze by combining brown sugar and hot water in a small saucepan. Bring to a boil over medium heat. When it boils in the center of the pan, add cold butter and stir until butter is melted. Remove from heat.

Sprinkle chopped pecans on bottom of baking pans. Barb uses three 8-inch round cake pans. Pour glaze over pecans and let stand 10 minutes.

Turn out dough onto a floured board, divide in thirds, roll each into a 12x17 inch rectangle. Spread butter sparingly or generously on dough, top with cinnamon and brown sugar to taste. (We like lots of cinnamon and not too much brown sugar.) Roll up dough and cut into 1 to 1-½ inch rolls. Place rolls cut-side up about 1 inch apart on top of glaze and let them sit in a warm place (75° to 80°) until doubled, about 1 hour.

Pre-heat oven to 350°. Bake until lightly browned, 20 to 25 minutes. Remove from oven and cool briefly on racks before turning out of pans onto a serving plate. Eat while warm, if possible. These freeze nicely after baking, thoroughly cooled and wrapped tightly in plastic or foil.

Emmy's Convenient Baked Toast

For breakfast, Emmy recommended this baked toast with good jam. Because it is so easy and can be prepared ahead of time, she said that it has often saved her life. • Substitute a baguette for sandwich bread and make great Melba toast for hors d'oeuvres.

Makes as much as you want

Best white sandwich bread or a baguette, sliced thinly (about ¼ inch)
Butter or olive oil

Pre-heat oven to 250°. Butter both sides of bread generously or drizzle with olive oil. Arrange on a cookie sheet. (Emmy preferred Pepperidge Farm's original thin-sliced white bread.)

Bake bread until nicely toasted, turning once and watching carefully until perfectly browned, about 10 to 15 minutes. Remove from oven and cool. Store in a covered tin. Freeze to keep perfectly.

CINNAMON TOAST

Re-heat baked toast at 300° until it smells great, about 10 minutes. Remove from oven and top with a mixture of equal parts powdered cinnamon and white granulated sugar. Serve immediately with tea. • Emmy reported that having this toast in the oven will help sell a house.

STRONG MEDICINE

John's grandfather, John Henry Strong, took up mountain climbing at age 57 after being diagnosed with a heart condition and told, "Not to walk against a strong wind."

He climbed 50 mountains in Switzerland, among them the Matterhorn and Mont Blanc, as well as many peaks in Colorado, the Tetons and the Canadian Rockies. Papa Strong, as he was called, started his daughter Betsy on her distinguished climbing career. He lived to be 93 proving that there's nothing like fresh air and deep breathing.

Connie's If-You-Don't-Like-to-Cook Frittata

A frittata is an omelette baked in the oven, an easy way to prepare eggs for a crowd. Making this frittata is almost as easy as not cooking which explains why Catherine's sister Connie asked for this recipe many years ago. Since then, Connie has learned to cook, especially on her treasured George Forman grill. Fortunately she continues with her original kitchen specialty, professional dish washing which is almost as important as being an appreciative eater. Connie scores a perfect 10 in both.

Serves 8-10

¼ c. butter (½ cube) or 4 T. olive oil
1 large onion, sliced thinly
10 eggs
1 t. baking powder
2 c. ricotta or cottage cheese (16 oz.)
¾ lb. cheese, about 3 cups grated
   (Monterey Jack, sharp cheddar,
   Gruyère, Stilton or a combination
   of cheeses)

<u>Options:</u>
1 green, red or yellow pepper,
   sliced thinly
½ lb. mushrooms, sliced thinly
   (about 2 cups)
3 leeks, well washed & sliced thinly
   (See page 75.)
½ lb. asparagus, steamed until tender
   (about 5 minutes) & cut in 1 inch pieces
1 bunch scallions, chopped
12 oz. can diced green Anaheim chiles
1 c. artichoke hearts, drained &
   chopped coarsely (See page 114.)
1 c. cooked chicken or ham, diced
¾ lb. hot Italian sausage, browned &
   drained thoroughly
½ lb. bacon (about 6 thick slices),
   cooked crisp & crumbled

Pre-heat oven to 350°. Grease a 9x13-inch baking dish or a large, shallow casserole. Melt butter over low heat in a frying pan and sauté onion until limp, about 5 minutes. In a large mixing bowl, beat eggs lightly. Add cooked onions and stir gently. Add baking powder, ricotta or cottage cheese and grated cheese. Mix together thoroughly.

Select options from the list. Add chopped peppers to onions after sautéing for several minutes and cook for several minutes more. Add mushrooms or leeks and do the same. Substitute leeks for onion. For asparagus, scallions, chiles, artichoke hearts, chicken or ham, cooked sausage or bacon, prepare as suggested above and then add directly to egg mixture after combining with cheese. Mix together gently.

Pour into prepared baking dish. Bake 30 to 40 minutes, until lightly browned and set. (Insert a knife in the center and it comes out clean.) Remove from oven, let sit for 5 minutes and serve.

Barbara's Huevos Rancheros

This recipe originated with Barbara's friend who comes from the town of Miguel Auza in the Mexican state of Zacatecas, northeast of Mazatlán.

Serves 1 or more

Black beans, cooked, ¾ c. per person
Warmed tortillas, 2 per person
Eggs, 1 or 2 per person
Chopped lettuce, 1 c. per person

Condiments:
Limes, ½ per person
Jalapeño peppers
Chopped onion
Salsa (See recipe on page 267.)

Barbara prepares her beans by soaking them in cold water overnight. The next day she drains them in a colander, rinses them in cold water and puts them in a soup pot. She covers them with plenty of cold water and cooks them until tender. Cooking time, she explained, depends upon the freshness of the beans, usually 1 to 2 hours. (See box below for more possibilities and another recipe on page 167.)

Wrap tortillas in foil and warm for 15 minutes at 250°. Prepare salsa or use a commercial one. (See recipe on page 267.) Chop lettuce and onion. Cut limes in quarters.

Poach or fry eggs. To poach eggs, bring a frying pan of water (about 1 inch deep) to a boil over medium heat, lower heat and maintain at a simmer. Break each egg into a cup, and gently pour it into simmering water. Spoon water over each egg as needed to cook the top. Cover pan, turn off heat and let sit until eggs are cooked as you wish, 1 to 2 minutes.

Assemble *huevos rancheros* by placing 2 warmed tortillas on each plate, top with lettuce, then black beans and eggs. Garnish with lime quarters and whole jalapeño peppers. Pass chopped onions and salsa.

GUATEMALAN BLACK BEANS

In Guatemala Barbara explained, black beans are called *frijol negro* in the singular. They are served three ways, *frijoles parados*, *frijoles colados* and *frijoles volteados*. *Parados* are "standing up" beans, cooked until tender but still whole. The next step would be to sieve or mash them and make *collados*. Then, Barbara's favorite, *volteados* or "turned" beans that are cooked still more by "turning" them in a frying pan until they are dry.

Barbara said these dry, condensed beans are even better the second day when they have a texture like peanut butter. *Volteados* are served spread on tortillas with fried *plátanos* (small bananas), *queso fresco* (a white, ricotta-like cheese) and scrambled eggs.

Paul's Peerless Potato Omelette

*Paul and John met on a school bus. In college they moved to freight trains and later a small plane that they flew through Canada. They also sailed through the night down the rugged, unforgiving Oregon coast. • Paul finds the waters less treacherous in the kitchen of the old farmhouse where he lives with his wife Anuncia and their son Tavi. • This recipe is Paul's adaptation of the Spanish classic **torta de patatas**, also called **tortilla española**, the national dish of Spain along with paella. **Torta** is eaten in Spain as a tapa or appetizer, but it also makes a fine breakfast, lunch or light dinner.*

Serves 4

4 medium potatoes   **6 T. olive oil**
1 large onion, chopped   **5 eggs**
4 cloves garlic, peeled & minced **Salt & pepper to taste**

Paul explained that traditionally the potatoes are fried, but he prefers to steam them. Peel and slice potatoes thinly and steam until tender but not soft, about 10 minutes. In a heavy 9-inch frying pan, sauté onion and garlic in 3 tablespoons of olive oil over medium heat until limp, about 5 minutes. In a mixing bowl, beat eggs and then gently add onions and potatoes. Season to taste with salt and pepper.

There are three ways to cook this omelette, the traditional method in a frying pan, a combination frying pan and broiler, and baked.

For the **traditional method**, heat 2 more tablespoons of olive oil in a frying pan over medium-high heat and pour in egg-potato-onion mixture. Cook without stirring until omelette forms a solid mass and is browned on the bottom. Adjust the heat as needed. It is very important to keep the omelette loose so that you can turn it. To do so, shake the pan across the burner from time to time and lift around omelette with a pancake turner. After several minutes, the omelette will be cooked on the bottom but still liquid on top. Then it's time for the big trick. Put a large plate on top of the pan and turn the omelette onto it. If you succeed the first time, give yourself an A+. Paul recommended using a frying plan with a non-stick surface and we agree. Once you have the omelette on a plate, add 1 tablespoon of olive oil to the pan and slip the omelette back. Cook briefly. Slip cooked omelette onto a serving plate and serve immediately.

FRYING PAN & BROILER METHOD • The frying pan must be ovenproof. Pre-heat broiler and position an oven rack about 5 inches below broiler. After cooking the bottom of the omelette as instructed above, place the frying pan under the broiler. Broil for 2 to 3 minutes until the top is set and nicely browned. Remove from oven and serve.

BAKED METHOD • Pre-heat oven to 400°. Grease an ovenproof casserole and pour in egg-potato mixture. Bake until omelette is set, 12 to 15 minutes. Be careful not to overcook. Remove from oven and serve.

Olga's Grateful Granola

We live in granola heaven, a town where everyone eats so much granola that half a dozen different local brands are available at the grocery store. This might make you think that granola is an esoteric substance, difficult to make. Not so. It is easy and Cousin Olga has provided us with a recipe that you can customize to suit your own taste.

Makes 22 cups

14 c. rolled oats
2 c. wheat germ
1 c. sesame seeds
1 c. sunflower seeds
2 c. nuts (8 oz.)
2 c. shredded unsweetened coconut
  (about 5 oz.)
¾ c. unflavored vegetable oil
1-½ c. honey
2 T. vanilla
1 t. salt

Optional:
2 c. raisins, currants, dried cranberries or other dried fruit,
  chopped coarsely

Pre-heat oven to 325°. In a very large bowl or soup pot, combine rolled oats, wheat germ, sesame and sunflower seeds, nuts and coconut.

In a saucepan, mix oil, honey, vanilla and salt and warm over medium heat until thoroughly combined, stirring constantly. Pour over dry mixture, and stir to mix thoroughly. Spread cereal mixture on 3 or 4 un-greased cookie sheets or baking pans.

Bake until lightly toasted, 30 to 40 minutes, stirring every 8 to 10 minutes. Remove from oven and cool on racks.

Add raisins, currants, dried cranberries or other dried fruit after baking. Store granola in tins or jars with tight fitting lids. Give a jar of granola as a gift.

THE RIDDLE OF BEES IN FLIGHT

What linked bees to Panama and San Jose, California in the nineteenth century? The answer is honey. On the site of the old terminal at the San Jose Airport, there were bees, bought in 1853 by an enterprising farmer from a New Yorker who lived in Panama. Enough of the bees survived the long trip to form one hive, thus beginning apiculture in California.

—From a historical marker at the San Jose Airport

Rice Pudding The-Way-Pop-Liked-It

Catherine's father, Frank, loved rice pudding. He wrote down the recipe in an old leather notebook that dates from his bachelor days on Rough and Ready Island near Stockton, California. His favorite recipes included tapioca pudding, 1943 Victory Cake, waffles, coconut cream pie, divinity and Spanish meatballs. • We think that rice pudding is too substantial to eat as dessert and prefer it for breakfast. Assembled the night before, refrigerated and then baked in the morning, it's a breakfast that makes you fit for important activities, such as Dog Rescue. John and Bruce Klepinger ate it the morning they rescued our border collie Lively from a tiny, precarious ledge where he had spent 17 hours. (See the story on pages 310-11.) • Rice pudding is a great way to use up leftover cooked rice. A second recipe for rice pudding on page 233 uses uncooked rice and bakes for many hours.

Serves 8

1 qt. milk
½ c. sugar
2 t. vanilla
Grated peel of 1 lemon
5 eggs

2 c. cooked rice
1 c. raisins (about 6-⅔ oz.)
  or currants (about 4-¼ oz.)
Freshly grated nutmeg

Pre-heat oven to 350° and bring a kettle of water to a boil. In a small saucepan, warm milk almost to a boil over medium heat (scald) and skim skin from surface. Remove from heat and add sugar, stirring well until it dissolves. Add vanilla and lemon peel.

Distribute rice evenly over the bottom of an ovenproof casserole or baking dish. Top with raisins or currants.

In a mixing bowl, beat eggs and then pour hot milk over them, mixing well. Pour gently over rice and raisins or currants. Grate fresh nutmeg on top

Set bowl in a baking pan, and fill the baking pan with about an inch of boiling water. Bake until custard is set, 50 to 60 minutes. Custard is set when a knife inserted in the center comes out clean. Remove from oven and cool. Rice pudding is best served warm but also delicious cold or at room temperature.

ADDING IT UP

I've come to believe that we become the sum total of those we love.

—Emmy Smith (April 7, 1995)

Beginning with Breakfast

Circa 1905 Applesauce

We have apple trees dating from the farm's beginning in 1905. One of them, with three varieties of apples grafted to it, thrives in spite of a completely hollow trunk. This remarkable tree produces fruit abundantly from late July through September. • Because apple fashions have changed so much over the years, we have been unable to identify all the varieties that grow here at the farm. We have both yellow delicious and Gravenstein as well as a small, tough-skinned November variety that stores well and makes fine juice. • We think the best applesauce in the world comes from **yellow transparent** *apples. Emmy called them June apples because in Kentucky her gnarly old tree bore fruit then. In our region, this variety produces apples in July on Nancy's tree in nearby Lorane. • We prefer Gravenstein, Newtown Pippin and Granny Smith for applesauce, the same tart varieties we use for pie and apple crisp. The beautiful, huge Rome Beauties are lovely for baking, and Pink Ladies get an award for their name and their flavor.*

Serves 6-8

12 green apples, washed & quartered
About ½ c. water
Juice of 1 lemon

1 t. cinnamon
½ t. each cloves, allspice & nutmeg
Brown sugar, if desired

Put apples in a soup pot and add water, about ½ cup, just enough to keep apples from sticking. Cover and bring to a boil, then reduce heat to low and simmer until the apples are soft, 20 to 30 minutes, stirring frequently to keep them from sticking to the bottom of the pan.

OVEN METHOD • Bake the apples in the oven at 325° in a covered casserole until they are very soft, about 1 hour, and you won't have to remember to stir them.

To remove skins and seeds, run cooked apples through a food mill. Or peel and core the apples initially, then slice and cook as directed and mash cooked apples with a potato masher. Stir in lemon juice and spices. Add brown sugar to taste, if you like.

WHAT HAPPENED?

We were astonished to learn that over 1,000 varieties of apples have been grown in North America. Yet we see so few of them in our grocery stores. If we can choose from hundreds of varieties, then why do we put up with the ubiquitous red delicious, a pitiful excuse for an apple that nearly always looks far better than it tastes?

We remember when Granny Smith was the "new" apple, imported from New Zealand and South Africa in the 1960s. Now we are grateful for Gala, Braeburn, Fuji and Pink Lady apples. The apple tide seems to be turning.

Fried Green Apples & Tomatoes

This is southern cooking at its best and simplest. Eat fried-green tomatoes and apples with bacon, eggs and cornbread for a breakfast that will keep you going all day.

Serves as many as you want

Green apples:
Green apples such as Granny Smith, Gravenstein or Newtown Pippin, 1 per person
Bacon grease or butter, about 1 T. per apple
Brown sugar to taste

Green tomatoes:
Green tomatoes, 1 per person
Bacon grease, about 1 T. per tomato

Optional:
Cornmeal

For fried green apples, allow 1 medium apple per person. Core apples and slice thinly, about ¼ inch thick. (No need to peel.) In a heavy frying pan, fry sliced apples in bacon grease or butter over medium heat until browned. Cover, lower heat and cook until apples fall apart, about 15 to 20 minutes. Then add brown sugar to taste. Serve immediately. These apples also re-heat nicely in a frying pan over low heat, stirring occasionally.

GREEN TOMATOES • Allow 1 medium green tomato per person. Slice tomatoes ½ inch thick. Coat tomato slices in cornmeal before frying, if you like. In a heavy frying pan, melt bacon grease over medium heat and cook tomatoes until they are "a little messy," directed Emmy. Serve immediately. No seasoning is necessary. Bacon grease is essential to the flavor of the tomatoes.

WORDS OF WISDOM

I can understand people who shun success. Many children do in school because, once they succeed, success will be EXPECTED. It is harder to fail after having succeeded than to have never succeeded at all. Fear of flying-kind-of-thing.

What you have to do is savor the pleasures of success, then you know it is worth the risk of failing once in awhile. If you have talent, you will succeed more than you fail, so long as you work hard at it. The only way to find out is to get out there and try. If you don't, some day you will regret not having done so.

—Barry Bingham, Jr.

Soups & Sandwiches for Lunch

Every pot must sit on its own bottom.

—Bessie Bankerd

Big-Bucks Chicken Stock

Chicken stock is a culinary resource that makes the difference between ordinary soup and something memorable. Stock in the freezer is like having big dollars in your savings account. • Even if you don't have celery, carrots and an onion, make stock with chicken parts and water. Or freeze chicken parts in a plastic bag and make stock when convenient.

Makes one or more quarts

Chicken carcass, bones, scraps & giblets
Water
2 carrots, halved
1 onion, peeled & quartered
2 stalks celery, halved
3 cloves garlic, peeled

1 sprig rosemary or 1 t. dried rosemary
1 sprig fresh parsley
6 peppercorns
1 sprig thyme or 1 t. dried thyme
1 bay leaf

Cover chicken parts with cold water in a large saucepan or soup pot. Add other ingredients and bring to a boil. Reduce heat, cover and simmer for 1 hour. Remove from heat, cool and strain through a colander. Discard solids. Chill stock and degrease. (See below.) Use stock immediately or freeze in tightly covered plastic containers.

DE-GREASING STOCK

De-grease stock by chilling it in refrigerator and then skimming thickened fat from surface with a spoon. A special measuring cup has its spout at the bottom, so you can pour liquid — meat juices or stock — from under the grease that accumulates on top. It's quick.

THE BEST ROUND-UP

For two days a yellow dog hung-out by the mailbox at the end of our driveway and cried. John put out dog biscuits, the only dog food we had after Ivy and Lively had died the previous year. The dog biscuits disappeared, but this dog would not come near the house.

Our cousin Andrea, her John Smith and their 3-year-old son Alex arrived for a visit. The boys went out to the barn where they could see the yellow dog hiding among the trees. John 2.0 and Alex turned their backs to the dog and John 2.0 said, "Do you want to go for a walk with us?" The dog raced to them. Then Alex ran into the kitchen, "Lady C, Lady C," he exclaimed, "here's your new dog."

We named our yellow Labrador retriever Harper after John's great mentor. He loves everyone and howls with guests when we say "grace" before a meal.

Quick & Dirty Soothing Soup

Nothing soothes like chicken soup. It's comfort food in the company of custard, milk toast, macaroni and cheese, mashed potatoes and brownies. Chicken soup is also nutritious, easy to digest and delicious.

Serves 2

3 c. chicken stock (See previous page.)
¾ c. pasta (*fusilli*, *penne*, bow
   ties, *cavatappi* or riso)

¾ c. frozen peas
Salt to taste
Freshly grated Parmesan cheese

Bring chicken stock to a boil in a covered saucepan over medium heat. Add pasta and cook covered for a few minutes less than the time indicated on package. Stir frequently to keep pasta from sticking to the bottom of the pan.

When pasta is cooked, add peas and stir. Add salt to taste and serve immediately with freshly grated Parmesan cheese.

VEGETABLE STOCK

We use powdered Rapunzel Vegetable Broth made in Switzerland as a substitute for homemade stock when needed. One tablespoon plus boiling water makes a quart of stock.

THE MANY LIVES OF SOUP

For Christmas dinner Bill Cadbury made a delicious risotto with kidney beans that was served in a whole, baked pumpkin. We froze the leftovers.

Months later, this tasty dish was reincarnated as soup, puréed with the addition of water and stock. We froze these leftovers, too.

About six weeks after that, we defrosted it again. This time we added sour cream, chicken stock, corn from two leftover cobs and more risotto. Voilà, another great soup and, finally, the end of Christmas dinner.

Emma's Best Bean Soup

Emma, a mainstay in the Smith family for most of her life, was the youngest of 15 children. She learned to cook when she was 16 under the guidance of her older sister, Mamie Harris. Emma and John's mother Emmy filled the kitchen with their delicious laughter and delectable food. • *This soup was John's father's favorite lunch with the addition of a few drops of Tabasco and a splash of sherry.* • *Emma reminded us that all soups and stews are better the next day.*

Serves 6-8

2 c. white navy or great northern beans
About 6 c. cold water
1-½ lbs. butt end of ham,
   ham hocks or ham bone
1 onion, chopped coarsely
4 or 5 stalks celery, chopped (about 2 c.)
1 large potato, peeled & cubed

14-½ oz. can "ready-cut" tomatoes
1 clove garlic, peeled & minced
1 T. parsley, minced
Salt to taste
¼ t. or more cayenne pepper

The night before, rinse beans in cold water, cover generously with cold water and soak overnight. The next day, drain beans in a colander, rinse and place in soup pot. Cover generously with cold water, about 6 cups. Bring to a boil over medium heat, reduce heat to low and simmer uncovered, stirring frequently and adding more water as needed. Cook until soft, about 2 hours.

While beans are cooking, wash ham and cover it generously with cold water in a big sauce-pan. Bring to a boil and cook uncovered until ham is tender. (If you use a ham bone, cook it with beans and omit this step.) Remove ham from broth, cool and cut in bite-sized pieces. Discard the fat and bone. Skim fat from ham broth and add broth to beans. (See page 68 for de-greasing stock.)

Add remaining ingredients, including ham, and cook 1 hour more. Adjust seasoning and serve hot. Soup freezes well in tightly covered plastic containers.

CHOPPING ONIONS

Cut off stem and root ends of onion. Cut it in half from stem to root. Peel off the outside layer of papery skin and one inner layer. Put onion cut-side down on a cutting board. Slice every ¼ inch or so parallel to the stem and root ends, and then slice crosswise for as fine a chop as needed. Repeat for second half.

THE LAST WORD

Even if you know many things, do not argue with the judge.

—An Ethiopian proverb

Alan's Father-Knows-Best Lima Bean Soup

Alan brought this soup — his own creation — for lunch one day when he was helping us remodel the house. We admire that he cooked with such originality after long days on the job. A gifted carpenter and a devoted father, he said that his daughter, Libby, preferred steak and potatoes to soup.

Serves 6

2 c. dried lima beans
1 large onion, chopped
2 T. vegetable oil
2 meaty ham hocks (about 1-½ lbs.)
6 c. cold water

2 large potatoes, diced
2 carrots, cut in ½ rounds
7 oz. can Anaheim chiles, diced
Salt & pepper to taste
1 t. paprika

The night before, rinse beans in cold water, cover generously with water and soak overnight. The next day, drain in a colander, rinse and put in a soup pot.

In a frying pan, sauté onion in oil over medium heat for about 5 minutes and then scrape into soup pot. In the same frying pan, brown ham hocks over medium-high heat and then add to vegetables and beans in soup pot.

Add cold water and remaining ingredients. Bring to a boil over medium heat, reduce heat to low and simmer uncovered. After about 30 minutes, skim foam from surface of the soup. Continue simmering soup uncovered for another 1-½ hours, adding water as needed and stirring frequently. When soup is nicely thick, remove ham hocks. Cool until you can handle them, cut up the meat, discard the bones and skin, and return meat to the soup. Adjust seasoning. Serve immediately or later.

Add a dash or two of Tabasco, Pickapeppa or other spicy sauce to this soup before eating. Cool thoroughly and freeze in tightly covered plastic containers.

THE PASSION OF WORK

Find the thing that needs no preparatory struggle and then do it for all you are worth if you can. There will always be black or gray moments when it is difficult to do even the thing you like.

—Gertrude Bell

From a letter to Edward Stanley
(*The Letters of Gertrude Bell*)

Bruce's No-Slouch Lentil & Spinach Soup

Bruce Klepinger was the leader of the trek in Nepal when John and Catherine met. His Sherpa friends of long-standing call him Ang Bruce out of respect. He is Mr. Bruce in India, said in a tone reserved for higher ups. Bruce is one of the premier mountaineering, trekking and river guides in the world. • He's also a no-slouch cook at home and on the trail. This is Bruce's version of a soup he enjoyed in a local restaurant.

Serves 6-8

3 c. yellow lentils
12 c. cold water & 1 T. chicken bouillon
   powder or substitute chicken stock
   for part of water
3 T. vegetable oil
2 large yellow onions, chopped
2 c. celery, chopped (4 or 5 stalks)
1 to 3 T. curry powder
1 t. turmeric

1 T. cumin seed
5 cloves garlic, peeled & minced
2 T. yellow mustard seed
1-½ to 2 lbs. chicken breast (about 2
   whole breasts), skinned, boned & cubed
1 bunch spinach, washed thoroughly
Juice of 1 lemon
Salt to taste
4 sprigs cilantro, chopped

The night before, rinse lentils thoroughly in cold water, pick out any stones, cover with cold water and soak overnight. The next day, drain in a colander, rinse and put in a large soup pot with cold water and bouillon powder or stock. Bring to a boil over medium heat, reduce heat to low and simmer uncovered, stirring frequently.

In a frying pan, sauté onion in oil over medium-low heat until transparent, about 10 minutes. Add celery and sauté 10 minutes more. Combine with lentils. Add curry powder to taste, turmeric, cumin and garlic. Stir well.

In a small, heavy-bottomed frying pan (cast iron is best), blacken mustard seeds by shaking pan over medium-high heat until nicely browned and fragrant, about 5 minutes. Add to soup.

Simmer soup uncovered for 2 hours, stirring frequently. Bruce lets his soup simmer uncovered all day, adding water occasionally for a total of 20 to 25 cups. Prepare soup to this point and then set aside to cool thoroughly, cover and refrigerate overnight. Re-heat over medium-low on cooktop, stirring frequently, or in oven at 300° for 30 to 45 minutes.

About ½ hour before serving, add cubed chicken to nicely bubbling soup and poach until the chicken is cooked, 15 to 20 minutes. Add spinach, lemon juice, salt and cilantro. Stir well and simmer gently for 5 minutes more. Serve with crusty bread.

Too much is never enough.

— One of Bruce Klepinger's mottos

"The higher you go, the higher you get" is another.

Birdlette's Red Lentil Soup

Birdlette is Mitzi who is also Maria Christina who became Mrs. Poetzinger and then Mom. It's not easy to explain how Catherine nicknamed her goddaughter Birdlette. It's easier to explain how Carol named her daughter Maria Christina. It's easiest of all to explain how Mitzi got to be Mrs. Poetzinger and then Mom. Fortunately, she is in the business of explaining things, having followed her mother into teaching. Mitzi is now a school psychologist as well as a gifted bilingual teacher. • The first time Mitzi came to visit the farm she brought a wonderful soup mix that we thoroughly enjoyed. This is our version of it.

Serves 6

2 c. red lentils
1 onion, chopped
2 T. olive oil
2 to 4 cloves garlic, peeled & minced
2 stalks celery, chopped (about ½ c.)

3 c. chicken stock or 3 c. cold water
  & 2 chicken bouillon cubes
Grated rind & juice of 1 lemon
Salt & pepper to taste
1 large chicken breast (2 halves),
  skinned, boned & cubed

The night before, rinse lentils thoroughly in cold water and pick out any stones. Cover with cold water and soak overnight. The next day, drain in a colander and rinse thoroughly.

In a soup pot, sauté onion in olive oil over medium-heat until transparent, about 10 minutes. Add garlic and cook 2 to 3 minutes more. Add drained lentils, carrots, celery, chicken stock (or cold water and bouillon cubes), lemon rind and juice. Bring to a boil over medium heat, reduce heat to low and simmer 1 hour uncovered, stirring frequently. Add more water as needed.

Season to taste with salt and pepper. Add cubed chicken and poach in gently simmering soup until chicken is done, 15 to 20 minutes. Serve immediately.

TAKE THAT, MICKEY MOUSE!

We were told of a loving grandmother who tucked a clove of garlic into the velcro tab of her five month old grandson's diapers to protect him from jealousy and the evil eye. After all, his mother was taking him to visit her office at the Disney Studios, and a careful grandmother owed him the best possible protection according to her Macedonian tradition.

George's Accidental Chicken Soup

Some people move to the country to get away from it all and seek isolation. Not us. We find there is nothing more important than good neighbors close by. George and his wife, Lorna, are the best. When an old pipe broke and produced a geyser in the front yard one summer while we were away, George helped stop the flood. George and Lorna pointed out that our "pregnant" cow wasn't pregnant just huge. They also rounded up their family to help rescue our cow Rosie from the stream where she'd fallen. And Lorna keeps John's hair trimmed, and George reminds us of important community meetings. We can't get along without them. • One snowy Saturday we scoured the cupboards and came up with this soup to take to George who was just home from the hospital.

Serves 4

1 c. red lentils
1 whole chicken breast (2 halves)
6 c. cold water
2 T. olive oil
1 medium onion, chopped

1 c. celery (about 3 stalks), chopped
1 carrot, quartered & sliced thinly
½ c. riso (small rice-shaped pasta)
¾ c. frozen peas
Salt to taste

Rinse lentils thoroughly in cold water, pick out any stones and drain in a colander. In a small soup pot, cover chicken with cold water, about 6 cups. Bring to a boil over medium heat, and skim foam from surface. Reduce heat, cover and simmer until the chicken is done, about 20 minutes. Remove chicken from stock and set aside. (See page 68 for directions on de-greasing chicken stock.) Add lentils to chicken stock and bring to a boil, remove from heat and set aside.

In a frying pan, sauté onion in olive oil over medium-low heat until transparent, about 10 minutes. Add celery and sauté 10 minutes more. Add carrots and sauté briefly. Add vegetables to lentils and chicken stock. Bring to a boil over medium heat, reduce heat, cover and simmer for 1 hour, stirring frequently. The lentils "disappear" and make a nicely thick soup. Add riso and simmer 10 minutes uncovered until pasta is cooked, stirring frequently to keep the riso from sticking to bottom of pan.

Skin, bone and cube chicken, add it to soup and heat thoroughly. Add peas, salt to taste and stir well. Serve immediately.

THE GREAT UNKNOWN

Men and melons are hard to know.

—Ben Franklin
Poor Richard's Almanac

Heart-Warming Leek Soup

On her first visit to Alexandra's family's home, Catherine looked at a beautiful antique rug and smiled. Her education had prepared her perfectly for such a moment. "Oh, what a beautiful rug you have hanging on your wall!" Catherine exclaimed in elementary Russian. She is still waiting to use a second obscure but crucial Russian phrase, "Be careful of the mushrooms with the white spots." • We love leeks and this unfailingly delicious soup is a favorite of ours, a variation on Alexandra's family recipe.

Serves 4

4 large leeks, chopped finely
2 medium potatoes, peeled & cubed
1 large carrot, sliced finely
2 c. chicken stock or
** 2 c. cold water & 1 chicken bouillon cube**

1 c. milk
¼ c. butter (½ cube)
Salt & freshly ground pepper to taste

In a medium saucepan, cover vegetables with chicken stock and bring to a boil. Lower heat and simmer 15 to 20 minutes until vegetables are soft.

In a second saucepan or soup pot, warm milk and butter together over low heat until the butter melts, stirring occasionally.

Purée cooked vegetables in 2 batches in a food processor or blender. Add purée to milk-butter mixture and season to taste with salt and pepper. Cook over low heat for 10 to 15 minutes more, stirring occasionally. Adjust heat as needed to avoid boiling. Serve immediately.

CLEANING LEEKS

Leeks need to be washed carefully because dirt seems to work its way in between the layers. Slice off root end, some of the top and cut in half lengthwise. Wash in lots of cold water and check between skins to make sure that all the dirt has been removed. Drain thoroughly and pat dry.

A good person earns more than wages.

—An Ethiopian proverb

From-the-Garden Squash Soup

We always grow lots of squash in our garden, hoping we'll have summer squash by the Fourth of July and enough winter squash to enjoy into the new year. We store our winter squash — acorn, Delicata, Hubbard and Sweet Mama hybrid, to name several favorites — in bushel baskets in our fruit room, an old milk shed insulated with four inches of sawdust in its wooden walls. • If you have the luxury of picking summer squash fresh from the garden, then its natural sweetness makes additional seasoning in this soup unnecessary.

Serves 6

3 T. butter or olive oil
2 onions, chopped coarsely

Winter Squash:
3 c. cooked winter squash or
raw winter squash, cubed
4 c. chicken stock or
4 c. cold water & 2 chicken bouillon
cubes

Summer Squash:
6 c. uncooked summer squash,
sliced thinly

Salt & freshly ground pepper to taste

Optional:
2 T. or more curry powder
Juice of 1 lemon
1 c. yogurt
½ c. chutney (See page 269.)
1 very ripe banana, mashed

In a large frying pan, sauté onions in butter or olive oil over medium-low heat until limp, about 5 minutes. Add curry powder if you wish and cook several minutes more. Add winter squash and chicken stock or summer squash. (Summer squash needs no additional water or stock.) Cook for 10 minutes uncovered, stirring occasionally. For uncooked winter squash, continue cooking 20 to 30 minutes more until tender.

Purée cooked vegetables in 2 or 3 batches in a food processor or blender. Return to soup pot and warm over medium-low heat. If desired, add lemon juice to either soup. Add yogurt, chutney or mashed banana to winter squash soup. Adjust seasoning and heat thoroughly, stirring frequently. Serve immediately.

Curried winter squash soup is delicious with cornbread on page 224. Summer squash soup is also very nice served cold on a hot day. Try swirling 2 to 3 tablespoons of pesto in it before serving. (See page 162.)

Photographs & ladies not allowed.

—Sign at Stok Monastery

During Buddhist initiation rites (Ladakh, India, 1984)

Susan's Zucchini & Brie Soup

There are people who putter around their houses fixing things up, there are serious do-it-yourselfers, and then there are Susan and Tom. Between them, they can do just about anything, including remodel a 1930's colonial house on a budget and in a style that would make Scrooge smile and Martha Stewart blush. • There are also plenty of people who give great parties. But no one has ever given a party quite like Susan and Tom's once-in-a-lifetime black tie affair for 12 guests. For this party in their rented cottage, they built a temporary dining-room complete with wallpaper and electricity. While listening to old favorites played on the baby grand piano by an amiable musician, we ate our oysters and drank our champagne in the living room and then dined in splendor on eight more courses in the new dining room. • This delicious soup has a wonderful flavor from the Brie, but we also make it with chèvre. Although peeling off the rind seems a very unkind thing to do to a fine Brie, it can be done nicely with a vegetable peeler when the cheese is cold.

Serves 4-6

**4 medium zucchini, sliced
  (about 4 cups)**
6 small potatoes, peeled & cubed
2 T. olive oil
2-½ c. chicken stock
**8 oz. ripe Brie, rind removed
  or chèvre (goat cheese)**

Salt & freshly ground pepper to taste

Optional:
½ c. cream
Cream sherry

In a large saucepan, combine zucchini, potatoes, olive oil and chicken stock. Bring to a boil over medium heat. Reduce heat, cover and simmer until potatoes are tender, 10 to 15 minutes, stirring frequently.

Purée cooked vegetables in a food processor or blender in 2 batches, adding half of the cheese to each. Return to pan, add salt and pepper to taste and cream, if desired. Warm thoroughly over low heat, stirring constantly. Serve immediately with a splash of sherry in each bowl.

THE HAT RACK THEORY

Alright, you are upset. Very. You will hang your upset on the first thing your eye lights on, i.e. the hat rack. Calm down! Chances are the source of your upset isn't close by. You do better to calm down, climb a tree, take a walk, think about it before you start tearing up turf.

—Emmy Smith

"Invented" with her older sister Betsy.

Alexandra's Earthquake Borscht

This Slavic minestrone with beet is usually called Ukrainian borscht to distinguish it from cold beet soup. The secret ingredient is celery root. • Many years ago on her first visit to California, Alexandra called her grandmother to get the recipe. She prepared borscht for the Manz family while we were staying in a beach cottage, and it was a big hit. So much so that early the next morning there was an earthquake, Alexandra's first. • We make our version of Alexandra's family borscht at least once each fall, using beets from the garden. There's nothing more delicious. • Alex reminded us that borscht is traditionally served with pirozhki, small meat filled pastries.

Serves 10-12

Beef stock:
3 or 4 meaty soup bones (about 2 lbs.)
14 c. cold water
1 large onion, quartered
2 bay leaves
10 whole peppercorns
1 t. salt

Garnish:
Sour cream
Sprigs of fresh dill

9 medium beets (about 5-6 cups),
   peeled & cubed
2 large white potatoes, peeled
   & cubed
2 onions, chopped
3 large carrots, peeled & sliced thinly
1 medium celery root, peeled & grated
   (about 2 cups)
2 large tomatoes, peeled, seeded &
   diced or 14-½ oz. can "ready-cut"
   tomatoes
6 oz. can tomato paste
2-3 c. shredded cabbage (1 small head)
4 cloves garlic, peeled & minced
Salt & pepper to taste
Several sprigs of fresh dill
   or 2 t. dried

In a large soup pot, cover beef bones with cold water. Add onion, bay leaves, peppercorns and salt. Bring to a boil over medium heat and skim foam from the surface as needed. Reduce heat, cover and simmer until meat is cooked, about 45 minutes. Remove meat and bones from stock and cool. De-bone and cube meat. Discard bones, gristle and fat. De-grease stock. (See method on page 68.) Return stock to soup pot.

Add cubed beets, potatoes, onions, carrots, celery root, tomatoes and tomato paste to the pot of stock. Simmer uncovered 45 minutes to 1 hour, until vegetables are nearly cooked, stirring frequently.

Add shredded cabbage, cubed meat, salt, pepper and dill. Simmer uncovered ½ hour more, stirring occasionally.

Adjust seasoning. Serve borscht hot topped with sour cream and dill. Borscht, like nearly all soups, tastes much better when re-heated the following day. It also freezes well in tightly covered plastic containers.

All-Seasons Chowder

This is a fast, hearty meal with lots of room for variation.

½ lb. bacon (about 6 slices)
2 large onions, chopped
1 green or sweet red pepper, chopped
3 white potatoes, peeled & cubed
¾ c. milk, half & half or cream

Options:
2 c. clam juice or cold water plus
    two 6-½ oz. cans minced or chopped
    clams OR
2 c. chicken stock or cold water plus
    17 oz. can corn (or 2 c. fresh kernels) OR
2 c. fish stock or clam juice or cold water
    plus 1-½ lb. fish filets (halibut, sea
    bass, lingcod), cut in 1 inch pieces

In a frying pan over medium heat, cook bacon until crispy. Remove from heat and drain on paper towels. Crumble and set aside.

Sauté onion in bacon grease over medium-low heat until limp, about 5 minutes. Add peppers and cook several minutes more. Add potatoes and cover with clam juice, stock or cold water. Simmer gently uncovered over medium-low heat until potatoes are tender, about 10 to 15 minutes.

Add clams, corn or fish and cook 5 minutes more, until clams or corn are hot, or fish is nearly cooked. Be careful not to overcook fish. Add milk or cream and crumbled bacon. Heat thoroughly, stirring gently and serve immediately.

THE JUDGE'S RECIPE

John's father, called "The Judge" by nearly everyone he knew, wrote us almost daily letters during the last years of his life. In warm weather, he sat in front of his manual Achiever typewriter on the back porch at 711, sipping Scotch, smoking his pipe and commenting on the world. Although a great appreciater of good food, he kept himself well out of the kitchen except when it came to mixing a drink. This is the Judge's only known recipe as related in his own words on January 26, 1983, just months before he died:

COG? Cognoscenti? No, a Mnemonic for Trappey's (tinned) Cajun Okra Gumbo . . . I have recommended it. I haven't read the label but long ago figured ONE should cook a couple of handfuls RICE to fill it out. I have had dreadful trouble remembering, Cajun, Okra, Gumbo. (John didn't like "OGRE.") Now I have it wrote down and maybe memorized?* [*Ogre was John's childhood pronunciation of okra.]

—Macauley Smith

Anuncia's Mother's Catalan Garlic Soup

When it comes to garlic, enough is never enough, and so we have two recipes for garlic soup. The first one is a Catalan recipe from Anuncia's mother. • This substantial soup makes a whole meal combined with salad and bread. • Breadcrumbs make a great thickening agent for soups and provide an excellent way to use up leftover crusts of bread.

Serves 6-8

⅓ to ½ c. olive oil
2 T. garlic, peeled & minced
   (about 12 to 15 cloves)
3 c. bread crumbs, finely ground
1 T. Spanish sweet paprika
6 c. cold water or chicken stock
   (See page 68.)

¼ t. cayenne pepper
Salt to taste
2 eggs
1 T. parsley, chopped finely

In a large frying pan or soup pot, sauté garlic in olive oil over low heat until golden, 2 to 3 minutes, stirring frequently. Add bread crumbs and cook until golden, adding more olive oil as needed. Add paprika, cold water or stock, cayenne pepper and salt. Bring to a boil over medium-high heat, reduce heat and simmer uncovered for 30 minutes, stirring occasionally.

Remove from heat and purée in a food processor or blender in 2 or 3 batches. Return to frying pan or soup pot and warm over low heat. In a small bowl, beat eggs gently and add to soup slowly, stirring constantly for 2 to 3 minutes. Ladle into soup bowls and top with parsley. Serve immediately

---

A SOFT LANDING

On the Fourth of July we were driving home from town when John spotted something white on the side of the road. He stopped and picked up a pitiful handful of burr-covered fluff that looked more like a dirty rag than a small poodle. The next day we spent hours picking burrs from the coat of this small, sensitive creature who sat patiently on our laps, grateful for the attention.

We called Paul and Anuncia who were looking for a puppy for their son, Tavi. They came right over. Anuncia sat down on a kitchen chair, the dog jumped into her lap and was adopted instantly. They named her *Capellades* after Anuncia's hometown, *Capé* (pronounced ká-peh) for short.

When we took *Capé* to Veneta for grooming, she was recognized as Babette, a former client of the dog beauty shop. Unlike most dogs that are cast out, *Capé* landed in the right lap and lived a long, happy second life in a home where devotion was plentiful.

Shirley's Clarion Garlic Soup with Pesto

Shirley was born in Clarion, Iowa, and her garlic soup features potatoes and pesto.

Serves 6-8

3 T. olive oil
2 T. minced garlic,
    (about 12 to 15 cloves)
6 c. chicken stock (See page 68.)
4 to 6 potatoes, peeled & cubed
    (about 4 cups)

¼ t. cayenne pepper
Salt to taste

6 to 8 T. pesto (See page 162.)

In a soup pot, sauté garlic in olive oil over low heat for several minutes until golden. In a saucepan, bring chicken stock to a boil over high heat. Pour boiling chicken stock gently into pot with sautéed garlic. Add cubed potatoes. Cover and cook over medium heat until the potatoes are tender, about 15 to 20 minutes.

Purée cooked vegetables in a food processor or blender in 2 or 3 batches. Return to soup pot and heat for several minutes over medium-low heat, stirring constantly.

Put 1 tablespoon of pesto in the bottom of each bowl and then ladle soup into it. Serve immediately with lots of crusty bread.

LIFE SAVING

To make ends meet after Catherine's grandfather died, her grandmother Marian Loberg Rowins ran a rooming house in the family home at 431 Summit Avenue in Pasadena. One of her renters was Mr. Paul Pauls, a German who had the first Volkswagen Beetle in Pasadena in the early 1950's.

Mr. Pauls told a remarkable story about his wartime experiences in Greece where he had served in the German army. Toward the end of World War II, he was stranded in Greece, sick and starving. A Greek peasant woman rescued him with a bag of onions — which must have been more valuable than gold at that time. She instructed him to eat one onion each day. He did and credited her kindness with saving his life.

Feeds-an-Army Cheese Soup

*It takes determination and desire to learn to cook. John had both plus Lisa as the best possible teacher. He progressed rapidly and was soon ready for a solo effort in the kitchen. Sopapillas looked good with a short list of ingredients. John did exactly as instructed, combining "all of the above ingredients," but something was wrong, very wrong. The batter was swimming in oil. John summoned Lisa who quickly diagnosed the problem. "All of the above" included a quart of oil in which the sopapillas were to be cooked. Lisa applied her considerable muscle to wringing oil from the batter as if it were an old dishrag. They rescued the sopapillas and created **dipstick bread**. • To follow directions, without judgment, can lead to trouble in all areas of life. • Lisa taught John to make this cheese soup as one of his early cooking efforts. This recipe may be an example of gonzo cooking. Try it and you may be surprised. To say it is filling would be an understatement.*

Serves 8-10

1 lb. spicy Italian bulk sausage
1 large onion, chopped coarsely
Two 14-½ oz. cans evaporated milk
2 lbs. Velveeta cheese, cut in chunks
Two 10 oz. packages frozen broccoli

11 oz. can mushroom soup
14-½ oz. can "ready-cut" peeled tomatoes
2 c. fresh mushrooms (about ½ lb.),
   sliced

In a large soup pot, brown sausage over medium heat. Remove sausage with a slotted spoon and set aside to drain on paper towels. Sauté onion in sausage drippings.

Add all other ingredients, including cooked sausage. Warm soup over medium-low heat, stirring frequently, until cheese has melted and broccoli is cooked, about 10 minutes. Serve immediately.

LOCAL COLOR

Lively and Ivy were barking wildly. We looked out the window and caught sight of a woman under an enormous blue and white golf umbrella walking along our road in the pouring rain. The neighbor's calves had also caught sight of her and were following her progress down the road from the confines of their pasture.

Barbara was close at hand with her dogs, Rita and Osa, who were giving this newcomer the once over. Barbara told the woman that she was the object of a great deal of interest. No response. She kept walking, deeply immersed in a book entitled The Seven Habits of Highly Effective People. We wanted to add an eighth to the list. Enjoy where you are.

High-Expectation Gazpacho

In the Pacific Northwest, we begin dreaming about tomatoes after Christmas. We order seeds in January, start them inside in February, transplant them to bigger pots two or three times, plant them in the garden in May with frost protection or early June after the danger of frost has passed. If we're lucky, we'll savor our first tomatoes by the end of July and by September we'll have them coming out of our ears. • Our son Nicholas will testify that there's nothing like tomatoes eaten directly from the plants, standing in the garden on a late summer afternoon. Our expectations are high because a warm tomato captures the essence of sunlight.

Serves 6

4 c. fresh tomato purée (20 to 25 Italian plum tomatoes, 3 to 4 lbs.)
1 cucumber, peeled, seeded & chopped coarsely
1 sweet red pepper, seeded & chopped coarsely

1 green pepper, seeded & chopped coarsely
1 medium red onion, chopped finely
2 cloves garlic, peeled & minced
¼ t. Spanish paprika, sweet or smoky
Salt & black pepper to taste

Measure tomato purée into a medium-sized glass, ceramic or stainless steel bowl. (Avoid aluminum because the acidity of the tomatoes may produce a chemical reaction.) Add chopped vegetables, garlic and seasoning. Stir gently. Cover and refrigerate at least 1 hour before serving. Serve chilled with croutons. (See recipe for croutons on page 203 and baked toast on page 59.) Fresh nasturtiums make a colorful garnish.

Catherine and Carol discovered a creamy gazpacho in Córdoba. The "cream" in **SALMOREJO CORDOBÉS** is stale bread soaked in water. Cut crusts from 5 or 6 large slices of stale bread and soak in water for 10 minutes. Squeeze as dry as possible. Put in bowl of food processor. Add ⅓ cup olive oil, 1 tablespoon sherry vinegar, 2 hard cooked eggs, then tomato purée, garlic and paprika. Process until smooth in 2 batches. Pour into serving bowl. Serve with chopped vegetables in small bowls on the side. Add chopped Serrano ham, too.

PEELING FRESH TOMATOES

FAST • We made tomato purée in a Victorio Strainer, a wonderful hand-cranked tool that separates tomato pulp and juice from the seeds and skins. Then Pat Harris gave us an attachment for our Kitchenaid Mixer, allowing us to produce gallons of fresh tomato sauce very quickly.

SLOW • Drop tomatoes into boiling water for 10 to 15 seconds to loosen the skins. Remove from boiling water with a large slotted spoon or pour into a colander. Peel off skins immediately. Cut tomatoes in half and scoop out seeds with a teaspoon or your fingers. Use as needed.

Doggone-Good Onion Sandwiches

An unexpected treat, these sandwiches were a staple in Louisville prepared by Emmy for tailgate parties at the end of Sunday afternoon beagling with the Finn Castle Beagles. John's father was fond of reminding Catherine that beagles are hounds not mere dogs, bred and trained to follow the scent of rabbits. Under the supervision of the green-jacketed Master of the Hounds and his assistant, the dogs track rabbits and the beaglers follow the dogs over miles of gently rolling countryside. The object of this sport is more gentle than it might seem, more in the spirit of fly fishing than trophy hunting, with emphasis on the cooperation of humans with dogs. After the rabbits retire to their holes, then everyone gathers for food and drink served out of the back of someone's vehicle.

Makes as many as you want

**1 or more red onions,
   sliced very thinly
Whole milk**

**Best rye bread
Mayonnaise (See page 266.)
Sliced tomatoes**

The day before, put sliced onions in a bowl or casserole and pour whole milk over them. Cover and refrigerate overnight. Whole milk is the secret ingredient because its fat works a miracle on the onions, bringing out their sweetness and taking away the smell. If onions are very strong, change milk once and soak for a full 24 hours.

The next day, drain onions in a colander and discard milk. Make sandwiches using very thinly sliced rye bread, homemade mayonnaise, garden fresh tomatoes and any other condiments you like.

CHAPTER 1:
FROM THE BEGINNING

When John was a student, he went to a Friday night "mixer" as they called those well-chaperoned college-sponsored dances in another era. At that mixer he met Mary.

Home he went to his roommate. "Jim, I've met a goddess," he reported. "She's perfect for you."

She was and still is. Jim and Mary married their senior year in college, more than 50 years ago.

2,000-Mile Sandwiches

If these sandwiches could talk, they would tell of back roads and adventures all over the United States. They've been packed in picnic lunches as a Smith family staple nearly as revered as chocolate sauce and much easier to eat on a serpentine road or halfway up a mountain.

Makes 6

6 English muffins
6-⅛ oz. can tuna, drained
⅔ c. cottage cheese

2 to 3 T. sour cream
1 t. dill weed
Ground black pepper to taste

Split muffins and toast well. Butter them, if you like. In a bowl, combine tuna, cottage cheese, sour cream, dill and pepper. Mix together nicely. Spread filling on bottom half of each toasted muffin, position the top and cut in half with a serrated knife. (Cutting these sandwiches is tricky because the filling wants to ooze out.) Wrap muffins individually, store in a cooler and head for the road.

Emmy also recommended using this filling on a fresh tomato or with tomato aspic. (See page 211.) She also reminded us that adding celery will make these sandwiches "too wet for traveling." Carry a small jar of chutney, a fresh tomato or some roasted red peppers to liven up these sandwiches.

CHAPTER 2:
HOW ONE THING LEADS TO ANOTHER

Catherine's roommate in San Francisco met Bruce Klepinger on one of his treks in Peru. Sometime later she brought him home for dinner because in those days Bruce needed both home and dinner. Those were the days when his home was a closet under the stairs in Berkeley and dinner was often a chancy affair. Between treks, Bruce continued coming to visit, eating Catherine's home cooking and telling his fabulous stories of exotic places.

Later when Catherine needed to figure out the next chapter in her life, she decided to go around the world. Because she wanted to see the highest place on earth, she selected a trek to the Base Camp at Mt. Everest led by her old friend Bruce. It happened to be the same trek that Jim Ottaway selected as a birthday present for John.

On the afternoon of Wednesday, March 19, 1984, Catherine walked from her room in Kathmandu's Mala Hotel to the lobby. She stood at the counter, looking at guidebooks for Nepal and then turned to the man standing next to her and asked his advice. They started talking and found out that they were on the same trek. Minutes later, John walked up. "Mac," said Jim, addressing John by his college nickname, "I want you to meet Catherine." That was it.

Melts-in-Your-Mouth Soufflé Bread

Called gougère, this hybrid of French bread and a soufflé comes from Burgundy. It is a perfect side dish with soup or roast chicken.

Serves 6-8

1 c. milk
4 T. butter (½ cube)
½ t. salt
Freshly ground black pepper
⅞ c. all-purpose white flour

4 eggs
⅔ c. Gruyère cheese (about 3 oz.), grated
   or freshly grated Parmesan cheese
1 T. heavy cream or sour cream

Pre-heat oven to 325° and grease a cookie sheet. In a heavy saucepan, combine milk, butter, salt and pepper. Bring to a boil over medium heat. Remove from heat and add flour all at once, stirring well. Return pan to medium-low heat and cook for 1 to 2 minutes, stirring constantly until the mixture comes away from sides of the pan and forms a ball.

Remove pan from heat and add eggs, one at a time, mixing well after each. Stir in half the cheese and all of the cream. Scrape batter onto a prepared cookie sheet and form into a big pancake about 12-inches in diameter. Sprinkle remaining cheese on top.

Bake 40 to 50 minutes, until puffy and lightly browned. Don't peek until at least 35 minutes have passed or gougère may fall. Remove from oven, cut into 6 or 8 wedges and serve immediately.

HORS D'OEUVRES PUFFS • Add all of grated cheese to the dough. Place soup spoonfuls of batter about 1-inch apart on greased cookie sheets. Bake about 20 minutes and serve immediately. This makes about 2 dozen.

TRAVELING LIGHTLY

When I lived on the road, I found I didn't miss familiar things or books. I couldn't carry much with me. There was instead great pleasure in simply sitting and remembering. I thought of memory as a blanket. I could take things out of my mind and handle them as though they were part of some beautiful fabric I carried with me, things that had happened long ago, the faces of people I loved, the words of a poem I had long since forgotten. This was something any nomad or illiterate peasant knew: the intangible treasure of memory, of memorized words.

—Suzanne Brind Morrow
From her book, *The Names of Things: A Passage in the Egyptian Desert.*

Afternoon Tea: Cookies, Cakes & Tea Breads

AVOIDING DETECTION

He looked about as inconspicuous as a tarantula
on a piece of angel food cake.

—Author unknown

Grandma Rowins' Original Oatmeal Cookies

*This recipe appeared in **Eats**, a small cookbook featuring 15 holiday recipes created by Catherine's grandparents, Marian and Howard Rowins, for Christmas 1905, the year they married. It was printed — probably by Grandpa Rowins who was a printer — on oatmeal colored paper with a red and green holly design on each page and tied together with red and green embroidery floss. The other recipes were cheese straws, nut bread, sour cream cake, a large white cake, a small white cake, fruit cookies, sugar cookies, chocolate pie, baked and boiled custard, orange marmalade and divinity candy. • These cookies are Manz family favorites.*

Makes 4-5 dozen

¾ c. butter (1-½ sticks),
   at room temperature
1 c. brown sugar
3 eggs
2 c. all-purpose white flour
¾ t. baking soda

¼ t. salt
1 t. cinnamon
2 c. rolled oats
1 c. raisins (about 6-⅔ oz.), chopped finely
1 c. nuts (4 oz.), chopped finely

Pre-heat oven to 350°. In a medium-mixing bowl, cream butter and sugar together. Add eggs one at a time, beating well after each.

In a second bowl, sift together flour, soda, salt and cinnamon. Add flour mixture to butter mixture and mix until flour disappears. Stir in oatmeal, raisins and nuts. Combine thoroughly.

Roll out dough about ¼ inch thick on a lightly floured board. Cut in circles with a cookie cutter or water glass. Place cookies on un-greased cookie sheets about 1-inch apart. Bake until lightly browned, 8 to 12 minutes. Remove from oven and cool on racks. Store in a covered tin. These freeze well.

CHOPPING RAISINS

Although nuts can be chopped well in a Cuisinart, raisins alone cannot. They get gummy or, if they are dry, spin around uselessly. If you add a cup of flour with the raisins (remembering to deduct it from the recipe), then the raisins chop nicely. Or chop raisins finely by hand with a chef's knife. Catherine remembers her mother grinding raisins for this recipe with a special attachment on her Sunbeam Mixmaster.

Carol's Serious Scotch Shortbread

Carol and Catherine have shared several lifetimes together, highlighted by hundreds of hours laughing in the kitchen while whipping up something to eat. They've passed recipes back and forth as often as advice. Carol has taken the art of recipe-writing to a new level of efficiency, giving Catherine a list of ingredients, usually abbreviated, and leaving the rest to her imagination. • These cookies are for people who are serious about butter and sugar. • In Edinburgh, we found a shortbread recipe that added cornstarch to give the texture more "shortness." The substitution of rice flour has a similar result.

Makes 3 dozen

1 lb. butter (4 cubes), at room temperature
1 c. white granulated sugar (superfine, if available)

½ t. vanilla
4 c. all-purpose white flour (Substitute 1 c. rice flour for 1 c. flour.)

Pre-heat oven to 300°. In a medium-mixing bowl, cream butter and sugar until light and fluffy. Add vanilla and mix well. Then gradually add flour (including rice flour, if desired) and mix gently until flour disappears.

Spread dough into an un-greased 9x13-inch baking pan. Press into place with your hands. Gently prick the top all over with the tines of a fork.

Bake until lightly browned, 35 to 45 minutes. Remove from oven and cool on a rack. Cut in squares while still warm. Store in a covered tin in the refrigerator. These also freeze well.

YES, INDEED!

One good thing about being alive is roses.

—Madeline Raff (Age 5)

Be of love a little more careful than of everything.

—e.e. cummings

Karen's Durable High Pass Biscotti

We rely on Karen and her husband, Tenold, for advice on everything — farming, cooking, canning, remodeling, car repairs, travel, boating, sewing and that's just the short list. Their daily lives are an inspired tapestry of fine art, fine living and hard work. Their farm on High Pass Road is an oasis for us and our children. Their influence is far-reaching and long-lasting. • These biscotti are one of Karen's minor inventions. We once found three of them left-over in a glass jar in our guest house. Months old, they were still well worth eating.

Makes 5-6 dozen

1-⅔ c. almonds (about 6-½ oz.),
   chopped
3 T. fennel seed
3 T. water
1 c. butter (2 cubes)
1-¾ c. sugar
6 eggs

¼ c. Ouzo
1 t. vanilla
5-½ to 6-½ c. all-purpose white flour,
   unsifted
2 t. baking powder

Pre-heat oven to 375°. Place chopped nuts on a cookie sheet and toast in oven until lightly browned, 7 to 10 minutes. Remove from oven and set on a rack to cool.

In a small pan, cover fennel seed with water, bring to a boil over medium heat. Remove from heat and set aside. In another small saucepan, melt butter over low heat.

In a large mixing bowl, combine melted butter, sugar, eggs, Ouzo, vanilla and boiled fennel seed. Add chopped almonds. Stir in 5-½ cups of flour and baking powder and mix until flour disappears. Dough should be soft. Depending on the weather and your flour, you may need part of the additional cup of flour. (See next page for note about flour.)

Divide dough into eight pieces. On a floured board, form each piece into a long, thin roll, approximately 2-inches in diameter. Place on un-greased cookie sheets about 2 inches apart.

Bake until lightly browned, about 20 minutes. Remove from oven and set on racks. Turn oven down to 150°. Cool rolls briefly until you can handle them. With a serrated knife, slice each roll diagonally into ½ to ¾ inch pieces. Place biscotti on cookie sheets cut-side up and return to oven until nicely dry, about 30 minutes. Turn them over once. (Or turn off oven and leave biscotti overnight.) Store in tightly covered tins or jars.

It frosts my cookies.

—Sally Cairnes-Wurster
Commenting on some political foolishness

LAVENDER BISCOTTI • We made these for Nancy when she had open garden days at her Sawmill Ballroom Lavender Farm by adapting Karen's recipe on the preceding page. Omit fennel, water, Ouzo and vanilla. Reduce sugar to 1-¼ cups, add ¾ cup of honey, 1 tablespoon of Nancy's own lavender buds, 4 tablespoons of grated orange peel and substitute hazelnuts for almonds.

CHOCOLATE BISCOTTI • Omit fennel, water, Ouzo and vanilla. Add 6 tablespoons of cocoa powder, 4 tablespoons of finely chopped orange peel and ¼ cup of Grand Marnier. Use almonds, hazelnuts or pecans. Go wild and add 6 ounces of bittersweet chocolate broken into small pieces.

THE MYSTERIES OF FLOUR

Flour is sensitive, its moisture content and, correspondingly, its volume may vary by as much as 20% depending on weather, storage and type of flour.

We once kept track of the flour we used to make Karen's biscotti. Karen in Junction City used 5-½ cups of all-purpose flour, Lisa in Edinburgh used 6-½ cups of local flour and Catherine in Crow used 6 cups of "best for bread" flour.

WHAT'S IN A NAME?

The name "Sawmill Ballroom Lavender Farm" was a metaphor for the community gathering place that Nancy and Joey hoped to create with their business:

SAWMILL • Honoring the timber interests that have been a big influence in our part of the world.

BALLROOM • A meeting place where we can kick up our heels and celebrate being together.

LAVENDER • Especially the Tuscan variety that Nancy hand-carried from Italy to begin the offerings at their farm.

Afternoon Tea   91

Emmy's Shoe Box Brown Sugar Squares

Emmy keeps a shoe box filled with these brown sugar squares and a second one of brownies, individually wrapped in wax paper, in her freezer at all times. She sends boxes of them to family members for state occasions and dispenses them freely to all friends and workers lucky enough to come through the screened back door at 711.

Makes 2 dozen

4 eggs, beaten
2 c. dark brown sugar
1 c. all-purpose white flour
1 t. baking powder
½ t. salt
1 t. vanilla
2 c. chopped nuts (8 oz.)

Optional:
½ c. butter (1 cube),
   at room temperature

Pre-heat oven to 325°. Grease a 9x13-inch baking pan. In a medium-mixing bowl, combine all of the ingredients. Stir until the flour disappears. (If you use butter, cream together with brown sugar and then combine with all other ingredients.) Scrape batter into prepared pan and smooth the top with a spatula.

Bake until lightly browned, about 20 minutes. Remove from the oven and cool in pan on a rack before cutting into squares. Cool thoroughly and store in a covered tin. These brownies freeze well.

DERBY BROWNIES

In Louisville "Derby pie" is a popular dessert named in honor of the horse race on the first Saturday in May. This pie features eggs, butter, flour, vanilla, bourbon, chocolate chips and pecans in a piecrust. Make "Derby brownies" with the following two additions to Emmy's brown sugar squares:

2 c. chocolate chips (12 oz. pkg.)

2 T. bourbon

GETTING DOWN

Leave her lay where Jesus flang her.

—Winn Allen

From Emmy Smith quoting a family friend who overheard this remark at a revival meeting in Kentucky in the 1930's.

Afternoon Tea

Emmy's Holland Butter Cookies

Another type of shortbread with cinnamon as the secret ingredient.

Makes 2 dozen

½ lb. butter (2 cubes),
   at room temperature
½ c. brown or white sugar
2 t. cinnamon
1 egg, separated

2 c. all-purpose white flour
1 pinch salt
1 c. unblanched almonds (4 oz.), filberts,
   pecans or walnuts, chopped

Pre-heat oven to 350°. Grease a 9x13-inch baking pan. In a medium-mixing bowl, cream together butter and sugar until light and fluffy. Add cinnamon, egg yolk, flour and salt. Mix until flour disappears. Press dough into prepared pan. With your hands or a rubber spatula, smear surface with slightly beaten egg white. Sprinkle chopped nuts evenly on top and press into dough.

Bake until lightly browned, about 20 minutes. Remove from oven and cut into squares immediately. Turn off oven and return pan to oven while it cools with the door open. When completely cooled, remove from pan. Store in a covered tin.

Emmy reminded us that **butter** may spoil in hot weather, so it's safest to store these and other butter cookies in the refrigerator or freezer.

VIEWS FROM THE PORCH

In spring and summer, while Emmy prepared meals, the Judge sat on their screened porch and wrote letters in his inimitable style:

We have always marveled at dear Mary Jackson's "dunce cap" to keep squirrels from Bird Feeder. This week 1st time THEY have conquered it. HOW they grasp edge, climb nearly vertical "tin" don't ask me. Michael was over, not full of ideas. Em says "hold on" & got a tin Crisco (successor to LARD). He smeared it on lower reaches of Dunce Cap. We have not seen a squirrel UP THERE, or falling off, but we saw one walking away, washing his hands in disgust. Maybe your Mother is a genius.*

DID I SAY last night GREATEST 1st time this season Imported GREEN Asparaguts. We used to say they melted in your mouth. DOUBT any home grown yet. (29 Mar 1992)

YIPPEE YIPPEE yest Fri SupperTime RELIABLY SAW a red rabbi [sic] coursing East along Rachel's DriveIn. (2 May 1992)

        —Macauley Smith

*To deter squirrels, Lisa uses Vaseline mixed with cayenne pepper
to grease the pole supporting her bird feeder.

Emma's Heirloom Pound Cake

Emma wrote down the recipe for this pound cake shortly before she died. She said that we HAD to have her recipe. Emma's version of the perennial favorite includes almond as its secret ingredient. • Pound cake topped with warm chocolate sauce is a superior treat.

Serves 18

1 lb. butter (4 cubes), at room temperature	¾ c. milk
3 c. sugar	1 t. almond extract
6 eggs	1 t. vanilla extract
4 c. all-purpose white flour	

Pre-heat oven to 325°. Grease and flour a 10-inch tube pan or two standard loaf pans. In a mixing bowl, cream butter and sugar until light and fluffy. Add eggs one at a time, beating well after each. Add flour a ½ cup at a time and milk about a tablespoon at a time, alternating flour and milk, and beating well after each addition. Add almond and vanilla extracts and mix thoroughly. Pour batter into prepared pan and smooth top with a spatula.

Bake until cake tests done, 80 to 90 minutes. (See page 47.) In two standard loaf pans, cake will cook faster, 60 minutes or so. Remove from oven and cool for 10 minutes on a rack before removing from pan. Serve warm or at room temperature. This cake is very fine served with chocolate sauce. (See page 40.)

MORE VIEWS FROM THE PORCH

The Judge was a keen observer of nature as well as a wordsmith:

Don't know whether Oregon has Mocking Birds. They were somewhat silenced by long excessive HEAT. NOW seem to start trilling beautifully AS ONE APPROACHES. They seem quite Human Conscious. (13 Oct 1991)

Did I say we have an Albino Sparrow (or somewhat) who flits congenially around with the others? Not outlawed as "Exceptional Child." (29 Oct 1991)

GEOGRAPHICALLY it might have been appropriate for you to name IVY EUREKA (CA) BUT I'm glad you did not: Eureka dead fish, Eureka pig effluent, Eureka skunk . . . . Not good. (25 Jan 1992)

—Macauley Smith

We found Ivy, our beloved border collie, along the side of the Interstate 5.
The Judge named her I-V, word play that became Ivy.

Andrea's Back-to-Basics Great Yellow Cake

When our cousin Andrea asked to bring her John Smith for his first visit, we knew that we were in for a treat. We figured that Andrea's great taste in basics such as yellow cakes must translate well into men named John Smith and it did. Her husband is now known to us as John Smith the Younger or John Smith 2.0. • Andrea heads for the kitchen when she comes to visit, baking up a storm, much to our delight.

Serves 10-12

2 c. sugar
4 eggs
1 c. unflavored vegetable oil
1 c. dry white wine, left-over
   champagne or lemon juice

2-½ c. all-purpose white flour
2-¼ t. baking powder
½ t. salt
1 t. vanilla

Pre-heat oven to 350°. Grease generously two 9-inch round cake pans, line bottom of pans with wax paper, grease paper and dust lightly with flour.

In a medium-mixing bowl, beat together eggs and sugar for 30 seconds. Add oil, wine, flour, baking powder, salt and vanilla. Beat for 1 minute. Pour batter into prepared pans. Place pans in the middle of the oven. Bake until the cake tests done, about 30 minutes. (See page 47.) Remove cake from oven. Cool for 5 minutes on racks before removing from pans. Cool thoroughly before frosting it.

FIT FOR THE QUEEN

1 yellow cake (2 layers)

¾ c. chestnut purée (See page 250.)

Chocolate frosting (See page 46.)

For a state occasion, spread sweetened chestnut purée between layers of this yellow cake. Top with chocolate frosting and serve to very important guests. (Buy chestnut purée in small cans in specialty stores, or make your own.)

KEEPING UP

Tidiness is never permanent.

—John Smith

Tee's Rose Bowl Brandied Fruitcake

This fruitcake scored with every bite at a party celebrating the University of Oregon Ducks' first Pac-10 college football championship in 37 years. At the Rose Bowl game on New Year's Day 1995, Tee's cake played so skillfully that it defeated the brownies, tempting the under ten crowd as readily as the adults.
• Tee took one of these cakes to Emmy whenever she was expecting important guests, and Emmy served it as lovingly as caviar. She often shipped one to us in John's duffel bag or by overnight mail. • If our University of Oregon football team had eaten 700 pounds of Tee's cake instead of 700 pounds of ribs before the Rose Bowl game, then they might have upset Penn State instead of giving them a good run for the money. • This "Friendship Cake," as it was originally called, requires time but is well worth the effort
.

Makes 3 bundt-style cakes, each serving 12-14

Day 1: STARTER FOR BRANDIED FRUIT
16 oz can crushed pineapple or other canned fruit & juice
2 c. sugar + 1 t. yeast
OR
1-½ c. fruit juice from previous batch of brandied fruit
2-½ c. sugar + 16 oz. can sliced peaches & juice

<u>Day 10:</u>
2 c. sugar
16 oz. can chunk pineapple or
   peaches & juice

<u>Day 20:</u>
2 c. sugar
30 oz. can fruit cocktail & juice
10 oz. jar maraschino cherries
   or canned cherries & juice

DAY 1 • Begin making brandied fruit a month or more before you plan to bake this cake. Prepare starter by combining crushed pineapple, sugar and yeast in a 1-gallon container such as a big glass jar. (Or if you have juice from a previous batch of brandied fruit, then combine it with sugar and sliced peaches.) Mix fruit thoroughly, cover loosely and let stand at *room temperature* for 30 days, adding designated fruit and sugar every 10 days and *stirring well every day*. The fruit ferments slowly at room temperature as sugar feeds the fermentation process. (Refrigeration stops fermentation.)

DAY 10 • Add sugar and pineapple, or if you used pineapple in your starter, then add sliced peaches. Stir well and cover.

DAY 20 • Add sugar, fruit cocktail and cherries. Stir well and cover.

DAY 30 • Drain juice from brandied fruit using a colander or sieve. Divide fruit and juice in thirds, about three 1-½ cup portions of juice and three 1-⅔ cup portions of fruit.

Place juice in airtight containers and give to friends with a copy of this recipe. This juice should be stored at room temperature and used within 5 days, not frozen. The brandied fruit freezes well, Tee explained. Use 1 batch for a cake immediately and then freeze the other two portions for future cakes, tightly covered in plastic containers.

THE FRUITCAKE

Cake:
1 yellow cake mix (18.25 oz.)
1 small pkg. vanilla instant pudding
  (3.4 oz.)
⅔ c. unflavored vegetable oil
4 eggs
1-⅔ c. drained, brandied fruit
1 c. nuts (4 oz.), chopped

Syrup:
½ c. water
1 c. sugar
¼ to ⅓ c. rum
OR
¾ c. orange juice
1 c. sugar

Pre-heat oven to 350°. Grease generously and flour a bundt-type cake pan. In a large mixing bowl, combine cake mix, vanilla pudding, oil and eggs. Beat thoroughly with a mixer for about 30 seconds. Add fruit and nuts and mix gently by hand until thoroughly combined. Pour into prepared pan. Bake until cake tests done, 50-60 minutes. (See page 47.)

While cake is baking, make syrup by combining water and sugar in a small saucepan. (Or substitute orange juice for both water and rum.) Bring to a boil over medium heat and boil for 10 minutes, stirring occasionally. Remove from heat. Cool syrup to lukewarm and then add rum. Because dark rum has a stronger flavor, use ¼ cup of it or ⅓ cup of light rum, Tee advised.

Remove cake from oven and set on a rack to cool. With a skewer or ice pick make a dozen holes in top of cake and pour warm syrup over it. When cake has cooled for about 10 minutes, remove it from pan. Cool thoroughly and serve. This cake also freezes beautifully, wrapped tightly in plastic and then foil.

For her 90th birthday, Emmy was delighted to have provided her own birthday cake, one of Tee's cakes sent by mail from Kentucky to the Redstone Inn in Colorado where we gathered for her Fourth of July celebration. Our waitress served it with candles at the end of Emmy's birthday dinner. The staff gobbled up the remainder, appreciating this terrific cake as much as we do.

Laney's Sure-Footed
Orange Peel Cake with Caramel Frosting

This orange cake with raisins, nuts and caramel frosting has become a favorite for festive occasions. •
Laney, a top hiker, was a fine cook. Walking along Teton trails with Laney always included discussions of
food and recipes. Laney and her husband Bill were still back-packing in their 70s.

Serves 12

Cake:
2 oranges or 1 c. candied orange peel
1 c. seedless raisins (about 6-⅔ oz.)
1 c. walnuts (4 oz.)
½ c. butter (1 cube), at room temperature
1 c. sugar
2 eggs, lightly beaten
1 c. orange juice & milk
2 c. all-purpose white flour
1 t. baking soda
1 t. baking powder
½ t. salt

Filling:
Orange-nut mixture (See below.)
¾ c. powdered sugar (about 3-¾ oz.)
¼ c. whipping cream

Caramel frosting:
⅓ c. whipping cream
1 c. brown sugar
½ t. baking powder

Pre-heat oven to 350º. Grease two 10-inch round cake pans, line with wax paper and grease the wax paper. Wash oranges in warm water with mild soap, rinse and dry. Peel rind from the oranges with a paring knife or potato peeler. Combine orange peel, raisins and nuts together in a food processor and process until coarsely chopped. Squeeze juice from oranges and add enough milk to make 1 cup.

In a mixing bowl, cream together butter and sugar until light and fluffy. Add eggs and mix thoroughly. Sift together flour, soda, baking power and salt. Add alternately with orange-milk mixture to creamed butter. Stir in about ¾ of orange peel mixture. Divide batter evenly between the 2 prepared pans and smooth tops with a spatula.

Place pans in center of oven. Bake 15 to 20 minutes or until top is lightly browned, and cake has come away from sides of the pans. Remove from oven and cool on racks for 10 minutes. Remove from pans and cool thoroughly. (See page 47.)

FILLING • In a mixing bowl, stir together remaining orange peel mixture with powdered sugar and cream. Place 1 layer of cake on a serving plate and spread filling on it. Top with second layer.

FROSTING • Combine cream and brown sugar in a small saucepan and boil until it forms a soft ball at 238º. (Use a candy thermometer.) Remove pan from heat and add baking powder. Beat until frosting seems ready to spread. Be careful not to beat it too long or it will get stiff and uncooperative. (If this happens, add 1 to 2 tablespoons of cream, then beat gently and briefly until it becomes manageable again.) Spread on top of cake. Serve immediately or refrigerate overnight.

Peg's Carrot Cake, Tavi's Birthday Cake & the Universal Wedding Cake

This recipe comes from Peg who baked it for Dean and Lisa's wedding, and Dean and Lisa made it for ours. After the cake was in the oven, Dean tasted the batter and discovered they had forgotten the sugar. Being resourceful cooks, they looked around the kitchen and decided the best bet was honey from their own bees, poured over the cake as soon as it came out of the oven. The new, improved version of this recipe was born. This was Tavi's birthday cake for years.

Serves 10-12

3 c. all-purpose white flour
¾ c. brown sugar
1 T. cinnamon
2 t. baking powder
2 t. baking soda
1 t. salt
4 eggs

⅔ c. buttermilk
1-½ c. unflavored vegetable oil
3 c. grated carrots
   (about 4 medium carrots),
1 to 2 c. nuts (4 to 8 oz.), chopped
1-½ c. honey

Pre-heat oven to 350°. Grease and flour cake pans, two 8 or 9-inch round pans for a layer cake or one 9x13-inch pan for a sheet cake.

In a large mixing bowl, combine dry ingredients. In a second bowl, beat eggs lightly, then stir in buttermilk, oil, carrots and nuts. Combine two mixtures and stir until flour disappears. Pour batter into prepared pans. Smooth top with a spatula.

Bake 40 to 50 minutes or until the cake tests done. (See page 47.) While cake is baking, warm honey in a small saucepan over low heat. Remove cake from oven, set on racks and immediately pour warm honey over the hot cake. Cool 10 minutes in pans. Remove from pans and cool completely before icing it. Serve at room temperature.

LEMON CREAM CHEESE ICING

Two 8 oz. pkgs. cream cheese (16 oz.), at room temperature

2 T. lemon juice & 1 T. grated lemon peel

1 t. vanilla

2 to 3 c. powdered sugar (about 10 to 14 oz.), sifted

Few grains of salt

Beat together cream cheese, lemon juice, grated rind, vanilla and salt. Add 2 cups of powdered sugar and mix well. Then add as much of the additional 1 cup of powdered sugar as needed to reach a suitable consistency.

Carol's Dreamed-Up Hazelnut Torte

Also known as filberts, hazelnuts are very popular in Europe but mysteriously underrated in the United States. We live in the largest filbert-growing region of the country, but we can't buy filberts in our nearest grocery store except briefly at Christmas. • This torte is Carol's invention.

Serves 8-10

**3 c. hazelnuts/filberts (¾ lb.),
  lightly toasted & finely ground**
9 egg whites
1-⅓ c. sugar

1 c. raspberry jam
**½ pint heavy cream whipped with
  1 T. sugar 1 t. vanilla**

Substitute almonds, pecans or walnuts for hazelnuts. Each has its characteristic flavor. The important part is toasting them lightly. Pre-heat oven to 400° and roast nuts on a cookie sheet for 7 to 10 minutes or until lightly browned. Remove from oven and cool. Grind finely in a blender or food processor in 2 or 3 batches.

Lower oven temperature to 350°. Grease three 8 or 9-inch cake pans, line bottom of each with wax paper, grease wax paper and dust lightly with flour.

In a large mixing bowl, beat egg whites at medium speed until they foam. Increase speed to high and beat until soft peaks form. Add sugar tablespoon by tablespoon and continue beating until peaks are stiff and glossy. Fold in nuts gently, mixing by hand. Pour ⅓ of batter into each pan. Smooth top of batter with a spatula.

Bake 25 to 35 minutes or until lightly browned. Remove from oven and cool on racks for 5 minutes. Remove from pans and cool thoroughly.

Just before serving, place a layer on a serving plate and spread with ½ cup of raspberry jam, top with second layer and remaining raspberry jam, then third layer. In a small mixing bowl, whip the cream, adding sugar and vanilla as it thickens. Top cake with whipped cream and serve immediately.

HAZELNUTS

According to Chinese lore, hazelnuts are one of five sacred nourishments given to man more than 4,500 years ago. • A member of the birch family, these nuts are a good source of protein as well as Vitamins B, C and E. • Turkey is the largest producer of hazelnuts in the world and Germany and England are the largest consumers. • The first hazelnut trees were planted in the Willamette Valley by a Frenchman, David Gernot, in 1876. • Hazelnuts can be stored at cool room temperature (70°) for several months or up to two years in the refrigerator.

From the brochure, "Sunnyland Nuts & Fruits," Vol. XI, Sunnyland Farms, Albany, GA

Maureen's Mother's Couturier Belgian Torte

When Maureen and Richard got married, we could not take our eyes off Maureen's mother's hat, an eye-catching confection of floral silk. Besides being glamorous, Mrs. Bender is an outstanding cook who has passed along to her daughter her love of cooking and many of her Belgian recipes, including this one. Maureen and her mother make you believe in a cooking gene. We hope granddaughters Gabriella and Adriana have it, too.

Serves 8-10

Torte:
½ c. butter (1 cube), at room temperature
5 T. sugar
4 egg yolks & 3 egg whites
10 to 15 T. all-purpose or cake flour
1-½ t. baking powder

Glaze:
½ c. currant jelly
2 t. lemon juice
Fresh strawberries or other seasonal fruit
½ pt. heavy cream, whipped, or sour
 cream

Pre-heat oven to 300°. Grease an 11-inch tart pan generously. (Our tin tart pan has fluted sides and a lift-out bottom.)

In a mixing bowl, cream butter and sugar until light and pale yellow. Add egg yolks one at a time, beating well after each addition. In a second mixing bowl, beat egg whites at medium speed until they foam, increase speed to high and beat until stiff peaks form. With a whisk, fold egg whites gently into butter-sugar mixture.

Sift together flour and baking powder. The amount of flour depends on the size of the eggs, all 15 tablespoons for extra large eggs, 12 for large eggs, etc. Add sifted flour tablespoon by tablespoon, folding gently after each addition until flour disappears. Scrape batter into prepared tin and smooth top with a spatula.

Bake 30 to 45 minutes or until lightly browned and springy when touched in the center. Remove from oven, immediately take out of pan and cool on a rack. When cool, place on a serving plate, flat side up and top with ¼ cup of currant jelly. Arrange fruit attractively, using nicely shaped strawberries, sliced peaches or nectarines, blueberries, grapes or other seasonal fruits.

In a small saucepan over medium heat, make a glaze by combining the remaining ¼ cup of currant jelly and lemon juice. Heat until bubbly and stir constantly. Paint glaze over fruit with a pastry brush or drizzle gently from a spoon. Serve with a bowl of whipped cream or sour cream.

TARTS 'N TORTES

According to Webster's Dictionary, a tart is a pastry shell filled with jam or jelly. A torte is a rich cake made with eggs, finely chopped nuts or crumbs and a little flour. We'll skip the legal definition of tort.

Leedy Garrison's
Original Gingerbread

Lisa collected her Grandmother Leedy's recipes in a book for her family. Of her gingerbread recipe, Leedy said, "This is mine." • A wonderful cook, Leedy lived in Blooming Grove, Texas and served her family from Franciscan apple pattern dishes, the same dishes which Marjorie Manz used in Pasadena, California. Leedy gave hers to Lisa before she died. • We remember Leedy's visit to Crow Farm when she advised us about the impending birth of a calf whom we named Garrison in her honor. We also remember Leedy spinning wool in the sun room with Barbara as her coach. Leedy said that our flowering quince, blooming during her visit, is called **japonica** *in Texas.*

Serves 8-10

½ c. shortening or butter,
   at room temperature
1 c. brown sugar
2 eggs
2 c. all-purpose white flour, sifted
2 t. baking soda

1-½ t. powdered ginger
1 t. nutmeg
½ t. salt
½ c. molasses
½ c. boiling water

Pre-heat oven to 350°. Grease and flour an 8x11 or a 9x9-inch pan. In a large mixing bowl, cream shortening (or butter) and sugar until light and fluffy. Add eggs one at a time, beating well after each.

Sift flour twice, the second time with soda, ginger, nutmeg and salt. In a small bowl, combine molasses and boiling water, stirring well. Add sifted ingredients alternately with molasses-water to creamed shortening or butter. Mix thoroughly until flour disappears. Pour into prepared pan and smooth top with a spatula.

Bake 30 to 40 minutes or until cake tests done. (See page 47.) Remove from oven and cool on a rack before removing from pan, or serve warm directly from pan.

Serve with applesauce on page 65. For an extravaganza, frost with chocolate frosting on page 46 or cream cheese icing on page 99.

HAVING YOUR CAKE & EATING IT, TOO?

Leedy's daughter, Ina Ruth, told a wonderful story about her mother's wedding day when Leedy's brothers kept badgering her to bake them a cake. After resisting mightily, Leedy finally relented and baked them their cake, filling it with dried beans. Their reaction was not recorded.

Wonder Woman Carol's
Whole Wheat Spice Tea Bread

Carol was an ace principal at a large inner-city elementary school in Southern California. Of her tremendous responsibilities, she said, "I prepared my whole life to do this. I loved my job." She dealt with staff, children, parents, neighbors, school administrators, local gangs, the police department, social workers, psychologists, coaches for after-school sports, local business people who ran a science education program for gifted kids, the head of the local zoo, alumni from her college, state school administrators, the community theater, health care professionals and even reporters on some days. It's an Olympian job, a close second to being President of the United States. • Carol also baked the best goodies for the staff lounge. This simple, healthy-tasting bread has long been a favorite. It toasts well, too.

Makes 1 loaf

2-½ c. whole wheat flour
1 T. baking powder
½ t. baking soda
½ t. salt
1 to 2 t. cinnamon

½ c. powdered skim milk
4 eggs
⅔ c. unflavored vegetable oil
1 c. dark brown sugar
1 c. buttermilk

Pre-heat oven to 350°. Grease a standard loaf pan. (We use Pam spray.) Sift flour, baking powder, soda, salt, cinnamon and powdered milk into a medium-mixing bowl.

In a small bowl, beat eggs lightly. Add eggs, oil, sugar and buttermilk to flour mixture. Mix until flour disappears. Scrape batter into prepared loaf pan and smooth top with a spatula. Bake 40 to 45 minutes or until bread tests done. (See page 47.) Remove from oven and cool 10 minutes on a rack before removing from pan. Serve immediately. Refrigerate wrapped tightly in foil or plastic after bread has cooled thoroughly.

¿Sólo así he de irme?
¿Cómo las flores que perecieron?
¿Nada quedará en mi nombre?
¿Nada de mi fama aquí en la tierra?
¡Al menos flores, al menos cantos!
—Cantos de Huexotzingo
A poem inscribed on the wall of the courtyard
in Mexico City's Museum of Anthropology:
So it will be when I've gone away?
Just like flowers which have died?
Nothing of my name will remain?
Nothing of my earthly fame?
Only flowers, only songs!

Pat's Thousands-of-Miles Banana Bread

If "nothing says loving like something from the oven," as the old Betty Crocker refrain went, Pat Harris has cornered the love market with her banana bread. She has been baking it for years, sending loaves all over the world to her traveling children. • Mace is a local addition.

Makes 1 loaf or 6-10 muffins

½ c. butter (1 cube) or
  ½ c. unflavored cooking oil
3 or 4 ripe bananas (about 1-½ cups)
2 eggs
1 t. mace or nutmeg
1 t. vanilla
¾ c. brown sugar

1 c. all-purpose white flour
2 t. baking soda
1 c. whole wheat flour
⅓ c. buttermilk or apple juice
1 c. nuts (4 oz.), chopped

Pre-heat oven to 325°. Grease a standard loaf pan or muffin tins. (We use Pam spray.) In a small saucepan, melt butter over low heat, remove from heat and cool.

Mash bananas with a fork in a medium-mixing bowl. Add eggs and mix well. Add mace and vanilla, then brown sugar and melted butter (or cooking oil). Mix well. Add white flour and soda and mix gently. Add wheat flour and buttermilk or juice. Mix briefly until flour disappears. Stir in nuts. Scrape batter into prepared loaf pan (or muffin tins) and smooth top with a spatula.

Bake bread for 1 hour or until top is browned and loaf tests done. (See page 47.) Bake muffins for 20 to 25 minutes. Remove from oven and cool 10 minutes on a rack before removing from pan. (Remove muffins immediately from muffin tin.) Serve immediately, if possible. Refrigerate wrapped tightly in foil or plastic after bread has cooled thoroughly.

GREAT EXPECTATIONS

"Catherine," queried Pat Harris with a very puzzled expression on her face, "what was the matter with those sweet potatoes you sent me? I cooked them and then I cooked them some more, but they were inedible." "Sweet potatoes? I don't know anything about sweet potatoes," I responded. "I'm talking about those brown tubers you sent to me last Christmas along with the garlic, winter squash and marmalade," Pat explained. Oh, no, the light was beginning to dawn. Our old and trusted friend — both a great gardener and a great cook — had prepared our red dahlia tubers for dinner.

Beebe's Zealous Zucchini Bread

Beebe is Catherine's best friend from college where they studied Russian and gave their first dinner party together. She recently wrote a letter reporting that she still uses the small paring knife and green enamel colander purchased for that historic dinner. • They continue their intense discussions of crucial matters such as food, recipes, kitchens, family life, politics and books. • Beebe's bread is one way of taming a zealous zucchini.

Makes 2 loaves

3 eggs
2 c. sugar
1 c. unflavored vegetable oil
2 c. raw zucchini, grated
   (about 2 medium zucchini)
1 T. vanilla
3 c. all-purpose white flour
   (or 2 c. white flour &
   1 c. whole wheat flour)

1 t. salt
1 t. baking soda
¼ t. baking powder
1 T. cinnamon
1 c. walnuts or filberts (4 oz.),
   coarsely chopped

Pre-heat oven to 350°. Grease 2 standard loaf pans generously. (We use Pam spray.) In a mixing bowl, beat eggs until foamy. Add sugar, oil, zucchini and vanilla and mix gently. Add flour, salt, soda, baking powder and cinnamon and stir until flour disappears. Stir in nuts and pour into prepared pans.

Bake 1 hour or until the bread is nicely browned and tests done. (See page 47.) Remove from oven and cool 10 minutes on racks before removing from pans. Serve immediately, if possible. After the loaves have cooled thoroughly, refrigerate wrapped tightly in foil or plastic.

WORKING MIRACLES

Pat Harris is a family therapist. We once watched her work her magic on an "impossible" person who happened to be staying with us. Pat's gently probing questions and our guest's unexpectedly eager and candid answers revealed a touching and sympathetic character who previously had been well hidden. It was a remarkable process.

AnnaDay's Sea Level Apricot Loaf

AnnaDay and her husband, David, live at 8,300 feet and spend more time in the out-of-doors than almost anyone else we know. This apricot loaf is their secret source of energy-providing carbohydrates. This is the sea level version of AnnaDay's densely delicious loaf.

Makes 1 loaf

1 c. dried apricots, quartered
  (about 6 oz.)
¾ c. water
½ c. frozen orange juice concentrate
1 egg
2 T. unflavored cooking oil
½ c. sugar

½ c. brown sugar
1 c. rolled oats
½ c. whole wheat flour
½ c. all-purpose white flour
1 T. baking powder
1 t. baking soda
1 c. walnuts (4 oz.), chopped

Pre-heat oven to 325°. Grease a standard loaf pan generously. (We use Pam spray.) Cut apricots in quarters or bite-sized pieces with scissors. In a small saucepan, cover apricots with water, and cook over medium heat until water is absorbed, about 10 minutes. Stir frequently to keep apricots from sticking to the bottom of the pan.

Add frozen orange juice to cooked apricots, and stir to cool apricots and melt frozen juice. In a small bowl, beat egg lightly and add to apricots. Add oil and mix thoroughly.

In a mixing bowl, combine dry ingredients. Add apricot-orange mixture and stir until flour disappears. Scrape the batter into prepared pan and smooth top with a spatula.

Bake 50 to 60 minutes or until loaf tests done. (See page 47.) Remove from oven and cool 10 minutes on a rack before removing from pan. Cool thoroughly. To serve, slice thinly. Refrigerate wrapped tightly in foil or plastic. It keeps for up to a week. Take on your next hike or picnic.

CHANGING TIMES

I think that YOU'VE probably changed more than the castle.

—Marjorie Manz

Responding to her 83-year old friend Mary Frances, who wondered if the Edinburgh Castle had changed much in the 30 years since her last visit in 1967.

Pre-Food: A Dinner Warm-up

As a child, Tavi coined the phrase "pre-food." Once upon a
time, pre-food was his favorite part of dinner . . . . well, at least
a close second to dessert. Things changed one Christmas when
he was observed chewing on a duck leg with total enjoyment, the
beginning of his expanded eating repetoire.

Anuncia's Levántate Sardine Dip

Anuncia could teach a rock to speak Spanish. Although she sometimes finds her students harder than rocks, Anuncia stays the course. She is a genius teacher with a flair for making language fun, immediate, interesting and accessible. • This dip is so unexpectedly delicious that it has fooled people who think they don't like sardines. It may also help with your Spanish. Levántate, siéntate . . . . (Get up, sit down . . . .)

Makes 1-½ cups

8 oz. cream cheese
3-¾ oz. can of sardines,
    packed in oil

Juice of 1 lemon
1 onion, chopped coarsely
2 or 3 cloves garlic, peeled

In a food processor or blender, combine everything, including oil from the sardines, and process until smooth. Serve immediately or refrigerate for an hour or overnight. This dip is very tasty with blue corn tortilla or other chips, crackers or raw vegetables. We also like to eat it on toast for lunch. Doubling the recipe works well.

SPEAKING TRUE

School is an extraordinary experience so far. They teach the Thai language using what they call the "Natural Approach." You learn to understand before you speak and not vice versa. In practicality this means that for 6-½ hours per day I listen to two Thais talk . . . talk during the first weeks about simple things like colored blocks over, under, longer, shorter, red, green, etc., but later about personal experiences, geography, folk tales, children's stories — in other words, the culture.

The teachers are, for the most part, extroverts, good actors and humorists who are able to keep you fascinated and determined to understand what (and not how) they are saying. Right from the start they talk at full speed though of course carefully limiting the vocabulary. It is, in theory, supposed to grow in your head until someday — miracle! — little words, like pearls, will dribble from your mouth!

They recommend 350-500 hours before speaking — the longer you wait the more "native" your accent and fluency will be — but it is sometimes hard not to try, not to consciously learn a word rather than let it grow by hearing it in context over and over. It's the only place in the world where a language is taught this way (though some places in California do teach a highly modified version of the method). Marvin Brown, a respected U.S. linguist who has lived in Thailand for 30 years, is the Director, and the Thai teachers, with a small smile and great deal of respect, call him a little ba or crazy. It's fascinating and I'm having fun!

—Bruce LeFavour

Bruce's Earthy Olivada

*You can always count on Bruce LeFavour for perfect flavors and textures. People are still talking about meals they ate and wine they drank years ago in his restaurants. Who else would have created a menu based on the Russo-Japanese War? • Good olives taste like the earth, their strong flavor and chewy texture bring to mind the dry, rocky, sun-drenched slopes where they grow. Eat them and smell the bay leaves and lavender that thrive in those same places. • Maybe the only way to improve an olive is to add garlic, olive oil and anchovies. So this is it, **olivada** or **tapenade**, the best of earth, sky and sea, also known as the "caviar of Provence."*

Makes 2 cups

½ lb. Kalamata olives, pitted   1 large clove garlic, peeled
8 anchovy filets   Pinch of salt
4 or 5 fresh oregano leaves, chopped   4 to 5 T. olive oil

Combine olives, anchovies and oregano leaves in a food processor. Process briefly. With a mortar and pestle, make a paste of garlic and salt. Add paste to olive mixture together with 3 tablespoons of olive oil, and process briefly. Add more olive oil as needed to make a chunky paste. Place in a small serving bowl. Refrigerate for several hours or overnight to let the flavors blend and then bring to room temperature before serving. Serve with crackers or baguette slices or big spoons. (See also recipe for baked toast on page 59.)

If you can't be persuaded to give anchovies a try, then substitute 2 to 3 tablespoons of capers for anchovy filets.

MANZ LORE

Of German stock, my grandfather Franklin Manz, was born in Lyons, Iowa in 1888. When he enlisted in the U.S. Army during World War I, they insisted that he adopt a middle name or initial. He chose the initial "P" which may have been a joke.

Gramp loved dogs and plants. For many years he raised wire-haired terriers and scotties at a kennel behind his home in San Gabriel, California. His most famous dog was Sheik, a champion wire-haired terrier who loved to eat the plums that fell to the ground in the orchard. Gramp's last dog and my first was Hansie, a patient black daschund who came to live with us when Gramp moved to our house after my grandmother died. Hansie spent many hours being dressed in my dolls' hats. He's surely a saint in Dog Heaven now.

Gramp's camellias, roses and dahlias filled the backyard of his home. When he retired from the Army Corps of Engineers in 1955, his colleagues gave him a $27 gift certificate for Simpson's in Pasadena. He bought three trees.

King Bee's Cheese Bits

The recipe for these spicy cocktail crackers originally came to Emmy from a favorite inn located in the Great Smoky Mountains of Tennessee. They were a staple in her freezer, prepared for many years by Emma who coached us on the method. These were a favorite of Barry B., also known as King Bee.

Makes 4 dozen

½ lb. butter (2 cubes),
  at room temperature
½ lb. sharp or very sharp cheddar
  cheese, grated (2 cups)
1 to 2 t. Tabasco sauce

2-⅓ c. all-purpose white flour
2 c. old style Rice Crispies cereal with
  no added sugar

Optional: Pecan halves

In a large mixing bowl, combine softened butter, grated cheese and Tabasco sauce thoroughly. We use our Kitchenaid mixer on low speed although Emma said mixing by hand was the secret.

Add half of the flour and keep working dough gently until it disappears. Work in 1 cup of Rice Crispies, then remaining flour and finally the second cup of Rice Crispies.

Taste dough and add more Tabasco sauce if needed, working it in thoroughly. Emma added Tabasco sauce until you could just taste it, giving the dough a slight bite. Cover bowl and chill for ½ hour.

Pre-heat oven to 350°. Form dough into walnut-sized balls and place on un-greased cookie sheets about 1-inch apart. Flatten each ball slightly with your thumb to make a small cracker.   (If you like, place a half pecan on top.) Bake 15 to 20 minutes or until lightly browned. Remove from oven and cool on racks. Serve at room temperature. Store in a tightly covered tin. They freeze well.

A CASE OF MISTAKEN IDENTITY

It is a well known and widely appreciated fact among our family and friends that we keep brownies and other treats tucked into the freezer in tins for emergencies.

Once when we were out of town, Victoria dropped by and found nary a brownie. Being resourceful, she kept digging until she found what she thought was a peanut butter cookie. Imagine her surprise when it turned out to be one of these spicy cheese crackers.

Our reputation at stake, we've tried to do better with the brownie supply. They are always kept in the black, red and gold tin with the Chinese motif.

Lynn & Anne's Re-Run Ricotta Cheese

Catherine met Lynn, Anne and Ruth in Ravello, Italy where they were caught after dinner watching re-runs of the television program "Dallas" in the former monastery where we were staying. Lynn, Anne and Ruth are Italian by choice, traveling to their homeland from the Pacific Northwest as often as possible. • This is Lynn and Anne's version of ricotta cheese.

Makes ¾ cup

1 quart whole milk
½ c. heavy cream
Juice of 1 lemon

Best olive oil
Several sprigs of fresh rosemary
Baguette or crackers

Line a sieve or colander with several layers of cheesecloth and position over a mixing bowl to catch the liquid whey that separates from the cheese curds.

In a large stainless steel saucepan or soup pot, bring milk and cream to a boil over medium-high heat, stirring occasionally with a stainless steel or wooden spoon. (Avoid using an aluminum pot or utensils because the acid in the lemon juice will react with the aluminum.) When milk boils vigorously, add lemon juice. Stir until curds and whey separate.

Remove from heat and immediately pour through the prepared sieve or a colander. Let drain for an hour or so. Place curds on a small plate. Discard whey. Cover and refrigerate if you are preparing well ahead or the day before.

To serve, shape cooled ricotta into a mound. Drizzle olive oil over it, and garnish with sprigs of fresh rosemary. Serve with baguette slices, crackers or baked toast (page 59) as an hors d'oeuvre. Or drizzle honey over ricotta, garnish with fresh fruit or berries, and serve as dessert.

YOGURT CHEESE

Emmy learned to make this easy, tasty cheese from a Scandinavian friend. One quart of unflavored yogurt makes about 1-⅔ cups (14 oz.) of cheese.

Line a medium strainer with cheesecloth or a clean square of muslin fabric and position over a bowl. Pour plain yogurt into the strainer. Cover and refrigerate overnight to drain thoroughly.

The next day, throw out liquid whey that has collected in the bowl. Store cheese curds in a covered container in refrigerator. Spread it on toast, crackers or sandwiches, or use it as the base for a dip.

Ruth's Roasted Garlic
& Goat Cheese on Proper Toast

*Ruth has immortalized the correct procedure for making a toast. Look deeply, meaningfully and wordlessly into the eyes of your partner and then clink glasses. A ritual for us now, **The Proper Toast** substitutes an important form of communication for a careless clash of crystal. • Tenold's variation for bigger groups is **The Toast Wave.** One person begins with **The Proper Toast** to the person on the right or left and that person then passes it on until the circle is completed.*

Serves 1 or more

1 bulb of garlic per person
Good olive oil
Baguette slices, nicely thin

1 oz. chèvre per person or substitute
    ricotta cheese (See recipe on previous page.)
Fresh thyme leaves

Pre-heat oven to 375°. Select a baking dish in which whole garlic bulbs will fit nicely. Remove a layer or two of the outer papery skin from each bulb of garlic. Drizzle a little olive oil over each bulb, enough so that garlic is sitting in a nice pool. Bake 45 minutes to 1 hour or until garlic is soft. For the diet version, bake garlic without olive oil but grease the bottom of the baking dish so garlic bulbs do not stick.

Brush oil from roasted garlic onto baguette slices and toast under the broiler or on the grill. (See also baked toast on page 59.)

Place cheese on a serving plate and top with fresh thyme leaves. To serve, pinch several garlic cloves out of their skins onto a slice of toast. Top with a spoonful of cheese and a few thyme leaves.

MANAGING PRIORITIES

I can't stop reading those books.
I only stopped to eat my favorite sausages.

—Julia Carol Poetzinger (Age 8)

Carol's granddaughter & Catherine's goddaughter

Carol's Subversive Guerrilla Guacamole

This is a delicious alternative to its classic cousin.

Serves 6-8

1 c. mayonnaise
½ pint sour cream (1 cup)
1 T. lemon juice
2 large ripe tomatoes, peeled, seeded
  & chopped (See page 83.)

1 crisp red onion, chopped finely
2 ripe avocados, peeled & cubed
Salt & pepper to taste

In a medium bowl, combine mayonnaise, sour cream and lemon juice, stirring well. Gently fold in chopped tomatoes, onion and avocados. Season with salt and pepper to taste. Serve immediately with tortilla or other chips and fresh vegetables.

CHANGING TIMES

Carol, her daughter Mitzi and I traveled to Europe the summer of 1982 after Mitzi graduated from high school. We called ourselves "Las Tres Sangrías," a tribute to our evening ritual in the plazas of Madrid, Toledo, Zaragoza and Santiago de Compostela.

We were treated with great politeness everywhere in Spain. A student walked blocks out of his way to lead us to our destination when we asked for directions in Vigo. Two men stopped to help us when our car overheated driving across the mountains outside Burgos. One of them, a truck driver, drove our car the last miles up and over the pass to make sure that we were safe. Our first day on the road I managed to drive the wrong way down a one-way street in Toledo and was called "*idiota*" which seemed like a fairly polite reprimand. We felt comfortable in Spain.

After a wild crossing of the Irish Sea by ferry, we took the train from Dublin to Donegal where a helpful publican directed us to a local bed and breakfast. We settled in comfortably for several days, the guests of a hospitable Irish family. By the second day, our hostess, also a wife and mother, worked up her courage to ask the question that must have been on her mind since our arrival. "Where are your men?" she inquired with some puzzlement. We had no answer for her.

Years later a friend told us about her travels as a single woman in Indonesia. She explained that she was routinely asked about her husband to which she finally worked out a satisfactory answer. "I killed him," she would reply which abruptly ended that line of inquiry.

Emily's Hot-Time Artichoke Dip

This favorite recipe was passed down from mother to daughter like many others in this cookbook. It's one of Emily's favorites that she treasures for its rich and elegant flavor as well as its memories of her mother Katy. This is serious party food.

Serves 8-10

Two 14-¾ oz. jars of artichoke
　hearts, packed in water & drained
3 T. mayonnaise
Juice of 1 lemon
1 small yellow onion, quartered
2 or 3 cloves garlic, peeled
1 c. Parmesan cheese (3 oz.),
　freshly grated

Sesame melba toast, crackers, chips
　(See baked toast on page 59.)
Fresh vegetables

<u>Optional</u>:
Chiles, such as 3 whole Anaheim chiles,
　roasted peeled & chopped or 4 oz. can
　diced Anaheim chiles

　　Pre-heat oven to 350°. Combine artichoke hearts, mayonnaise, lemon juice, onion, garlic and Parmesan cheese in a blender or food processor and process until smooth. Stir in chopped chiles, if desired. Pour into a 9x9-inch baking pan or a small ovenproof casserole.

　　Bake 30 to 40 minutes or until hot and bubbly. Serve immediately with melba toast or other crackers, chips or fresh vegetables.

BEGINNER'S LUCK

Grinning from ear to ear, our grandson Cole started pulling crumpled bills from his pocket. "Let's see, that was $15 for the club's caddy fee, then a $65 tip, plus $10 from another guy, and $5 for winning a bet. That makes $95."

At age 11 Cole had successfully launched his caddy career with his friend Joe. The previous weekend the boys had passed their test with flying colors and then set-up shop at a Denver country club on the Friday before Easter. In the morning there were no takers for their newly minted services, but after lunch the boys were snapped up by a four-some.

Cole and Joe were beaming when we arrived to pick up Cole about 5pm. We quickly learned that carrying a fully loaded golf bag for 18 holes was a serious task for a 90-pound lad. Still grinning from ear to ear, Cole was sound asleep in the back seat of the car before we got home.

Andy's Gold Medal Chicken Liver Paté

Andy Loebelson's recipes are alive and well at Crow Farm, reminding us of a friend with whom we've lost touch. He once whipped up this paté easily for a wedding crowd.

Serves 10-12 (4 cups)

¾ lb. chicken livers
1 c. heavy cream
6 double graham crackers
4 anchovies or 3 T. anchovy paste
2 eggs

1 small onion, chopped coarsely
1 T. all-purpose white flour
Salt to taste
½ t. black pepper

Pre-heat oven to 250°. Grease paté mold or standard loaf pan. Bring a kettle of water to a boil. Wash chicken livers thoroughly in cold water, drain and pat dry with several paper towels.

In a blender or food processor, combine all ingredients and purée to total smoothness. Pour into prepared mold or loaf pan, cover with wax paper and set in a 9x13-inch baking pan. Pour boiling water into the baking pan to a depth of about 1-inch. Bake 1 hour. Uncover and bake ½ hour more. Remove from oven, cool, un-mold, chill and serve.

Paté freezes perfectly **before** cooking, not after. If using frozen paté, thaw completely and then cook as directed.

NAME THE DOG

Sound carries in our small valley and sometimes it carries with it a few surprises. Our relationship with a neighbor began over sound waves at dawn and bedtime when they would call their dog repeatedly, something that sounded like R-i-v-e-t, R-i-v-e-t. Pretty soon we concluded that Rivet, as we nicknamed him, had a mind of his own which did not include a shared agenda with his family.

Rivet turned out to be neighborly in his own way, appearing in our yard from time to time to exchange dog tales with Lively and Ivy. He seemed to like them, but he never paid any attention to us. At the end of his visit, we would hook him up to a leash and walk him home. It was always an oddly agreeable process. Rivet was a Schnauzer, a breed of terrier that seems peculiarly immune to humans -- not unfriendly or aggressive in any way — simply oblivious.

We found out that Rivet's name was really Griffin, perfect for a dog who seemed more like a walking gargoyle than a household pet.

Poor Man's "Caviar"

*In Russian, it's known as **baklazhanaya ikra** or eggplant caviar. It's called **caponata** in Italian and **baba ghanooj** in Arabic. First cousins are the French **ratatouille** and the Romanian **ghivetch** with zucchini as an added ingredient. Its origins are certainly Middle Eastern. • Delicious on sesame crackers or with fresh vegetables, it also makes a great sandwich spread and travels well on picnics.*

Makes about 2 cups

1 large eggplant or 2 medium
3 T. olive oil
1 large onion, chopped
1 large green pepper, chopped
1 sweet red pepper, chopped

6 cloves garlic, peeled & minced
6 oz. can tomato paste
1 T. lemon juice
1 t. sugar
Salt & pepper to taste

Pre-heat oven to 450°. Wash eggplant in cold water, drain and pat dry. Prick skin of eggplant in several places with a fork. Place in an un-greased baking pan and bake 45 to 55 minutes or until eggplant is soft and collapsed. Remove from oven and cool slightly. Peel off skin. Purée eggplant in a food processor or blender. Set aside.

In a large frying pan, sauté onion in olive oil over medium-low heat until limp, about 5 minutes. Add chopped peppers and cook 5 minutes longer. Add puréed eggplant, minced garlic, tomato paste and mix thoroughly. Lower heat and simmer covered for 45 minutes, stirring occasionally.

Add lemon juice and sugar, then salt and pepper to taste. Cook uncovered for 15 minutes more, stirring from time to time. Remove from heat and cool. Serve at room temperature or chilled.

At the end of the summer when we have lots of small Japanese eggplants and plenty of fresh tomatoes, we make lots of this "caviar" to freeze. Instead of baking the eggplant, peel and cut each small one in half lengthwise and then into ½ inch slices. Sauté with peppers. Substitute 2 cups of fresh tomato purée for the tomato paste and cook the vegetables **uncovered**, instead of covered, for 45 minutes. Omit lemon juice and sugar because garden fresh vegetables have plenty of flavor and sweetness.

HOME ALONE

Peace, perfect peace with loved ones far away.

—Emmy Smith
Quoting a favorite hymn

Sally's Elegant Caviar Pie

Sally Harper used to prepare this caviar pie for parties in San Francisco before she ran away to the Galapagos Islands. She eventually returned with a handsome son to settle in the Pacific Northwest. • This hors d'oeuvre was also Jim Ottaway's maiden effort in the kitchen, prepared for John and Catherine's wedding lunch at Crow Farm.

Serves 8-10

6 hard boiled eggs, peeled
   & chopped (See page 208.)
1/3 c. best mayonnaise (See page 266.)
1 onion, minced
3/4 c. sour cream

3-1/2 oz. jar caviar, red or black
Parsley
Toast triangles or crackers
   (See baked toast on page 59.)

In a medium bowl, combine chopped eggs, mayonnaise and minced onion. Mound onto a serving plate and shape into a circle about 6-inches in diameter. Cover with sour cream. If you are making this ahead, cover and chill for several hours or overnight.

Just before serving, spread caviar evenly on top. (If you put caviar on top too soon, it "bleeds" messily into the sour cream.) Garnish with parsley and serve with toast triangles, crackers or baked toast.

SPICY PEANUTS
An Indian snack re-created from travel notes

Makes 2 cups

2 c. raw peanuts (8 oz.)

2 T. unflavored oil

1/4 c. red onion, finely chopped

1 Serrano chile, minced

1-1/2 inches fresh ginger, peeled & minced

Juice of 1 lime

In a cast iron frying pan, toast peanuts over medium-high heat until lightly browned and aromatic, shaking pan across the burner. Remove toasted peanuts from pan and set aside. In the same pan, sauté onions in oil over medium-low heat until limp, about 5 minutes. Add minced chile and ginger, and cook several minutes more. Add peanuts, and stir well to coat them thoroughly. Squeeze lime juice over peanuts and stir. Remove from heat. Pour into a serving bowl and serve immediately.

Goddaughter Day's Letter

WATER, WATER, EVERYWHERE

Right now I am writing by candlelight and watching the rain come down in torrents outside my window. We are in the midst of the worst rainstorm here since 1914. We have had 12 inches of rain since 7:00 last night and it is now 3:30 p.m. Mom and Dad just got back from trying to save our driveway from being washed away. I spent the morning listening to the radio reports and answering the phone from distressed neighbors wanting to know how we are. I always answer with, "Well, we're cold and wet and without electricity, but pretty much we feel like the smart little piggies who built the brick house on top of the hill." "Well, great," they say. "Call us if you need any help." "OK," I say.

Our neighbors all have different stories. Of waking up at 3:00 a.m. and bailing out your living-room, or sliding out in mud with sandbags to save the hill behind your house, or watching the little stream that ran beside your house carry away boulders, trees and maybe your driveway.

It makes you pull together and work as a community and although it's a bit nerve-wracking at the time, I wouldn't miss it for the world. Well, when it rains, it pours. As Mom said, "It makes you feel like a tick on the back of a giant dog. The dog is going to go wherever he wants and you better hang on for the ride."

—Day Rose Kornbluth

From a letter written by our then 13-year-old goddaughter in 1995, describing the wild floods in Southern California. • Day's family lost their Santa Barbara dream home in the Jesuita Fire of May 2009, just a few months after Day's marriage to Max Pitman on August 15, 2008 in the most beautiful wedding of all time. Day's parents, Story and Peter, are rebuilding their home. • The legendary brownies on page 41 come from Day's grandmother and Story's mother Laura.

Fish

> *There is a time for laughing*
> *and a time for not laughing.*
> *This is not one of them.*
>
> —Inspector Clouseau

Carol's Bountiful Bouillabaisse

Carol launched Catherine making bouillabaisse decades ago. Catherine still remembers with amazement hearing Carol's sons, 10 year-old Doug and 9 year-old Eric, asking their mom for leftover bouillabaisse the night after a big party. Smart kids. • This is our daughter Emily's favorite Crow Farm dinner and one we enjoy on state occasions.

Serves 8-10

2 large onions, chopped coarsely
3 to 4 T. olive oil
1 large green pepper, chopped coarsely
1 large sweet red pepper, chopped coarsely
4 cloves garlic, peeled & minced
28 oz. can "ready-cut" tomatoes
6 c. fish stock (See next page.)
1 c. white wine
¼ t. saffron threads
Juice of 1 lemon & 2 lemons cut in wedges

1-½ lbs. assorted fish filets (cod, haddock, halibut, perch, snapper, sea bass, shark or other firm fleshed white fish; see page 123 for note about shark)
1 lb. shrimp, peeled & de-veined
1 lb. scallops
18 clams
½ lb. squid tubes (calamari), cleaned & cut in ½ inch rounds (See page 182.)
Fresh parsley, chopped

In a soup pot over medium heat, sauté onion in olive oil until transparent, about 10 minutes. Add peppers and garlic and sauté 2 to 3 minutes more. Stir in tomatoes, fish stock and white wine. Bring to a boil over medium-high heat, lower heat, cover and simmer for 30 minutes.

Wash fish and seafood in cold water and drain. Cut fish into bite-sized chunks. Scrub clams thoroughly with a brush.

Pulverize saffron threads in a mortar with a pestle. Dissolve powdered saffron in a spoonful of hot stock and add to the pot. Stir in lemon juice and increase heat to high.

When soup is boiling rapidly, add clams. As soon as they open, remove them with tongs or a spoon. Discard any that don't open. Add fish, then a minute or two later shrimp, scallops and squid. Let the fish and seafood poach in simmering soup for several minutes until cooked. Be careful not to overcook it. Serve immediately in soup bowls garnished with opened clams, lemon wedges and parsley, accompanied by lots of garlic bread (page 226).

VARIATIONS FROM TOM & ANGELA

Tom makes a delicious bouillabaisse without saffron, seasoning with fennel, oregano and basil in addition to garlic and lemon juice. He also uses tomato sauce in the base rather than tomato chunks. • Angela tops her bouillabaisse with *rouille*, a mayonnaise with garlic, saffron and cayenne smeared on a slice of grilled bread.

Fish

Functional Fish Stock

The secret ingredient of bouillabaisse is fish stock, the better the stock the better the soup. • *At our excellent fish store in Eugene, we can sometimes get fish skeletons or collars, primarily salmon and halibut. Salmon makes a delicious, oily stock that must be well skimmed. Often we settle for a 46 oz. can of sea clam juice. Simmer the skeletons or collars and/or clam juice with water and vegetables. The vegetables contribute great flavor.* • *Like chicken stock, fish stock is another priceless resource for your freezer. When you cook a whole fish, save the skeleton in a plastic bag. When you have several, make stock.*

Makes at least 1 quart

Head, tail & bones from several
  large fish
6 c. or more of water or a mixture
  of water, clam juice & white wine
2 celery stalks, cut in 2 inch segments

2 carrots, cut in 2 inch segments
2 onions, quartered
2 leeks, coarsely chopped
8 whole black peppercorns

Put fish parts in a large soup pot and cover with cold water, clam juice and white wine. Add vegetables and peppercorns. Bring gently to boil over medium heat. Reduce heat, cover and simmer for an hour. Cool and strain. Discard solids. Use stock immediately, or cool and freeze in tightly covered plastic containers.

GONE FISHING

Nicholas loves to fish. In Haines, Alaska before a float trip on the Alsek and Tatsheshini Rivers, Nicholas went fishing while the rest of us went on a hike. He returned to a good spot he had found the day before, prepared with fishing lures recommended by the locals. He landed a dozen salmon.

Fish in hand, Nicholas thought about what his father might say if he arrived at our rustic hotel with a dozen raw fish. Hmm, perhaps not.

Fortunately he had noticed that there was a makeshift fish camp in the grassy field in front of our hotel, a summer tourist attraction where you could eat salmon dinners prepared in the Native American fashion, marinated and grilled. Nicholas approached the two young women chefs with his problem and a lot of charm. They agreed to prepare two of his salmon in exchange for the other ten.

Nicholas returned that evening with a big smile on his face and two large foil wrapped packages in his arms, packages that even a persnickety father would love. And love it we did. We picnicked in grand style, sitting in the grass, eating Nicholas' salmon while praising his fishing abilities, his brains and his charm. We were still eating salmon the next day.

Fish Filets à la Vaudoise

This is the classic recipe for perch from Lake Geneva as Lac Leman is known in the Swiss Canton of Vaud. In 1975 a student in Catherine's advanced English-as-a-second-language class gave her this recipe. • We have substituted filets of sole or sand dabs for the lake perch, unrelated to ocean perch, a whole different kettle of fish.

Serves 4

About 1-½ lbs. filets of sole
   or sand dabs
Juice of 1 lemon
3 T. all-purpose white flour
2 to 3 T. unflavored vegetable oil

Sauce:
2 tomatoes
2 T. butter
2 oz. mushrooms, chopped finely
   (about ½ cup)
½ c. white wine
Fresh parsley, chopped finely
Salt & pepper to taste

Peel and seed tomatoes as directed on page 83. Dice and reserve for sauce. Rinse fish in cold water and pat dry with paper towels. Squeeze lemon juice over fish. Dust a plate with 2 tablespoons of flour and roll the fish in it to coat lightly.

In a frying pan over medium-high heat, brown the fish on each side in hot oil. Remove the fish from the pan and keep warm while making the sauce.

For the sauce, melt the butter in a frying pan, add 1 tablespoon of flour and stir until thickened. Add white wine, stirring well. Then add diced tomatoes and mushrooms and continue cooking briefly. Add parsley, salt and pepper to taste. Pour sauce over the fish and serve immediately with rice or steamed potatoes.

COME ON, FREEDOM OF SPEECH!

CENSORSHIP OF ART: What a dull controversy. You call me ambivalent or equivocating BUT I grew up from an early age exposed to Classical ART that was pretty faithful to the Human Form. I can't see that it made me depraved. PER CONTRA I was totally against the Cincinnati Gallery and Nat'l Fdn for Arts promoting the "black" photographer capitalizing on the vulgarity of an "artistic" photo of a Crucifix immersed in human urine. The Human Form (not deformed) need not be veiled. Being nasty should not be subsidized . . . COME ON "Freedom of Speech." SAY IT AGAIN.

—Macauley Smith (September 21, 1991)

Story's Friendly Shark Tacos

Story claims she doesn't cook, but whenever we visit the food is unforgettably delicious. One year it was a divine roasted red pepper soup that must have taken days to make. Another time it was baked halibut and once these tacos. Story's daughter, Day Rose, our goddaughter, was well on her way to becoming a great cook before she was 12. Her first specialties were banana bread and rice pudding. Natty, Day's younger sister, has taken up cooking, and her tamales are tops.

Serves 6

1-½ lbs. shark, cut in bite-sized
   pieces
2 c. milk or water &
   juice of 1 lemon or 1 T. white vinegar

Condiments:
12 tortillas, warmed
Salsa (See page 267.)
Sour cream

2 to 3 T. olive oil
1 large onion, chopped finely
1 green pepper, chopped finely
4 cloves garlic, peeled & minced
2 large tomatoes, peeled, seeded
   & diced (See page 83.)
   or 14-½ oz. can "ready cut" tomatoes
3 T. cilantro, chopped finely
3 T. lemon juice
Salt & pepper to taste

    Rinse shark in cold water and put in a baking dish. In a small bowl, combine milk or water with lemon juice or vinegar, stir and pour over shark. Cover and refrigerate for 1 hour. This will remove the slight ammonia flavor from the shark. Drain shark, rinse in cold water, drain again and pat dry with a paper towel. Cut in 1-inch cubes.

    In a frying pan, sauté onion in olive oil over medium-low heat until limp, about 5 minutes. Add green pepper and garlic and sauté several minutes more. Add diced tomatoes, shark, cilantro, lemon juice, salt and pepper to taste. Simmer uncovered until shark is just cooked, about 5 minutes. Serve immediately with warmed tortillas, salsa and sour cream.

ADDING IT UP

Now, the average comic strip only takes about ten seconds to digest, but if you read every strip published in The Washington Post, as Ronald Reagan claims he did while President, it takes roughly eight minutes a day. Which means, by my tally, that the Former Leader of the Free World spent a total of 2 weeks, 2 days, 5 hours and 20 minutes of his presidency reading the comics. Which explains a lot.

—Garry Trudeau
From his remarks on Yale Class Day (May 26, 1991)

Joey's Father-Son Scientific Seviche

*Joey wears many hats, writer, educator, farmer, track and field umpire, baseball player/coach, carpenter and more. In his chef's hat, he made Julia Child's **boeuf bourguignon** for 14 for Nancy's birthday and **paella** for 20 cooked outside on a cold November evening because his daughter Ruby wanted the full wood smoke flavor for her 21st birthday party. Now that's love and fine cooking. • Can food determine your future? Joey became a marine biologist after his father Sam, a chemist, served this **seviche**, a notably exotic choice for a single parent in the 1970s. Let science explain this connection. • Joey and Nancy brought this **seviche** to Crow Farm for a memorable winter Sunday lunch after we had returned from a long trip. Let friendship explain this delight. • Joey and Nancy have special hand-made bowls in which to serve **seviche** for special occasions, such as birthdays. This is a serious party food.*

Serves 8-10

2 lbs. large or jumbo shrimp, cooked
¾ c. lime juice (about 6 large limes)
1 lb. sea scallops, raw
Flexible amounts according to taste:
  6 T. red onion, diced
  6 T. red bell pepper, chopped coarsely
  6 T. cilantro, chopped
½ c. olive oil
½ t. oregano
Splash of Tabasco sauce

Garnish:
3 avocados, peeled & sliced
1 lemon, cut in wedges

Optional:
Pepperoncini

Peel and de-vein shrimp. (Save shells in a bag in the freezer to use in fish stock.) In a large pot, steam shrimp over simmering water until they turn pink. Cool and cut shrimp in thirds. Put in a bowl with lime juice to marinate. Cut raw scallops into thin slices and add to shrimp and lime juice. Cover and marinate in the refrigerator for 1 to 1-½ hours.

Drain shrimp and scallops. (Discard lime juice.) Add red onion, red bell pepper, cilantro, olive oil, oregano and Tabasco. Toss gently and marinate in the refrigerator for at least 1 hour more. Serve with avocado slices, lemon wedges and pepperoncini, if you like.

PULLING OUT THE STOPS

Dear John stop
Can't come to mtg stop
Queen B has 2 much cntrl over honey stop
No May Day yet stop
With you all in spirit stop
Rear Admiral Joey

—Joey Blum
Why he missed a meeting of the Hell & High Water Boys' Club.

Fish

Maureen's Back-to-the-Barn Baked Salmon

On her first visit to the farm, Maureen spent nearly all her time in the barn playing with our two black lambs, Lillian and Chops. She was content with the smell of hay and those soft lips nibbling on her fingers. • Serve Maureen's salmon with steamed new potatoes, fresh asparagus and crusty French bread for a total extravaganza.

Servings vary with size of fish

1 whole salmon, cleaned & butterflied
Mayonnaise
Bacon (6 to 8 thick slices, ½ to ¾ lb.)

Lemons, thinly sliced & cut in wedges
Onions, thinly sliced
Fresh rosemary, thyme & parsley

Pre-heat oven to 400°. Wash fish in cold water and pat dry with paper towels. Spread a sheet of heavy-duty aluminum foil over a baking pan or cookie sheet large enough to hold the whole salmon. Place fish on foil and rub with mayonnaise, inside and out. Put several slices of bacon under the salmon. Open fish and layer onion, lemon slices and fresh herbs. Close salmon and top with remaining slices of bacon. Seal foil tightly.

Bake salmon, allowing approximately 10 minutes for each 1-inch thickness of fish. Don't overcook. We like our salmon best when it's still pink in the center. Transfer baked salmon to a platter, remove foil (or fold it back) and garnish with lemon wedges and fresh parsley. Serve with steamed potatoes and basil-garlic mayonnaise on page 266.

SOMETHING'S FISHY

Tom and Susan pulled off the biggest fish trick of all time. About 3 a.m. Tom caught a gorgeous 9 lb. steelhead in Puget Sound. He had it iced and packed at Johnny's Dock and loaded onto the 10 a.m. southbound train designated as "camping equipment" to skirt the prohibition on shipping food. Susan called to tell us dinner was on the way.

Story was running late when she arrived to retrieve our shipment in Eugene. Doors locked, she anxiously circled the station and finally found a lone clerk in the back room who handed over our "camping equipment." She drove this cargo home where our precious steelhead sat on ice in its cooler on our north porch. Bhagwan Bruce LeFavour poached it to perfection the following night. A meal we'll never forget!

Boatwright Andy's Low Octane Oysters

Andy Erickson is one of the most naturally gifted teachers of all time. He handles tools like Segovia handled his guitar. Always exploring new disciplines, Andy is a master mechanic, an experienced shipwright, a skilled wood worker and a licensed pilot. • He wears a ring on each hand, one signifying his marriage and the other his connection to the Great Spirit.

Serves 3-4

¾ lb. fresh oysters
1 c. beer
3 T. all-purpose white flour
1 egg

3 T. cornmeal
3 T. butter
2 lemons, quartered

In a small bowl, cover the oysters with beer and marinate for several hours or overnight in the refrigerator. (Beer removes any slightly bitter, fishy flavor.) Drain oysters and pat dry with a paper towel.

Dust a plate with flour. In a small bowl, beat the egg lightly with a fork. Sprinkle cornmeal on a second plate. Roll oysters in flour, dip in beaten egg and roll in cornmeal. Set on a platter.

In a frying pan, melt butter and sauté oysters over medium heat until brown, 3 to 4 minutes on each side. Serve immediately with lemon quarters and spicy tomato sauce.

SPICY TOMATO SAUCE

½ c. catsup or tomato sauce

1 T. Dijon mustard

1 t. Tabasco sauce

1 t. Worcestershire sauce

Combine the ingredients and mix well. For variety, add 1 tablespoon of horseradish or 1 teaspoon of anchovy paste to the sauce.

SMOKE SIGNALS

*If it's smokin', it's cookin'.
If it's burnin', it's done.*

—Andy Erickson's cooking motto

Bill's New Orleans' Oyster Loaf

Bill White created a great restaurant that looked 100 years old the day it opened on Santa Barbara's State Street. • One summer he worked wonders on our Crow's Nest guesthouse when he visited for a month, adding the kitchen, bathroom and outdoor shower. Years later Bill returned to help with the construction of a cabin he had designed. "That's the first time anyone ever used one of my designs," he reported. • Bill and his wife, Sue, built an extraordinary house in Willits, California that gradually incorporated the small, existing house. These days he is finishing a small straw bale house on the same property. • Bill has fascinating ideas about lifestyle and politics as well as the world's largest collection of beautiful old doors. He introduced us to the rural Italian mid-day meal with pasta, salad, bread, wine and a nap. • Bill's mother's family hails from Shreveport and this is his version of a New Orleans' favorite.

Serves 3-4

1 baguette or loaf of French bread or sourdough rolls
1 recipe of Andy's oysters & spicy tomato sauce (See recipe on previous page.)

Pre-heat oven to 350°. Cut bread in 5-inch sections and halve each section lengthwise. Scoop or cut away bread to make a trough in the center of each piece. (Save bread chunks in a plastic bag in the freezer for crumbs or turkey stuffing.)

Warm bread uncovered in the oven at 200° while you prepare the oysters. Place cooked oysters in the trough of the bread, top with spicy tomato sauce and serve immediately with lemon wedges.

UP IN SMOKE

Dear Katrink:

In keeping with the ecology kick and the need to use everything to the bitter end, I couldn't think of a more appropriate way to say "thank you" for the cigar sent in your care package. As you can see, I gave up on the utter [sic] side as the ecologists apparently don't realize that if the ink don't stick, I can't write.

Love,
Yer Fadder

A note to Catherine from her father Frank Manz, written on both sides of a Santa Fe cigarillo box, thanking her for a Havana cigar purchased in London in 1971 and smuggled home wrapped in a shower cap.

The Bhagwan on Cooking Crabs

There is good crabbing along the Oregon coast. Old timers like our neighbor Lorna keep a bag of chicken fat in the freezer ready for use as bait for their crab traps. • John took Jeff and Tavi crabbing at Salmon Harbor one day, and they were so successful that they had crabs scrambling all over the deck of the boat. We had sublime crab cakes for dinner that night prepared by Jeff's wife, Victoria. • We rely on our cooking guru, Bhagwan Bruce LeFavour, for advice on important matters such as the proper way to transport and cook crabs.

Buy or catch live crabs and take them home in a cooler with ice on the bottom, then a layer of damp newspapers, the crabs, another layer of damp newspapers and a sprinkling of ice on top. Bruce instructed that crabs must travel right side up or they'll die. Also, avoid plastic bags that will suffocate them.

Bring your largest kettle of water to a boil over high heat. Use enough water to cover the crabs generously and salt it to taste like sea water. This will require lots of salt. Cover the pot.

As soon as the water comes to a boil, immerse the live crabs upside down so that each body is well submerged. (The body requires the longest time to cook.) Return water to a boil uncovered. When the water boils again, set the timer for 8 to 12 minutes: 8 minutes for 1-½ pound crabs, 11 to 12 minutes for crabs over 2 pounds. At the end of this set time, turn off heat and let crabs sit in the water for 1 to 2 minutes more.

Remove crabs from the water and cool them on a platter for 2 to 3 minutes or until you can handle them comfortably with a dishtowel.

To clean the crabs, set them on their backs. Locate the protuberance from the rear end that fits in the groove on the bottom of the shell. Lift and tear off, making a small hole. Insert your thumb in the hole and pry off the back of the shell, leaving the legs and body in one piece.

With your hands, scrape off the gills (lungs) and the green and white body fat. Bruce reminded us that although we discard this — it's called *tomalley* — the Vietnamese consider it a delicacy.

Break the crab in half with your hands, leaving two legs and equal parts of the body on each half.

Remove the stomach located near the head. It's obvious. You'll want to clean the crabs carefully with your hands so that you won't have to rinse them. Rinsing them washes away flavor, Bruce cautioned. (If you must rinse them, then use the cooking water sparingly.)

The crabs are now ready to eat. Nutcrackers and nut picks make useful tools for prying open crab legs.

Crab Violet Ray

This is our celebrity recipe. Violet Ray is an artist whose collages commenting on American consumer culture have been exhibited in New Mexico, California and Oregon. In a later life, Violet Ray was an outstanding soccer coach for his son's team. • Violet considers this a Kentucky recipe because he ate it first with Kentucky friends in New York City. Such is the way recipes travel.

Serves 2

2 T. olive oil
1 medium onion, chopped finely
2 cloves garlic, peeled & minced
8 oz. can tomato sauce
½ t. fresh tarragon or ¼ t. dried

½ t. fresh thyme or ¼ t. dried
¼ lb. fresh crab meat
  or 6-⅛ oz. can crab meat

2 c. cooked rice

See instructions for preparing fresh crab on the previous page. In a medium frying pan over medium-low heat, sauté onion and garlic in olive oil until onion is limp, about 5 minutes. Add tomato sauce and herbs. Simmer uncovered over low heat for 10 minutes, stirring occasionally. Add crab meat and simmer uncovered 10 minutes more, stirring frequently. Serve immediately over rice.

WITH GRATEFUL THANKS

Just before my sixteenth birthday I was selected to be an exchange student in the American Field Service Program. The cost of this program was $750, a princely sum in 1964 and nearly my father's entire monthly salary. Before my parents had time to worry about financing this opportunity, a check arrived in the mail from Uncle Bill and Aunt Frances, my mother's older sister and her husband.

Uncle Bill's gesture was more than generosity. He had been a student in Paris in the 1920's when American ambulance drivers from World War I created the beginning of what became the American Field Service student exchange program. Uncle Bill was really my predecessor a student abroad.

My uncle and aunt's gift insured that I would have the same kind of experience that had been so important to him and that my parents wouldn't be in hock because of it. I'll never forget how much his support meant to me, and I'll never know the relief my parents probably felt at my Uncle and Aunt's easy generosity.

 Fish

Just-Trapped Crab Vermouth

This is a nicely messy do-it-yourself crab-picking meal.

Serves 4

3 T. olive oil
1 large onion, chopped coarsely
2 cloves garlic, peeled & minced
1 c. vermouth or dry white wine

1 c. clam juice or water
Juice of 1 lemon
2 cooked, cracked crabs (See page 128.)
2 T. parsley, chopped

In a medium soup pot over medium-low heat, sauté onion in olive oil until limp, about 5 minutes. Add garlic, vermouth, clam juice and lemon juice. Bring to a boil over medium-high heat, reduce heat, cover and simmer gently for 10 to 15 minutes.

Add cooked, cracked crabs, cover and simmer gently until crab is thoroughly warmed, 5 to 10 minutes.

Serve in soup bowls, topped with parsley and accompanied by plenty of French bread to soak up the broth and big napkins to mop up messy fingers. Nut crackers and picks make good crab-eating tools.

THE PROMISE OF SPRING

It was snowing when Howard and Edith put me on the train back to Boston laden with bulbs and branches. Having grown up in Southern California, I was unprepared for what a bowl of fragrant paper-white narcissus and a vase of delicate yellow forsythia blossoms might mean in mid-winter in my student apartment. Of course, they meant everything with their promise of spring.

I finally understood the excitement of a scene in a Russian novel portraying Moscow street vendors selling sprigs of mimosa in late winter. I also learned about dwarf Alpine jonquils sold on street corners in Lausanne, Switzerland, available by the dozen along with a small box in which to mail them to loved ones.

At the end of my first real winter, I stood with Edith at her kitchen window as she pointed to purple crocus poking their bright heads up through the new snow on an April morning. At that moment, I knew anything was possible.

Poultry

LIFE IN THE WILD

Jack and Henrietta arrived on Christmas morning, survivors of rural warfare in which a hawk and a weasel had picked off their flock-mates one by one. They traveled in style in a wood-slatted box, delivered by John Jones from his neighboring farm to their new home in our barn.

Jack was a handsome Araucana rooster and his partner Henrietta, a pert, brown-spotted charmer named for Catherine's mother's best friend. They lived happily at the farm for several years, raising their two daughters, "The Clucks." The hens provided us with many dozens of beautiful brown eggs. Jack was our alarm clock, hailing in the dawn each morning in his pure voice.

Henrietta lost her head, we think, to a weasel that probably burrowed under the aged wooden walls of the barn. Some months later Jack went out in the line of duty, sounding the alarm in the middle of a rainy winter night, trying to protect the rest of his small flock. The next morning we found his body next to the stream where it had been dragged by a hungry raccoon.

Swamp Chicken

This easy, soothing dish is a variation on chicken soup, perfect for those times when you need comfort food.

Serves 4

2 T. olive oil
1 large onion, chopped
1 sweet red pepper, sliced in thin strips
1 qt. chicken stock (See page 68.)
2 whole chicken breasts (4 halves),
  skinned

2 cloves garlic, peeled & minced
About 4 c. cooked rice
1 c. broccoli florets
Salt & pepper to taste

In a small soup pot or a large frying pan, sauté onion in olive oil over medium-low heat until limp, about 5 minutes. Add sliced red pepper and sauté several minutes more. Pour chicken stock over vegetables and bring to a boil over medium-high heat. Add chicken breasts and minced garlic. Return to a boil, reduce heat, cover and simmer gently for 15 to 20 minutes, until chicken is cooked.

Add cooked rice and broccoli, and cook briefly until broccoli is tender. Adjust seasoning and serve in soup bowls with crusty French bread.

THE CROW FARM GAZETTE

Jack and Henrietta are well established in the barn, choosing not to emerge and tempt the local raptors. Jack is sick and tired of losing his ladies to predators. Henrietta has no urge to tempt the fates either, being a wise and wary Araucana. She now sleeps in the tiny brace at the very top of the barn roof. Very safe. Jack, being more of a middle-age-spread kind of guy, can only make it to the first pole, but I suspect he's safe as can be, too. Henrietta attacks cats, we also noticed. She'll be a great mom come spring.

Jack and Henrietta have scratch, but one suspects that cracked corn is what they truly desire, as the wheat remains much longer on the tray. They now have a dish of water that needs replenishing only about every third or fourth day. They simply aren't ready to venture out to the running water of the brook. It's hard to convey human logic to chickens, so we compromised.

—Barbara Rattenborg

From her handwritten Gazette in which she offered "all the news you would want to know —NEVER any crime, economic news, terrorist updates or bad news of any kind."

Garlicky Lemon Chicken

A favorite for years, this easy recipe is a good beginning for several meals. Roast chicken can be followed by a chicken curry or chicken salad from the leftovers and then chicken stock from the bones.

Serves 4

1 whole chicken
1 or 2 lemons
**Fresh herbs (sprigs of rosemary,
   thyme or tarragon)**

**4 to 6 cloves garlic, peeled &
   sliced thinly**

Pre-heat oven to 325° to roast chicken for 2 hours, or 375° to roast chicken for 1 hour. Wash chicken in cold water, drain and pat dry with paper towels. Remove chicken fat and discard. (Wash and reserve giblets for chicken stock; see page 68.)

Wash lemons, dry and poke holes all over them with a fork or paring knife. Put lemons and herbs inside chicken. Loosen skin on the chicken breast by pulling it gently and insert garlic slices.

In a baking pan, position chicken breast-side down on a rack, and place in center of oven. Half-way through roasting, turn chicken breast-side up. Roast chicken for approximately 2 hours at 325° or approximately 1 hour at 375°. Adjust time according to size of chicken. Chicken is done when the juice runs clear from a knife prick at the joint between the body and the leg. Serve with roast potatoes on pages 198-9.

THE BAD ACTOR

We should have paid attention when told that she didn't like Comb Boy, the striking black and fluorescent green Australorp named by Ruby when he was the Number 2 rooster at her family's farm. In spite of Ruby's opinion, Comb Boy moved to Crow Farm to become our Number 1 rooster and, as it turned out, Public Enemy Number 1.

Our hopes for Comb Boy's redemption were short-lived as he attacked whomever whenever he felt like it, making our orange broom the weapon of choice when we approached the hen house.

One day Comb Boy made his last mistake. John was delivering a bag of feed to the chickens and Comb Boy attacked John's leg with his sharp spurs. John simply turned and dropped the 50 lb. bag on top of the indiscreet rooster and whacked his head off neatly with a machete. That was the end of Comb Boy. As we say here at the farm, bury the beak that bites you.

Andy's Chicken with Black Bean Sauce

Andy Loebelson introduced us to fermented black beans, the not-so-secret ingredient in this recipe. They are available in Asian grocery stores. • This is a good, last minute dish — fast and tasty.

Serves 4

1 whole chicken, cut in serving pieces
   or 3 whole chicken breasts (6 halves)
   or assorted chicken parts
3 to 4 T. unflavored vegetable oil
1 medium onion, sliced finely
2 cloves garlic, peeled & minced
2 T. cornstarch

1-¼ c. hot water
2 T. soy sauce
1 inch of fresh ginger, peeled & chopped
   finely
⅓ c. oriental fermented black beans

About 4 c. cooked rice

In a large frying pan, brown chicken pieces in oil over medium-high heat. Remove chicken and set aside. In the same pan, reduce heat to medium-low and brown onions with garlic, about 5 minutes. Add additional oil as needed.

In a small bowl or measuring cup, dissolve cornstarch in hot water and pour over onions. Bring to a boil over medium heat, stirring constantly until thickened.

Add soy sauce, ginger, black beans and chicken. Stir well. Cover and simmer over low heat, stirring occasionally, for 20 to 30 minutes or until chicken is tender.

Remove chicken to a warm platter. Reduce the sauce by boiling vigorously over high heat for several minutes, stirring constantly. Pour sauce over the chicken and serve with rice.

CELESTIAL MAINTENANCE

What each of us does with our time here on Earth —our actions as well as our thoughts — affects us, others, the planet and the universe itself. Thus each of us is involved in the maintenance of the cosmos at each moment simply by taking care of ourselves and others.

In addition, each of us is given a special assignment to carry out during our time on earth. It is our job to discover our personal assignment and to pursue it to the best of our ability.

—An Old Crow

Klepinger's Kumquat Chicken

Kumquats are a treat eaten whole like candy, sliced thinly in salads or pickled. Bruce Klepinger created this recipe with a gift bag of kumquats fresh off a Southern California tree.

Serves 4

Pickled kumquats:
1 c. kumquats (about 18 to 25)
½ c. cold water
⅓ c. lemon juice
½ c. sugar

2 whole chicken breasts (4 halves)
**   or assorted chicken parts**
¾ c. white wine

About 4 c. cooked rice

Wash kumquats in cold water, drain and remove stems. In a small saucepan, combine kumquats with water, lemon juice and sugar. Bring to a boil uncovered over medium heat, reduce heat and continue boiling vigorously until kumquats swell up, about 15 minutes. Reduce heat to low, cover and simmer 15 minutes more.

Pre-heat oven to 350°. Place chicken breasts with meat side up in a baking pan or casserole. Arrange the kumquats attractively on top of chicken. Pour pickling juice and white wine gently over the top. Bake uncovered for 45 minutes or until the chicken is nicely browned, basting with liquid every 10 minutes or so. Serve immediately with rice.

CELESTIAL MAINTENANCE VISITING

Run to the covered bridge,
slowly.
Enjoy the daffodils reborn,
joyfully.
Pick some weeds in the garden,
carefully.
Take a shower in the fresh air,
wonderfully.
Talk long with John and Catherine,
gratefully.

—Jim Ottaway, Jr.
Found in the Crow's Nest after Jim & Mary's visit.
(Easter 1991)

Maya's Marinated Yogurt Chicken

Because food does provide comfort, it is often offered in sympathy. After Nicholas' mother died, this delicious dish was the main course of a dinner prepared for us by the mother of his students, Ben and Ruth.

Serves 4

Marinade:
1 c. yogurt
½ c. lime juice (about 3 limes)
3 cloves garlic, peeled & minced
½ to 1 t. salt
½ t. powdered ginger
1-½ t. coriander
1 t. cumin
½ t. cayenne pepper

1 whole chicken, cut in pieces
3 whole chicken breasts (6 halves)
or assorted other parts

About 4 c. cooked rice

In a large bowl, combine ingredients for marinade and mix thoroughly. Add chicken and stir to coat thoroughly. Cover and marinate in the refrigerator for 1 to 2 days.

Transfer chicken and marinade to a baking pan. Pre-heat broiler and set oven rack lower than usual for broiling to keep the yogurt marinade from burning. Broil chicken in marinade for 10 to 15 minutes on each side or until chicken is golden brown. Serve immediately with rice.

LIFE-LONG LEARNING

It's a heavenly feeling when suddenly the thing jumps at you and you know you understand. I dare say you don't, but it doesn't matter, the feeling is there. I don't think you get it out of books a bit, though books help to strengthen it, but you certainly get it out of seeing more and more, even of quite different things. The more you see, the more everything falls into a kind of rough and ready perspective, and when you come to a new thing, you haven't so much difficulty in placing it and fitting it into the rest. I'm awfully glad you love the beginnings of things — so do I, most thoroughly, and unless one does, I don't believe one can get as much pleasure out of the ends.

—Gertrude Bell

From a letter to her sister Elsa
(*The Letters of Gertrude Bell*)

Alexandra's Grand Jeté Moroccan Chicken

Alexandra is Catherine's best friend from graduate school where they read Bulgakov and Dostoyevsky together as well as gave weekly dinner parties. It was Alexandra who introduced Catherine to rare roast beef with horseradish, prepared to perfection in her tiny student apartment kitchen, proof that good cooks can cook well anywhere. This recipe comes from one of their unforgettable graduate student dinner parties. • Alexandra has been helping run the U.S. government's international programs for doctors and scientists for more than 30 years, an absolute ace in this work as she was in the academic world. • With Alex, you can do grand jetés on side streets in suburban Maryland or discuss the importance of red shoes. She once rode in an elevator with Rudolph Nureyev and much later sent us photos of his extraordinary tomb outside Paris. It is draped with an intricate oriental rug, a magic carpet fashioned by a friend out of thousands of pieces of glass, a fitting tribute to this legendary artist and his passion for oriental rugs.

Serves 4-6

1 whole chicken, cut in pieces or
   3 whole chicken breasts (6 halves)
¼ c. unflavored vegetable oil
2 small onions, chopped coarsely
4 cloves garlic, peeled & minced
½ c. almonds (2 oz.), chopped coarsely
2 c. cold water
½ c. raisins (about 3-⅓ oz.)

3 apples, unpeeled, cored & sliced
2 t. cinnamon
3 T. honey
1 t. powdered ginger or 1 T. fresh
   ginger, peeled & minced
Salt & pepper to taste

Whole wheat bread, thickly sliced

In a large frying pan, brown chicken in oil over medium-high heat. Lower heat, and add onions, garlic and almonds. Sauté several minutes. Then add water, cover and simmer for 15 minutes.

Add raisins and apples and simmer 20 minutes longer. Test if chicken and apples are done. If so, add cinnamon, honey and ginger. Season to taste with salt and pepper. Serve with thick slices of whole wheat bread to mop up juice.

FAMILY VALUES

Everyone talks values as if they were computer skills. We would rather create memories: butter-dipping raw folds of Parker House Rolls on Thanksgiving morning; clipping sprigs of basil before the first frost; stirring the batter for your sister's devil's food birthday cake. In food, there is so much to learn about life. As with good friends, the best foods are the simplest and most honest.

—Christopher Kimball

From an editorial entitled "Letter to My Younger Daughter" by the editor & publisher of *Cook's Illustrated* (January/February 1994).

Mama's Nine Bowl Chicken Curry

On important occasions when we were growing up, Mama would make a beautiful curry served with nine different condiments, each in its own small bowl waiting to be piled on top of the curried chicken. • We like Paul's version of chicken curry, too, with lime juice as its secret ingredient. Curry gives the cook lots of room to experiment. • Curry powder itself is a virtual grocery store of spices, including turmeric, cumin, coriander, cloves, mustard, ginger and cayenne pepper, as many as 40 different ones.

Serves 8

Chicken stock:
3 whole chicken breasts (6 halves)
10 black peppercorns
1 small onion, peeled &
   studded with 6 whole cloves
1 small carrot, quartered
4-½ c. cold water

Sauce:
2 T. unflavored vegetable oil
1 large onion, chopped coarsely
2 T. or more curry powder

Original version:
3 to 4 c. chicken stock
1 very ripe banana, sliced
1 apple, peeled, cored & diced
¾ c. chutney (See page 269.)
¾ c. golden raisins (about 5 oz.)
Juice of 1 lemon

Paul's version:
2 c. or more chicken stock
1 c. coconut milk
3 T. crystallized ginger, chopped finely
1 T. fresh mint, chopped
¼ t. ground cloves
⅛ t. ground black pepper
Juice of 1 lime
½ c. cream or sour cream

About 8 c. cooked rice

Condiments:
3 hard boiled eggs, peeled & chopped
2 fresh tomatoes, chopped
½ lb. bacon (about 6 thick slices),
   cooked crisp & crumbled
6 green onions, chopped
¾ c. shredded coconut (about 1-⅞ oz.)
8 oz. can crushed pineapple
1 c. peanuts (8 oz.), chopped
1 green pepper, finely chopped
Chutney (See page 269.)

In a soup pot, combine chicken, peppercorns, onion, cloves, carrot, and cover with cold water. Bring to a boil over medium-high heat, skim foam from the surface, lower heat, cover and simmer for 20 to 30 minutes or until the chicken is done. Or turn off the heat after it comes to a boil, cover and let sit for an hour. (On an electric burner, remove pot from heat and set aside to cool.)

Remove chicken from stock. Cool, skin, and bone. Shred or cut in bite-sized pieces. Strain chicken stock, de-grease it (see page 68) and set aside. (Extra chicken stock freezes nicely in old yogurt or cottage cheese containers.)

In a large frying pan over medium-low heat, sauté onion in oil until transparent, about 10 minutes. Add curry powder and cook several minutes more, stirring constantly. Add chicken stock, banana, apple, chutney, raisins and lemon juice. Lower heat, cover and simmer for 30 minutes. About 5 minutes before serving, add cooked chicken. Serve with rice and condiments.

PAUL'S CHICKEN CURRY • After cooking onion and curry powder for the sauce as explained on the previous page, add chicken stock, coconut milk, crystallized ginger, mint, cloves and pepper. Lower heat, cover and simmer for 30 minutes. Just before serving add lime juice, cream and cooked chicken.

BIRDS OF A FEATHER

I still laugh when I think of the pleasure my father got from his relationship with our pet bird. This bird flew in the window of my sister's second grade classroom, presided over by the white-haired dowager, Mrs. Pernot. My sister Connie raised her hand to volunteer the antique brass birdcage that Mama had brought home to fill with ivy. (Where did Mama get such an idea decades before Martha Stewart?) Mama then brought the birdcage to Hamilton Elementary School and the visiting canary came home with us. He had a leg band with a number and I remember Mama making phone calls to trace him. Nothing came of that.

Naming our new bird was an event in our household. Mama wanted to call him Caruso and she did. Pop preferred Seagull or Birdbrain. I felt strongly about Oriole although looking back that seems like a peculiar choice even for a kindergartner. His full name ended up Enrico Caruso Oriole Seagull Birdbrain Manz.

Pop and Seagull began their day together in our breakfast room. "Okay, Seagull, what's up?" Pop would greet the bird before feeding him bits of bacon and crusts of toast. In the evenings, they shared a passion for westerns, Pop from his easy chair in the living room and Seagull from his cage in the breakfast room where he would burst into song during the shoot 'em up scenes.

One evening Seagull emitted loud, unnatural squawks that aroused Pop's attention. After careful analysis, my father determined that the carved pumpkin placed on the breakfast table was disturbing our bird. Pop promptly rescued his friend by moving the offensive pumpkin out of sight. And peace was restored to our household.

Combined-Forces: Karen's Garlic Chicken with Sally's Miracle Garlic

Garlic is a miraculous substance. We believe in its health-giving properties, so much so that we grow about 60 feet of it in a large 20-foot square bed near our vegetable garden. • Karen, ever the sorceress in the kitchen, created this winning dish using garlic from our garden which Sally Cairnes-Wurster had pickled for each of us as a Christmas gift.

Serves 4

2 c. chicken stock (See page 68.)
2 whole chicken breasts (4 halves)
¼ to ⅓ c. unflavored cooking oil
¼ c. water
12 shitake mushrooms, sliced
⅔ c. pickled garlic cloves (See below.)

1 c. green onions, sliced
2 T. fresh ginger, peeled & thinly sliced
2 T. cornstarch
¼ c. pickling liquid from garlic
⅓ c. soy sauce
About 4 c. cooked rice

In a saucepan over high heat, bring chicken stock to a boil and boil vigorously until volume reduces by half.

In a frying pan over medium-high heat, sauté chicken breasts in 3 to 4 tablespoons of oil, browning the skin side first, then turning them over. Reduce heat, add water and simmer until chicken is tender, about 15 minutes. Remove chicken from pan and keep warm.

In the same pan, sauté shitake mushrooms in 2 tablespoons of oil over medium-high heat. Lower heat to medium, add whole, pickled garlic, green onions and ginger, and sauté until onions are wilted, about 5 minutes.

Add reduced chicken stock, cornstarch, soy sauce and pickling liquid, and cook over medium heat for several minutes until thickened, stirring constantly. Pour over chicken and serve immediately with rice.

SALLY'S MIRACLE PICKLED GARLIC (*Makes 3 cups*)

3 c. garlic cloves, peeled

1-½ c. white vinegar

½ c. sugar

½ t. salt

Make a pot of tea and sit in a comfortable chair. Or, better yet, invite a friend to help peel the garlic. It's time-consuming but worth it. Peel all the garlic cloves and set aside. Combine vinegar, sugar and salt in a saucepan and bring to a boil. Add peeled garlic and boil 1 minute. Remove from heat and spoon into 3 clean ½ pint jars. Keep in the refrigerator. Eat like candy or use in salads.

Bad Boy Tom's
Tantalizing Turkey Cutlets Piccata

Tom, our favorite boat captain and high school special education teacher, has managed to make a virtue of being a bad boy. There is a particularly good story about Bad Boy Tom and the strip poker game that changed his domestic fortunes forever. We love his stories about the intricacies of fishing rights in the state of Washington, about himself and his life with Susan and his daughter, Lizzy B. • A variation on the classic veal piccata, this dish is also a marvelous way to prepare calamari steaks.

Serves 4

4 turkey cutlets
3 T. all-purpose white flour
3 T. olive oil

Option:
Substitute calamari steaks (often sold pounded tender)

Place each cutlet between 2 pieces of wax paper and pound until very thin. (Pounding tenderizes meat or poultry and allows you to cook it very quickly.) Dust flour on a plate and roll the cutlets in it. In a large frying pan, heat olive oil over medium-high heat and sauté cutlets for several minutes on each side until lightly browned. Remove to a warmed platter and prepare the piccata sauce.

PICCATA SAUCE
¼ c. lemon juice
¼ c. sherry
2 T. capers
1 T. liquid from capers

Add lemon juice and sherry to frying pan in which cutlets have been cooked. Warm over medium heat for several minutes, scraping flour from the bottom of the pan and stirring well until thickened. Add capers and caper liquid and stir gently for a minute or two. Pour sauce over prepared cutlets and serve immediately.

HIGH LIVING

Aren't we magic?

—Emmy Smith

A favorite remark as she delights in the best meal ever eaten, the best conversation ever spoken or the best visit ever shared.

 Poultry

Lisa's Tex-Mex Chili & Beans

Lisa's family always serves this chili with pinto beans on Christmas Eve and we have celebrated the New Year with it. It's a great antidote to the excesses of the season. • Make a double batch of beans and freeze some for later.

Serves 8

Beans:
3 c. pinto beans
6 c. cold water
1 onion, quartered
Salt to taste (1 t. or so)
1 jalapeño pepper, chopped finely
   or ½ T. cumin
   or 1 T. chili powder

Condiments:
1 large onion (about 1 cup), chopped
4 fresh tomatoes (about 2 cups), chopped
1 head of lettuce, chopped
2 c. cheddar cheese (½ lb.), grated
Salsa (See page 267.)
Sour cream or yogurt
Tortilla chips

Chili:
Salt
16 cloves garlic, peeled & minced
2 lbs. ground turkey (or beef)
⅓ c. or more chili powder
1 c. cold water or so

The day before, pick any rocks out of the beans, then rinse in two changes of cold water and drain in a colander. In a large soup pot, combine beans, water and onion and bring to a boil over medium-high heat. Remove from heat, cover and let sit overnight. (See box below.)

The next day, add salt, chopped jalapeño pepper (or cumin and chili powder). Cook beans uncovered over low heat until tender, 2 hours or more.

For chili, heat up a large, heavy frying pan over medium-high heat. (Cast iron is best for this.) Dust the bottom with salt, add minced garlic and cook briefly until golden. Be careful not to burn the garlic making it bitter.

Add ground turkey and brown it over medium-high heat, stirring constantly. There won't be much juice from ground turkey because it is so lean. Add chili powder until the browned turkey becomes a deep, dark red. Add 1 cup of cold water and simmer uncovered for 30 minutes, stirring occasionally and adding more water as needed. Chili should be moist but not soupy. Serve with beans and condiments.

SOAKING BEANS

Lisa explained that beans left to soak too long may begin to ferment. Bringing them to a boil before leaving them to soak prevents this.

Meat

TODAY'S JOKE

Question: What did the Buddhist say to the hot dog vendor?
Answer: Make me one with everything.

—Author unknown

Sent by Faith for inspiration

Aunt Frances' Beneficial Beef Burgundy

Catherine's mother's older sister, Frances, was a fine cook and an excellent letter writer. Her weekly letters often included a new recipe such as this one which became a Manz family favorite, often the chosen meal for birthdays or other important celebrations. • *In retirement Uncle Bill, Aunt Frances' husband, became a master cook. Catherine treasures his well-used copy of Julia Child's* **Mastering the Art of French Cooking.** • *Use good red wine for this stew, a burgundy, cabernet, pinot noir, syrah or merlot.*

Serves 4-6

**2 lbs. lean stewing beef, cut in
  1-inch cubes
5 T. olive oil or bacon grease
3 large onions, chopped coarsely
4 cloves garlic, peeled & minced
1 bay leaf**

**1 bottle good red wine
1/2 c. sherry or Cognac
Salt & pepper to taste**

About 6 cups of cooked rice

Pre-heat oven to 325°. Pat meat cubes dry with paper towels. This important step makes it easier to brown the meat well. In a large frying pan, brown meat in 3 tablespoons of olive oil or bacon grease over high heat. Put browned meat into a large heat-proof casserole with a tight fitting lid.

Add 2 tablespoons of oil or bacon grease to the same frying pan and sauté onions over medium-low heat until transparent, 7 to 10 minutes. Add garlic and sauté several minutes more. Add bay leaf, wine, sherry or Cognac, and beef stock and bring to a boil.

Pour onion mixture over meat, cover and set in the middle of the oven. Cook several hours. Check the liquid level in the casserole every hour or so. Add more wine or stock as needed.

Remove casserole from oven. Ladle some of the liquid from the casserole and pour through a mesh strainer into a large saucepan. Bring to a boil and reduce volume by half. Return the thickened liquid to the pot and mix well. Serve with rice.

Make this stew the day before and then re-heat it for an hour at 325°. Everyone always eats more of this than you expect, so make lots. It freezes very well.

LIVE IT UP

Live, don't know how long;

And die, don't know when;

Must go, don't know where;

I am astonished I am so cheerful.

—Maximilian I Hapsburg

Recorded by our friend Jimmy Stewart from a charcoal inscription on the cellar wall at Schloss Tratzberg.

Meat

Anonymous Carbonada Criolla

*We don't know how we got this recipe but we're glad we did. • It's especially tasty in the fall with the last of our corn, our own potatoes and winter squash. • **Carbonada** means literally "browned" in Spanish, referring to the preparation of the meat for a stew. **Criolla** means "creole," a Spaniard born in the Americas. In this case, it refers to a stew born in the Americas featuring the indigenous corn.*

Serves 6

1-½ lbs. stew meat, cut in 1 inch cubes
2 T. olive oil
2 cloves garlic, peeled
3 T. butter
l large onion, chopped
2 tomatoes, peeled, seeded & chopped
   (See page 83.)
   or 14-½ oz. can "ready-cut" tomatoes
Salt & pepper to taste
4 peaches or mangoes, peeled & cubed
   or 16 oz. can sliced peaches
   or 1 c. dried mangoes, cut in bite-sized
   pieces

3 medium white potatoes, peeled
   & cubed
17 oz. can corn or 2 c. fresh kernels
   (about 6 ears of corn)
2 c. beef stock
1 pumpkin, about 10 inches in diameter
   or 2 to 3 c. winter squash, peeled &
   cubed

Pat meat cubes dry with paper towels. This important step makes it easier to brown the meat well. In a large frying pan or medium soup pot, brown meat in olive oil over medium-high heat. Remove meat with tongs or a slotted spoon and set aside.

In the same pan, melt butter and sauté whole cloves of garlic over medium heat until well browned. Remove garlic and discard. Add chopped onion and sauté for several minutes, adjusting heat as needed. Add tomatoes, browned beef, salt and pepper. Cook for 15 minutes, stirring occasionally.

Add peaches or mangoes, potatoes, corn and stock (or a combination of stock and liquid from canned peaches and corn). Lower heat, cover and simmer until tender, an hour or more, stirring occasionally and adding more stock as needed.

Pre-heat oven to 350°. Cut off top of pumpkin and scoop out seeds and membranes. Salt and pepper the inside of the pumpkin and butter the cut edge. Cover pumpkin with foil and bake on a cookie sheet for 45 minutes or until tender but not too soft.

When the *carbonada* is ready, ladle it into the cooked pumpkin and place in a warm oven until ready to serve. When serving, scoop out some of the pumpkin with each serving. We prefer to skip the whole pumpkin and add cubed winter squash together with the potatoes.

Can't-Miss
Family Pot Roast

We found this easy method for cooking pot roast in Emmy's recipe file, its origins unknown.

Serves 6

4 strips bacon (about 6 oz.)
2 carrots, sliced
2 onions, chopped
4 lbs. rump roast or round of beef
Salt to taste

Freshly ground black pepper
½ c. beef stock or bouillon
1-½ c. dry wine, red or white
½ c. brandy

Pre-heat oven to 450°. Line the bottom of an ovenproof covered casserole with bacon, sliced carrots and onion. Add the meat and season with salt and pepper. Pour in beef stock and place casserole uncovered in a hot oven for 15 minutes.

Lower heat to 300°. Add wine and brandy. Cover and cook for 4 hours. Remove from oven and skim grease from the surface. Adjust seasoning. Emmy added several good splashes of Pickapeppa sauce.

Lift roast onto a platter, slice and serve in soup bowls with some of the broth and lots of crusty bread.

FAX MAGIC

Left Firenze in a light rain. Went on the fastest train yet. It would hit the tunnels and feel like entering a decompression chamber. Great countryside, decaying castles and farms hundreds of years old but everywhere re-building. In fact, Firenze looks a little like a Christo piece gone wild. There was no building without a drape or scaffolding. The results, however, were very sparkling and bright. It will look good when done but Italy is losing its patina. I don't know which I prefer, old or new.

You would have been proud of us walking everywhere — even hiked to the Piazza Michelangelo on one of the prettiest days I've seen — full of sun and blooms and promise. Met a charming couple selling alabaster who also had Pirenese-type doggies. [Karen and Tenold have Great Pyrenees dogs, Gladys, Iris, now Lili and Soufi.] Needless to say, a few lies were swapped until he told us of his other dog which hunts up baskets of truffles for them. Then it was just pure envy. Beautiful people.

The noise in the cities hovers around loud to louder. However, we could easily stop that with a couple million roles of duct tape to tape everyone's hands to their sides. Then we'd see if they could yell and scream or even talk.

—Tenold & Karen Peterson

Fax to Crow Farm from the Hotel Carriage in Rome (April 26, 1996)

Meat

Susan's Fit-for-a-Queen (or a Quarterback) Beef Tenderloin with Pasta

If queens or presidents or divas or patriarchs or equestriennes or mule drivers or boat captains or snow boarders or saints or virtuosos or ballerinas or bird watchers or CEO's or beaus or mothers-in-law or hungry gardeners come to dinner, serve this. The pasta by itself makes a delicious meal.

Serves 6

Beef:
2 lbs. beef tenderloin, trimmed of fat
1 T. whole coriander seeds
½ t. whole black pepper
1 t. coarse kosher salt
1 T. extra virgin olive oil

Pasta:
12 oz. pasta (*penne* or *fusilli*)
¼ c. olive oil from sun-dried tomatoes
4 large shallots, thinly sliced
4 cloves garlic, peeled & thinly sliced
½ c. oil packed sun-dried tomatoes, drained & thinly sliced
⅓ c. kalamata olives, pitted & quartered
¼ c. Italian parsley, chopped
Freshly ground pepper to taste

Pre-heat oven to 425°. For pasta, begin heating a large pot of water with splash of oil and a big pinch of salt.

Put tenderloin in a small roasting pan. In a mortar with a pestle, grind whole coriander, black pepper and kosher salt. Add 1 tablespoon of olive oil to make a paste. Rub on meat with your hands. Cook meat as desired, using a meat thermometer. (For medium rare, the internal temperature should be about 125° and the cooking time about 20 minutes.)

In a frying pan over medium-low heat, sauté shallots and garlic in 2 tablespoons olive oil until limp but not brown, about 5 minutes. Add tomatoes, olives, parsley and remaining olive oil. (If you don't have oil-packed tomatoes, soak dried ones in ½ cup of red or white wine for ½ hour. Drain and use as needed.) Warm sauce thoroughly over medium-low heat.

Remove meat from oven. Set on a cutting board, cover with foil and let rest for 10 minutes. Cook pasta according to directions on the package. Drain by tossing gently in a colander. Put pasta in a warm serving bowl. Add meat juice to the tomato sauce, stirring well. Pour sauce over the pasta. Slice the tenderloin and serve immediately.

> *Plates should be hot, hot, hot;*
> *glasses cold, cold, cold;*
> *and table decorations low, low, low.*
>
> —Elsie de Wolfe

Norma's Very-Near-the-Border Fajitas

Lisa's mother, Norma Lively of Euless, Texas, is the source of many outstanding recipes. Lisa prepared these fajitas for us on our first visit to Edinburgh, warming up for her program to introduce as many Scots as possible to Tex-Mex food, an undertaking which we believe has had a favorable impact on Scottish politics.

Serves 4

Marinade:
½ c. olive oil
¼ c. red wine vinegar
⅓ c. lime juice
3 cloves garlic, peeled & minced
3 onions, sliced thinly in rings
¼ t. cumin
1 t. sugar
1 t. oregano
½ t. salt
½ t. black pepper

2 whole chicken breasts (4 halves),
   skinned & boned or 1 lb. round steak

Condiments:
8 flour tortillas
Chopped tomatoes & green peppers
Chopped lettuce
Salsa (See recipe on page 267.)
Grated sharp cheddar or Monterey
   Jack cheese

In a bowl, combine ingredients for the marinade. Cover boned chicken breasts or steak with marinade and marinate at least 3 hours or overnight in the refrigerator. Steak should be no more than ½ inch thick for best results when marinating; cut or pound as needed.

Pre-heat oven to 200°. Prepare condiments and put in small bowls. Warm tortillas wrapped in foil in the oven for about 15 minutes.

Remove chicken or meat from marinade. In a frying plan, cook marinade over high heat until liquid is reduced and onions are golden, about 5 to 7 minutes.

Grill chicken or meat until cooked as you like it. (About 6 to 10 minutes on each side for the chicken and 5 minutes or more for the steak.) Cut chicken or steak into ½ inch strips.

Make fajitas by layering a tortilla with chicken or meat plus onions and condiments. Roll tortilla and pick it up to eat.

REASONABLE GOALS

I'm going to be a strong woman when I grow up.

—Zoë Livelybrooks (Age 3)

Meat

Mama's Mainstay Meatloaf

Catherine's Uncle Ed told of going to the corner grocery store as a child to order fresh ground meat for his mother's meatloaf. This is his younger sister's version of the family recipe. • John usually makes this meatloaf when Catherine is out of town, providing himself with a good company dinner and then lots of sandwiches.

Serves 6-8

1 lb. each ground beef & ground pork
  or substitute sausage for pork
8 oz. can stewed tomatoes or
  8 oz. can tomato sauce
1 small onion, chopped coarsely

2 eggs
1-½ c. bread crumbs or cracker crumbs
  or rolled oats
Salt & pepper to taste

Pre-heat oven to 350°. In a medium bowl, combine all the ingredients using your hands. Form into a loaf and place in a standard loaf pan. Bake 1 hour. If needed, pour off grease after 30 minutes.

This meatloaf is especially good served with baked potatoes or sliced thinly in sandwiches the next day.

TOPPED WITH BACON

For extra flavor, Sofia puts 3 or 4 strips of bacon on top of her meatloaf before cooking.

ESCAPE HATCH

Oh, I'm so relieved that I won't have to find a new dress.

—Marjorie Manz

Catherine's mother's response to the announcement by long distance telephone that her daughter had just married John.

Pop's Frankly Not-from-Spain Spanish Meatballs

Frank, Catherine's father, had two cooking specialties, these meatballs and a great Spanish omelette that he sometimes made for Sunday supper. His other favorite foods were rice pudding and peanut butter sandwiches. • Pop was finicky about his sandwiches. They had to be made with Laura Scudder's smooth-grind peanut butter (crunchy was anathema) on thin sliced rye bread with mayonnaise and thin sliced onions or bananas. • Because of its great importance in the Manz household, peanut butter was served at breakfast, lunch and dinner in a Limoges porcelain jar hand-painted by Pop's grandmother. • Pop like to tell of carrying Campbell's tomato soup in the hip pocket of his trousers when he left the Sacramento River's Rough and Ready Island each day after work, heading to nearby Stockton for dinner in a cafe with an uncertain menu. Be prepared was his motto.

Serves 4-6 (about 20 meatballs)

1 lb. ground round steak
1 small onion, chopped finely
5 soda crackers, crushed finely
　(about ⅓ c.)
1 egg

2 T. uncooked rice
Salt & pepper to taste
Two 11 oz. cans Campbell's tomato soup
2 T. cold water

Pre-heat oven to 400°. In a medium bowl, combine the meat, onion, crackers, egg, rice and seasoning thoroughly with your hands. Form into walnut-sized meatballs and place in a heat-proof casserole.

In a small bowl, stir together the tomato soup and water. Pour over the meatballs and bake uncovered for 15 to 20 minutes at 400°. Reduce heat to 350° and continue cooking for approximately 1 hour. Serve immediately with baked potatoes.

KITSCH-EN DECORATING TIPS
Catherine rode a bus near Ravello, Italy decorated with the following:
A potted spider plant perched on a shelf.
Numerous decals, including one of Jesus & one of Mt. Vesuvius.
A rosary hanging from the rearview mirror.
A giant pencil topped by a clown head. • Family photos & other snapshots.
A bouquet of fresh pansies & carnations. • Italian & British flags.
A sign in English reading "Not eat on buss."
A sign in Italian,
"Si prega di non parlare al conduttore,"
or
"Don't talk to the driver."

Emma's Essential Chili

Emma's chili feeds a crowd easily. Freeze it and be prepared for a big party whenever you want. Emmy always has tubs of this chili in her freezer for easy entertaining. For many years, it was her preferred birthday dish on the Fourth of July.

Serves 18-20

4 lbs. lean ground round steak
3 T. or more chili powder
⅓ c. olive oil
6 large onions, chopped coarsely
2 green peppers, chopped coarsely
10 cloves garlic, peeled & minced
Two 28 oz. cans whole tomatoes
Two 15 oz. cans tomato sauce
Two 12 oz. cans tomato purée
Two 6 oz. cans tomato paste

Other seasoning: Emma used 2 pkgs. of chili condiments which contain various combinations of powdered chiles & oregano, basil, coriander, cumin, cayenne pepper & masa/corn flour to thicken. Create your own favorite combination. Here's ours:
    4 oz. can diced Anaheim chiles
    2 T. or more chili powder
      (in addition to chili powder above)
    3 T. ground cumin
    2 T. basil
    1 T. oregano
    1-½ T. ground coriander

In a large frying pan, brown meat topped with chili powder over medium-high heat. If necessary, use two frying pans or brown meat in 2 batches. Put browned meat in a large soup pot or two smaller ones.

In the same frying pan(s), sauté onions over medium-low heat in olive oil until limp, about 5 minutes. Add garlic and green peppers, and sauté several minutes more. Add cooked onions and peppers to the meat in the soup pot plus tomatoes, sauce, purée, paste, and whatever other seasoning you may choose. Stir well. Simmer chili uncovered over low heat for two hours or more. Stir frequently and add water as needed. Chili should be very thick.

Emma's chili is better made ahead of time, cooled, refrigerated overnight and then re-heated. It also freezes beautifully. It is very nice served on top of angel hair pasta (*capellini*) with sour cream, grated Parmesan or sharp cheddar cheese, finely chopped onions and chopped black olives.

CHILI WITH BEANS

For chili with beans, add 2 large cans of kidney beans (27 oz. each), drained, about a ½ hour before serving. OR soak 4 cups of dry kidney beans overnight, then drain and rinse with cold water. Add the soaked beans plus 8 cups of water with the canned tomatoes and cook as directed above.

 Meat

Balboa Island Yacht Club
Enchilada Pie

Carol's children, Doug, Eric and Mitzi, spent their childhood summers participating in the swimming, boating and social activities of the Balboa Island Yacht Club, a remarkable kids' organization run by the kids themselves. This is the casserole from their Friday evening potluck dinners. • Now all eight of Carol's grandchildren have romped on the same beach under her watchful eye.

Serves 8-10

2 lbs. lean ground beef (or turkey)
1 large onion, chopped
3 c. spaghetti sauce
   (one 26 or 30 oz. jar)
1 c. sliced black Oberti olives
   (two 4.25 oz. cans)
Salt & pepper to taste
1 dozen corn tortillas, cut in 1 inch
   strips
1-½ c. sharp cheddar cheese (6 oz.),
   grated
¾ c. cold water

Tamale pie:
1 green pepper, diced
17 oz. can whole kernel corn, drained
1 to 2 T. chili powder
½ recipe of cornbread on page 224

Vegetarian version:
Substitute 4 cups of cooked rice for meat
Add 13 oz. can black beans, drained

Pre-heat oven to 350°. In a large frying pan, brown meat and onions over medium heat. Add spaghetti sauce and olives and warm thoroughly. Season to taste.

In a casserole, layer tortillas, meat sauce and then cheese, ending with a layer of cheese. Pour water gently over the top. Bake 25 to 30 minutes or until bubbly. Serve immediately.

TAMALE PIE • Sauté green pepper with onions. Add corn with olives. Omit tortillas. Top with ½ recipe of cornbread batter and smooth top with a spatula. Bake as directed above.

VEGETARIAN VERSION • Omit meat. Add cooked rice and beans with spaghetti sauce. Proceed as directed above.

THE HEART OF THE MATTER

On the subject of good marriages, Carol once succinctly advised, "Sex and sandwiches," cryptically leaving much to the imagination.

Meat

Lew & Cathy's Good-Enough-for-the Dog Lamb Meatballs

This recipe came from friends of Lew and Cathy's and, before that, from friends of those friends. It's the usual genealogy of a favorite recipe. • Lew rode his bicycle 500 miles across the desert at least four years in a row. He must have eaten a lot of these meatballs to have that kind of stamina. • These are the meatballs which our border collie, Ivy, stole off the countertop when visiting in Pasadena. When traveling, she did not eat much except when opportunity knocked.

Serves 6 (about 25 meatballs)

1-½ lbs. ground lamb
2 T. chopped parsley
1 onion, minced
1 t. dried mint
2 eggs, beaten
Salt to taste
½ t. freshly ground pepper

4 T. all-purpose white flour
½ t. baking soda
About 2 T. cold water
1 T. butter

In a mixing bowl, combine lamb, parsley, onion, mint, eggs, salt and pepper with your hands.

In a small bowl or measuring cup, mix flour and soda with enough cold water to make a paste. Add to meat mixture and mix thoroughly. Form into walnut-sized meatballs.

Melt butter in a frying pan and cook meatballs until nicely browned, about 10 minutes. Serve immediately with rice pilaf or feathered rice on page 195.

STANDING ROOM ONLY

Victoria, our Dorset sheep named for the British queen whom she resembled, was a gift from Karen and Tenold. Victoria was delivered at dinnertime one evening, standing regally behind them in their old luxury car, the backseat conveniently removed for her comfort and a feed sack discreetly placed on the floor in case of an accident.

 Meat

Beebe's Resourceful Roast Leg of Lamb

Dijon mustard and coffee work well with lamb and garlic in Betsy's old favorite recipe. • Karen and Tenold, and Barbara have given us peerless meat from their homegrown lambs each year, the most succulent lamb we've ever tasted. We save the legs of lamb for state occasions.

Serves 6-8

⅓ c. Dijon mustard
2 to 3 T. strong coffee
5 cloves garlic, peeled & minced

3 T. fresh rosemary
4-½ lb. leg of lamb

Pre-heat oven to 425°. Combine mustard, coffee, garlic and rosemary in a small bowl. Rub paste on leg of lamb with your hands. Place lamb in a roasting pan. Roast about 45 minutes to an hour. A meat thermometer helps determine the desired outcome.

COOKING ROASTS

Remove meat from the refrigerator about two hours before cooking so that it is at room temperature when you put it in the oven. This is important.

We invested in a small probe thermometer that gives an instant temperature reading when inserted in the meat. It seems to be more reliable than our old meat thermometer that cooked along with the roast.

The temperatures for doneness given for both roast beef and lamb in our old resource cookbooks seem to be too high and produce over-cooked meat. We prefer lamb on the rare side with an internal temperature about 120°. For medium, the internal temperature should be about 140° and for well-done, 160°.

The pleasure of eating meat, especially rare meat, depends on knowing where it comes from and how it has been handled.

EGG-STATIC?

In spring, according to an old Hungarian folk custom, young men sprinkle women with perfume and then receive red eggs in return.

Meat

Caroline's Mesmerizing Mississippi Pork

Caroline makes music out of numbers in the finance department of our school district. She's a whiz. •
Her family recipe for braised pork comes from her father, Christy Morgan, a retired Presbyterian minister
in Corinth, Mississippi. He uses Wicker's Original Marinade & Baste, a commercial product from a
secret family recipe that lists vinegar, salt and spices as the ingredients. We get Wicker's by mail order
from Missouri. • *This is an improvised basting liquid for slow oven-braising of a pork roast.*

Serves 6-8 (4 cups of marinade)

3-½ c. white wine
½ c. cider vinegar
2 T. dried shallots, pulverized
1 heaping T. sweet paprika
1 t. chile powder
1 t. oregano
1 t. savory

½ t. allspice
½ t. cumin
1 bay leaf
Several sprigs of fresh thyme

3-½ to 4 lb. pork shoulder or loin roast

Combine wine, vinegar, shallots, herbs and spices together in a glass jar. Shake well.
This braising liquid keeps in the refrigerator for several weeks.

Remove pork roast from refrigerator an hour or so before cooking so it can come
to room temperature. Pre-heat oven to 275°. Place the roast fat side up in a covered
casserole. Pour braising liquid over roast to a depth of 2 inches. Cover and let sit 1 hour.
Roast for 4 hours, basting several times.

Remove roast from oven. Lift onto cutting board and cool enough to handle. Strain
and de-grease braising liquid, and pour into a small pitcher. Pull meat apart, discarding
bone and fat. Arrange shredded meat attractively on a serving platter. Pour some braising
liquid over meat, and serve with remainder.

This eats well with baked grits on page 173 or mashed potatoes on page 247 and
cornbread on page 224 or biscuits on pages 223 and 229. It is also delicious with cooked
greens. If you're feeling wild, serve **one** of John's mint juleps to each guest before dinner.
(See page 275.)

SUDDEN INSPIRATION

"What is the meaning of life?," Sally Cairnes-Wurster asked
unexpectedly one day while I was folding laundry and she was
cleaning the kitchen sink. I laughed at the audacity and timing
of her question. Then she answered herself brilliantly, "Life is the
meaning of life." We can't argue with that.

 Meat

Triumphant Hungarian Goulash
à la Elelmiszer

Catherine and Carol traveled to Hungary during the spring of 1998 to celebrate Carol's retirement as an elementary school principal. • Carol had mastered enough Hungarian to keep them out of trouble, and the language proved to be a fascinating challenge. One of Catherine's first words in Hungarian was **elelmiszer,** *which she excitedly understood to mean "elephant" because a pachyderm was hanging on the sign next to this exotic word. It actually means "grocery store," a more useful word for travelers in search of a picnic. • Carol reminded Catherine that Hungary is the land of soups. Their two favorites were mushroom with paprika and sour cream, and pheasant consommé with liver dumplings. • In the dessert division, Szamos torte with its layers of rich chocolate cake and cream filling dotted with marzipan was the hands-down winner. Dobos torte finished second. • Goulash was a treat with its flavorful, tender chunks of pork. The not-so secret ingredient was paprika, the taste of which was so flavorful, a perfect complement to cabbage. This is our version of goulash.*

Serves 6

1 medium head green cabbage, shredded (about 8 cups)	1 t. hot Hungarian paprika (*csípös*)
½ lb. bacon (about 6 thick slices)	1 t. or more salt
2 large onions sliced thinly	2 to 2-½ c. dry white wine
2-½ t. sweet Hungarian paprika (*édes*)	3 T. vegetable oil
	1-½ lbs. pork tenderloin, cubed

In a mixing bowl, cover the shredded cabbage with cold water and soak for about 1 hour. Drain in a colander. In a frying pan, cook the bacon until crisp. Remove with tongs, drain on paper towels and break into 1-inch bites.

In the same pan, sauté onion in bacon grease until limp, about 5 minutes. Add cabbage and continue cooking for several minutes more. Season with paprika and salt. Add 2 cups of white wine, cover and simmer for ½ hour, adding more wine as needed.

In another frying pan, brown pork in vegetable oil over high heat. Add to cabbage along with bacon, and simmer covered for ½ hour more. Serve with the traditional *spätzle* (German short egg noodles) or rice.

Sweet the air of May, lightly, gently blowing,

Fragrant as the lilac spray at my doorstep growing,

White and ghostly in the gloom stand the apple trees in bloom.

—A Hungarian round

Carol learned this song at camp many years ago and has been teaching it to her students ever since. It seems to capture the Hungarian character, at once romantic and melancholy.

Mardy's Beach House Indonesian Noodles with Pork & Shrimp

*Mardy, an American Field Service exchange student in Indonesia in the 1960s, brought back this recipe for a classic dish called **bakmi goreng**. She prepared it for a gathering at the French's beach house on Long Island where Catherine was also a guest of Howard, Ecith and their daughter Serena.*

Serves 6-8

1 lb. boneless pork, trimmed of fat
  & cubed
⅓ c. unflavored cooking oil
6 T. soy sauce
3 large onions, chopped
2 cloves garlic, peeled & minced
¼ c. green onions, chopped
½ to 1 lb. cooked shrimp

4 T. fresh ginger root, peeled &
  minced or 1 T. powdered ginger
½ lb. fresh bean sprouts
  or 8 oz. can, drained
½ lb. very fine egg noodles
3 c. cabbage, finely shredded
  (about 1 small head)

For the noodles, bring a large pot of water to a boil. In a large frying pan, brown pork in 2 to 3 tablespoons of oil over medium-high heat. Add 3 tablespoons of soy sauce and cook for several minutes more. Remove pork from the pan with tongs or a slotted spoon and set aside.

In the same pan, sauté onions, garlic and green onions in the remaining oil over medium heat. Add shrimp, ginger, 3 tablespoons of soy sauce, bean sprouts and cabbage, and simmer uncovered gently over low heat, stirring occasionally.

Cook egg noodles according to directions on the package and then drain well in a colander. Alternately add noodles and cooked pork to vegetables and shrimp in the frying pan in small amounts. Stir gently and simmer 10 to 15 minutes more. Serve immediately.

THE PRAYER OF SOCRATES

Socrates: O beloved Pan and all ye other gods of this place, grant to me that I may be made beautiful in my soul within, and that all external possessions be in harmony with my inner man. May I consider the wise man rich; and may I have such wealth as any the self-restrained man can bear to endure. Do we need anything more, Phaedrus? For me that prayer is enough.

Phaedrus: Let me also share in this prayer; for friends have all things in common.

—Plato
From *Phaedrus*

Reflections on Women's Suffrage

At age 17, halfway through the second semester of my freshman year in college, I married a good-looking senior, nine years older than I. No, it was not Stanley! I became pregnant almost immediately. The doctor said, "Of course you cannot go to school in the Fall." That was 1931, so I thought I had to believe the doctor. I had a 4-H scholarship for my sophomore year, but sorrowfully, I passed it to the alternate.

My daughter was born at my parents' home. The doctor and a neighbor woman spent the night eating popcorn and telling jokes while I begged to call the whole thing off.

When my daughter was six months old, it had become abundantly clear that the marriage was a huge mistake. I confided in some friends that I was contemplating a divorce, a scandal! The word reached my 4-H agent, a divorced woman with a daughter older than I. She was a Presbyterian and she hurried to my home to discourage me from taking that step. "We do not have the right to marry again while the husband is still living. It is a long, lonely road to travel." Since I had no definable religion, I ignored her advice, became a "divorcée," and moved back home with my baby.

I was ill prepared for the reaction of former friends and neighbors. My mother's friend told her that her husband said a woman might as well stay married because divorced women never amounted to anything anyway. The members of mother's extension unit, most of whom had known me for years, suddenly saw me as evil. Pointed remarks were made in meetings; clippings from Baptist newsletters were read aloud at meetings and appeared in our mail. My favorite college professor told my friend that she doubted that I would ever return to school.

It took two years, but I did return. It was 1934, deep depression, dust bowl days. My father's expertise as a master carpenter was not needed — who would build houses in such times? There were no unemployment funds, no aid to dependent children, no food stamps. There was no financial aid or student loans either. But some people still had salaries and hired household help at 25¢ an hour. The college extension division had mail room work and filing at 20¢. After working all summer cooking for a boarding house, I had enough money to pay fees and buy books and $13 left-over. Thank goodness for my parents' foresight in keeping that house near the university where we could live and their willingness to provide child care.

Fall semester 1936. I was finishing work for a Bachelor of Science degree in Home Economics. I was so worried that I might not find a job that it was hard to concentrate on classes and assignments. Then, out of the blue, the Dean told me that Kansas Gas & Electric Company in Wichita, Kansas, had asked her to send a couple of applicants to be interviewed for positions as "home service advisors." She suggested that I go, which I did.

I was told, before time to start home, that I had the job and should report mid-January after the end of the semester. The sales manager said that I must leave my daughter, now five years old, with my family until I had become acquainted and adjusted to the job. I returned to school too excited to concentrate!

When my daughter was ready to start first grade she joined me in Wichita. The search for child care ended with hiring a teenage girl to come to the house in the afternoons. I never met another single mother during the five years that I was there. In fact, I never met a working mom — working for money that is. In some ways it was comforting to know that neighbors up and down the block were home with their children. In case of emergency, someone would help.

When, after ten years as a single mom, I was ready to marry Stanley, I had to give up my job. Married women still could not work at Kansas Gas & Electric in 1941!

—Gladys Belden

Written in honor of the 75th anniversary of women's suffrage.
(See Gladys' recipe for bread on page 216.)

Meat

Pasta, Beans & Cheese

Life is the combination of magic and pasta.
—Federico Fellini

De Cecco pasta, our favorite, comes conveniently dried in a bright turquoise blue and yellow box featuring a cheerful peasant woman bringing in the sheaves of wheat. It's as good as most fresh pasta and sits patiently on the shelf until needed. Allow 2 oz. of dried pasta for each serving as a first course and 3 oz. as a main course.

Mary Lou's Love Affair Clam Spaghetti

Beautiful, red-haired Mary Lou has had a lifelong love affair with Italy and Italians. This old family recipe is the legacy of a love affair. (Too bad love affairs don't always produce such comforting results.) •
We try to keep the ingredients for this favorite meal on hand at all times.

Serves 4

½ c. butter (1 cube)
2 or 3 cloves garlic, peeled & minced
Two 6-½ oz. cans minced clams
1 lb. linguini, spaghetti or fettuccine
Green onion tops from one bunch,
  chopped finely

2 c. Parmesan cheese (about 6 oz.),
  freshly grated
Dried red pepper flakes

For pasta, bring a large pot of water to a boil with a splash of oil and a big pinch of salt. In a small saucepan, melt butter and add minced garlic. Bring to a boil. Add juice from one can of clams and bring to a boil once again.

Cook pasta as directed on the package. While pasta is cooking, add clams to butter and garlic and heat thoroughly. Drain pasta thoroughly by tossing gently in a colander.

Pour clam sauce over pasta. Toss in green onion tops, 1 cup of Parmesan cheese and red pepper flakes to taste. Serve immediately in a pre-heated bowl with remaining cheese and plenty of hot bread.

Look to this day!
For it is life, the very life of life.
In its brief course
Lie all the verities and realities of your existence:
The bliss of growth
The glory of action
The splendor of beauty,
For yesterday is but a dream
And tomorrow is only a vision,
But today well-lived makes every yesterday a dream of happiness
And every tomorrow a vision of hope.
Look well, therefore, to this day!
Such is the salutation of the dawn.

—Kalidasa

A favorite poem by a poet & dramatist regarded as the greatest figure in classical Sanskrit literature.

Maureen's Pasta with Leeks & Bacon

In this fat-gram counting era in which we live, it's a great relief to savor a cream sauce occasionally. No, we don't want to eat rich food every night, but we're also not willing to give it up entirely. • Thanks to Maureen, an inspired gardener and cook, we can sometimes enjoy our favorite winter vegetable with bacon in a cream sauce.

Serves 4

½ lb. bacon (about 6 thick slices),
   cut into 1 inch pieces
3 or 4 large leeks, sliced finely
1 T. fresh parsley, chopped
⅛ t. nutmeg, freshly grated
Salt to taste
12 oz. pasta (6 oz. each of regular
   & spinach, if you like)

2 T. butter
½ c. heavy cream
¾ c. Parmesan (about 2 oz.),
   freshly grated
Freshly ground pepper

For pasta, bring a large pot of water to a boil with a splash of oil and a big pinch of salt. Wash leeks thoroughly in cold water and drain. (See page 75.)

In a medium frying pan, cook the bacon over medium heat until crisp. Remove with tongs and drain on paper towels. Set aside.

Slice leeks finely, including most of the green tops. Sauté over medium-low heat in 2 tablespoons of bacon grease until limp, about 5 minutes. Add parsley, nutmeg and salt.

Cook pasta as directed on the package. Drain pasta thoroughly by tossing gently in a colander.

Melt butter in a soup pot. Add pasta and toss lightly. Add leeks, bacon, cream and half of the Parmesan cheese. Toss together and warm gently over low heat for 2 minutes. Sprinkle with remaining cheese and freshly ground pepper. Serve immediately in a heated bowl.

UNEXPECTED TREAT

Wrap Parmesan rinds in plastic and save in the refrigerator. Add to soup as you wish. In Italy, the well-cooked rind is considered a treat for the cook.

Essence-of-Summer Pesto

The perfume of basil is like summer itself, strong but fleeting. We plant two or three dozen basil plants in the garden each year in anticipation of pesto, and then we freeze large amounts to savor during the winter. • Catherine has carried lots of fresh basil to her sister in Pasadena. It travels beautifully with the leaves rolled in a damp dishtowel and sealed in a plastic bag.

Serves 6

2 c. fresh basil leaves
⅓ c. pine nuts (about 1-½ oz.)
⅓ c. best quality olive oil
6 cloves garlic, peeled
½ c. Parmesan cheese (about 2 oz.),
  freshly grated & additional cheese

1 lb. fettuccine or other pasta
Freshly grated Parmesan cheese

Pick basil leaves from stems, discard stems and flowers, wash leaves in cold water and dry thoroughly. Toast pine nuts briefly until lightly browned in a small cast iron pan over medium heat or in the oven at 350° for 7 to 10 minutes.

In a blender or food processor, combine basil and olive oil and process briefly until basil is chopped coarsely. (Basil may be frozen at this point. See page 306 for freezing tips.) Add garlic, toasted pine nuts and Parmesan cheese. Process to a thick paste.

For pasta, bring a large pot of water to a boil with a splash of oil and big pinch of salt. Cook pasta as directed on the package. Drain pasta thoroughly by tossing gently in a colander. Combine pesto and pasta, mixing thoroughly with a spoon. Serve immediately with more grated Parmesan cheese.

USING PESTO

CHICKEN SALAD • Cook a whole chicken breast (2 halves) on the grill, or wrap in foil and bake at 350° for 25 minutes. Cool and cut chicken in ½ inch chunks. Combine with pasta and pesto. Serve at room temperature or chilled.

PESTO DIP • To one batch of pesto, add 8 oz. of ricotta or cream cheese and process until well combined. Thin with milk or cream as needed. Serve with crackers and raw vegetables.

Valentine Pasta

This was a red and white invention on Valentine's Day, prepared to eat after planting peas, lettuce and spinach in the garden.

Serves 4-6

½ c. pine nuts (about 2 oz.)
1 large red onion, sliced finely
3 T. olive oil
4 oz. oyster mushrooms, sliced
   (about 1 cup)
4 oz. sun-dried tomatoes, chopped
   coarsely (about ¼ cup)

½ c. white wine
4 oz. goat cheese, crumbled
1 lb. tomato fettuccine
Freshly grated Parmesan cheese

Pre-heat oven to 350° and toast pine nuts until lightly browned, 7 to 10 minutes. For pasta, bring a large pot of water to a boil with a splash of oil and a big pinch of salt.

To make sauce, sauté onion in 2 tablespoons of olive oil in a frying pan over medium-low heat until limp, about 5 minutes. Add the mushrooms and another tablespoon of olive oil. Sauté for several minutes until the mushrooms are soft. Add tomatoes and white wine. Cover and simmer over low heat until tomatoes are tender, 10 minutes or so. Add goat cheese. Stir gently until warm.

Cook pasta as directed on the package. Drain pasta thoroughly by tossing gently in a colander. Toss with sauce in a pre-heated bowl. Top with toasted pine nuts and serve immediately with freshly grated Parmesan cheese.

RUBY KNOWS BEST

At age six Ruby observed to her mother that it was frankly "shocking" that Valentine's Day wasn't a national holiday considering how important it is. Take that, Uncle Sam.

Mother Nature intervened in the discussion that year, 1994. It snowed about 8 inches the day before Valentine's Day, enough snow in our area to close the schools and just about everything else. Thus Ruby got her wish for a Valentine's Day holiday.

Faith's Pasta Nada

*Faith came up with this dish one night when she had "nothing" in the house to eat. She explained its fine combination of flavors and textures depends on using the best ingredients — pasta, salt, pepper, olive oil, walnuts, herbs, olives and Parmesan cheese. This is the place to use your best extra virgin olive oil for its pure taste. • Faith and her husband, Bruce LeFavour, served us another version of this pasta topped by a handful of chopped arugula leaves under which we delighted in the taste of a few homegrown, dried **sungold** cherry tomatoes. • Our favorite tomatoes for drying are **Principe Borghese**, a small Italian variety slightly larger than a cherry tomato.*

Serves 2

6 oz. fettuccine
¼ c. walnuts (1 oz.)
2 T. whole Italian parsley leaves
2 T. best extra virgin olive oil
⅛ t. or more non-iodized kosher flaked salt (a few shakes from a salt shaker)

¼ c. Parmesan cheese (1-½ oz.), freshly grated
Fresh, coarsely ground black pepper

For pasta, bring a large pot of water to a boil with a splash of oil and a big pinch of salt. Toast walnuts by shaking them in a heavy, hot frying pan over medium heat until they begin to brown and become aromatic. Or roast in the oven at 350° until lightly browned, about 7 to 10 minutes. Wash parsley, remove stems and pat dry.

Cook pasta as directed on the package. Drain thoroughly by tossing gently in a colander. Return pasta to the hot pot and toss with olive oil.

Arrange pasta individually on each plate. Top with a shake of salt, then freshly grated Parmesan cheese, parsley, fresh pepper and toasted walnuts. Serve immediately.

EARLY SPRING PASTA NADA

3 T. dried black olives (about 12 to 15 olives), pitted & quartered

3 T. fresh sage leaves

Substitute sage and olives for parsley in the above recipe. Make a chiffonade of fresh sage by removing leaves from the stems, mounding them together and slicing lengthwise into thin strips. Proceed as above.

Beebe's Well-Written Lasagna

Catherine treasures the original copy of this recipe, part of a letter now smudged, blurred and sticky with its own culinary history. It's written in Beebe's unmistakable script, that cheerful round handwriting that keeps cropping up in the recipe drawer.

Serves 12-15

Tomato Sauce:
1 lb. Italian bulk sausage
28 oz. can "ready-cut" tomatoes
Two 29 oz. cans tomato sauce
12 oz. can tomato paste
2 large onions, chopped coarsely
2 green peppers, chopped coarsely
½ lb. mushrooms, chopped coarsely
  (about 2 cups)
6 cloves garlic, peeled & minced
2 T. basil
2 t. oregano

1 lb. lasagna noodles, uncooked
2 lbs. mozzarella cheese, grated
2 lbs. ricotta cheese
¼ lb. Parmesan cheese (a heaping cup),
  grated

In a large frying pan, brown sausage over medium heat. Transfer it to a large soup pot with a slotted spoon. Add tomatoes, tomato sauce and tomato paste to the pot. Bring to a boil over medium heat, stirring occasionally. Reduce heat to simmer.

In the same frying pan, sauté onions in sausage drippings over medium-low heat until limp, about 5 minutes, adding olive oil as needed. Add green pepper and sauté several minutes more. Add mushrooms and garlic and sauté several minutes more. Add cooked vegetables to tomato mixture. Season with basil and oregano. Simmer uncovered for 2 hours, stirring occasionally. The sauce shouldn't be too thick because the uncooked lasagna noodles will absorb moisture from it while baking.

When sauce has thickened nicely, pre-heat oven to 350°. In a large, deep casserole, two 9x13 inch baking pans or a disposable 18x13 inch heavy foil baking pan, assemble the lasagna in layers, beginning with several ladles of sauce, then a layer of uncooked lasagna noodles, mozzarella and ricotta cheeses, and finally more sauce. Beebe recommends using the thickest parts of sauce on the bottom layer, saving the more liquid part for the upper layers. You need at least two full layers. Top with noodles, sauce and finally Parmesan cheese. Bake lasagna until hot and bubbly, 30 to 40 minutes. Remove from oven and let sit for 10 minutes before cutting and serving.

Lasagna keeps well in the refrigerator overnight before baking. It also freezes well **after** baking for 25 minutes. Cool completely, cover or wrap tightly in plastic or foil. Individual slices freeze well, too. Thaw lasagna overnight in the refrigerator and re-heat for 30 minutes at 300°.

Everything-Under-the-Sun Spaghetti Sauce

Spaghetti sauce is fun because you can improvise by adding what you find in your pantry and refrigerator. Connie, Catherine's sister, cautions her from time to time not to get carried away. They both remember the worst meal of their childhood when True Kellogg fixed her infamous scrambled eggs that actually did include everything in the refrigerator and a few things that shouldn't have been.

Serves 6 or more

1 lb. Italian bulk sausage
2 large onions, chopped coarsely
1 c. celery & celery tops (about 3 stalks), chopped coarsely
1 large green pepper, chopped coarsely
½ lb. mushrooms, sliced finely (2 cups)
2 T. olive oil
1 large carrot, sliced finely
28 oz. can "ready cut" tomatoes
12 oz. can tomato purée

1 c. red wine
½ c. fresh basil or 2 T. dried
1 small sprig fresh oregano or 2 t. dried
Salt & pepper to taste
6 cloves garlic, peeled & minced
1 T. lemon juice
12 sun-dried tomatoes, diced
Freshly grated Parmesan cheese

In a large soup pot, brown sausage over medium heat. Remove it with a slotted spoon and drain on paper towels.

In the same pot over medium-low heat, sauté onions in sausage drippings until limp, about 5 minutes. Add celery and green pepper and sauté several minutes more. Then add mushrooms and olive oil and cook until mushrooms are soft. Add carrots, tomatoes, tomato purée, red wine, basil, oregano, salt and pepper. Mix thoroughly. Reduce heat to low and simmer uncovered for 1-½ hours, stirring occasionally.

Add garlic, lemon juice and sun-dried tomatoes. Stir well. Adjust seasoning and simmer 30 minutes more. Serve over pasta cooked as directed on the package. Top with freshly grated Parmesan cheese.

AN EDITORIAL ON HOME COOKING

It's not an accident that chicken soup and apple pie are icons in our society. Food is central to our lives. We eat more, waste more, diet more and weigh more than any other nation in the world. We throw away enough to feed a whole country. We may even buy enough diet food to balance the budget. Yet somehow we are not satisfied.

In spite of the abundance, we are hungry because we don't eat properly. All that fast food adds up to very little. We need more than calories. We need the loving support suggested by chicken soup and apple pie. These icons speak volumes about home cooking and what it means to our well-being.

Pat's Tunnel Rock Black Beans

According to legend, when Pat LeFavour got married, her mother gave her money for a wedding dress, but she bought a 16-gauge shotgun. • Pat fixed these beans for us in her house on the Salmon River near a great old fishing hole. We've been making them ever since.

Serves 10-12

4-½ c. black beans
4 T. butter
4 medium onions, chopped coarsely
8 c. cold water or beef stock
   (If you use water, add 4 to 6 beef
   bouillon cubes.)

⅓ c. cumin
1 heaping T. ground oregano
10 large cloves garlic, peeled & minced

Optional:
6 T. lard

The night before, sort through the beans, throw out any rocks, rinse, cover with cold water and soak overnight. The next day, drain beans in a colander, rinse in cold water and drain again.

In a large soup pot, sauté onions in butter over low heat until transparent, about 10 minutes. Add beans and stir to coat with butter. Add water to cover, about 8 cups. Bring to a boil over medium heat, reduce heat to low, cover and cook for 2 hours, stirring occasionally and adding water as needed.

Add cumin and oregano and continue cooking until the beans are soft, 1 hour or more. Mash the beans with a potato masher and add minced garlic (and lard if desired) and stir well. Continue cooking for another ½ hour or so.

Serve with rice and tortillas or fajitas on page 150 or huevos rancheros on page 61 or rice on page 194.

THE GUATEMALAN BEAN TEST

Black beans are a staple in the Guatemalan diet, Barbara learned firsthand as a Peace Corps volunteer living in the village of Cubulco in the Baja Vera Paz region. In the marketplace, she learned to test for good beans by taking sample bites from each vendor's supply. If she could bite through a bean, then it was fresh enough. She also had to inspect the beans carefully for mold.

Trail Creek Ranch Sunday Beans

This recipe reminds us that eating from cans can be tasty. At Trail Creek Ranch, these beans are served with hamburgers at the Sunday evening barbecue. The same recipe came to us a second time from a friend of a friend who grew up in Wyoming not far from the ranch.

Serves 10-12

15 oz. can lima beans
Two 15 oz. cans kidney beans
40 oz. can pork & beans
1 T. Worcestershire sauce
½ c. catsup

¼ c. brown sugar
¼ lb. bacon (about 3 thick slices), diced
1 onion, chopped
½ c. molasses
½ t. dry mustard

Pre-heat oven to 325°. Combine all of the ingredients in a large casserole. Cover and bake 1-½ hours. Remove from oven and serve immediately with grilled meat or chicken.

A LOVE LETTER

Dear Lil' Bit:

I am asking John & Catherine to give this enclosure to you. As you live in "the sticks," I am not sure you realize what a fine doggie like you is entitled to. See this picture of a poodle getting some special dog perfume. So, when next your friends go East, have them take you to the dog beauty shop which is called "Le Chien" or possibly "La Biche" and get the full treatment — in Manhattan, of course.

Pup & Queenie miss having you around. Running Bear doesn't because he is a cat & is allergic to dogs. Anyway, the Trail Creek dogs send their best.

And love,
Betty

A letter from Betty Woolsey to our dog, Lil' Bit, who enchanted Betty during several visits to her great Wyoming ranch.

Pasta, Beans & Cheese

Carol's Germane German Lentils

This is another of Carol's German recipes. • Lentils are certainly important, nutritious, easy to prepare and beautifully colored in reds, yellows, browns and greens. Although this recipe is typically made with brown lentils, it is also very attractive made from red or yellow ones as well as the small, speckled French lentils. Carol's daughter-in-law, Kate, likes to add a bay leaf to the lentils while cooking. • These lentils make a thick soup, but you can also serve them as a main course with German spätzle (short egg noodles) and beer.

Serves 4-6

4 c. cold water
1-½ c. lentils
l onion, chopped coarsely
Celery tops &/or green onion tops

1 t. salt
2 T. butter
2 T. all-purpose white flour
1 to 2 T. vinegar

In a medium saucepan, bring cold water to a boil. While water is heating, rinse lentils in cold water and drain in a colander. Add lentils to water as soon as it boils and remove from heat. Let lentils sit for one hour. Add onion, greens and salt to the lentils. Cook uncovered slowly over low heat for ½ hour or so.

Melt butter in a small saucepan and stir in flour to make a paste. Add vinegar and combine well. Add to lentils, mixing well. Simmer lentils over low heat for 15 minutes more, stirring frequently. Serve immediately or later.

Schlafen Sie voll,

Essen Sie Kohl,

Trinken Sie Bier,

Lieben Sie mir.

Emmy's favorite quote from her father, Papa Strong:

Sleep well,

Eat cabbage,

Drink beer,

Love me.

Can't-Live-Without-It Cheese Soufflé

Cheese soufflé makes an easy dinner. Total preparation and cooking time is about 1 hour and 15 minutes.

Serves 2 (or more, up to 8)

2 T. butter
2 T. all-purpose white flour
⅔ c. milk
1-½ cups sharp cheddar cheese (6 oz.),
   grated
4 eggs, separated
⅛ t. cayenne pepper
¼ c. Parmesan cheese (1 oz.), grated
¼ t. cream of tartar

<u>Each additional serving (up to 8):</u>
1 T. butter
1 T. all-purpose white flour
⅓ c. milk
2 eggs, separated
¾ cup cheddar cheese (3 oz.), grated
Pinch of cayenne pepper
Pinch of cream of tartar

Pre-heat oven to 350°. In a small saucepan, melt butter over low heat and add flour, stirring quickly to form a paste. Add milk and cook, stirring constantly, until thick and smooth, about 5 minutes. Add grated cheese, stir until melted and remove from heat. Add egg yolks and cayenne pepper, stirring well. Cool for 10 to 15 minutes.

Grease a 2-quart soufflé dish or casserole and coat with grated Parmesan cheese. In a mixing bowl, beat egg whites until soft peaks form. Add cream of tartar and continue beating until egg whites are stiff but not dry. Add ⅓ of egg whites to cheese mixture and fold together gently with a wire whisk. Then add this mixture to the rest of the egg whites and fold together gently until the egg whites disappear.

Pour into prepared container. Bake until beautifully risen and golden brown on top, 30 to 45 minutes, depending on the size of the soufflé and your preference for consistency. Like an omelette, a soufflé can be soft or hard cooked. Serve immediately with a green salad and crusty bread.

USING LEFTOVERS

Try different types of cheese or a mixture of leftover cheeses in your *soufflé*. • Add 1 cup of cooked crab, ham or chicken in bite-sized pieces to the cooled cheese-egg yolk mixture. • Add a tablespoon of fresh herbs, chives, parsley, basil, oregano, tarragon or sage, chopped finely.

Heavenly Aunt Lucille's Easy Soufflé

Catherine's Aunt Lucille was a great spirit and a marvelous cook, baking her own bread, trying new recipes and feeding her family splendidly, including the challenge of adapting to low fat/low salt cooking in her later years. She provided the relish plate for all holiday gatherings, always on the same sectioned glass plate which she filled with carrot and celery sticks, black and green olives, and pickles, including her favorite watermelon pickles. • Aunt Lucille's father Dakota Stookesberry, called Coa, was named after the territory in which he was the first white child born, according to the family lore. Her beautiful mother Christina Davidson, was one of four daughters of Scottish parents who had settled in Arizona. Catherine remembers their Oswego Street home in Pasadena with the adjacent lot planted in California poppies.

Serves 4

3 eggs
1-½ c. milk
Pinch of dry mustard or cayenne pepper
2 c. fresh bread cubes (about 7 inches
   of baguette)
2 c. cheddar or Gruyère cheese (½ lb.),
   grated

Options:
7 oz. can diced Anaheim chiles
½ lb. bulk sausage, cooked & drained

Pre-heat oven to 350° and grease a 2-quart soufflé dish or casserole. In a medium bowl, beat eggs well, and add milk and seasoning. Stir in bread cubes and cheese. (Add chiles and/or sausage.) Pour into prepared casserole. Bake immediately or cover and refrigerate several hours or overnight. Bake until soufflé is lightly browned and set, 30 to 45 minutes. Soufflé is set when a knife inserted in the center comes out clean. Serve immediately with a green salad and crusty bread.

BAKED CHILE RELLENO CASSEROLE

Serves 3-4

½ lb. sharp cheddar cheese, thinly sliced
7 oz. can whole green Anaheim chiles or
6 fresh chiles, roasted, seeded & peeled
2 eggs, lightly beaten
¼ c. all-purpose white flour
1 c. milk or half & half

Pre-heat oven to 350°. Grease a 2-quart casserole. Arrange half of the cheese slices on bottom of casserole. Layer chiles on top and then remaining cheese. In a small bowl, combine eggs, milk and flour thoroughly. Pour gently over chiles and cheese.

Bake 45 to 55 minutes until lightly browned and custard is set (a knife inserted in the center comes out clean). Remove from oven and serve immediately with warm tortillas or cornbread on page 224.

Cauliflower Soufflé

Dijon mustard is the secret ingredient in this recipe, its bite perfect with the cauliflower.

Serves 4

1 large cauliflower
4 T. butter (½ cube)
½ c. Parmesan cheese (1-½ oz.),
  grated
¼ c. Dijon mustard

4 eggs, whole or separated
¼ c. lemon juice (1 or 2 lemons)
2 c. grated cheese (½ lb.), Monterey Jack,
  cheddar, fontina, etc.

Rinse cauliflower in cold water and drain. Cut or break cauliflower into florets and steam until tender, about 15 to 20 minutes.

Pre-heat oven to 350°. Boil a kettle of water. Butter a 2-quart soufflé dish or casserole with 1 tablespoon of butter. Coat the bottom and sides of the soufflé dish with ¼ cup of grated Parmesan cheese.

In a food processor or blender, purée cauliflower with remaining butter in 2 batches and transfer to a large mixing bowl. Add mustard, egg yolks and lemon juice. Mix thoroughly. Stir in grated cheese.

In a mixing bowl, beat egg whites at medium speed until they foam, increase speed to high and beat until stiff peaks form. Fold gently into cauliflower mixture. (Omit this step and use whole eggs, lightly beaten, in the previous step. The soufflé won't be as puffy.) Pour into prepared container. Top with remaining ¼ cup Parmesan cheese.

Place soufflé dish in a 9x13 inch baking pan and fill baking pan with boiling water to a depth of about 1 inch. Bake until top of soufflé is lightly browned, 50 to 60 minutes. Remove from oven and serve immediately with a green salad and crusty bread.

FEET OF MAGIC

After dinner Uncle Ed was sitting comfortably in the living room at Mama's house. Suddenly our dog Lil' Bit spun-around and leapt into the octogenarian's lap. We watched with amazement as Uncle Ed stroked Lil' Bit tenderly and called her "darling."

With her finely tuned sensibilities, Lil' Bit had heard Uncle Ed's unspoken request and jumped at the chance to demonstrate that he was a "dog person" at heart.

Elida's Fortune 500 Baked Grits

*During World War II, Elida was an economist and a crack research writer on the editorial staff of **Fortune** magazine. Later Elida, Emmy and a few other friends would get together in the spring and fall to talk food for the coming season with the fervor of a hot editorial meeting. • Elida's baked grits, also called grits pudding or cheese grits, is a classic southern dish made from coarsely ground white corn. It's a splendid first cousin to a soufflé, a main dish for a light supper served with a green salad or a side dish for a Kentucky dinner of sliced country ham, "greasy beans" and cornbread. • We have Albers Quick Grits in our pantry, finally located in the hot cereal section of our local grocery store. A true southerner would sneer at quick grits.*

Serves 6

1 c. uncooked grits (about 4 c. cooked)	3 eggs
½ c. butter (1 cube), cut in chunks	½ lb. sharp cheddar cheese, grated
A scant ¼ c. milk	(2 cups)

Pre-heat oven to 400° and grease a 2 quart casserole. In a saucepan, cook grits as directed on the package, but remove from the heat after 15 minutes for regular grits and 3 minutes for quick grits.

Add butter to grits, stirring well until it melts, and then add milk, mixing thoroughly. Beat in eggs, one at a time. Stir in grated cheese, mixing thoroughly until it has melted. Pour into prepared casserole. Bake until lightly browned on top, about 1 hour. Serve immediately.

Grits pudding is very tasty fried-up in bacon grease for breakfast and served with warm syrup. It also freezes well **before** baking.

THE EGG MAN

Each Friday afternoon the egg man arrived at Catherine's childhood home in Pasadena, delivering to her family a dozen or two eggs fresh from his farm in Covina, a farming community about 18 miles to the east where Catherine's mother had once taught school.

This weekly egg delivery was a fact of life in the 1950's, but in retrospect it seems like an astonishing luxury. No one else we knew had an egg man although that was still the era of back porch deliveries of milk in glass bottles with heavy cream floating on top. The why's and how's of this unusual arrangement are lost in time but a sense of wonder remains.

Instructions for an 80th Birthday

To Whom It May Concern:

On the chance you are one who makes a fuss over an 80th:
Mine is July 4, 1988.

Preface:
At 711 we have too many things.
We shed possessions whenever possible and appropriate.

Therefore:
You are asked to do for yourselves (NOT for me).
Whatever $$$ you might have blown on me, blow for you.
When informed (envelope enclosed) what heart's desire you have chosen
and executed (if possible), all the pleasure will be mine.
I need NOT un-wrap. You need NOT wrap.
I need NOT express ecstatic gratitude by pen, telephone or in person.
You will remember me when you eat it, sip it, wear it, enjoy it.

The Great Devising here outlined will go down in history as
A MAJOR BREAK-THROUGH, IMPORTANT.
The date will be remembered as
the invention of the cotton gin by Eli Whitney (1794),
Paul Revere's ride (April 18)
or the Magna Carta.

Instructions: *Study list for inspiration. Add to it. Take your time.*
Report decision (or problem) postmarked not later than June 30 midnight.
To be opened on July 4.

P.S. A birthday letter will be 100% acceptable
and avoid trouble and worry in lieu of this challenge.

Inspiration List: *New pot for stove, a recording for machine, costly soap (for a change), upgraded bottle (for a change), trip around the world, trip to somewhere else, theater tickets, fine restaurant dinner, subscription to a magazine, a lilac, a rose bush, a tree, contribute to a worthy cause, contribute to an unworthy cause, new shoes for jogging or dancing, new car?*

—Emmy Smith
From a letter describing her wishes for her 80th birthday.

Paella

WELL DONE

I never eat when I can dine.

—Maurice Chevalier

Paella History, Lore & Rules of the Road

The smell of an apple wood fire and the aroma of garlic, spicy sausage and chicken mingle in the hot air of a late August afternoon as the large cast iron skillet of saffron rice is lifted to the table. We top it with slices of roasted red pepper, sprigs of parsley, lemon wedges, grilled shrimp, clams and green-lipped mussels. Our paella is ready to eat.

Paella isn't a recipe but a way of cooking rice with vegetables, meat and seafood, using what you have at hand and what is in season. As our Catalan friend Anuncia explained, even the same person using the same ingredients will make different paellas on different days.

Named for the specialized pan in which it is traditionally cooked, paellas range in size from about 12 inches to 8 feet or more in diameter. During the Arab occupation of Spain from the 8th to the 15th centuries, rice paddies were established in La Albufera outside Valencia, and rice became a dietary staple. Paella evolved as a combination of rice plus assorted garden produce, even snails. By the twentieth century paella had become Spain's national dish with variations from region to region and household to household.

Ingredients

Anuncia's mother, María, made a paella extravaganza with *sepia* (cuttlefish), *escamarlanes* (squilla), *calamares* (bigger than our calamari), *gambas* and *langostinos* (shrimp and prawns) — heads intact — all with the Mediterranean's distinct salty flavor. Thursday was the day to make paella in Capellades, Anuncia's hometown, because the seafood was fresh.

Our paella adventure began after eating Anuncia's adaptation of her mother's paella based on local ingredients, including brown rice in the years before paella rice was available, frozen calamari and headless shrimp. Our "sanitized seafood" is a mystery to Spaniards because the heads and skeletons of seafood can provide significant flavor for paella and many other dishes.

Anuncia's old friends and our new ones, Maribel Giner and August Gil, brought us a helpful book about paella entitled *El libro de la paella y los arroces* (Alianza Editorial, Madrid, 1994). According to the author, Lourdes March, a typical **paella valenciana** today combines rice, chicken, rabbit, snails (or fresh rosemary), two kinds of beans (*judías verdes "ferraúra"* and *judías de grano tierno "tavella"*), tomatoes, olive oil, paprika, saffron, salt and water. Rosemary is an essential ingredient because snails in Valencia feed on that herb, giving its distinctive flavor to the local paella.

Anuncia reminisced about paella with rabbit, sparerib tips (called *cap de costella*), artichokes, peas and roasted peppers and another favorite with lima beans. We've made paellas with cauliflower, broccoli and garbanzo beans. We add Kentucky ham when we have it, more lemon juice with more seafood and hot paprika when we want to spice it up.

Rice

The best Spanish paella rice still comes from the paddies of La Albufera where it is produced in different grades with the top one called "extra." Like its Italian counterpart *Arborio* rice, paella rice is *medio grano* or medium grain, thicker and shorter than American white rice. As soon as Arborio rice became readily available in local grocery stores, we could throw out our brown rice paella that took too much cooking. Fortunately, we can now get paella rice at our fish store in Eugene, Oregon.

Anuncia carried home a bag of top grade paella rice — SOS brand — from Barcelona so that we could make paella with visiting Spanish friends, Maribel, whose family comes from the homeland of paella in the Alicante, and her husband, August. A marvelous cook, Maribel guided the preparation of two paellas, one with rabbit, sausage, green peppers, tomato sauce, peas, garlic and parsley and the other with prawns, steamed clams and mussels, ham, green peppers, artichoke hearts, peas, saffron, parsley, garlic and lemon wedges.

We used Spanish rice for one paella and Italian *Arborio* rice (Beretta superfino) for the second. The Spanish rice cooked faster and was easier to work with than the *Arborio* rice with its listed moisture content of 14.5%. (Señora March explained in her book that the moisture content of Spanish paella rice is at least 20% when harvested.) We concluded that Anuncia's hand-carried rice contained more moisture and was fresher than the *Arborio* rice from our grocery store.

How much rice?
Allow about ¼ cup of rice per person (more for big appetites).

The Pan
A shallow pan with a large surface area for cooking is essential for paella because the rice cooks by evaporation from its surface and by absorption. A wok is an unsuitable design, but a cast iron frying pan works well. Although traditional paella pans are steel, Anuncia has concluded that cast iron, which is not available in Spain, cooks at least as well.

Size of pan = how many servings?
11-inch cast iron frying pan • 1 to 1-½ cups of rice • Serves 4-6
13-inch paella with non-stick surface* • 1 to 2 cups of rice • Serves 4-8
(*Made by Atlas Metal Spinning Co. of San Francisco.)
14-inch Spanish steel paella • 1 to 2 cups of rice • Serves 4-8
17-inch Spanish steel paella • 2 to 3 cups of rice • Serves 8-12
20-inch Lodge cast iron skillet** • 4 to 6 cups of rice • Serves 16-24
(**Special-ordered from a local cookware shop; weighs 25-lbs.)

Cooking Techniques
Don't wash paella rice because it needs to absorb all of its moisture while the paella is cooking.

Paella is best cooked over an open fire. In the kitchen, use a gas burner, if possible, because electric burners create a hot spot in the middle of the pan that can burn the rice. In Spain, you can buy a special gas burner with two or three rings of gas jets to disperse the heat evenly under the paella.

 Paella

To release the flavors of the paella's ingredients, Maribel explained, you must sauté them in olive oil over high heat until the water in them has evaporated and the garlic, vegetables, meat or seafood begin to brown.

It is preferable NOT to stir the paella once the boiling liquid has been added to the rice because stirring disrupts cooking and may change the texture of the rice. We confess that we stir the rice to make sure that it cooks evenly and to keep it from burning, particularly over an open fire.

A crust, called the *socarat,* may form on the bottom of the paella, and it is considered a treat. There is a fine line between forming this crust and burning the bottom of the paella. It may take several paellas before you figure out the correct heating adjustments on your stove or over an open fire.

The finished paella should be somewhat dry, Anuncia advised. Remove paella from the fire when the rice is dry but still chewy, and cover it with a hot, damp towel, followed by several sheets of newspaper, nicely tucked in, for insulation. The paella can sit "until the late children arrive," explained Maribel. Her husband added that a left-wing newspaper would hold the heat better.

HOW BATHTUB BARBIE GOT HER NAME

We had just finished creating our new outdoor barbecue when Jane Bartlett, our Australian niece, and Jason Wagoner arrived from Canberra on their engagement tour. It was a beautiful early spring evening. We were outside standing on the new slab and admiring the old bathtub topped with firebricks and the Tuscan grill.

"That's definitely Bathtub Barbie," Jane observed, using the popular Aussie slang for barbecue. You can always trust Jane to sum things up. (See page 15 for more about the construction of Bathtub Barbie.)

And you can trust Jason to build a fine fire, a skill that he was able to demonstrate to his soon-to-be-fiancée for the first time while helping to prepare Jane's birthday dinner at Camp Sherman in Oregon's Cascade Mountains.

Tips for Cooking Paella over a Wood Fire

Paella cooked outside over a wood fire is serious party food in the same league as roast pig at a Hawaiian luau. Allow 2 hours for preparations, fire building and cooking. This is many-handed cooking at its best.

ORGANIZE • Cooking paella over a wood fire can be a scramble at times, so you need to be organized. Have all your ingredients ready and at hand when you begin cooking.

TIMING • Start the fire approximately 45 minutes before you cook. Build a wood fire in a barbecue large enough to accommodate a cast iron frying pan or other heavy pan suitable for cooking directly over the fire. We once hung our 20-inch cast iron skillet over the top of a 22-½ inch Weber barbecue without the grill rack. At home, we build a fire in our backyard fireplace. (See previous page for details.)

WOOD • We think fruit wood gives the best flavor so we horde fallen limbs and pruned branches from our apple and pear trees.

GRILL RACK • As soon as the fire is going strong and the grill is hot, begin cooking. (Description of our Tuscan grill on page 280.) Grill red peppers until completely charred. (Method on page 188.)

CHARCOAL • Add charcoal briquettes to fire, about one-third the volume of wood. This helps stabilize the fire for more even cooking. Once the fire has burned down to hot coals, grill chicken breasts, about 6 to 8 minutes on each side. Cut chicken into bite-sizes pieces and set aside. Chicken will cook again with rice, so it can be pink inside.

CAST IRON • If you are using a cast iron pan, warm it slowly next to the fire before setting it on a rack directly over the coals, or it may crack. Begin cooking sausage or onions as directed in recipes on the following pages. Follow the order of preparation indicated in the recipe.

THE FIRE • We haven't yet figured out how to build the perfect fire for cooking paella, and sometimes we count on fast action with our Chinese wok spatula to keep things from burning. (John likes to put a long stick in the handle to extend its range. Long-handled barbecue tools are helpful.) If the paella gets too hot, we lift the pan off the fire using pot-holders, heavy welder's gloves or Tenold's homemade "paella hooks," a pair of metal hooks with wooden handles, copied from a magazine, that fit perfectly into the handles of our big cast iron skillet. Let the paella cool briefly until the fire settles down. Keep a small stack of wood of various sizes nearby; kindling one-inch in diameter comes in handy for a quick boost to the fire.

Have heated stock in a pan and a kettle of hot water nearby for the paella. Add initial liquid. The total amount will depend on the rice and the fire. The classic paella method requires adding liquid and then letting the paella cook without stirring. In practice, we find this impossible over an open fire. We stir the rice as needed.

About 7 to 10 minutes after adding the initial liquid, the rice will still be tough. Add more stock or water (or white wine or beer as Joey does). When paella returns to cheerful bubbling, arrange prawns and/or clams directly on top of rice. Let the paella cook for about 5 minutes without stirring.

When the rice is dry but still chewy, remove the paella from the fire and add peas, if you are using them. Cover the paella with a towel soaked in hot water and wrung out, and several sheets of newspaper, tucked in around the pan, for insulation. Let the paella sit for 10 minutes while rice finishes cooking and flavors blend.

If you are NOT already cooking the shrimp, mussels and/or clams on top of the paella, then grill or steam them while the paella is resting. (Discard mussels or clams that fail to open.) Arrange red pepper slices and lemon wedges on top and serve paella immediately.

LEFTOVER PAELLA

Anuncia remembers eating leftover paella at her Aunt Filomena's house on Sunday evenings. We enjoy leftover paella at room temperature or warmed in a covered casserole in a 300° oven for 20 to 25 minutes.

PROFESSIONAL PAELLA ADVICE

Rule 1 • Don't eat paella in the dark. Traditionally, it is eaten in the afternoon, not at night. Paella is too beautiful not to be admired in good light.

Rule 2 •Don't eat paella with salad. Its complex flavors deserve to be savored without the distraction of vinegar.

—Maribel Giner & August Gil

BIG IMPROVEMENTS

Anuncia has greatly enriched the English language. Thanks to her, we have *chopping*, a much more enjoyable form of shopping and, most importantly *burrocrats*, to describe those stubborn, hide-bound characters who sometimes make our lives miserable. *Happy as a clown* is a big relief, too. (We never did understand "happy as a clam.") *Chaterina* certainly improves "Catarina."

Paella Possibilities: Be an Artist

Paella is one of the most sensuous dishes in the world because of its colors, textures and taste. We encourage you to experiment making paella with your own favorite combination of ingredients. Be the artist in your own marvelous creation. (See recipes on following pages.)

VEGETABLES	RICE
Artichoke hearts	Allow ¼ cup of un-cooked paella rice or Arborio rice per person.
Broccoli	
Carrots	
Cauliflower	
Fava beans	Cook rice with chicken stock or beef stock or fish stock or vegetable stock or cooking liquid from beans or vegetables.
Garbanzo beans	
Green beans	
Lima beans	
Leeks	
Onions: yellow, red or white	
Peas, including snow peas	
Peppers: red, green, orange or yellow	
Tomatoes: fresh or sun-dried	
Turnips	
Kale	
Mushrooms	
Olives	

MEATS	SEASONINGS	SEAFOOD
Chicken	Garlic	Calamari
	Paprika	
Ham	Saffron	Clams
	Rosemary	
Pork	Bay leaf	Mussels
	Parsley	
Rabbit	Salt	Prawns/Shrimp
	Lemon juice	
Sausage	Clam juice	Scallops
	Tomato sauce	
	White wine	

Anuncia's Parking Lot Paella

Our paella odyssey began with Anuncia's efforts to create a version of her mother's paella using ingredients readily available in our local grocery stores. Our paella-making has improved in direct relation to "chopping" in Eugene. • We prepared this paella and the next one in the parking lot of our favorite grocery store on a blustery Sunday afternoon for the spring Food Fair. We got lots of attention with two Weber barbecues smoking from fruitwood fires built by John and Paul. Anuncia used her Spanish steel paella pan and we used our American cast iron one. We talked about paella and answered questions as we cooked. When the paellas were done, we served them to more than 100 people in small plastic cups.

Serves 8-10

4-½ c. chicken or vegetable stock or water
1 whole chicken breast (2 halves),
   skinned, boned & cubed
   (For cooking over a wood fire, keep
   chicken breast whole.)
3 to 4 T. olive oil
2 large onions, chopped finely
3 cloves garlic, peeled & minced
2 c. freshly made tomato sauce
   or 15 oz. can tomato sauce
   (See page 83.)
1 lb. calamari, cleaned & cut in rings
   (See next page.)
2 c. paella rice or Arborio rice
1 t. sweet paprika (Spanish or Hungarian)

¼ t. saffron threads, pulverized with
   mortar & pestle; then dissolved in
   ½ c. hot water
Salt to taste
2 sweet red peppers, roasted
   & cut in strips (See page 188.)
1 c. green peas, fresh or frozen
½ lb. Italian sausage
¾ lb. shrimp
12 to 20 clams or mussels

<u>Garnish</u>:
Parsley
Lemon wedges

Bring a kettle of water to a boil. If you are using stock, then also bring it to a boil in a small saucepan and maintain at a simmer.

In a paella or large, heavy frying pan or other shallow, flat bottomed pan, brown the chicken quickly over high heat in 2 tablespoons of olive oil. Remove chicken from the pan with tongs or a slotted spoon and set aside.

If you use sausage, brown it now, remove from pan with a slotted spoon and set aside. In the same pan, sauté onions over medium-low heat in sausage drippings or 2 tablespoons of olive oil until limp, about 5 minutes. Add garlic and sauté several minutes more.

Add the tomato sauce, browned chicken pieces, calamari, rice, boiling water or stock, paprika, the saffron solution and salt to taste. If you are using cooked sausage, add it now. Bring the paella to a boil uncovered over high heat, lower the heat to medium-high and simmer for 10 minutes. Stir only as needed to cook the rice uniformly.

Reduce heat to medium or medium-low and cook for 10 minutes more. Check rice occasionally to make sure there is enough liquid to finish cooking it, adding hot stock or water as needed. A crust may form on the bottom of the paella. This is desirable, but there is a fine line between forming a crust and burning the paella. Learning to "manage the fire" comes with practice.

While the paella is cooking, roast the red peppers and cut in strips. (See method on page 188.) If you are using shrimp, clams or mussels, steam them in a large frying pan or soup pot. Shrimp are done when they turn pink and clams or mussels when they open. (Discard any that fail to open.) Set aside.

Remove paella from the heat when the rice is dry but still chewy, stir in peas, cover with a warm, damp towel, followed by several sheets of newspaper. Let it sit covered for 10 minutes while the rice finishes cooking and the flavors blend. Garnish with roasted red pepper strips, seafood, sprigs of parsley, and lemon wedges. Serve immediately.

CALAMARI

We buy squid tubes, supposedly cleaned, then rinse them in cold water and make sure that the fingernail-like membrane has been removed from inside. These pull out easily.

SAFFRON FOR TOURISTS

Saffron is the bright orange stigma of a fall blooming crocus — Crocus sativus, — that thrives in Spain, Turkey and throughout Asia Minor. One acre of plants — about 70,000 — produces a pound of saffron, making it more costly than gold, the most expensive spice in the world.

Although saffron gives paella a vibrant yellow color, Anuncia explained it is a poor substitute for other ingredients that give rice a superior flavor, such as stock made from the heads of prawns and skeletons of fish. Anuncia first tasted "yellow rice" for lunch at school. The verdict? Not impressed. Her mother never used saffron in paella. In Barcelona, Anuncia jokes, saffron is for tourists.

NEWS FLASH: ANOTHER PAELLA EXPERIMENT

We made paella with chanterelle mushrooms, sausage, kale, leeks, a Maui onion, garlic, rosemary and vegetable stock. We sautéed salted mushrooms in a dry pan until they released their moisture and set aside, adding them to the paella with cooked sausage. We sautéed kale in sausage drippings, removed it from the pan and added it after removing paella from the heat.

 Paella

Imagination Rules:
Garrulous Garbanzo Bean Paella

Substitute broccoli or cauliflower for carrots. Add cubed turnips. Substitute red onions for yellow. Omit leeks and use sweet Walla Walla or Vidalia or Maui onions. Add chopped fresh tomatoes. Substitute fresh fava beans for garbanzos. Add chopped salami. Experiment to discover your own favorite combinations. (See notes on page 181.)

Serves 6-8

4 c. vegetable stock
¾ c. artichoke hearts
Juice of 1 lemon
3 T. olive oil
1 large onion, chopped
2 leeks, chopped finely
2 carrots, diced (about 1 cup)
1 c. cooked garbanzo beans
8 oz. can tomato sauce
1 c. white wine

1 t. sweet paprika (Spanish or Hungarian)
2 cloves garlic, peeled & minced
2 sprigs parsley, minced
1 T. fresh rosemary, minced
Salt to taste
2 c. paella rice or Arborio rice
1 c. shelled peas, fresh or frozen
3 sweet red peppers, roasted & cut in
   strips (See page 188.)

Bring stock to a boil in a saucepan and maintain at a simmer. Cut artichoke hearts in quarters. Place in a small bowl, and cover with lemon juice. (See note about artichoke hearts on page 114.)

In a paella or large, heavy frying pan or other shallow, flat-bottomed pan, sauté onions in olive oil over medium heat until limp, about 5 minutes. Add leeks and sauté 5 minutes more.

Add carrots, garbanzo beans, tomato sauce, paprika, garlic, parsley, rosemary, white wine and salt to taste. Simmer uncovered over medium-high heat for several minutes. Add artichoke hearts, lemon juice, simmering stock and rice. Bring to a boil over high heat, reduce heat to medium-high or medium and cook uncovered for 10 minutes. Stir only as needed to cook the rice uniformly.

Reduce heat to medium or medium-low and cook for 10 minutes more. Check rice occasionally to make sure there is enough liquid to finish cooking it, adding hot stock as needed. A crust may form on the bottom of the paella. This is desirable, but there is a fine line between forming a crust and burning the paella.

Remove paella from the heat when the rice is dry but still chewy, stir in the peas, arrange the roasted peppers nicely on top and cover it with a warm, damp towel, followed by several sheets of newspaper. Let it sit covered for 10 minutes while the rice finishes cooking and the flavors blend. Serve immediately.

Paella

Fideuà: Ariadna's Mother-Daughter Pasta Paella from Catalonia

For many years, Anuncia had described fideuà *to us longingly. In 1999 we faced our own plates of* fideuà *while seated next to Anuncia's mother Maria at a restaurant in Capellades called "The House of a Piece of Rabbit." Oh, my, we finally understood Anuncia's longing for the savory richness of this dish — pasta infused with fish stock, given subtle texture with a nutty garlic paste, and served with a rich, garlicky mayonnaise called* alioli *in Catalan • When Ariadna, Maribel and August's daughter, came to visit in 2009, she gave a memorable cooking lesson about* fideuà*. She brought special "Fideo No. 2" pasta and her trusty cookbook, a well-used notebook penned in her mother's distinctive script. • This delectable dish is the favorite of Ariadna's daughter Violetta. Her little brother Leo prefers blueberries. • "Fideuà" is pronounced* fee-day-waugh *(as in the author Evelyn Waugh) with the accent on the last syllable.*

Serves 6-8

6-8 c. fish stock (See page 121.)

"Paste":
1 T. each, pine nuts, almonds & filberts,
 lightly-toasted
2 T. parsley
3 cloves garlic, peeled
½ piece of toast

Optional seafood: Prawns, scallops, fish, prepared as you wish; also bay shrimp may be added before serving.

Alioli: (Method on page 266.)
1 egg
1 T. lemon juice or sherry vinegar
½ c. olive oil
5 cloves garlic, peeled
Salt & pepper to taste

Pasta:
3 T olive oil
2 cloves garlic, unpeeled
1 lb. pasta: spaghetti or capellini
 broken into 1-inch lengths, two 7-oz.
 pkg. Mexican "Fideo" pasta, or 500
 grams Spanish "Fideo No. 2" pasta
1 cube of concentrated fish stock
 (See note on next page.)

Bring the fish stock to a gentle simmer in a medium soup pot over medium heat.

"PASTE" • Combine ingredients in a food processor or blender. Process until well crumbled. Set aside.

ALIOLI • Make this sauce using the above ingredients as instructed on page 266. Anuncia's mother always makes her *alioli* in a mortar with a pestle, creating a thinner sauce. Refrigerate *alioli*, if you are making it well ahead.

Break spaghetti or capellini into 1-inch lengths. (Mexican "Fideo" is the correct shape but finer than Spanish "Fideo No. 2." Spaghetti is thicker, capellini finer.)

In a paella or other shallow, wide-bottomed pan, heat olive oil (enough to cover the surface of the pan) and garlic over medium-high heat. Remove garlic when brown. Add pasta and brown it nicely, stirring constantly. Add "paste" and 1 cube of fish stock. (Note: Knorr's fish cubes are not available in Eugene; substitute a teaspoon of concentrated vegetable stock.) Stir well. The *fideuà* may be prepared to this point and finished later.

Add simmering fish stock to cover pasta. Raise heat and maintain a vigorous boil for about 10 minutes. (Mexican "Fideo" pasta cooks faster than broken spaghetti; spaghetti cooks longer than capellini or Fideo #2. Adjust cooking times accordingly.) Rotate pan on burner. Use two burners at the same time, as needed for extra heat, if you have a large pan. Add more stock as needed.

Remove pan from heat and set on a wet towel. Place two wooden spoons on top of pasta and cover with a lid. Wrap covered pan with several sheets of newspaper, tucking the ends under the pan and making a tent. Let rest for 10 minutes. Unwrap, pasta should be "standing up." If not, don't worry; this is a fine point of style. Serve immediately with *alioli*.

ABOUT HAPPINESS

Be willing to be happy.
Don't expect someone else or something to make you happy.
Forgive yourself and others easily and often. • Laugh at least once a day.
Take good care of yourself physically. • Breathe slowly and deeply.
Eat well, sleep well and exercise regularly.
(Another formulation: Eat good food, tell the truth and be kind.)
Make sure that you do at least one thing each day that makes you happy.
Claim your private space for regeneration.
Be grateful. If it helps, keep a record of what you're grateful for each day.
Identify frustrations in life and eliminate them whenever possible.
Accept what IS and go forward from there.
Recognize that we cannot change others, but when we change ourselves,
then we also change our relationships with others.
Identify things NOT to do.
Be thoughtful. Tell other people (even strangers) good things often.
Examine your intentions and aim for the highest and best for all.
Look outside often and carefully to gain perspective about yourself.
Celebrate change. • Never say never.
Discover your unholy thrills,
such as loving to wear raggedy clothes, taking a long, quiet bath
while reading a good book, keeping chickens, admiring the behavior of ducks.

—An evening's wisdom from a group of friends

Paella

Vegetables, Rice & Potatoes

Moo, moo, what to do?

—Ruby Blum (Age 6)

Very High Roasted Red Peppers

We love roasted sweet red peppers, especially the ones from our own garden during those brief but much anticipated days in late August and September. Nothing tastes better. Roasting seems to release the full flavor of sweet peppers.

Approximately ½ pepper per person for salad

Red, yellow or orange sweet peppers
Garlic, peeled & minced
Good olive oil

Wash peppers and dry. Use whole peppers or remove the stem and seeds and cut into strips before grilling. Place whole peppers or strips of peppers on the grill or under the broiler, turning with tongs until blackened completely on the outside.

Remove charred peppers from heat and immediately seal in a plastic bag, a brown bag or a tightly covered container. Let peppers steam for at least 10 minutes to loosen the charred outer skins. Peel off skins with your fingers and a paring knife, remove seeds and use as desired. DO NOT RINSE because water washes away flavor.

RED PEPPER SALAD • Slice peppers into ½ inch strips and arrange nicely on a plate. Sprinkle minced garlic over the top and drizzle with good olive oil.

CHICKEN NOT-SO-LITTLE

It did look just like a broody hen, her grayish feathers all fluffed out, sitting on her nest. But this "hen" was an impressive mushroom perched on the roots of a large up-turned oak tree on the shore of Laurel Lake in southeastern Kentucky. It was quite a sight among the bright fall foliage of the hardwood forest there.

We had come ashore from our houseboat for a walk when John spotted it. Barry broke off a piece to take back to the boat for identification from Edie's mushroom book. Later that day, we learned that we had a rare delicacy, a hen-of-the-woods mushroom.

John and Barry returned for the remainder of our treasure, an estimated 25 pounds. In the kitchen, we carefully broke off several "feathers" and steamed them for 10 minutes as instructed in the mushroom book. Edie sautéed them in butter, and we served them with risotto and roasted red peppers, a meal fit for a queen. The delicious taste of our "hen" captured the essence of the woods.

Emmy's Baked Tomatoes Baltimore Style

Emmy lived in Baltimore from age 8 to 16 when her father Papa Strong, a Baptist minister, had a church there. • Over the years, Emmy has recreated this favorite Baltimore recipe, adding a little of this and a little of that until she got it just the way she remembered it. • Emmy reminded us to cook plenty of these tomatoes because everyone always wants more.

Serves 6-8

Two 28 oz. cans "crushed" tomatoes
1 large onion, chopped coarsely
¾ c. brown sugar
1 to 2 c. croutons, old toast, stale
   bread or crackers

3 T. butter
Ground black pepper to taste

In a saucepan or heat-proof casserole, combine tomatoes and onion. Simmer uncovered over medium heat for an hour or so until juice is considerably reduced.

Pre-heat oven to 300°. Add brown sugar, croutons (or bread cubes or crushed crackers) for thickening, a "big chunk" of butter and ground pepper to tomatoes. If you are using a saucepan that can't go into the oven, transfer tomatoes to an oven-proof casserole. Cover and cook tomatoes "indefinitely" in a slow oven. If you need to keep track of time, cook them for an hour at 300°. Serve hot. Baked tomatoes keep well in the refrigerator for several days. They also freeze well.

BALTIMORE MEMORIES

It couldn't matter to the production of stewed tomatoes, but I lived 8 years in Baltimore. The lively angle is that we had come from near a year in Germany and I couldn't speak English. We brought a Fraulein with us.

There's fun to tell about that as World War I started and a German ship was captive in the harbor and where did she take me? You guessed it. I entertained the sailors while she (in her own way) kept them "company," is my guess.

Baltimore was a wonderful city and it was a wonderful time there to grow up. All safety. All available. Trolley cars. Roller skates. My school was a nice walk. The alley behind our house at 1517 was all Black, houses and garages. The Fire Department still had horses, white ones.

—Emmy Smith

More-Precious-Than-Gold Stuffed Tomatoes

*Anuncia carried tomato seeds from Capellades, her family home outside Barcelona. These specialty tomatoes, called **tomatos vacíos de Montserrat** (or empty tomatoes), are for stuffing. They are lighter with less internal structure than other tomatoes. • We planted the seeds, produced several strong plants and fussed over them in this strongly dissimilar climate. The tomato fairy looked kindly on our cross-cultural experiment and finally rewarded us with several dozen ripe fruit at the end of the summer. We were unprepared for the amazing flavor of these tomatoes. They were sweeter when cooked. Oh, the wonderful surprises in this world.*

For 1 serving

1 tomato suitable for stuffing	**½ stalk celery, chopped finely**
1 T. pine nuts	**1 T. sweet red pepper, chopped finely**
1 slice of wheat bread, toasted &	**1 T. chicken stock**
cut in ½ inch cubes	**Pinch of celery seed**
1 T. olive oil	**Pinch of *herbes de Provence***
3 T. onion, chopped finely	**Salt & pepper to taste**

Pre-heat oven to 350°. Cut off top of each tomato and scoop out seeds and membrane. Drain upside down on a paper towel for several minutes.

Spread pine nuts on a baking sheet and toast briefly in oven until lightly browned, 7 to 10 minutes.

Sauté onion in olive oil over medium-low heat until limp, about 5 minutes. Add celery and red pepper, and cook a few minutes more. Add bread cubes, chicken stock and pine nuts. Mix well. Add seasoning and stir. Stuff tomatoes and place them on a baking sheet. Bake 20 minutes. Remove from oven and serve immediately.

MIND OVER MATTER

*When they take away all of your freedoms,
you still have one last freedom,
the freedom to choose your own attitude
under any set of circumstances.*

—Viktor Frankl

From *Man's Search for Meaning*

Emmy's Red Cabbage Casserole

This delicious, long-cooking casserole is a perfect side dish with meat or poultry. Emmy said that she always doubled the recipe. It also freezes well. • Bhagwan Bruce LeFavour served red cabbage with pork tenderloin grilled in the fireplace on his Tuscan grill. He sautéed thinly sliced red cabbage and onions in olive oil, added sliced apple and cooked it briefly.

Serves 8

**4 to 6 c. red cabbage (1 small head),
  shredded**
2 medium onions, chopped coarsely
2 T. bacon fat or vegetable oil
2 tart apples, cored & sliced
2 T. brown sugar
2 t. or more salt
Freshly ground pepper to taste
¼ t. cloves

¼ t. nutmeg
½ c. water
½ c. red wine

Optional:
**1 to 2 dozen chestnuts,
  roasted or boiled,
  peeled & quartered
(See page 250.)**

In a large bowl, cover shredded cabbage with cold water, soak for an hour and then drain thoroughly in a colander.

In a large frying pan, sauté onions in bacon fat over medium-low heat until limp, about 5 minutes. Add sliced apples and cook 5 minutes more. Add cabbage, brown sugar, salt (lots), pepper, cloves, nutmeg, water and wine. If you are using chestnuts, add them now. Cover and simmer gently for 1 hour or more. Adjust seasoning and serve hot.

Instead of simmering on top of the stove, cook this casserole in a slow oven — about 300° — "for as long as you have," explained Emmy. One hour will do.

---

*I shall go down again to the valley of concern.
I shall return to the rage of change.
But it is today that is forever and forever,
And I can hold the sun and the moment
In the wink of my eyes.*

—William D. Mundell

A favorite poem of Emmy's from *Hill Journey*

Pat's Summer Squash Casserole

Every gardener has a stories about Giant Zucchinis run amok in the garden. If only we could figure out some creative uses for surplus squash: making zucchini paper or paying off the national debt in zucchini dollars or building zucchini log homes. • Although Pat LeFavour's original recipe calls for yellow squash (and they do look beautiful in this casserole), zucchini, patty pan or any other summer squash will do equally well.

Serves 6 -8

2 or 3 leeks or 2 medium onions,
chopped coarsely (See note about
leeks on page 75.)
4 T. butter (½ cube) or olive oil
2 or 3 assorted peppers, chopped
coarsely (red or green, hot or sweet,
depending on your taste or what's
available) or 4 oz. can Anaheim
diced green chiles

6 c. summer squash, sliced or cubed
17 oz. can whole kernel corn, drained
or 2 c. fresh corn kernels (about 6 ears)
1 c. Asiago or Parmesan cheese, grated
(about 3 oz.)

Pre-heat oven to 300°. In an oven-proof casserole, sauté leeks or onions in butter or olive oil over medium-low heat until limp, about 5 minutes. Add peppers and sauté 5 minutes more. Add squash and cook until squash is thoroughly warmed but still crisp. Add corn and mix gently. Top with grated cheese.

Warm uncovered in oven until the cheese melts and gets bubbly, about 20 minutes. Serve immediately.

BASIC STRING BEANS

Fresh string beans are almost as important to our summer garden as tomatoes. We think there's nothing to improve the perfect natural flavor of summer beans just picked from the garden.

After stringing them, drop a few handfuls into a pot of rapidly boiling, well-salted water. Cook them briefly until they are bright green but still crunchy. Drain in a colander, rinse with cold water immediately and let them dry thoroughly wrapped in a kitchen towel. (Be careful that a tidy helper doesn't try to hang up the towel.)

Put beans in a serving dish, top with a splash or two of your best olive oil, a few grindings of black pepper and a big pinch of salt. (We like the sudden crunch of coarse salt.) Toss and serve.

Beebe's Thank-God-I'm-40 Vegetable Curry

The colors and textures of this beautiful curry come from its rich assortment of vegetables. Like Beebe herself, it's colorful, stylish and interesting. • Beebe said that it was such a relief to turn 40 because she finally had permission to be completely herself, the "more so" of getting older, as Beebe described it. At 50, she reported that she was even more "unabridged." After all, 40 was merely a warm up. We can hardly wait for 80.

Serves 8

4 T. butter (½ cube) or olive oil
2 large onions, chopped coarsely
Tops & leaves from 1 bunch
    of celery, chopped
3 carrots, sliced finely
1 red pepper, cut in thin strips
1 cauliflower, broken into florets
1 small eggplant, peeled & cubed
1 or 2 zucchini or yellow squash,
    sliced
1 c. raisins (about 6-⅔ oz.)
1 c. peanuts (4 oz.)

¾ c. chutney (Any kind but plum,
    Beebe advised.)
3 to 4 c. chicken or vegetable stock
2 T. or more curry powder
⅛ t. or more cayenne pepper

About 8 cups cooked rice

Optional:
3 whole chicken breasts, skinned,
    boned & cubed

In a large soup pot, melt butter over medium-low heat. Sauté onions in butter (or olive oil) until limp, about 5 minutes. Then add celery and sauté a few minutes more. Add carrots, followed by red pepper, cauliflower, eggplant and squash, cooking each a few minutes before adding the next.

Stir in raisins, peanuts and chutney. Then add enough stock to come ¾ of the way up the vegetables. Add curry powder and cayenne to taste. Mix well. Cover and simmer 1-½ hours over low heat, stirring occasionally.

If you want to add chicken cubes, do so approximately 20 minutes before serving, and poach gently in the simmering curry. Serve over rice. This curry does not freeze well, Beebe advised.

VERY FINE TUNING

Humor: Is is maybe the equivalent of perfect pitch in music?

—Emmy Smith

Emily's Maverick Rice

Emily Wells is the great-granddaughter of Sam Maverick, the Yale-educated Texas War of Independence hero who gave the English language his last name as a term indicating a willingness to do things one's own, unconventional way — the original maverick. He defied Texas ranching tradition by running his calves unbranded. • We admire the independent spirit we've observed in his family, his great-great-granddaughter Marsha and great-great-great-granddaughters Melissa and Emily.

Serves 6

1-½ c. long grain white rice
   (Texmati rice is recommended.)
¼ c. vegetable oil
1 small onion, coarsely chopped
1 clove garlic, peeled & minced
3-½ c. chicken stock (See page 68.)
Salt to taste

<u>Optional:</u>
1 or more Serrano chiles, seeded &
   chopped

Cover rice with cold water and soak for 1 hour or so, then rinse and drain thoroughly in a wire mesh strainer. (The holes in our colander are too big.)

In a large, heavy frying pan, heat oil almost to the smoking point over high heat. Fry rice until pale gold, stirring frequently. Reduce heat to medium-low. Add onion and garlic, and sauté for 5 minutes.

Stir in chicken stock and salt. Add chopped chiles, if you like. Cook uncovered over medium heat until most of the liquid has been absorbed or evaporated, 15 to 20 minutes. Reduce heat to lowest setting, cover and cook 5 minutes more. Remove from heat and let stand covered for 30 minutes. Serve immediately.

ETERNAL MYSTERIES

*Love confounds all notions of time,
effaces all memory of a beginning,
all fear of an end.*

—Mme de Staël

Emmy's Dynamite Rice

This recipe produces feathered rice by cooking it twice, the first time roasted dry and the second time steamed. The result is a different, lighter texture that John described as "exploded." It's delicious.

Serves 4

1 c. white rice
2 T. butter
2-½ c. boiling water

Salt to taste
¼ c. fresh parsley, chopped

Pre-heat oven to 375°. Spread rice in a shallow pan and bake until rice is golden, about 10 to 15 minutes. Stir or shake the pan occasionally. Remove from oven and lower the heat to 350°.

Pour rice into a casserole with a tight fitting lid. Add 1 tablespoon of butter and boiling water. Stir well and cover. Bake 30 minutes. Remove from oven and add remaining 1 tablespoon of butter, salt and parsley. Mix gently. Serve immediately.

LEFTOVER RICE

Emmy reported that rice is even better the second time around: Freeze leftover rice in a plastic bag. When you want to use it, bring a pot of water to a boil. Add rice to boiling water, return to a boil, give rice a quick stir, remove from heat, drain in a colander or a wire mesh strainer, and serve immediately. This also works for leftover pasta, cooked but undressed, frozen or not.

MORE MYSTERIES

You're so tall . . . . Are you married?

—Nepali laundry lady

Greeting Catherine at the Mala Hotel
(Kathmandu, 1984)

Ann's Effortless Brown Rice Casserole

Lawn mowing can be a drudge for the suburban homeowner. Not so for our cousin Ann who solved her grass problem by inviting a flock of sheep to mow around her beautiful old house in the Boston area. On a summer visit, we fell asleep to the sweet sound of a tinkling bell and the soft crunching of her lawn sheep that were kept in range by an electric fence. We thought this was an inspired solution. • This rice dish is also an inspired solution to the question of dinner. Keep the ingredients for it on your pantry shelf and in your refrigerator for an easy, last minute meal.

Serves 3-4

1 c. brown rice
2-½ c. stock or cold water (See page 68.)
2 large onions, chopped coarsely
   (about 2-½ cups)

3 T. butter or olive oil
1 c. grated cheese (4 oz. of Gruyère,
   3 oz. of Parmesan)
1 c. chopped parsley or frozen peas

The volume of chopped onions and cooked rice should be roughly equal. Cook rice in stock or water as directed on the package. Pre-heat oven to 300°. Grease an oven-proof casserole.

Sauté onions in butter or olive oil over medium-low heat until limp, about 5 minutes. Add cooked rice and mix together nicely. Scoop into oven-proof casserole. Bake 20 minutes. Remove from oven and mix in cheese and parsley or peas. Cover, let sit 5 to 10 minutes and serve.

POINT OF VIEW

"That's not really a treasure," I observed as Zoë twirled the twist tie on her finger. We were studying the objects, including an assortment of jewelry, in a wooden music box while the strains of "More" tinkled in the background. "Twist ties are used to close up those small plastic baggies for sandwiches," I explained.

There was a pause while Zoë contemplated my words with the full intensity of her three and a half year old mind. "You could put a peanut butter and jelly sandwich in one of those bags and take it with a girl to the coast," she proposed. Oh, yes, the makings of a treasure were inherent in that twist tie all along.

To celebrate her fourth birthday, we did take Zoë to the coast with a peanut butter sandwich in a baggie with a twist tie.

Vegetables, Rice & Potatoes

Ruth's Easy-Does-It Risotto

The classic method for cooking Italian Arborio rice involves the slow addition of boiling chicken stock, half cup by half cup, to perfectly preserve the integrity of the rice. Ruth's version is less fussy and produces good results.

Serves 3-4

2 T. butter
1 T. olive oil
1 small onion or 2 shallots,
  chopped finely
1 clove garlic, peeled & minced
1 c. Italian Arborio rice
2-¼ c. chicken stock (See page 68.)
¼ t. saffron threads

¼ c. white wine or vermouth
¼ c. or more Parmesan cheese,
  (1 oz. or more), grated

Options:
¾ c. peas, fresh or frozen
1 c. cooked chicken or ham, diced
½ lb. cooked shrimp

In a small saucepan, warm chicken stock to a simmer over medium heat. In a mortar with a pestle, crush saffron threads to make a powder. Dissolve pulverized saffron in ¼ cup of hot chicken stock and pour back into simmering stock.

In a heavy-bottomed casserole, melt butter over medium heat and add olive oil. Sauté onion and garlic for several minutes. Add rice and stir to coat well. Add hot chicken stock to rice and bring to a boil over medium-high heat. Reduce heat to low, cover and simmer gently until rice is chewy, about 20 minutes.

Add white wine, stir and remove from heat. Stir in Parmesan cheese. Add peas, chicken, ham or shrimp. Cover and let sit for 5 minutes before serving.

MAÑANA AT THE FARM

Friends visiting one Christmas kept mentioning the porch at the Crow's Nest where they were staying. "You should probably take a look at the porch," they suggested one day. Later after receiving no response, they pressed gently again, explaining that they could no longer use the front door because of the porch. "You really need to take a look at it," they advised.

On Christmas morning, it got serious, "You've got to look at the porch right away." So, we walked up to the Crow's Nest and were amazed to find that the porch had broken off completely from the cabin and tipped vertically like a sinking ship.

Belatedly, we got out the jack and a come-along to shore up the porch until it could be re-built.

Edie's Organizational Genius Potatoes

In another life, Edie must have been a general with all five stars. She can organize anything, do it beautifully and make it seem effortless. It's amazing to watch. A wedding for 350? No problem. A brunch for 200? A piece of cake. A dinner dance for 250? Easy as falling off a horse. A fund-raiser for charity? Record breaker. Dinner for four? Perfection. Ask a favor? It's done. She inspires us in more ways than one. • We love to eat in Edie's cozy kitchen with its 12-foot high ceilings, cheery blue and yellow color scheme and the big table right where it should be — in the center of the room. • If you prepare Edie's potatoes, your organizational abilities will improve. Guaranteed.

Serves 6

3 T. olive oil
8 medium potatoes, peeled or not
   & sliced thinly

8 cloves garlic, peeled & minced
2 T. butter
Salt & pepper to taste

Pre-heat oven to 400°. Pour 1 tablespoon of olive oil into the bottom of an oven proof pan or casserole. Make a nice layer of potatoes, overlapping the slices attractively. Drizzle with olive oil, sprinkle with garlic, and season with salt and pepper. Repeat the layers and dot the top with butter. Bake until top is browned and crispy, 45 minutes to 1 hour. Remove from oven and serve immediately.

BUZZARDS OF A FEATHER

The problem began with a gift to our neighbor's father many years ago. A pair of peacocks, native to the Indian subcontinent, proved adaptable to our distinctly different climate, and their offspring became a flock of several dozen marauding birds. Lloyd, our neighbor, attempted to keep the birds in check by feeding them grain during the winter. Come spring bands of males made forays into the neighborhood scouting potential food sources and devastating local plant life. Roses were a particular favorite.

One spring morning, John looked out the window of the sun room to find a peacock staring at our tomato and pepper plants that were nearly ready to be transplanted into the garden. That was a declaration of war.

We called in Barry for a hunting expedition. He bagged two birds before lunch. We ate one for dinner, marinated in plum wine and braised. It was tasty.

Later in a conversion with Lloyd, John mentioned our peacock meal. Lloyd narrowed his eyes and looked at John skeptically. "Tastes too much like buzzard for me," he said.

The peacock feathers were priceless, Bruce Klepinger explained. He agreed to carry a box of them to the Buddhist monastery in Thami, a village near Mt. Everest, as a gift from our local flock. The monks were delighted.

Mary Jean's 6-foot-5-inch Roast Potatoes

A time management study would establish that Mary Jean, Catherine's Australian sister, has no time to cook. In spite of that, she produces remarkable home-cooked meals for her family day after day and runs the family business with her husband. Of course, Mary Jean never sleeps. but that is a small price to pay to be Super Woman. • Nobody likes Mary Jean's potatoes better than her 6 foot 5 inch son Michael, 23 years old and still growing. (That was 1998; full-grown now, he's the father of two sons.) • We can't promise these potatoes will make you tall because, after all, Michael's big sister Jane is the family midget at 5 feet 9-1/2 inches. There was also Ludwig the Cat who measured 1 foot 1 inch with four on the floor.

For each serving

**1 to 3 potatoes per person, depending
  on the size of the potatoes &
  the size of the person
Olive oil
Salt & pepper to taste**

**Optional:
Minced garlic, chopped rosemary,
  tarragon or parsley**

Pre-heat oven to 400°. Wash potatoes, drain and dry them on a tea towel. Cut potatoes in uniform pieces based on the size of the potatoes, quarters, eighths, etc.

Place potatoes on a cookie sheet or in an ovenproof casserole. Drizzle with olive oil and toss to coat thoroughly. Season to taste with salt and pepper. Bake potatoes until nicely browned, turning them with a spatula every 10 minutes, 40 to 50 minutes total cooking time. Remove from oven and toss with garlic and/or chopped herbs. Serve immediately.

OTHER VEGETABLES • Roast turnips (cut in quarters or eighths), parsnips and carrots (cut in 2-inch chunks) and onions (cut in quarters). Add red peppers (seeded and cut in 1-inch strips) half-way through roasting.

---

*There once was a girl from Australia
Who went to a dance as a dahlia.
The petals revealed what they should have concealed
And the dance as a dance was a failya.*

—Author unknown

Recited by Emmy Smith on learning that we would visit Australia.

Anuncia's Legendary Potato Roll

Called Brazo de Gitano or Gypsy Arm, this favorite Catalan dish is delicious and beautiful with its garnish of red pepper strips and yellow aioli, the colors of the Catalan flag. Served many times at her son Tavi's birthday parties in Eugene, it met with great success among guests from age three on up. • It can be served as an hors d'oeuvre or lunch, but it also makes a fine supper with a bowl of soup and salad. • Re-designated **The Slug,** *we have adopted it as local cuisine of the Pacific Northwest.*

Serves 6-10

5 to 8 medium-sized potatoes
2 to 3 T. milk
1 T. butter
1 or 2 cans oil-packed tuna
(6-⅛ oz. each)

1 c. aïoli (See page 266.)
2 red peppers, roasted & peeled
(See page 188 for method.)
2 dozen good Spanish, Greek, French
or Italian black olives

Use 5 potatoes for a smaller roll or 8 for a larger one. Peel potatoes, cover with cold water in a large saucepan or soup pot. Bring water to a boil, reduce heat, cover and cook until potatoes are tender but firm when pricked with a fork or paring knife, about 15 to 20 minutes.

Drain potatoes in a colander. Return to pot and mash by hand with a fork or a potato masher, or use a ricer or food mill. (A food processor is too harsh.) Add milk a little at a time and then butter, stirring with a wooden spoon. These mashed potatoes should be thicker than regular mashed potatoes in order to hold their shape when formed into a roll. The consistency is correct when you touch the potatoes with a spoon and they stick to it.

Anuncia recommended using Portuguese tuna packed in olive oil, but any kind of oil-packed tuna will do. (Tavi urged us to use dolphin-safe tuna.) Use 1 can of tuna for a small roll and 2 cans for a larger one. Drain oil from tuna and mix it into the potatoes with a fork.

Turn out potato-tuna mixture onto a clean dishtowel and form into a roll by patting into shape through the towel. Slip the roll onto a large serving platter and gently pull the towel away. Pat the roll with the towel to smooth its surface.

Cover roll with aioli, and arrange the strips of red pepper about ½ inch apart. In between red pepper strips, place black olives. If you wish to make a "slug," reserve two olives for the eyes and make a cut in that end for the "slug's" mouth. Use a strip of red pepper for the tongue. Serve immediately or refrigerate for 1 to 2 hours before serving. To serve, cut in slices about ½ inch thick.

Salads

*To make a good salad is to be a brilliant diplomatist —
the problem is entirely the same in both cases.
To know exactly how much oil
one must put with one's vinegar.*

—Oscar Wilde

Two Salad Dressings:
Vinaigrette & Cissy's Anchovy Special

A fine French chef who served a memorable bouillabaisse shared his garlic secret with Emmy's friend, Sacha, who then passed it on to her. Remove green center shoot from each clove of garlic. Voilà! You can eat garlic like peanuts with no afterglow.

Enough for a large salad

¼ c. olive oil
1 to 2 T. t. vinegar (wine, rice or
  balsamic) or lemon juice
  or a combination

1 T. Dijon mustard
2 cloves garlic, peeled & minced
Salt & pepper to taste
Favorite fresh herbs

Combine ingredients in a small jar and shake well. (An old 8 oz. Dijon mustard jar is a perfect size.) The amount of vinegar depends on the type and your taste. Add favorite herbs or omit mustard. Season to taste.

EASY DRESSING • Karen taught us to dress a salad by drizzling a little good olive oil and a splash of balsamic vinegar directly on salad greens. Then toss.

CISSY'S ANCHOVY SALAD DRESSING

Cissy ran a 1,000-acre farm in the heart of the Kentucky Blue Grass. Her competence extends to the kitchen, too. This is a favorite recipe of her. • We never look at a sea lion without thinking of Cissy's love of these creatures, a love affair that began on the Oregon coast many years ago.

Makes enough for 1 large salad

2 oz. tin of anchovies packed in oil & well drained

1 T. lemon juice

2 T. grainy Dijon mustard

⅓ c. buttermilk

2 T. fresh dill

1 scallion, minced

Combine all ingredients in a food processor or blender and process until smooth. Chill and serve with fresh greens.

Caesar's All-in-the-Family Competition Salad

Family dynamics can lead to competition. Competition can lead to innovation. Innovation can lead to improvements. Each of the three Watchie sisters claims to have the BEST recipe for Caesar salad. This one comes from Chris. She advised, "When in doubt, add more lemon juice," and the correct quantity of Parmesan is "LOTS." • The Caesar of this salad is Caesar Cardini, the Italian-born Mexican who created it, but the other Caesar deserves the last word and a gold star for political acuity. "Men willingly believe what they wish," Julius Caesar observed, or "Fere libenter homines id quod volunt credunt" in the original.

Serves 8-10

2 large heads Romaine lettuce
   (or 3 small)
Lots of Parmesan cheese,
   freshly grated (at least 1 c.,
   about 3-oz.)

Optional Croutons:
French bread, about 1-½ c., cubed
3 T. olive oil
3 whole cloves of garlic, unpeeled

Dressing:
¼ to ½ c. olive oil
¼ to ½ c. lemon juice
2 T. Dijon mustard
2 T. red wine
1 to 2 t. Worcestershire sauce
4 or 5 big cloves garlic, peeled
1- 2 oz. tin anchovies
1 egg

Wash lettuce in cold water, tear into bite-sized pieces, then spin or shake dry. Wrap in a tea towel and crisp in refrigerator while making dressing.

For dressing, combine olive oil, lemon juice, mustard, red wine, Worcestershire sauce, garlic, anchovies and egg in a food processor or blender and process until smooth. (For a coddled egg to use in place of a raw one, place cold egg in a small bowl and cover with boiling water. Let sit for 10 minutes. Use as directed above.)

In a salad bowl, toss greens with Parmesan cheese and then toss again with dressing. Serve immediately.

For croutons, cut bread in 1-inch cubes. In a frying pan, sauté garlic cloves briefly in olive oil over medium heat until they begin to brown. Remove garlic, add bread cubes and brown them nicely. Drain on paper towels and add to salad.

WISE WORDS

Pleasure is in the repetition.

—Don Julio Cobos
Frequently quoted by Bruce Klepinger

Em's Big-Hearted Greens
with Yellow Peppers & Caramelized Almonds

Emily is required by popular demand to bring this beautiful salad to family gatherings and potlucks. • At her home in Denver, it's a pleasure to open the refrigerator because it is always filled with good food, the makings for salads and sandwiches, milk, syrup, eggs, cheese, juice and homemade pesto in the freezer. Emily is a working mom who manages to feed our two grandsons good, home-cooked food. • In her non-spare time she organizes major charitable activities at the boys' school, her big heart as full as her frig.

Serves 8-10

8 c. mixed field greens or 2 large heads
   of Romaine, shredded
3 yellow peppers, sliced in thin strips
12 mushrooms ("good & firm"), sliced
½ red onion, sliced very thinly
8 oz. feta cheese, crumbled

<u>**Caramelized Almonds**</u>:
⅔ c. sugar
⅓ c. water
1 c. blanched, slivered almonds

<u>**Dressing**</u>:
See recipe on page 202
           or
Commercial vinaigrette
(such as Newman's Own, Em's favorite)

    Wash greens, spin or shake dry. Wrap in tea towel and crisp in refrigerator. In a heavy saucepan or cast-iron frying pan, melt sugar over high heat, stirring constantly with a wooden spoon. Add almonds and continue stirring until almonds are thoroughly coated and richly brown, about 10 minutes total time. Remove from heat, and immediately pour onto a cookie sheet. Spread nuts into a single layer. Cool briefly until you can handle nuts and break them apart. (Don't wait too long, or you'll need a sledgehammer, advised Emily.)

    Combine lettuce, sliced peppers, mushrooms, red onion, crumbled feta and caramelized almonds in a large salad bowl. Pour dressing over salad and toss. Serve immediately.

BIG JOKE FROM A SMALL JOKER

I was in the kitchen with Macauley, our 28-month old grandson and Em's son, on Thanksgiving morning. He was sitting at the table drinking juice and I was across the room working on dinner.

He coughed a couple of times and I asked if he had a frog in his throat. Mac looked at me squarely with the full blue-eyed intensity of his two years. "Yes," he said. There was a pause for reflection and then he added, "Rivet, rivet." For emphasis, no doubt. I'm still laughing at this perfect, first joke. That's our boy.

Marsha's Transcendental
Baked Goat Cheese Salad with Good Olives

*She has the voice of an angel! Move over Marlene Dietrich, move over Lauren Bacall, it's Marsha we yearn to hear at the end of the phone line. • Needless to say, Marsha took France by storm, making a particular friend of the olive merchant in downtown Avignon. He oversaw an empire of olives, literally dozens of varieties, each offered in its own barrel. And the names, Kalamata, Niçoise, Arnaud, Sicilian and Aromatique, Marsha's favorite. • This salad has long been one of Marsha's favorites, but living in Provence sealed its place in Marsha's culinary repertoire. When she wanted to prepare it for a special lunch, she asked the advice of the lady in the convenience store across from her apartment. The "Casino lady," as Marsha called her after the name of the grocery store chain, recommended using fresh thyme. Marsha prefers **herbes des Provence**, a mixture of marjoram, basil, savory, thyme, rosemary and even lavender. Marsha makes vinaigrette with lots of Spike that includes sea salt and "about 50 herbs."*

For 1 serving

1 oz. chèvre per person
1 baguette
Best olive oil
Big pinch of thyme or
   herbes des Provence
1 clove garlic, peeled & crushed

1 to 2 c. greens per person,
   washed & dried
Vinaigrette dressing
   (See pages 202 & 206.)
Good olives

    Pre-heat oven to 400°. Slice chèvre into rounds, four or five rounds from a 5-oz. cheese. Slice baguette into thin rounds. Place each round of chèvre on top of a baguette slice, making small open-face sandwiches, and set on a small baking pan. Top each round of chèvre with a few drops of olive oil and a big pinch of thyme or herbes des Provence, and crushed garlic. (If you have fresh herbs such as chives, thyme, parsley and rosemary, mince ½ teaspoon for each serving.)

    Bake until chèvre is warm and soft, 10 to 15 minutes. While chèvre is baking, wash and dry greens, dress with vinaigrette and arrange nicely on individual plates.

    Remove chèvre "sandwiches" from oven and place each in the center of a plate of greens and garnish with olives. Serve immediately with remaining baguette slices.

THE EPITOME OF STYLE

I want to look good when I go out.

—Marshall Wells

Marsha's father explained to his family why he had to dress impeccably to be admitted to the hospital.

 Salads

Anne's Oasis Avocado & Mango Salad

Lucky you if you're invited to Anne and John's house in Melbourne on a hot summer day. Their patio garden, Anne's perfect creation, provides coolness, comfort and inspiration among the hanging baskets, roses, gardenias, fuschias and even a topiary giraffe. Fortunately, Anne and John think nothing of inviting 80 people for afternoon tea, giving the pleasure of their hospitality to many. • If you're really lucky, their daughters Belinda and Suzanne will fill you in on the finer points of cricket, including the answer to the great question, "When is an over over over there?" • John Kumnick is Catherine's Australian brother and Anne his wife. • Anne served this marvelous salad on a hot summer evening, and it is forever associated with the pleasure of sitting in their sweet garden oasis. • This is high on our list of porch food.

Serves 6

1 head of butter lettuce
½ lb. bacon (about 6 thick slices),
   cut in 1-inch pieces
2 ripe avocados, peeled & cubed
2 mangoes, peeled & cubed
   (See method on page 297.)
½ c. whole walnuts (2 oz.)

Dressing:
¼ c. olive oil
2 T. lemon juice
1 t. Dijon mustard

    Wash lettuce thoroughly, tear into bite-size pieces and spin or shake dry. Wrap in a tea towel and crisp in refrigerator while cooking bacon. Cook bacon in a frying pan over medium-high heat until crisp. Drain on paper towels.

    Put lettuce in a serving bowl and arrange bacon, avocados, mangoes and walnuts attractively on top of it. Combine ingredients for dressing in a small bowl or jar. Shake or whisk thoroughly. Drizzle over salad and serve.

MAKING PLANS

In January 1984 Shelley and I had hatched a plan to meet at the Athens airport in May. Shelley would arrive from California and I would already be in Athens at the end of my trip around the world. With our combined imaginative powers, Shelley and I could not have pictured John as a player in that future reunion. (John and I had met in Nepal in March.)

With a bunch of iris bought from a street vendor en route to the airport, I stood waiting expectantly, scanning the crowd. There she was at the long appointed hour, her smile and enthusiasm matching my own, our reunion a triumph of hopes and plans. Shelley carried all the news of my previous life in San Francisco plus an envelope of love offerings from John in Oregon who had already established communication with my family and friends.

It's magic. You create a plan, write something expectantly on your calendar, make the arrangements and then, lo and behold, that plan becomes a reality in an airport halfway around the world.

Generic Salads

Catherine grew up eating her mother's coleslaw, carrot-raisin and Waldorf salads. These salads still evoke pleasant memories. • The grown-up Catherine once had the pleasure of staying at the Waldorf Astoria Hotel in New York City on a business trip. At the end of the day, she traded business-wear for her flannel nightie, called room service and ordered a Waldorf salad and a split of champagne for dinner. The business long forgotten, this dinner remains a happy memory of a perfect meal accompanied by Glenda Jackson as Hedda Gabler on public television. A night on the town.

Serves 6

Cole Slaw:
1 small head of cabbage, grated or
    shredded (about 6 cups)
1 carrot, grated
1 apple, peeled, cored & diced
1 t. celery seed

Carrot & Raisin:
5 or 6 carrots (about 6 cups), grated
½ c. walnuts or pecans (2 oz.), chopped
½ c. raisins (about 3-⅓ oz.)

Waldorf:
3 large, tart green apples, cored & diced
    (Granny Smith, Newtown or Pippin)
1 c. celery (2 stalks), thinly sliced
½ c. nuts (2 oz.), chopped
½ c. currants (about 2 oz.)

Dressing:
8 oz. can crushed pineapple
¼ c. plain yogurt or sour cream
¼ c. mayonnaise

Choose your salad and combine ingredients in a serving bowl. For dressing, mix together pineapple (including juice), yogurt or sour cream, and mayonnaise in a small bowl. Pour over salad and mix well. Serve immediately or chill and serve.

AN EDITORIAL ON FAST FOOD

Fast food is an egregious oxymoron. You can eat fast food, as most do, on the run and in your car, but under such adverse conditions, it is not food. Fast — yes, convenient — yes, calories — yes, food — no. Someday it will be proved that meals are less nutritious eaten on the run, standing up or in front of a television set. How can anyone digest food eaten while watching a discussion of hemorrhoids, athlete's foot, dandruff or headaches?

Non-dairy creamer takes another piece of the cake in the oxymoron division. It makes you wonder, doesn't it, about who's been smoking what for how long? Meanwhile, please do NOT pass the salt-free salt or the bottle of I Can't Believe It's Not Butter.

Marjorie's LoCal Potato Salad

We've tried many recipes for potato salad, but we always return to the one Catherine remembers from childhood, her mother Marjorie's. It's the basic American salad of its era. • LoCal was John's father's designation for Southern — as in Lower — California. • In our low fat era, we also find it a great relief to eat a lot of mayonnaise once in awhile. This salad offers the perfect opportunity.

Serves 12

12 medium potatoes, russet, white
    or red (Marjorie always used
    russets.)
8 eggs
2 bunches of scallions, chopped finely
1 medium bunch of celery, chopped
    finely (include leaves)
1 red or yellow onion, chopped finely

Dressing:
1-½ c. good mayonnaise (See page 266)
    (Substitute plain yogurt for
    ½ c. mayonnaise.)
½ c. Dijon mustard
4 medium dill pickles, chopped finely
    or ½ c. dill pickle relish
Sweet Hungarian or Spanish paprika

In a medium soup pot, cover potatoes with cold water and bring to a boil. Reduce heat, cover and cook until potatoes are tender but firm when pricked with a fork or paring knife, about 15 to 20 minutes.

In a saucepan, cover eggs with cold water and bring to a boil. If you have an electric burner, turn it off as soon as the water boils, cover and let the pan sit on the hot burner for 8 minutes. If you have a gas burner, reduce heat to low and simmer for 8 minutes. Remove eggs from hot water immediately, immerse in cold water for several minutes, then drain, peel and chop.

Drain potatoes in a colander. Cool until you can handle them comfortably, peel and cut in ½ inch cubes. In a large serving bowl, combine potatoes with hard-boiled eggs, scallions, celery and onions. Add mayonnaise, mustard and pickles. Mix gently until thoroughly combined. Top with a generous sprinkling of paprika. Cover, chill for several hours and serve.

GRACE NOTES

Our yellow Labrador retriever Harper took up singing before dinner when we have company. This tradition began as John's impromptu invitation for Harper to join our conviviality in his own language. Much to our surprise he responded enthusiastically and developed confidence in his own soaring vocals, including a kind of canine vibrato. Now even when we do not have company, he sometimes gives us a woof that indicates his wish to sing with us, his head back and nose pointed upward for the descending chords of his rich, rolling baritone.

Salads

Elemental Beet Salad

Beet-lovers ourselves, we know that the world is divided into beet-eaters and non-beet-eaters. Although this line is rarely crossed, sometimes this salad has lured a non-beet-eater. • The secret ingredient is balsamic vinegar. Use a good quality one. • We grow several varieties of beets in our garden each year, including winter-keeper, golden and early wonder tall tops. • John is convinced that eating a fresh, steamed beet makes him feel like Popeye after his spinach.

Serves 6-8

8 medium beets
⅓ c. balsamic vinegar
2 sprigs parsley, chopped finely

Remove greens from beets leaving about 1-inch of stems. Scrub beets in cold water. Steam them in a soup pot on top of the stove until tender, 20 to 40 minutes, depending on the size of the beets. Or pre-heat oven to 400°. Place beets in a casserole with about 1-inch of water and a tight fitting cover. Steam beets in oven for 20 to 40 minutes.

Remove from heat. Peel beets as soon as they are cool enough to handle and cut into bite-sized pieces. In a medium-sized serving bowl, immediately toss warm beets with balsamic vinegar. Garnish with chopped parsley and serve at room temperature or chilled.

THE ROOT OF THE MATTER

We never thought much about turnips until we arrived in Scotland in December. There we watched sheep feed contentedly in fields spotted with uprooted turnips, one of the earliest cultivated vegetables and actually an enlarged stem, not a root. In spite of the enthusiasm showed by these sheep, we did not have much interest in turnips.

Then we met Bobby Mann who grew up near Tillamook, Oregon. As a child, when he was supposed to be practicing his violin, he was off fishing with his brother fortified by raw turnips scavenged from the surrounding fields where they were grown as cattle fodder.

When Bobby Mann came to dinner at Emmy's, she remembered his love of turnips and secured one through a phone call to a friend with a garden. She placed the fresh turnip in the middle of a plate surrounded by tortilla chips and guacamole. Bobby took the turnip in hand, quickly peeled and sliced it with the deftness of a master. He ground fresh pepper on the first slice and bit into it with relish, a smile spreading across his face. Then we followed his example, amazed by the delicate, sweet crispness of a perfect, fresh turnip.

Carol's Bush-Proof Broccoli Salad

If you serve this salad, you'll be safe from politicians like George H. W. Bush who once publicly eschewed broccoli. • Carol first tossed this salad together for a family gathering in the late spring, liking the combination of colors, textures and flavors. A little of this, a little of that and she gave us a new favorite. • Hide the toasted cashews because they've been known to disappear while the guests were visiting in the kitchen before Easter brunch.

Serves 6-8

Salad:
7 to 8 c. broccoli florets (about 3
   large bunches of broccoli)
2 sweet red peppers, chopped coarsely
   or roasted and cut in small squares
   (See page 188.)
1 medium red onion, sliced thinly
¾ c. cashews (3 oz.), freshly roasted

Optional:
2 c. cooked chicken, cubed

Dressing (About 1 cup):
⅓ c. oil (Combine peanut & sesame
   with an unflavored oil.)
⅓ c. rice vinegar
2 T. honey
2 T. marmalade or substitute grated
   peel of 1 orange or lemon
2 T. soy sauce
1 t. Worcestershire sauce
4 cloves garlic, peeled & minced

Optional:
1 T. Cointreau

Combine broccoli florets, red pepper and onion in a medium serving bowl. For a more substantial salad, add cubed, cooked chicken.

To make dressing, combine the ingredients in a small saucepan. Heat until bubbly. Remove from heat and add Cointreau, if desired. Mix gently and pour over broccoli. Toss and let sit for an hour or so at room temperature.

Pre-heat oven to 350° and toast cashews lightly for 7 to 10 minutes. Just before serving, top salad with roasted cashews and serve.

In summer when we have abundant broccoli in the garden, we make a batch of this dressing and keep it in the refrigerator in a small jar. Then we're ready to make this salad quickly by re-heating the dressing and tossing with fresh broccoli.

But I wanted Tutu to live to be 1200 years old.

—Madeline Raff

Five-year-old Madeline responding to news of her great-grandmother's death at age 91 in 1997.

Emmy's Winter-Relief Tomato Aspic

Emmy recommended making tomato aspic in winter when store-bought tomatoes aren't worth their salt. • She also urged us to grow our own sprouts and proudly demonstrated how to separate the sprouts from the un-sprouted seeds using her salad spinner.

Serves 8-10

4 c. tomato or V-8 juice
      or
4 oz. tomato paste & 1 c. stock &
2-½ c. tomato or V-8 juice

2 T. unflavored gelatin
1 T. Dijon mustard
2 t. Worcestershire sauce
½ t. Tabasco sauce
Juice of 1 lemon

1-½ c. mixed chopped vegetables:
    celery, carrots, green onions &/or
    mushrooms, thinly sliced

Optional:
1 avocado, peeled & cubed
Juice of 1 lemon

Endive, lettuce, arugula or sprouts
Mayonnaise (See page 266.)

In a small saucepan, warm ½ cup of juice or stock over medium heat and dissolve gelatin in it, stirring well. Remove from heat and cool.

Pour remaining juice, tomato paste or stock into a serving bowl. Add mustard, Worcestershire and Tabasco sauces. Stir well. (If you use the well-flavored "Snappy V-8," then you may want to omit all or part of the additional seasoning.) Add cooled gelatin mixture and mix well.

Prepare vegetables and add to the aspic. Mix together gently. In a small bowl, coat cubed avocado with lemon juice and add to tomato mixture in serving bowl. Stir to distribute evenly. Cover and chill aspic for several hours until firm. Serve with endive, lettuce leaves or sprouts, and top with homemade mayonnaise.

MOLDED ASPIC • Oil a 2-quart mold lightly and pour tomato-vegetable mixture into it. Chill thoroughly.

GELATIN GYMNASTICS

To un-mold aspic, fill sink with several inches of hot tap water. (Depth depends on size of mold.) Set chilled mold in hot water for 15 seconds, taking care not to splash aspic. Remove mold from water, top with a serving plate and invert quickly. If aspic does not release right away, repeat water bath for another 10 seconds. Garnish with greens and serve immediately.

 Salads

House Whiskey Chicken Salad

For many years, Laney and Bill House were our fearless leaders on hiking trails in the Grand Tetons. At the ranch we visited with Emmy and the Judge, everyone affixed name labels to their own liquor bottles that were stored at the bar. Laney and Bill wondered why their bottle was always empty until they realized that "House Whiskey" always goes first.

Serves 6-8

4 c. cooked chicken, cubed
  (2 whole chicken breasts)
1-½ c. seedless raisins (about 10 oz.)
2 c. celery (about 6 stalks), chopped
Chutney (See page 269.)

Dressing:
¾ c. homemade mayonnaise
  (See page 266.)
¼ c. sour cream
1 t. lemon juice
2 t. or more curry powder

In a mixing bowl, toss together chicken, raisins and celery. In a small bowl, combine all of the ingredients for dressing and mix well. Pour dressing over salad and toss. Cover and chill thoroughly. Serve with chutney.

Exultation is the going
Of an inland soul to sea,
Past the houses — past the headlands —
Into deep Eternity —

Bred as we, among the mountains,
Can a sailor understand
The divine intoxication
Of the first league out from land?

—Emily Dickinson
(1859)

Emmy sent this note in 1995: "I learned it! Not (nothing!!) easy. Does it grab you? Having poems stored in your head is the best of resources."

Cheerful Chinese Chicken Salad

This recipe came from a friend of a friend of Dean and Lisa's. We first ate it in the dead of winter during a snowstorm, cheered by its beautiful colors and textures. We like the combination of intense ginger pickles, spicy chicken and crisp lettuce. It is another great salad for summer evenings on the porch.

Serves 4-6

Chicken:
3 or 4 half chicken breasts
　　(about 3 c. cooked & shredded)
¼ c. soy sauce
¼ t. powdered ginger
½ t. powdered garlic

Dressing:
18 oz. jar of sweet preserved red
　　ginger slices (pickled ginger)
2 T. unflavored vegetable oil
1 T. powdered mustard

1 small head of lettuce, chopped
　　(We like Romaine, but the original
　　recipe called for iceberg.)
5 green onions, slivered in 1-½ inch
　　lengths
½ c. cilantro, coarsely chopped
1 medium carrot, grated
½ sweet red pepper, thinly sliced
1 to 2 T. sesame seeds, freshly toasted
　　(Toast in the oven at 400° for 2-3
　　minutes or in a frying pan over
　　medium-high heat.)

Look for pickled red ginger slices in Asian grocery stores; Tung Chun and Mee Chun are two brand names that we have found.

Pre-heat over to 350°. Remove skin from chicken breasts. Coat with soy sauce, sprinkle with powdered ginger and garlic. Wrap chicken in foil or place in a covered casserole. Bake 20 to 30 minutes until done, but not overcooked. Remove from oven and cool. Shred by hand.

Drain preserved ginger and chop coarsely in a food processor. (It's messy by hand.) In a serving bowl, toss shredded chicken with chopped ginger, oil and mustard. Prepare ahead to this point, cover and refrigerate for several hours or overnight.

Wash lettuce thoroughly in cold water and spin or shake dry. Chop into ½ inch shred. Wrap in a tea towel and crisp in the refrigerator.

Before serving, toss chicken-ginger mixture with lettuce and remaining ingredients. Serve immediately.

SOUND ADVICE

Ride my curves gently.

—Sign on a high mountain road between
Leh & Lekir in Ladakh, India.

The Gypsy Bhagwan's Shrimp Salad

There was a young lady from Crow
Who went to the ocean real slow.
She got to Smith River,
There met a high liver
Who showed her where doublewides go.

—The Gypsy Bhagwan,
an alias of Bruce LeFavour

Serves 4 as a main course
or more as an appetizer

1-½ lbs. cooked bay shrimp
Juice of ½ lemon
⅓ c. good mayonnaise (See page 266.)

1 to 2 T. Thai sweet chile sauce
2 shallots or 1 bunch of green
onions, chopped finely

Combine ingredients in a serving bowl. Toss together gently. Serve immediately or chill before serving. This is a great summer dinner salad or an easy appetizer served on crackers or toast triangles. (See baked toast on page 59.)

THE VISION THING

One summer evening I spotted a young deer in our upper pasture, probably the one who had been pruning our newly planted trees. I called Ivy, our border collie, and pointed in the direction of the deer. Off she went and the deer, seeing a dog heading its way, made haste for quieter pastures. Ivy stopped abruptly and gave me one of her "what on earth are you trying to tell me" looks. She ran because she had been directed to run, but she hadn't seen the deer at all. She didn't have eyes for deer.

Sheep, now that was quite another matter. Ivy definitely had eyes for sheep. Riding in the car, she would spot sheep in a distant pasture and be riveted until they disappeared from view. She used to spend hours monitoring Barbara's flock of sheep in the pasture next door. She wasn't allowed into that pasture so she had to work "her" sheep from our side where she beat a path along the fence line.

We once took our dog Lil' Bit to visit Bruce and Faith. Faith's great old dog Wiggins came out to greet us. Lil' Bit walked up to Wiggins and stood directly in front of her. Wiggins was oblivious. We looked at Faith puzzled. "Oh," explained Faith, "she only sees big male dogs." Lil' Bit wasn't on her screen.

Ivy and Wiggins reminded us that we only see what we want to see or what we're trained to look for.

Bread

> *And they lived happily ever after and chewed bread together.*
>
> —An ending of Russian fairy tales

NOTES ON BREAD-MAKING

YEAST • Yeast is sensitive to heat. It begins working at about 50°, thrives between 75° and 80°, and dies above 120°. Proof yeast by adding it to warm water (about 75°) and stirring gently. Then let it sit until the yeast begins to work and the mixture becomes bubbly.

FLOUR • Use special bread flour milled from wheat, including red wheat, which produces more gluten in the bread-making process. The moisture content of flour varies by as much as 20% depending on weather, storage and type of flour, so you need to learn to gauge how much flour is required in a given recipe.

KNEADING • To knead, fold dough in half, push it with the heels of the palms of both hands, then pull dough back on top of itself, rotate ¼ turn and repeat until dough is smooth and elastic.

Gladys' Presidential Bread

Gladys was the mother of four children, wife of a political activist, an award-winning home economics teacher and a lifelong member of the League of Women Voters. She worked diligently for children's rights in Oregon. (See her thoughts about women's rights on page 158.) • We wanted Gladys to be President of the United States. In a perfect world, she would have been elected by a land slide, the first woman to hold that office. • Gladys was a great cook. There has never been better food than a slice of this bread with her home-churned butter.

Makes 2 loaves

2 c. milk
2 T. butter
$\frac{1}{4}$ c. honey
1-$\frac{1}{2}$ T. yeast
$\frac{1}{4}$ c. warm water (about 75°)
2 to 3 c. bread flour
 (See previous page.)

2 c. whole wheat flour
1-$\frac{1}{3}$ c. rye flour
$\frac{1}{3}$ c. oat flour
$\frac{1}{3}$ c. soy flour
$\frac{1}{4}$ c. sesame seeds
2 t. salt

In a small saucepan, bring milk almost to a boil over medium heat (scald) and skim skin from surface. Remove from heat, stir in butter and honey. Cool to lukewarm.

Add yeast to warm water in a measuring cup. Stir gently to dissolve and let sit until bubbly.

Combine 2 cups of bread flour and all of the other flours, sesame seeds and salt in a large mixing bowl. Stir in milk and yeast mixture. Mix until flour disappears. Turn dough onto a floured surface and knead until smooth and elastic, about 5 minutes, adding more bread flour as needed. (See previous page.)

Put dough in an oiled bowl or soup pot, and grease its top. Cover with plastic wrap, a towel, dinner plate or lid. Let rise in a warm place (approximately 75° to 80°) until dough has doubled, about 1-$\frac{1}{2}$ to 2 hours.

Turn dough onto a lightly floured surface and punch it down, divide in 2 equal parts, shape into loaves and place in oiled loaf pans. Cover with a towel or greased plastic wrap. Let rise in a warm place until doubled, approximately 1 hour.

Pre-heat oven to 350°. Bake until loaves are lightly browned and nicely crusty, about 50 minutes. Remove from oven and cool briefly before removing from pans.

KEEPING CURRENT

Make a new, young friend every year.

—Emmy Smith

One secret of a happy old age.

Mrs. Pfister's Nova Scotia Bread

Mrs. Pfister used to deliver loaves of her Nova Scotia bread to Marjorie and other friends who were recovering from an illness or surgery. A sure way to make you feel better! • Mrs. Pfister wrote that she liked the "evening assembly of ingredients" for this bread because she could have it ready for lunch the next day, filling her house with the delicious aroma of freshly baked bread.

Makes 4 loaves

2-¼ t. yeast (¼ oz. pkg.)
½ c. warm water (about 75°)
1-½ c. rolled oats
5 c. boiling water
2 T. butter
2 T. salt

2 T. honey
1 c. molasses & ½ c. brown sugar
  or ½ c. molasses & 1 c. brown sugar
14 to 15 c. bread flour
  (about 3-½ lbs.)

The evening before, add yeast to warm water in a measuring cup. Stir gently to dissolve and let sit until bubbly.

Combine rolled oats and boiling water in a large mixing bowl. Stir in butter and salt, then honey, molasses and brown sugar. Cool to lukewarm, about 15 minutes.

Add yeast to well cooled oat mixture. Then add 11 cups of flour all at once, stirring until flour disappears. Mrs. Pfister would then put dough in a large, oiled soup pot and cover it, letting it sit at room temperature overnight.

Mrs. Pfister wrote, "In the morning, you'll find this a sticky sponge and you'll need considerably more flour to get the dough to where you can handle it and make loaves without your hands being covered with sticky, wet dough." To do this, turn dough onto a well-floured surface and knead until smooth and elastic, about 5 minutes, adding more flour as needed, approximately 3 to 4 cups. (See page 215.)

Divide dough into 4 equal parts and shape into loaves. Put in oiled loaf pans, cover with a towel or greased plastic wrap, and let rise in a warm place (75° to 80°) until doubled or tripled once again, about 1-½ hours.

Pre-heat oven to 325° and bake until lightly browned and nicely crusty, 60 to 70 minutes. Remove from oven and cool briefly before removing from pans.

CLARITY WITH STYLE

I couldn't agree less.

—Betsy Strong Cowles Partridge

John's aunt's response to opposing points of view.

Aunt Solange's Honestly French Bread

Aunt Solange was Lisa's French aunt, an important distinction because Lisa also has a non-French aunt who lived with her husband on a houseboat in Paris for many years.

Makes 6 small loaves

1-½ T. yeast
2-¾ c. warm water (about 75°)
7 to 8 c. bread flour

1 T. salt
Cornmeal

In a small bowl, add yeast to ½ cup of warm water. Stir gently to dissolve and let sit until bubbly. In a large mixing bowl, mix 7 cups of flour, salt and remaining 2-¼ cups of warm water. Stir until flour disappears. Add yeast mixture and combine thoroughly.

Turn dough onto a floured surface and knead until smooth and elastic, about 3 minutes, adding more flour as needed. (See page 215.) Divide dough in half and place in two large, oiled bowls or small soup pots. Cover each with greased plastic wrap, a towel, dinner plate or lid. Let rise in a warm place (75° to 80°) at least 3 hours or overnight in the refrigerator.

Turn dough onto a lightly floured surface. Punch it down and divide into 6 equal parts. Roll each piece into a rectangle, then roll up and pinch together to make a loaf shaped like a large cigar. Sprinkle cornmeal onto 2 un-greased cookie sheets and set 3 loaves on each, about 2 inches apart. Make shallow, crosswise slices in the top of each loaf, every inch or so. Let rise uncovered in a warm place for l hour.

Pre-heat oven to 450°. Bake until tops are lightly browned, 30 to 35 minutes, and loaves sound hollow when tapped. Remove from oven and cool. These loaves freeze well after baking and may be re-heated, uncovered, at 450° for 10 minutes.

DEFINITIONS

"Do you do cocktails?" the American lady asked Mike Smith, the bartender at the Glendruidh House Hotel in Inverness, Scotland. "Yes," he answered, "I've been known to put water in whiskey."

Susanna's Bernese Braided Egg Bread

Susanna, a classmate of Catherine's in college, came from Switzerland and she taught her college friends how to make this traditional bread from Berne, called in German, Sonntigszoepfe. At Easter, she explained, the same dough is used to form Easter pigeons and on December 6th, little bread men — Grettibanze — are made from it.

Makes 1 braided loaf

½ c. milk
2-¼ t. yeast (¼ oz. pkg.)
1 T. sugar
¼ c. warm water (about 75°)
1 t. salt

1 whole egg & 2 egg yolks
3 to 3-½ c. bread flour
2 T. melted butter
1 egg white & 1 T. water

In a small saucepan, warm milk to lukewarm (about 75°) over low heat. In a mixing bowl, combine yeast and sugar and stir in warm milk. Add warm water, salt, whole egg and egg yolks. Mix thoroughly. Add 3 cups of flour and stir until it disappears.

Turn dough onto a floured surface and knead until smooth and elastic, about 3 minutes, adding more flour as needed. (See page 215.)

Put dough in an oiled bowl or a small soup pot. Cover with greased plastic wrap, a towel, dinner plate or lid. Let dough rise in a warm place (75° to 80°) until doubled, about 1-½ hours.

Turn dough onto a lightly floured surface, punch it down and divide into 3 equal parts. Shape each piece by rolling it with your hands into a 14-inch long rope. On a greased cookie sheet, braid the 3 ropes as you would hair. Brush braided bread with melted butter and let it rise again in a warm place until doubled, about 45 minutes to 1 hour.

Pre-heat oven to 375°. In a measuring cup or a small bowl, beat egg white with 1 tablespoon of water and brush over loaf to make it shiny. Bake until very well browned, 25 to 35 minutes, and the loaf sounds hollow when tapped. Remove from oven and cool.

FRESH AIR

If you must say something bad, say it out of doors.

—Emmy Smith

"Let's-Play-Neighbor" Focaccia

"Neighbor," Ruby's favorite game, was created by her mother Nancy. It began, "Let's play neighbor." To which the response was, "Hello, Neighbor." Then we employed all the fantasy or reality we wanted. Ruby sometimes "had" two babies, a newborn and a five month old. "Neighbors" were often returning from exotic vacations with stories of faraway places or we "went" to each other's houses, drank tea and chatted about our children. Ruby's children included Maria, Brown Baby, Josefina and Sniffy. Yes, Sniffy. • Sniffy, the Syrian hamster, was born simultaneously in Damascus and Ruby's father's imagination. Joey began Sniffy's saga as a bedtime story for Ruby and his legendary activities grew as much as Ruby did. Sniffy traveled frequently, including an important trip to Peru to help the government. He would also speed over to Crow Farm in his red sports car, his black van or his private airplane. His best exploit was riding around in Carmen's dress during the New Year's Eve performance of Bizet's opera. • As a reality check, Ruby began cooking with her parents. This focaccia is a family favorite. Nancy explained that she would measure while Ruby "dumped and pressed the buttons on the 'Squeezinart,'" Ruby's term for their food processor. Ruby advised that counting to five is enough time to process this dough, 10 would be way too much.

Serves 6-8 as an appetizer

Dough:
1 c. warm water (about 75°)
2 t. yeast
1 T. sugar
1 t. salt
3 T. olive oil
2-½ to 3 c. all-purpose white flour

Garlic oil:
3 cloves garlic, peeled
3 T. olive oil

Topping:
1 big sprig fresh rosemary
Coarse salt & freshly ground pepper

Make garlic oil by slicing garlic and combining it in a small bowl with olive oil. Set aside. For dough, add yeast and sugar to warm water in a measuring cup and stir gently to dissolve. Let sit until bubbly. (Nancy and Ruby skip this step.)

Measure 1-½ cups of flour into a mixing bowl or the bowl of a food processor. Add salt and yeast mixture. (Nancy and Ruby pour water, yeast, sugar and salt directly on top of flour in the food processor.) Mix until flour disappears or process briefly, no more than 5 seconds. Add olive oil and another ½ cup of flour and mix or process briefly. Scrape sides of bowl. Add ½ cup more flour and mix or process briefly.

Turn dough onto a lightly floured surface and knead for several minutes until dough is smooth and elastic. Place dough in a lightly oiled bowl, oil top of dough and cover with a dishtowel or plastic wrap. Let sit in a warm spot (75-80°) to rest until doubled in size, about 1-½ hours. Nancy and Ruby like to put this dough on a sunny windowsill, next to the wood stove or on top of the clothes dryer when it's running.   Turn dough onto a lightly floured surface, punch it down and knead briefly. Set it in the middle of an oiled baking sheet or cast iron griddle. Press it into an 8-inch round, let it rest for 5 to 10 minutes and then press it into a larger 12-inch circle.

Cover with oiled plastic wrap and let rise a second time in a warm place until doubled in size, about 45 minutes. Nancy explained that she sometimes omits this second rising to save time and bakes her focaccia immediately.

Pre-heat oven to 400°. Remove sliced garlic from olive oil and save to eat. Poke surface of dough with your fingers to make nice dimples an inch or so apart. Pour or brush olive oil over surface of dough. Break rosemary into individual leaves and scatter on top. Sprinkle with coarse salt and freshly ground pepper.

Bake focaccia until golden brown, about 20 minutes. Remove from oven, cut in wedges and serve immediately.

NEW PUP

Our border collie, Lively, looks the part of a comic creature with his "permed" fur and wild amber eyes. He comes from a farm near the Old Peoria Road in Harrisburg. He was one of four remaining pups from a litter double that size, born to a sweet, wild-eyed mom who didn't like seeing Lively leave home one bit. Lively's dad was a champion herd dog, we were told. He was once put on a sit-stay in the field and Sam, his master, forgot to release him. Sam returned hours later to find him in exactly the same place. This fine dog was shot in what Sam described as a neighborhood drug bust several months before Lively was born.

When we drove up to Sam's farm, we noticed puppies racing through the fields outside the barn. When Sam directed us to the barn to see the puppies in their pen, we laughed. As we entered the barn, the last puppy was struggling over the gate into the pen. All were breathing hard. Sam gave Lively credit as the leader of the pack. Sam's favorite and ours, too, Lively came home with us, sitting anxiously on Catherine's lap for his first agonizing car ride.

Lively was confused about his new life and John slept with him on the back porch for his first nights. It took Lively weeks to work up his courage to come inside the kitchen. It took him months to like riding in the car. It took him years to walk upstairs in the house. And he was never comfortable going down. He would get "stuck" on the last step that required leaving the comfort of brown stairs for the scary cream-colored linoleum floor of the front hall.

Bhagwan Bruce's Pizza

The paragon of international chefs, Bruce LeFavour always arrives at the farm with his small Honda filled to the roof with fine wines, the best breads the Bay Area has to offer, an ice chest chock full of provisions and his favorite books. He cooks beside us in the kitchen as if he were a mere mortal. He hasn't fooled anyone yet. No one makes pizza or anything else like Bhagwan Bruce. • The long, slow rising of this dough creates a delightfully chewy crust.

Makes two 10 inch pizzas

Dough:
½ t. (level) yeast
1 to 1-½ c. warm water (about 75°)
2-½ c. unbleached all-purpose
  white flour
½ c. whole wheat pastry flour
1 t. (heaping) salt
1 T. (generous) olive oil

Toppings:
Goat cheese
Mozzarella or fontina cheese, thinly
  sliced or grated
Shallots, thinly sliced or minced
Dried black olives, pitted & quartered
Fresh thyme, rosemary, sage, chopped
Olive oil
Fresh parsley, tarragon, basil or garlic
  chives, chopped

Begin making this pizza dough very early on the day you want it or the night before. Add yeast to ½ cup of warm water in a measuring cup. Sir gently to dissolve and let sit until bubbly. Combine flours and salt in a large mixing bowl.

Add olive oil to another ½ cup of warm water. Pour this and the bubbly yeast mixture over the flour and mix until the flour disappears. Add more warm water as needed.

Turn the dough onto a floured surface. Knead for several minutes until the dough has some bounce. Rest 3 minutes and knead again briefly until it feels right. (Yes, this is the tricky part.)

Place the dough in a well-oiled, straight-sided container, cover it and set in a cool place (approximately 60°) until it triples in bulk, about 12 hours. The slow rising produces a chewier texture. (If you use the same container for raising the dough as you mixed it in, then wash it, rinse in cold water and dry it well before oiling it again.)

Turn the dough onto a lightly floured surface, punch it down and let it rise again, covered with a tea towel, in a warm place (75° to 80°) until double in size, about 1-½ hours.

Pre-heat oven to 450°. Divide dough in half and form two balls. Roll each ball into a 10-inch circle and top with your favorite combination of cheeses and herbs. Drizzle olive oil over the top. Bake approximately 12 to 18 minutes. Remove from the oven and top with chopped fresh parsley, tarragon, basil or garlic chives and serve immediately.

Betty's Best Not-for-the-Dog Biscuits

We loved our visits with Betty in her Montana log cabin not far from the Lolo Pass. It was a cozy place, filled with dogs — Peaches, Albert and Murphy — and great views of the Bitteroot Valley. • Betty and her husband Billy had been out-of-touch with John for many years after they all left Colorado. Finally they tracked John down at the farm and drove up unannounced one Saturday. It was both a remarkable reunion for John and a great introduction for Catherine, the beginning of a new chapter in old friendships. • Peaches, Betty and Billy's diminutive white dog, raced into the hayfield, stood paw to hoof with three horses and looked them straight in the eye. When the horses took flight so did Peaches in a mad dash back to the house. That was the end of her brief career as a cow dog. • These biscuits are worth staying home for because they melt in your mouth and warm your hands.

Makes 18

1-½ c. all-purpose white flour	4 oz. cream cheese
1-½ T. sugar	1-½ T. butter
1-½ t. baking powder	1 egg, beaten
½ t. cream of tartar	⅓ c. buttermilk
¼ t. baking soda	Coarse kosher salt

Pre-heat oven to 450°. Sift together flour, sugar, baking powder, cream of tartar and soda into a medium-mixing bowl. (If you don't have a flour sifter, simply shake this mixture through a wire mesh strainer.)

With a pastry blender or your hands, work in cream cheese and butter gently until mixture resembles coarse cornmeal. With a fork, work in egg and buttermilk briefly until flour disappears. (Too much handling makes biscuits tough.)

Turn out dough onto a lightly floured surface and knead briefly until smooth, 5 or 6 times. Roll out dough into a rectangle ¼-inch thick. Cut in 2-inch squares, sprinkle with salt and lift onto an un-greased cookie sheet with a pancake turner, leaving 1-inch between biscuits. Bake until lightly browned, 12 to 15 minutes. Serve immediately with butter and honey.

RIDING LESSONS

It looks like he got rode hard and put away wet.

—Sally Cairnes-Wurster

Commenting on a photograph of San Francisco 49er quarterback Steve Young in an advertisement for milk. (*The New Yorker*, Fall 1995)

Leedy's Skillet Cornbread
& Kate's Mother-of-the-Princess Spider Cake

This family recipe comes from Lisa's grandmother, Leedy Garrison of Blooming Grove. Lisa explained that cornbread is part of the Texas tradition of soul food and is served with pinto beans cooked with salt pork and onion, a bit of green tomato chow-chow (chutney) and iced tea. The cornbread is used to sop up yummy bean juice. "Besides being tasty," Lisa wrote, "it is economical. Leedy and Great Aunt Nora claimed they funded their travel habits with soul food." • Leedy used white cornmeal and added a teaspoon of sugar. Lisa's mother omits the sugar. Nancy adds more eggs, corn and cheese to her cornbread.

Serves 6-8

¼ c. bacon grease or unflavored vegetable oil
1-½ c. cornmeal
½ c. all-purpose white flour
1 T. baking powder
1 t. salt
½ t. baking soda
2 eggs
1-½ c. buttermilk

Optional:
1 t. sugar
2 more eggs
1 c. corn kernels or creamed corn
1 c. cheese, grated

Pre-heat oven to 450°. Melt bacon grease in a large cast iron skillet in the oven. Combine dry ingredients in a large mixing bowl. In a second, smaller mixing bowl, beat eggs lightly and then add buttermilk. Mix thoroughly. Pour egg mixture into dry ingredients. (Add optional sugar, or corn and cheese.) Stir briefly until flour disappears. Pour melted bacon grease (or oil) into batter and mix briefly. Pour batter into hot, greased skillet. Bake 15 to 20 minutes until lightly browned. Remove from oven, cut in wedges and serve warm with butter and honey.

This cornbread makes a hearty breakfast served with butter and warm maple syrup, easier for a crowd than pancakes.

SPIDER CAKE

The "spider" in spider cake refers to a type of cast iron skillet with legs that was used for cooking in the fireplace. Kate, the highly accomplished mother of six-year-old Princess Madeline, gave us this old recipe for a sweeter version of cornbread that can be served as a cake, bread or a substitute for pancakes.

Substitute ¼ cup of butter for bacon grease, add ½ cup of sugar, ½ cup of flour and ½ cup of sweet milk to the above ingredients and mix as directed. Before baking, pour 1 cup of sweet milk gently over the top of the batter.

Bake at 450° for 10 minutes. Turn oven down to 350° and bake until cake tests done, 20 to 30 minutes. Remove from oven, cool briefly and serve warm.

Bread

Stella's Ageless
New Mexican Corn Bread

Catherine met Stella in New Delhi en route to Ladakh in Northern India where they visited winter festivals at Tibetan Buddhist monasteries. High on the Tibetan plateau, it was well below freezing as we admired the colorful ceremonial dancing in open-air courtyards. The intrepid Stella, then 75, was still riding her bike around New York City when she wasn't traveling or working in her dark room to process her remarkable black and white photographs. • She introduced us to this favorite recipe on a visit.

Serves 6-8

2 c. yellow cornmeal
1 t. baking soda
½ t. salt
2 eggs
½ c. unflavored vegetable oil

1-½ c. milk or buttermilk
17 oz. can creamed corn (about 2 c.)
1 to 2 T. dried red chile flakes or
   7 oz. can diced Anaheim green chiles
1 c. sharp cheddar cheese (4 oz.), grated

Pre-heat oven to 400°. Grease a 10-inch iron skillet, spring-form pan or oven-proof casserole. In a small bowl, combine cornmeal, soda and salt. In a larger bowl, beat eggs lightly and then add oil and milk. Mix thoroughly. Stir in creamed corn, then cornmeal mixture and mix well. Mix in half the dried chiles and half the grated cheese. (If you are using Anaheim chiles, add all of them now.)

Pour batter into the prepared container. Sprinkle remaining cheese and chiles on top. Bake until a knife inserted in the center comes out clean, about 40 minutes. Remove from oven, cut in wedges and serve immediately.

IN THE BAG

Sun hat, denim skirt, sweater, cotton jacket, shorts, jeans, 3 t-shirts, sleeveless top, skirt and top from New Delhi bazaar, batik sundress from Sri Lanka, bathing suit, bathing suit cover-up, running shoes, sandals, dress flat shoes, socks, 3 scarves, underwear, tights, leotard, diarrhea pills, face cream, shampoo, toothpaste and toothbrush, contact lenses and saline solution, flashlight and extra batteries, sewing kit, birthday present for sister Connie, Buddhist book, wooden mask of Buddhist god Sakra, Sri Lankan cookbook, guidebook to Sri Lanka, novel *The Name of the Rose*, book about Indian history, book about memsahibs in India, writing paper and pens, string bag, cocoa, curry powder, 1 kg. of tea, assorted sea shells, 1 water buffalo vertebrae, audio tape of Sinhalese music, camera, 8 rolls of exposed film, whistle & water purifying kit.

—Contents of Catherine's suitcase as she left Sri Lanka
during her trip around the world in 1984.

Fundamentalist Garlic Bread

Absolutely no substitutions or additions are permitted. If you're going to be a fundamentalist, garlic and butter are worthy fundamentals.

Makes 1 loaf

½ c. butter (1 cube)
10 cloves garlic, peeled & minced
1 loaf sourdough or French bread

Pre-heat oven to 350°. In a small pan, melt the butter over low heat and stir in minced garlic. Slice the bread in half lengthwise. Drizzle garlic butter over each half of the bread, arranging the minced garlic evenly with a fork. Put the halves of bread together and slice crosswise in thick pieces with a serrated knife. Wrap the loaf in foil. Heat until nicely toasty, abut 20 minutes. Remove from the oven and serve immediately.

DIET GARLIC BREAD

Garlic cloves, peeled

Olive oil

Sourdough or French bread, sliced

Cut cloves of garlic in half and rub on sliced bread. Brush olive oil on each slice of bread. Toast or grill bread. Serve immediately.

PERSPECTIVES ON PACKING

When John travels, he always packs a bathing suit and long underwear, covering the bases for extremes in temperature.

His mother, Emmy, always traveled with a compass, a whistle, a thermometer and a metal Sierra cup.

Catherine's mother Marjorie took a folding metal cup that she could easily fill from a water fountain.

Catherine carries extra underwear because the first time she packed her own suitcase for a family vacation she didn't take any, and it became a family joke. She also takes several books so she'll never be stranded without a good read.

Desserts

Do not try to taste honey if you see it on a thorn.

—An Ethiopian proverb

Marjorie's Appealing Apple Crisp
with Laura's Secret Sauce

Our food likes and dis-likes as children are powerful. Although we grow out of some tastes, such as Catherine's early passion for peanut butter and sweet pickle sandwiches, others stay with us. This apple crisp remains Catherine's sister's favorite non-chocolate dessert. • In the chocolate department, we loved Mama's "chocolate sandwiches," sweetened whipped cream between layers of thin chocolate wafers topped by a maraschino cherry. Yum! • Apple crisp is best made with tart green apples such as Granny Smith, Newtown or Pippin. • Our goddaughter Day Rose and her sister, Natty, get excited at the mere mention of their grandmother Laura's secret sauce for pies, crisps and cobblers of all types.

Serves 6-8

8 apples (about 6 cups),
   peeled & sliced
¼ c. cold water
¼ c. brown or white sugar or honey
2 t. cinnamon

Optional:
½ t. nutmeg, cloves or allspice

Topping:
1 c. all-purpose white flour
½ c. brown or white sugar
6 T. butter or Crisco
9 double graham crackers, finely crushed
   (about 1-½ cups) (See page 42.)

Optional:
½ c. chopped nuts, rolled oats or
   coconut

Pre-heat oven to 350°. Place sliced apples in the bottom of a shallow oven-proof casserole or baking dish. Pour water over apples and sprinkle with sugar, cinnamon and other spices.

For topping, combine flour, sugar and butter in a mixing bowl or food processor. Mix together with a fork or process briefly until it is the consistency of coarse cornmeal. (Add chopped nuts, rolled oats or coconut, if you like, and mix or process briefly.) Spread this mixture evenly over apples and top with crushed graham crackers. Bake until nicely bubbly, about 1 hour. Serve warm with Laura's sauce.

BLACKBERRY CRISP • Substitute 6 cups of blackberries for apples and omit water.

LAURA'S SECRET SAUCE

Make sauce by adding brown sugar to sour cream gradually until you like the taste. Stir well. Cover and chill before serving.

Desserts

It-Must-Be-Spring
Strawberry Shortcake

Catherine remembers eating strawberry shortcake for dinner on Sunday evenings in late spring after driving home from visiting Uncle Ed and Aunt Lucille in Ventura, California. We usually bought a flat of perfect strawberries from a roadside stand and ate at least half of them in the car. • Another favorite Sunday supper was waffles with bacon, and sometimes Mama made corn fritters. We looked forward to our oddball Sunday suppers.

Serves 8

Biscuits:
1-½ c. all-purpose white flour
2 t. baking powder
½ t. salt
2 T. sugar
Finely grated peel of 1 orange
¼ c. butter (½ cube), chilled
½ c. & 1 T. milk or buttermilk

3 pints strawberries (6 cups)
2 t. sugar
1 T. Grand Marnier

½ pt. heavy cream (1 cup)
1 T. sugar
1 t. vanilla

Wash strawberries in cold water and drain well in a colander. Remove stems and slice into a bowl. Add sugar and mash several times with a potato masher or fork. Stir in Grand Marnier and let sit. We prefer berries at room temperature.

For biscuits, pre-heat oven to 450°. Sift flour, baking powder, salt and sugar twice into a large mixing bowl. (If you don't have a flour sifter, simply shake flour mixture through a wire mesh strainer.)

Add orange peel and then cut in butter with a fork or pastry blender until the mixture resembles coarse cornmeal. Add ½ cup of milk. With a fork, work gently to make soft dough, adding the remaining tablespoon of milk if needed. (Too much handling makes biscuits tough.)

Turn out dough onto a lightly floured surface and knead briefly until smooth, 5 or 6 times. Roll dough about ½ inch thick and cut into 2-½ inch biscuits with a cookie cutter or water glass. Arrange biscuits on an ungreased cookie sheet with 1-inch between them. Bake until lightly browned, 10 to 12 minutes. Remove from oven and cool.

In a mixing bowl, whip cream, adding sugar and vanilla as it thickens. When biscuits are cool enough to handle, split them. Place the bottom of a biscuit on a plate or in a soup bowl, fill with strawberries and top with the other biscuit half, more strawberries and whipped cream. Serve immediately.

SAVORY BISCUITS • Omit sugar and orange peel, and proceed as directed.

Margot's Worth-the-Trip Pavlova

A 7,000 mile plane ride is a small price to pay for one of Margot's Pavlovas, the delectable meringue, whipped cream and fresh fruit confection which is Australia's great gift to dessert lovers. Margot's granddaughter Jane explained that passion fruit is the secret ingredient in Pavlova. Available in cans in Australia, we haven't been able to locate it here. • The name honors the great Russian ballet dancer Anna Pavlova (1881-1931) who was as light on her feet as the best meringue.

Serves 8

Meringue:
4 T. cornstarch
3 egg whites
1-⅓ c. powdered sugar (about 6-¼ oz.)
Pinch of salt
2 t. lemon juice or white vinegar
1 t. vanilla

Strawberries, kiwi, bananas, blueberries, peaches, passion fruit, grapes or other fresh fruit, sliced as needed

Lemon custard:
3 egg yolks
⅔ c. sugar
1 T. butter
Finely grated rind of 1 lemon
¼ c. lemon juice

½ pt. whipping cream (1 cup)
1 T. sugar
1 t. vanilla

Pre-heat oven to 250°. Spread foil on baking sheet, grease it generously and mark a circle 9-inches in diameter (11-inches for a double meringue). Dust with 2 tablespoons of cornstarch so it's easier to remove meringue after baking.

For meringue, beat egg whites in a mixing bowl at medium speed until they foam, increase speed to high and beat until stiff peaks form. Sift together powdered sugar, remaining 2 tablespoons of cornstarch and salt. Add gradually to beaten egg whites and mix gently with a wire whisk. Add lemon juice and vanilla, mixing briefly. Spread meringue on prepared foil in a circle, mounding around the circumference to make a shell.

Reduce heat to 200° and bake meringue for 1-½ to 2 hours or until lightly browned. Check to make sure the meringue is not cooking too quickly. Long, slow cooking is the secret, Margot advised. Remove meringue from oven, invert on a cooling rack and peel off foil carefully. Turn right side up and cool thoroughly.

LEMON CUSTARD • While meringue is baking, make lemon custard by lightly beating together egg yolks and sugar in the top of a double boiler. Add butter, grated rind and lemon juice. Mix thoroughly. Place the top of the double boiler top over gently simmering water. (See page 236 for double boiler technique.) Cook until custard thickens, about 7 to 10 minutes, stirring constantly. Remove from heat and cool.

Set meringue on a serving plate. Spread lemon custard over the bottom of it. In a small bowl, whip cream, adding sugar and vanilla as it thickens. Fill meringue shell with whipped cream. Arrange fruit of your choice attractively on top of the cream and serve immediately or refrigerate briefly before serving.

Desserts

Pat's Thrillingly Therapeutic Cheesecake

Pat Harris, the eldest of 15 children, raised four fine children of her own and at the same time became an outstanding family therapist. If this isn't miraculous enough, she's a fabulous cook who has provided remarkable meals for her family and friends on land and at sea. Pat is the only person we know who has cooked a hot breakfast while sailing offshore around Cape Blanco in calamitous weather. • This cheesecake is her family's favorite birthday cake.

Serves 12

Crust:
½ c. butter (1 cube)
9 double graham crackers, finely crushed
    (about 1-½ cups) (See page 42.)
¼ c. powdered sugar (about 1-¼ oz.)

Optional:
Seasonal fruit

Filling:
Three 8 oz. pkgs. cream cheese at
    room temperature
4 eggs
¾ c. sugar
2 t. vanilla
Grated peel of 1 lemon
1 pint sour cream (2 cups)

Pre-heat oven to 350°. To make crust, melt butter in a small saucepan. Add crushed graham crackers and powdered sugar to melted butter and mix until butter disappears. With your hands, press crust into the bottom of an 8, 9 or 10-inch spring-form pan.

To make filling, combine one 8 oz. package of cream cheese and 1 egg in blender or food processor. When thoroughly combined, add 8 oz. more cream cheese and second egg. Mix thoroughly. Then add last 8 oz. cream cheese and third egg. Mix well. Add the last egg, sugar, vanilla, lemon peel and blend well. Pour into crust.

Bake 50 minutes or until cheesecake is set. Remove cheesecake from oven and top with sour cream. Return to oven for 8 minutes. Remove from oven and cool on a rack.

Run a sharp knife around cheesecake to loosen it from the spring-form pan before releasing the spring. Gently lift off pan and set cheesecake on a serving plate, leaving the bottom of the spring-form pan in place. Cool thoroughly and then refrigerate for at least an hour. Serve chilled. Just before serving, garnish with fresh berries or other seasonal fruit.

MOCHA-KAHLÚA CHEESECAKE • Make syrup by combining 1 tablespoon of instant coffee, 2 tablespoons of cocoa and 3 tablespoons of Kahlúa in a measuring cup or small bowl. Mix together thoroughly. Before baking the cheesecake, pour this syrup over the top of the batter and swirl by running a knife through it, gently making small loops on the surface. Take care not to cut the crust. Bake as directed above.

PUMPKIN CHEESECAKE • Substitute 36 gingersnaps for graham crackers in crust. Omit lemon peel in filling; add 2 teaspoons of cinnamon, 1 teaspoon of powdered ginger and ¼ teaspoon each of cloves and allspice to filling. Continue as directed above.

Luscious Lemon & Pine Nut Cheesecake

This light and lemony cheesecake has the distinctive flavor of toasted pine nuts.

Serves 8-10

Crust:
⅓ c. pine nuts (about 1-½ oz.)
6 T. butter (¾ cube)
2 c. all-purpose white flour
⅓ c. sugar

Filling:
Finely grated peel & juice of 2 lemons &
  water as needed to make ½ cup
1 c. sugar
8 oz. cream cheese
16 oz. ricotta cheese
4 whole eggs & 3 egg yolks
⅓ c. pine nuts (1-½ oz.)

Pre-heat oven to 350°. On a baking sheet, lightly toast all of the pine nuts (⅔ cup total) until lightly browned, 7 to 10 minutes. Remove from oven and cool. Chop ⅓ cup finely for the crust and set aside the remaining ⅓ cup for the filling.

To make the crust, melt butter in a small saucepan. Add chopped pine nuts, flour and sugar to melted butter. Mix until flour disappears. With your hands, press crust into the bottom of an 8, 9 or 10-inch spring-form pan. Refrigerate for 10 minutes.

Cover chilled crust with a round of aluminum foil, wax paper or cooking parchment and top with pie weights, dried beans or rice. Bake crust for 15 minutes. Remove from oven, lift off foil and pie weights. (Discard beans or rice.) Return crust to oven until lightly browned, about 10 minutes. Remove from oven and cool on a rack.

For filling, make syrup in a small saucepan by boiling together lemon juice, water and sugar for 1 to 2 minutes. Stir constantly to dissolve sugar. Remove from heat and cool.

In a food processor or mixing bowl, cream two cheeses, eggs and yolks thoroughly. Gradually add syrup, mixing well. Stir in lemon peel. Pour into baked crust and sprinkle toasted pine nuts on top. Bake until lightly browned but still soft in the center, 30 to 40 minutes. Remove from oven and cool to room temperature on a rack.

Run a sharp knife around cheesecake to loosen it from the spring-form pan before releasing the spring. Gently lift off the pan and set cheesecake on a serving plate, leaving the bottom of the spring-form pan in place.

We prefer to eat this cheesecake at room temperature. Refrigerate it if you make it well ahead and then remove it from the refrigerator an hour or so before serving.

Desserts

Aunt Helen's Baked Rice Pudding

Carol said this recipe was "quintessentially Aunt Helen — simple, classic and trustworthy — with more layers than would appear on the surface." • Carol's Aunt Helen once explained that the success of this dish was measured by the layers of crust, the more the better. Long, slow cooking condenses the milk and produces a fine caramelized flavor.

Serves 8

6 c. milk
¾ c. sugar
½ c. uncooked rice
1 t. vanilla

<u>Optional</u>:
½ pt. heavy cream, whipped

    Pre-heat oven to 250°. Pour milk into a saucepan, add sugar and warm over medium heat, stirring constantly until the sugar dissolves. Remove from heat. Add uncooked rice and vanilla. Mix well. Pour into a baking dish, stirring to arrange rice evenly.

    Bake 3 to 5 hours, very slowly, stirring in the brown crust that forms from time to time. Milk will reduce by about 50% during cooking. (It took about 3 hours in Carol's conventional oven and 5 hours in our convection oven.) Pudding is done when it is thickened nicely, and rice is well cooked. Serve warm with whipped cream.

WISE WAYS

Sometimes in the middle of the night we hear the magic voice of an owl. The h-o-o-o-o-t, h-o-o-o-t is barely audible above the thick stillness of the dark. We listen hard to catch this call.

In the barn, we sometimes find owl pellets that contain the digested and regurgitated remains of past dinners, small museum displays of rodent bones encased in fur. They are quite beautiful. There have also been a few brown and white feathers scattered discreetly like treasures.

John once felt an owl fly noiselessly past him at the open end of the barn. Once Lisa and Zoë heard a hoot-hoot while they were in the barn. Thinking it was John imitating an owl, they hooted back and forth with the real thing. When John and I were walking by the apple tree, the owl flew over us swiftly and noiselessly in a friendly, aerial salute.

There does seem to be great wisdom in speaking just loudly enough to be heard, recycling your trash in tiny, tidy bundles and revealing your presence by the soft sound of your wings brushing through the air.

Memories-of-Childhood Floating Islands

Catherine's mother served floating island pudding in a cranberry glass bowl that had belonged to her mother. It was beautiful and soothing, her childhood favorite.

Serves 6

Custard:
3 c. whole milk
½ c. sugar
6 egg yolks, lightly beaten
Finely grated peel of 1 lemon
1-½ t. vanilla

Islands:
6 egg whites
Pinch of salt
¼ t. cream of tartar
¼ c. sugar
½ t. vanilla

Burnt sugar syrup (See following page.)

For custard, warm milk almost to a boil (scald) in a saucepan over medium-high heat and skim the skin from the surface of the milk. Pour scalded milk into the top of a double boiler and place over — not in — gently simmering water. (The water must simmer gently to cook the custard, **not** boil vigorously which can curdle it.) Add sugar and mix well to dissolve.

In a small bowl or measuring cup, beat egg yolks lightly and pour them into the scalded milk. Cook, stirring constantly, until the custard thickens, about 10 minutes. This custard will be thin. Remove from heat. Add lemon peel and vanilla and stir well. Cool. Serve at room temperature or cover and chill thoroughly for several hours or overnight.

FLOATING ISLANDS • Pre-heat oven to 250°. Spread a piece of foil on top of a cookie sheet and sprinkle 1 tablespoon of cornstarch over it. This makes it easier to remove the meringue "islands" after baking.

In a mixing bowl, beat egg whites at medium speed until they foam. Add salt and cream of tartar, and beat at high speed until soft peaks form. Add sugar tablespoon by tablespoon and then vanilla. Beat until the peaks are stiff and glossy. Scoop egg whites onto the prepared cookie sheet, making 6 or more nicely mounded meringue "islands."

Bake until a knife inserted in the center of one comes out clean, about 20 minutes. Remove from oven, lift gently off the foil with a pancake turner and cool briefly on a rack. Serve as soon as possible.

To serve, pour custard into a beautiful serving bowl or individual bowls. Float meringue "islands" in the custard. Drizzle burnt sugar syrup attractively over the top. Serve immediately.

Emmy's Back-Doorstep Burnt Sugar Syrup

Emmy put this syrup in jars and left it on the back doorsteps of friends together with a few cups of baked custard. Hmm, sweeter than flowers.

Makes 3 cups

3 c. boiling water (or substitute strong coffee for part of water)
3 c. white sugar

Measure 3 cups of water (or water and coffee) into a small saucepan and bring to a boil over high heat. Reduce heat to a simmer.

In a large cast iron frying pan, melt sugar over moderate heat, stirring constantly with a heavy spoon. This takes 10 to 15 minutes. Once melted, the sugar is a rich brown color. Pour boiling water (or water-coffee mixture) into melted sugar slowly, stirring constantly. Be very careful because melted sugar is extremely hot, and it bubbles wildly as water is added. For your protection, wear a cooking mitt on your stirring hand. Cook syrup over medium heat until it is the consistency of maple syrup, about 6 to 8 minutes. Remove from heat and cool.

Serve with ice cream or baked custard below. This delicious syrup keeps indefinitely in a covered jar in the refrigerator.

BAKED CUSTARD *(8 servings)*

Pre-heat oven to 375° and boil a kettle of water. Scald 3 cups of whole milk as described on the previous page. Add ½ cup of sugar, mixing until it dissolves. In a mixing bowl, lightly beat 5 whole eggs. Add them gently to the milk, stirring to combine thoroughly. Add 1-½ teaspoons of vanilla and mix well.

Pour custard through a strainer to remove bubbles, and then pour into a baking dish or individual custard cups. Top with freshly grated nutmeg. Set the dish or custard cups in a 9x13-inch baking pan, and pour boiling water into the baking pan to a depth of about 1-inch.

Bake until custard is set, about 1 hour, or 20 to 30 minutes for cup custard. Custard is set when a knife inserted in the center comes out clean. Remove from oven, lift out of baking pan and cool on a rack.

For an easy *crème brûlé*, substitute cream for half of the milk in this recipe. Serve with burnt sugar syrup.

 Desserts

Bessie's Fashionable Vanilla Ice Cream

Catherine was 7 when the Manz family moved to South Holliston Avenue in Pasadena. Our new neighbor Bessie Bankerd was still glamorous at 70 although her red hair had faded. She and her daughter Lois loved beautiful clothes and hats and still bought them frequently at elegant department stores called I. Magnin and Bullock's Wilshire. From time to time, the Manz girls would get a telephone call inviting us across the street for a "showing" of the latest fashions. A black velvet hat given to Mama by Mrs. Bankerd rested on the shelf of her closet awaiting an Audrey Hepburn moment. • Mrs. Bankerd was an excellent cook, and this ice cream was one of her specialities.

Makes about 1-½ quarts

2 cups whole milk
6 egg yolks
1-½ c. sugar

1 pt. whipping cream (2 cups)
2 t. vanilla
Peel of 1 lemon, finely chopped

To make custard for ice cream, warm milk almost to a boil (scald) in a saucepan over medium-high heat and skim the skin from the surface of the milk. Pour scalded milk into the top of a double boiler and place over — not in — gently simmering water.

Beat egg yolks lightly in a small bowl. Add yolks and sugar to milk. Make sure the water in the bottom of the double boiler does not touch the bottom of the pan. (Water must simmer gently to cook the custard, **not** boil vigorously which can curdle it.) Cook, stirring constantly, until the custard thickens, about 10 minutes. Custard will be thin.

Remove from heat and add cream, vanilla and lemon peel. Stir well. Cool to room temperature. Cover and chill several hours or overnight in the refrigerator. Freeze according to the directions for your ice cream maker. Serve with chocolate sauce on page 40 or burnt sugar syrup on previous page.

We have a small Krups electric ice cream freezer with a double walled bowl filled with a liquid that must be frozen before use. We fill the frozen bowl about ⅔ full with chilled custard. (Ice cream puffs up as it freezes.) The freezer compartment of our refrigerator does not cool this bowl adequately for making ice cream although it's fine for sorbet. Fortunately, our chest freezer does the trick.

BEYOND SWEET DREAMS

"It would be my complete honor and joy to make you just what your heart desires for your Christmas Eve birthday," wrote Andrea. And the sumptuous choices were chocolate peppermint cake; *crème brûlé*/chocolate *pot de créme*/butterscotch custard; triple chocolate peppermint trifle; gingerbread layer cake with cream cheese frosting; bittersweet chocolate *soufflés* with caramel sauce; sweet and salty cake (chocolate cake with caramel/*fleur de sel* frosting and chocolate *ganache*) or chocolate *mousse* cake with *ganache* and caramel sauce. And the winner was bittersweet chocolate *soufflés* that made our taste buds feel gloriously operatic.

Brazenly Blackberry Sorbet

*Blackberries grow like weeds in Oregon. Although we spend more time cutting them back and digging them out than we do eating them, the eating of a plump, sun-warmed blackberry straight from the vine is incomparable. • Old-timers argue about berries, comparing the more common big-berried Himalayan variety (**Rubus procerus**) with the native smaller-berried Pacific blackberry (**Rubus ursinus**). No comparison, they say, the native one wins, and judging by the name, local bears must agree. Introduced in 1885, the Himalayan blackberry was developed by Luther Burbank from stock sent to him from India, hence the name. • We're not too picky when it comes to berries for this sorbet which highlights the best of our summer produce, the blackberry, be it native or not. This sorbet captures the intensity of blackberry flavor and its rich color.*

Makes about 1-½ quarts

8 cups blackberries (4 pint boxes)
1-½ c. sugar
3 T. lemon juice

In a food processor or blender, purée blackberries in 2 batches. To remove seeds, force purée through a medium wire mesh strainer into a bowl, stirring and pushing the fruit pulp with a wooden spoon until you have released as much fruit as possible, about 6 cups. Discard seeds. Add sugar and lemon juice and mix thoroughly.

Cover and chill the fruit purée for at least 1 hour. You can freeze purée at this point, then thaw and use at a later time. Pour purée into bowl of an ice cream freezer and freeze according to its directions.

THE ROCKY ROAD

Mama's great friend Marian Reed used to invite my sister and me to take turns going for an overnight visit to her house in Covina, California, then out among the orange groves east of Pasadena. It was always a great treat to spend time with Marian because as a teacher and elementary school principal, she knew everything about kids.

On one of those adventures Marian introduced me to real ice cream at one of the new Baskin-Robbins stores. I was overcome by 31 choices and after long deliberation selected vanilla out of desperation. Marian was horrified and ordered rocky road for each of us. It was a turning point in my life to discover nuts and marshmallows in ice cream.

Lois-Bug's One-Shot Date Torte

The richly talented and entertaining Lois Bankerd, nicknamed Lois-Bug, did not cook. She did play the piano and sing like an angel . . . well, perhaps more like Billie Holiday than an angel. • After her mother died, Lois came to Marjorie — the Manzes lived across the street from the Bankerds — to get her mother Bessie's recipe for this date torte. Lois learned to make it for holiday gatherings, her solo effort in the kitchen besides broiling lamb chops for a succession of impossible wire-haired terriers named Tuffy, Brandy and Saddle.

Serves 8

3 eggs
¾ c. sugar
3 T. all-purpose white flour
1 t. baking powder
Pinch of salt
1 c. dates, pitted & chopped, 12-15 whole
  dates (about 5 oz.)
1 c. nuts, chopped

½ pint whipping cream (1 cup)
1 T. sugar
1 t. vanilla

Pre-heat oven to 325°. Grease two 8 or 9 inch round cake pans. Line with wax paper and grease again.

Combine eggs and sugar in a mixing bowl and beat until light and fluffy, about 5 minutes. Sift flour, baking powder and salt together. Sprinkle over egg mixture and fold in gently. Stir in chopped dates and nuts. Pour into prepared pans and smooth the tops with a spatula.

Bake until the torte is lightly browned and has pulled away from the sides of the pans, 25 to 35 minutes. Remove from oven and remove from pans immediately. Pull off wax paper and cool on racks.

Just before serving, whip cream in a small bowl, adding sugar and vanilla as it thickens. Place one layer of date torte on a serving plate. Top with half of whipped cream, position the second layer and then top with remaining whipped cream. Serve immediately.

COMPLICATED FRIENDSHIPS: IVY & EASTER

Our border collie, Ivy had a love affair with a brown-spotted, lop-eared rabbit named Easter. Easter lived at Ruby's house and was —you guessed it — a gift to her from the Easter Bunny one year. Whenever we would visit Ruby and her parents, Ivy would jump from the car and race out back to check on her friend Easter. It was her duty and, perhaps, her pleasure.

Ruby's mom Nancy reported that Ivy once spent three hours sitting patiently below Easter's cage. Finally Nancy had to separate Ivy from Easter because all of that dogged devotion was making Easter anxious.

Desserts 🐦

Sofia's Championship Baklava

We love the story of Sofia's father Tommy Galson winning his national boxing title in the 1920's and then going home to Greece to bring back his bride, Sofia's mother Evagelia. • We think Sofia herself is a champion in the kitchen and everywhere else. After a brief flirtation with law school, Sofia went to work as a "go-fer" at the bottom of the corporate ladder. Within ten years, she was named Assistant Treasurer, a role in which she had to dine with bankers in New York City instead of fetching sandwiches. From there she went on to become the Chief Financial Officer of the Pacific Stock Exchange. Then she added wife and soccer mom to her resume.

Makes 30

Syrup:
1-½ c. water
2 c. honey or sugar
8 or 10 whole cloves

½ lb. sweet butter (2 cubes)
1 lb. phyllo pastry leaves

Filling:
1 lb. shelled walnuts (4 cups), chopped
1 c. sugar
8 oz. Zwieback crackers or
   2 c. bread-crumbs, finely ground
1 T. cinnamon
Dash of nutmeg

The day before, make syrup by combining water, honey and cloves in a saucepan and bringing to a boil over medium heat. Boil 10 minutes, skimming foam and stirring well. Remove from heat, cool to room temperature. Refrigerate while preparing the filling, assembling and baking the baklava. Pre-heat oven to 300°.

FILLING • Combine chopped walnuts, sugar, crumbs, cinnamon and nutmeg in a mixing bowl. Toss together thoroughly.

In a small pan, melt butter. Brush a 9x13-inch baking pan with melted butter. Keep phyllo pastry leaves moist under a damp tea towel. Lay two pastry leaves on the bottom of the baking pan and brush with melted butter. Add two more pastry leaves and brush with butter again. Sprinkle the filling evenly over buttered phyllo. Repeat two layers of pastry leaves, butter and filling until you have used up everything, ending with four phyllo leaves on top, brushed with the last of the butter. (Sometimes we have a few pastry leaves left over.)

Bake baklava until lightly browned, about 45 minutes. Remove from oven and pour cold syrup over baklava immediately. Let baklava sit overnight. With a sharp knife, cut in diamonds or squares, remove from pan and store in an airtight container.

The main thing an old cat remembers is how to meow.

—A Bulgarian proverb

From Amos Oz' novel, *Fima*

Lisa's Well Polished Pie Crust

No one handles a chain saw or a classroom or a child or a goose or a computer or a problem like Lisa. She is the original Jack-of-all-trades. When she was applying for her first teaching job in the public schools, John wrote a recommendation that said Lisa's involvement with any undertaking would guarantee success. She's that good. He also wrote that she would be teacher-of-the-year within three years. She was. Soon after, she was called to Washington to receive a national award for the energy conservation program that she designed and implemented in our school district. These are the least of her accomplishments. Now there is Zoë, her daughter and our goddaughter. Zoë at age 5 was nearly 42. Now at 17, she's the valedictorian of her high school graduating class.

Makes one 8 or 9 inch pie crust

⅓ c. Crisco or butter (about 5-½ T.)
1 c. all-purpose white flour
½ t. salt
3 T. cold water

Sally's variation:
½ T. more shortening or butter
½ t. vinegar, white or cider

Mix Crisco or butter, flour and salt together with a fork or pastry blender until the mixture resembles coarse corn meal. Add water and mix gently until the dough forms. With your hands, shape the dough into a ball, handling as little as possible. (Handling or working the dough too much makes the pie crust tough, not flaky.) Wrap the dough tightly in plastic and chill in the refrigerator for at least 30 minutes.

The precise ingredients in pie crust continue to be a matter of discussion among those who bake. Lest you think there is a last word, we have included Sally Cairnes-Wurster's variation. Vinegar is the secret ingredient in her crust. For more about discriminating taste, see Lisa's family story on the next page.

Roll out the dough between two sheets of wax paper until it is about one inch larger than the diameter of your pie pan. Don't linger over rolling or the crust may stick to the wax paper.

Remove top layer of wax paper and lift dough gently into pie pan, wax paper side up. Remove second piece of wax paper and shape dough to the pan. For fluted edges, press the index finger of your left hand on the edge of the crust while pinching the dough between the index finger and thumb of your right hand. Continue around the crust. Poke holes in the bottom of the crust with a fork and chill at least 30 minutes. Overnight is fine.

PRE-BAKED CRUST • Pre-heat the oven to 400°. Bake crust until the edges are lightly browned, 12 to 15 minutes.

A PIE CRUST TIP

Lisa keeps her crust crisp by spreading a little egg white evenly over the bottom of it and then letting it dry before baking.

Desserts

Norma's Stolen-from-the-Crows Texas Pecan Pie

This recipe is the result of extensive testing by Lisa's mother, Norma, and her mother, Leedy. They concluded that white corn syrup was better than dark and the initial baking at high temperature is essential to toast the nuts and set the crust. The secret ingredient is white vinegar that cuts the sweetness.
• Norma explained that she uses an extra half-cup of nuts in her pecan pie in good years when she gets her share of the pecans before the crows. Although chopping the pecans makes the pie easier to cut, "at covered dish dinners, the pie with the whole pecans goes first," observed Norma. Esthetics count.

Serves 8

3 eggs
1 c. white corn syrup
¼ c. sugar
1 to 1-½ c. whole pecans

2 T. melted butter
1 capful white vinegar
1 t. vanilla
1 unbaked pie shell (See previous page.)

Pre-heat oven to 450°. In a medium-mixing bowl, beat eggs together by hand and add corn syrup, sugar, pecans, melted butter, vinegar and vanilla. Mix gently. Norma cautioned against using a mixer because vigorous beating causes the top of the pie to have "an unattractive, bubbly appearance." Pour filling into an unbaked pie shell.

Bake 5 to 7 minutes. Then lower the temperature to 300° and continue baking until the pie is lightly browned and set in the center, about 30 to 40 minutes. Remove from oven, cool on a rack and serve.

PECANS

A native American tree, the pecan is a member of the hickory family which grows wild from Illinois south to the Gulf Coast, including forests along the river banks of the lower Mississippi River Valley. Georgia is home to the largest orchards of cultivated trees. Pecans are a rich source of Vitamin B-6.

1 cup of pecans = 3-½ oz.

1 lb. of pecans = about 4-½ cups

From a brochure entitled "Sunnyland Nuts & Fruits," Vol. XI
(Sunnyland Farms, Albany, Georgia)

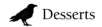

Henrietta's Perfection Berry Pie

As Marjorie would have been happy to tell you, her college sorority sister Henrietta was the best friend you could possibly have. She was also an exceptionally fine school psychologist and a wonderful cook. We love photos of Henrietta as a little girl feeding chickens in her backyard in Los Angeles and as a newlywed smiling joyously at her husband Bob. • *Henrietta's original pie recipe called for boysenberries or youngberries, but it's great for blackberries, too.*

Makes 1 pie

2 pint boxes of berries
  (about 4 cups)
1 to 1-½ c. sugar
1 c. water
¼ c. cornstarch, sifted

1 baked pie shell (See page 240.)
Whipped cream

We prefer NOT to wash our berries whenever possible. If you must rinse them, do so immediately before using them with cold water in a colander. (Store unwashed berries in the refrigerator until needed.)

Pour about half the berries (2 cups) into a medium saucepan and crush with a potato masher or fork. Add sugar, adjusting the amount of sugar based on the sweetness of the berries and your own taste. Then add water and cornstarch and cook over medium heat until thick, about 7 minutes, stirring constantly. Remove from heat and cool.

Pour half of the cooked berry mixture into the bottom of a baked and cooled pie shell, then add remaining fresh berries and top with second half of cooked berry mixture. Chill and serve with whipped cream.

If you have extra berries to freeze for pies, then mix each quart of fruit with ½ cup of sugar and freeze tightly sealed in plastic bags or small plastic containers.

THE WELL-CROSSED MARIONBERRY STORY

The Loganberry is a cross between a blackberry and a raspberry. It was crossed again to produce the Olallie and the Chehalem varieties. Then these two were crossed to create the Marionberry, named for Marion County, Oregon where it was grown for the first time in 1956. The Marionberry is Oregon's original contribution to the world of blackberries.

Holiday Foods

Who's going to raise the turkey?

—Marjorie Manz

A fundamental question asked by Catherine's mother while planning Thanksgiving dinner from her hospital bed.
(May 1996)

Beauty Queen Cranberries:
Sauce, Relish, Orange Jelly & Salad

On a holiday table lit by candles, cranberry sauce in a glass bowl is the beauty queen. You can't beat it for color or taste. • Orange juice and peel are secret ingredients in our cranberry sauce. • Cousin Ann gave us this easy recipe for a delicious, uncooked cranberry relish. Her orange jelly recipe makes a light dessert or a marvelous holiday salad with the addition of ground cranberries, oranges and pineapple.

Serves 8-10

Cranberry sauce:
Two 12 oz. bags cranberries
  (about 6 c.)
2 c. orange juice
2 c. sugar
Grated peel of 3 or 4 oranges

Cranberry relish:
12 oz. bag cranberries
$\frac{1}{2}$ c. sugar
$\frac{1}{2}$ t. cinnamon
$\frac{1}{8}$ t. cloves

Orange jelly:
2 T. unflavored gelatin
$\frac{3}{8}$ c. cold water
$\frac{3}{4}$ c. boiling water
$\frac{3}{4}$ c. sugar
$\frac{1}{2}$ cup & 1 T. lemon juice (9 T.)
3 c. orange juice
$\frac{1}{4}$ t. salt

Cranberry salad:
1 recipe orange jelly
2 oranges
12 oz. bag cranberries
1 c. sugar
16 oz. can crushed pineapple with juice

Pick through cranberries, discarding spoiled or discolored ones. Wash in cold water and drain in a colander.

CRANBERRY SAUCE • Bring orange juice and sugar to a boil in a small soup pot. Add cranberries and simmer uncovered until cranberries have popped, about 10 minutes. Remove from heat and cool. Stir in orange peel. Pour into a serving bowl, cover and chill until firm. Serve chilled

CRANBERRY RELISH • Combine washed cranberries, sugar, cinnamon and cloves in a food processor or blender. Process briefly to make a pleasant texture. Serve immediately or chill for several hours.

ORANGE JELLY • Pour gelatin into cold water in a small bowl and stir. Add boiling water and mix thoroughly to dissolve gelatin. Add sugar, lemon juice, orange juice and salt. Mix thoroughly until sugar dissolves. Pour into a 2-quart mold or serving dish, cover and chill until set. (See page 211 for instructions on removing gelatin from a mold.) For a simple dessert, serve orange jelly topped with blueberries and whipped cream.

CRANBERRY SALAD • Prepare orange jelly as instructed above. Wash whole oranges and cut into quarters or eighths. In a food processor or blender, process oranges, cranberries and sugar until nicely chunky. Add cranberry-orange mixture and crushed pineapple, including juice, to the orange jelly. Mix well and pour into a 3-quart mold or serving dish. Cover and chill until firm. Serve chilled.

Holiday Foods

All Things Considered:
Tip-Top Turkey Dressing

This recipe for turkey dressing evolved over many Thanksgivings with the addition of something one year, another thing the next until this version became the family favorite.

Fills a large turkey & more

**8 c. old bread, torn into bite-sized
  pieces (white, wheat, corn, rye,
  sourdough; mixed bread is best)**
1 c. currants (about 4-¼ oz.)
¼ c. brandy, rum or bourbon
1 lb. spicy Italian bulk sausage
¼ lb. butter (1 cube)
**4 c. onions (about 4 large onions),
  chopped coarsely**

**3 c. celery, including leaves
  (most of a bunch), chopped coarsely**
**2 large apples, cored & thinly sliced
  (peeled or not)**
1-½ c. whole pecans (about 5-¼ oz.)
¼ c. fresh sage or 2 T. dried
Big sprig of fresh thyme or 1 T. dried
Small sprig of fresh rosemary or 1 t. dried

Save old bread, including crusts, in a plastic bag in your freezer. About three or four days before roasting your turkey, thaw bread and tear it into pieces in a large bowl. Turn bread occasionally to dry it out. (You can also dry bread in the oven by lightly toasting it on cookie sheets for about 20 minutes at 300°.) Soak currants in brandy in a covered container for several hours or overnight.

On the day you roast your turkey, brown sausage in a large frying pan. Remove sausage with a slotted spoon and drain on paper towels. Set aside.

Sauté onions over medium heat in sausage drippings and butter until transparent, about 10 to 15 minutes. Add celery and sauté 5 minutes more.

In a large bowl, toss dried bread cubes, currants, sausage, onions, celery, apples, nuts and seasoning together until well mixed. Stuff your bird. (To contain this messy process, we usually position the bird in the sink while stuffing it.)

Put extra dressing into an oiled casserole, pour 1 cup of water or stock over the top and bake covered for 1 hour at 325°.

A PROPOSAL OF DUBIOUS DISTINCTION

Let's take a walk and I'll teach you Greek history.

—A Greek man
In conversation with Catherine
(Athens, 1984)

Paul's Museum-Quality
Mastodon Mashed Potatoes

Paul's research in American history led to his understanding of the origin of American consumer culture through a line connecting mastodons, the founding fathers, P.T. Barnum and his Fiji Mermaid. • Keep an eye out for Paul's provocative bumper sticker, "Mastodon Nation," the meaning of which is debated in parking lots. • Paul has taken ordinary mashed potatoes and transformed them into something as exciting as the Fiji mermaid riding bareback on a mastodon. • Onion is his secret ingredient.

Serves as many as needed

1 medium potato per person, peeled
1 medium onion for each 4 to 5
   potatoes, peeled & quartered
Salt & pepper to taste

Butter (3 to 4 T. for 5 potatoes)
Milk or cream
   (scant ¼ c. for 5 potatoes)

    White potatoes and elbow grease help make good mashed potatoes. White potatoes seem to work better because they have more starch than other types.

    In a saucepan or soup pot, cover potatoes and onion with cold water and add a big pinch of salt. Bring to a boil, reduce heat, cover and simmer until potatoes are soft when pricked with a fork or paring knife, about 15 to 20 minutes.

    Drain potatoes in a colander and discard onion. (Save potato water for soup.) Return potatoes to the pot and mash thoroughly with a potato masher. Running the potatoes through a ricer or a food mill makes the potatoes very light. (A food processor is too powerful.) Add butter and some milk, beating by hand with a wooden spoon and gradually adding more milk as needed until you reach the desired consistency and lightness. Season to taste with salt and pepper. Serve immediately.

CONNECTING THE DOTS

On a trip to the beach when he was about 18 months old, Tavi stared at the Pacific Ocean. He then announced to his parents, Paul and Anuncia, "It looks like apple juice." Nicholas, at about the same age, declared that the Great Salt Lake "tastes like potato chips."

WARNING

Anecdotal evidence indicates that it is possible to gain weight from reading certain recipes. To avoid extra pounds, read our extreme recipe on pages 324-25 of *The Spectacular Appendix.*

The Foster's Traveling Cranberry Pudding
with Heart Attack Sauce

The Fosters know how to eat and how to celebrate. This recipe came from a friend of Angela's mother-in-law who then famously baked it in a coffee can and carried it to the Caribbean in 1969. Angela continued the family tradition by carrying it on the train from Glenwood Springs to Oakland for many years. • *Once you've tasted it, you'll understand why the Fosters and Smiths cannot live without it.*

Serves 8-10

Pudding:
2 c. fresh cranberries, washed
   & picked over
1-½ c. flour
2 t. soda
½ t. salt
½ c. dark molasses
½ c. hot water

Flambé:
1 c. brandy, whiskey or rum
¼ c. sugar

Sauce:
1 c. sugar
1 c. heavy cream
½ c. unsalted butter
Pinch of salt
1 t. vanilla

Special utensils:
Covered pudding mold or a bundt pan
   or a coffee can & parchment or foil
Large covered pot, big enough to hold
   pudding steamer

Coarsely chop the cranberries in a food processor. (It is tedious by hand and risky in a blender.) Grease generously the pudding mold or bundt pan or coffee can, including the lid or a piece of parchment or aluminum foil to make a cover. Bring several inches of water to a boil in a large covered pot with a rack in the bottom. (Canning jar lids made a good substitute rack.)

Put the chopped cranberries in a medium-mixing bowl. Sift the flour, soda and salt onto the cranberries. Combine the molasses and hot water in a measuring cup. Add to the cranberry mixture and stir well. Pour into the prepared pudding mold. Cover with lid or make a lid with parchment or aluminum foil, tenting the top with a double pleat to allow for the pudding to rise, and then affixing it with a rubber band or string. Set pudding on rack in the large pot. Cover and steam for 2 hours at a steady simmer. Check occasionally and add hot water as needed. The pudding can be made as long as a week ahead and stored in the refrigerator. Remove from refrigerator two hours before serving and re-heat for 30 minutes in steamer.

SAUCE • Combine sugar, cream, butter and salt in the top of a double boiler or a saucepan pan with a heavy bottom over low heat. Stir. When butter is melted, add vanilla. Keep warm or re-heat before serving.

FLAMBÉ • To serve, unmold pudding on a serving platter. In a small saucepan, warm brandy, whiskey or rum with sugar. Stir gently until sugar dissolves. Carefully ignite and immediately pour flaming mixture over pudding. Serve rapidly with lavish amounts of sauce. Expect applause.

Excessively Well-Sauced Persimmon Pudding

The Smith family requires two sauces for our persimmon pudding. • The large fruited Japanese persimmon Hachiya becomes sweet as it ripens, and two or three will make a cup of purée. The smaller Fuyu, edible while firm, makes a cup with four or five fruit. • In Kentucky, John once filled his baseball cap with dozens of the walnut-sized native persimmon, Diospyros virginiana, picked on a walk in the woods. Then Emmy got out her Chinois sieve to make purée that we carried home for Thanksgiving, frozen in a plastic container. • Because competition may be a form of flattery, we hereby announce a contest with the Fosters to determine the most dangerous pudding.

Serves 8

1 c. persimmon purée	2 T. brandy or sherry
2 t. baking soda	1 c. all-purpose white flour
½ c. butter (1 cube),	2 t. cinnamon
at room temperature	¼ t. salt
1 c. brown sugar	1 c. currants (about 4-¼ oz.)
2 eggs	½ c. pecans (1-¾ oz.), chopped
1 T. lemon juice	½ c. dried persimmons (about 2-¾ oz.),
2 t. vanilla	chopped

Ripen persimmons at room temperature. The Hachiya variety is usually very hard and very tart when we buy them at the grocery store, but they ripen in a week or so. The Fuyu fruit may be eaten while still firm.

To make persimmon purée, peel the ripened fruit and purée pulp in a food processor or blender, or put them through a sieve or food mill.

Pre-heat oven to 350°. Grease a 9x13-inch baking pan. In a small bowl, combine persimmon purée and soda. Set aside.

In a medium bowl, cream butter and sugar until light. Add eggs, lemon juice, vanilla and brandy and beat until well mixed. Stir in persimmon purée and then flour, cinnamon, salt, currants, pecans and dried persimmons. Mix until flour disappears. Scrape batter into the prepared pan and smooth surface with a spatula.

Bake until pudding tests done when a knife or cake tester inserted in center comes out clean, 45 minutes to 1 hour. Serve pudding warm with sauces on the next page.

STEAMED PUDDING • Grease generously a 6-inch covered mold or bundt pan. Bring several inches of water to a boil in a large covered pot with a rack in the bottom. (Canning jar lids made a good substitute rack.) Scrape batter into prepared mold or pan, and cover tightly. (See instructions on previous page.) Set pudding on rack in the large pot. Cover and steam for 1 hour at a steady simmer. Check occasionally and add hot water as needed. Serve immediately.

Holiday Foods

HARD SAUCE

Makes 1 cup

½ c. butter (1 cube), at room temperature
1 c. powdered sugar (about 5 oz.), sifted

3 T. brandy

Cream together in a food processor or mixer. Scrape into a serving bowl. Serve at room temperature for a soft sauce. Cover and chill for an hour or overnight for a "hard" sauce.

LEMON SAUCE

Makes 2 cups

½ c. butter (1 cube)
1-½ c. sugar
Juice & finely grated rind of 2 lemons
¼ c. water
2 eggs, well beaten

Melt butter in a small saucepan over low heat. Add sugar, lemon juice, rind and water. Increase heat to medium, bring to a gentle simmer and stir well until sugar dissolves. Reduce heat, add beaten eggs and stir constantly until thickened, about 5 minutes. Keep heat low so eggs won't scramble. (If that does happen, you can rescue the sauce by processing it until smooth in a blender or food processor.) Remove from the heat and serve warm.

One must allow that a certain amount of carelessness
in one's nature often accomplishes
what the will is incapable of doing.

—Jane Bowles

Spoken by Miss Goering in her novel, *Two Serious Ladies.*

Barry's Quintessential Low Fat Chestnuts

In late fall, we looked forward to a "Priority Mail" package of freshly harvested chestnuts from Barry in Louisville. Chestnuts, Barry reminded us, have the lowest fat content of any nut, a boon for the health conscious. • He prefered his chestnuts roasted over an open fire. We also like chestnut purée, both savory and sweet. • Peeling chestnuts is hard work but worth it. Two of us can peel a pound in about 20 minutes. It's a good activity to share with friends over conversation and cups of tea. • To roast chestnuts, pierce them as instructed below and then roast in the oven at 450° for 20 to 30 minutes.

Makes about 2 cups

1 lb. fresh chestnuts (about 4 cups or 60 nuts, un-shelled)

Savory:	Sweet:
1-½ c. beef stock	**1-½ c. milk**
Several sprigs of parsley	**¼ c. sugar**
1 bay leaf	**1 vanilla bean**
3 T. butter	**2 T. butter**
Salt & pepper to taste	

Pierce each chestnut on its flat side with the tip of a paring knife or the point of kitchen scissors. (Chestnuts expand when heated and need an outlet so they won't explode.) Place chestnuts in a saucepan or soup pot and cover with cold water. Bring to a boil and simmer for 10 minutes.

Remove from heat and leave chestnuts in hot water, removing 3 or 4 at a time to peel. This important step keeps the skins soft so you can peel them more easily. Insert the point of a paring knife in the pierced hole and enlarge it enough to release the nut. Often the inner skirt of the nut comes with it. If not, rub nut between your fingers to remove it.

SAVORY CHESTNUTS • Cover peeled nuts with stock in a sauce-pan, add parsley and a bay leaf. Bring to a boil over medium heat and simmer covered until nuts are tender, about 45 to 60 minutes. Nuts should be soft when pierced with a knife. Drain in a colander. Purée chestnuts in a food processor or blender, adding 2 tablespoons of butter and stock as needed to make a purée the consistency of mashed potatoes. Season to taste with salt and pepper. Serve immediately or scoop into an ovenproof casserole, top with 1 tablespoon of butter in dots and re-heat covered at 250° for 25 minutes.

SWEET CHESTNUTS • Cover peeled nuts with milk, add sugar and vanilla bean. Bring to a boil over medium heat and simmer covered until nuts are tender, about 45 to 60 minutes. Drain in a colander and reserve milk. Purée chestnuts in a food processor or blender, adding milk as needed to make a purée the consistency of mashed potatoes. Use **sweet purée** as desired for cake filling or serve as mousse, topped with whipped cream. (See page 95 for yellow cake recipe using sweet chestnut purée as filling.)

MONT BLANC

In honor of the great peak that towers 15,771 feet over south-eastern France & northern Italy.

Serves 10-12

2 lbs. chestnuts for sweet chestnut purée (See previous page.)
•
Meringue shell (See page 230.)
•
4 oz. unsweetened baking chocolate
¾ c. sugar
3 T. butter
•
1 pt. whipping cream (2 cups)
2 T. sugar
1 t. vanilla

Peel chestnuts as directed on previous page and cook with milk, sugar and vanilla bean as directed for sweet purée.

Prepare meringue shell as instructed on page 230.

Melt chocolate in a small saucepan with a heavy bottom over low heat or in the top of a double boiler over gently simmering water.

In a food processor or blender, purée ⅓ of cooked chestnuts at a time, adding proportional amount of melted chocolate, sugar and butter to each batch. Using a ricer or spatula, create the slope of a mountain in the baked meringue shell, leaving a small central chimney for whipped cream. Prepare ahead and refrigerate at this point.

Just before serving, whip cream, adding sugar and vanilla as it thickens. Fill the chimney in the chestnut purée with whipped cream and serve immediately.

It's not what you do that makes you tired,
it's what you don't do.

—Emmy Smith

Quoting her friend, Fannie Brandeis.

A Christmas Stollen for Heroic Huskies

During World War II, a stuffed dog who resided at the Smithsonian Institution in Washington, D.C., found his way into the car of a Smith family friend who was doing Artic research for the U.S. Army on the design of back packs for dogs in the mountain corps. This friend dropped by for a Christmas visit. From the window, John and his sister Rachel spied the dog in the car and begged for him to be brought in. In he came. He was introduced as Balto and became their canine Christmas tree be-decked with ribbons, presents at his feet and a bottle of whiskey tied around his neck. • The Balto of John's memory was a St. Bernard, not the black-coated husky of the historic Nome photos. The hometown was wrong, too. Balto of Nome fame was by then residing in the Cleveland Museum of Natural History, not the Smithsonian. So, who was this dog named or nicknamed Balto? • This easy fruit bread might have been a favorite for a hungry dog or a tired musher. You can make it ahead and pull it out of the freezer when needed.

Makes 1 or 2 loaves

1-½ c. pine nuts (about 6-½ oz.)
1-½ c. all-purpose white flour
1 c. rye or wheat flour
2 t. baking powder
1 t. mace
½ t. cardamom
½ c. butter (1 cube)
½ to ¾ c. brown sugar
1 c. currants (about 4-¼ oz.)

1 c. candied lemon or orange peel, chopped (about 5 oz.)
1 c. dried cranberries (about 5 oz.)
1 c. sour cream or cream cheese (8 oz.)
1 egg
2 t. vanilla
1 t. almond extract
2 T. rum or bourbon
   (& a big shot for the musher)

Pre-heat oven to 350°. On a baking sheet, toast pine nuts until lightly browned, for 7 to 10 minutes. Remove from oven and cool. Chop 1 cup finely and leave the remaining ½ cup whole. Cover a cookie sheet with brown paper. (A grocery bag will do nicely.)

Combine white flour, baking powder and spices with cold butter in a medium mixing bowl or a food processor. Process until it resembles coarse cornmeal. In a second bowl, combine dried fruit, ground and whole nuts and rye or wheat flour. Add flour-butter mixture and mix well.

In a small bowl, combine sour cream or cream cheese, egg and flavorings. Stir in brown sugar and add to flour-fruit mixture. Mix together gently until flour disappears. Form dough into a ball and turn out onto a lightly floured surface. Flatten dough, fold it back on itself, kneading 6 to 8 times. Roll dough into an 8x10-inch oval, or divide and roll into two 5x9-inch ovals. Crease dough slightly off center and fold along crease with the smaller segment on top. Lift onto paper covered baking sheet.

Bake until lightly browned and a toothpick inserted in the center comes out clean, about 45 minutes. Remove from oven and serve warm. Or cool and wrap tightly in plastic or foil to freeze. Thaw and re-heat at 250° for 20 minutes.

Togo's Triumph: Revising the Balto Legend

We got interested in Balto because of John's early encounter with him. (See previous page.) Our investigations led us into spell binding dog territory.

At 5:30 am on January 31, 1925 the precious vials of diphtheria serum were delivered into the hands of Dr. Curtis Welch in the snowbound city of Nome, Alaska, the last stop of a grueling 674-mile overland journey. Twenty mushers and their dogs had carried the serum in relays from the railhead at Nenana where it had been shipped from Seward. Dr. Curtis had radioed for the experimental anti-toxin at the outbreak of what threatened to become a fatal epidemic in Nome, the isolated Inuit community of 1,700.

A black-coated husky named Balto and musher Gunaar Kaasen carried the fur-wrapped cargo on the final 55 mile leg of the journey and became the public heroes of this "Great Race of Mercy," now commemorated annually by a sled dog trail race called the Iditarod. Balto was a hero but not top dog.

The laurels of this epic journey belong to an intrepid 12 year-old Siberian husky named Togo, who weighed in at a scrawny 48 pounds, and Leonhard Seppala, Nome's best musher and three-time winner of the All Alaska Sweepstakes races in 1915-17. Seppala, a hardy Norwegian immigrant, set out from Nome with a pack of 20 dogs, including his prize dog Togo. Balto, a second stringer, was left at Bluff to provide relief on the return journey. When Seppala and Togo picked up the serum in Shaktoolik, they had already traveled 150 miles, including a crossing of the treacherous Norton Sound. They turned around for the return journey in a blizzard. With visibility negligible, Seppala simply trusted his amazing lead dog to pick the way through the fracturing sea ice in a perilous effort that might easily have ended in disaster.

At Golovin, Seppala passed the serum to Charlie Olson who relayed it 25 miles to Bluff where Gunaar Kaasen hitched up Balto, borrowed at the last minute as lead dog. Although their 55-mile run in blizzard conditions was impressive, it does not touch the astonishing 260 mile loop, crossing and re-crossing the Norton Sound, made by Togo and Seppala.

Seppala was angered by the omission of Togo from public credit for his amazing feat. Although Togo never raced again, he lived several years more and sired a line of sled dogs that race in Alaska today. Seppala lived to be 90.

Balto didn't fare so well. He ended up in a "dime-a-view" museum in California from which he and six teammates were rescued by school children in Cleveland. On hearing of the dogs' plight, they collected enough money to bring them to the mid-west where they lived at the Cleveland Zoo. After his death six years later, Balto was stuffed and moved to the Cleveland Museum of Natural History where he resides today.

Sources: An article by Paul McHugh (*San Francisco Chronicle*, March 16, 1998) and an Associated Press wire service report (*The Eugene Register-Guard*, March 1998)

Alice's Poem

STUFFED*

This is just to say
I made the stuffing
from your Crow Farm Cookbook,
the one with the calories
and currants and brandy
and five kinds of bread
and so much to dice, slow-cooked together
outside the bird, then slathered with
gravy and cranberry sauce
that I made like you said.

Such a memory feast,
comfort food for old crows
like us – and like you!
Thanks be for such tastes,
and for leftovers,
and old days, old friends,
a communion of flavors
that grow better each day.

Forgive me for
eating so much, and
forgive that I let my children
believe the stuffing this year
was one of my creations.
What's left
in the fridge
three days later
is still so delicious,
so sweet
and so cold.

—Alice W. Vining

Alice of Ann Arbor, Michigan wrote this poem as a
thank you for the cookbook. Alice also thanks William
Carlos Williams for inspiration. We hereby thank her.

*See note about "stuffed" on page 45.

Christmas Cookies

Christmas would not be Christmas without cookies. Some of us have vivid memories of our childhood homes filled with smells of holiday baking and then the delicious pleasure of eating the results, hoping to rescue enough for festive plates wrapped in colored cellophane to give to neighbors and friends. Gifts of holiday cookies can't be beat.

The recipes that follow come from several families and friends, old favorites based on recipes handed down from generation to generation. We've emphasized gingerbread because it is a favorite and, as Carol explained, every German family has its own special recipe. There are other German cookies plus several other European varieties.

Be sure to look at the cookie recipes at the front of the cookbook for shortbread and other varieties on pages 41-45 and 88-93.

A Quartet of German Gingerbreads

*This recipe for **Honig Lebkuchen** — honey gingerbread — came from Carol through her German mother-in-law Ilse Raff. As a bride and novice in the kitchen, Carol learned a lot about cooking from Ilse whose heirloom recipes include the almond gingerbread on the next page, hazelnut macaroons on page 260 and the torte on page 48. • German cookies are traditionally made weeks before the holidays and stored in tightly covered tins to "mellow."*

Makes 7-8 dozen

1 lb. honey (1-⅓ c.)
½ c. brown sugar
½ c. grated orange peel
   (6 to 8 oranges)
Juice & rind of 1 lemon
1 t. cinnamon
½ t. cloves
½ t. nutmeg or ginger
2 t. baking soda

½ t. cream of tartar
2 T. brandy
¾ lb. almonds, finely ground (3 c.)
About 1 lb. all-purpose white flour,
   (3 to 4 c.) (See pages 91 & 215.)

<u>Powdered sugar glaze:</u>
2 c. powdered sugar (about 10 oz.), sifted
4 T. lemon juice

Begin a day or two before you want to bake this gingerbread. In a large saucepan or soup pot, combine all ingredients **except** almonds and flour. Warm over medium-low heat until mixture foams, stirring constantly. Remove from heat and cool.

Add ground almonds all at once and then 3 cups of flour gradually, mixing well. Add additional flour (from the remaining cup) as needed to make a stiff dough. Divide dough in half and roll out ½ inch thick on two un-greased cookie sheets. Cover each with a tea towel and set in a cool place to rest for 12 to 24 hours. (Instead of rolling out dough, Carol suggested that you let it rest in the covered soup pot and then before baking, form it into walnut-sized balls.)

Pre-heat oven to 325°. Bake gingerbread until lightly browned, about 15 to 20 minutes. Remove from oven and cool on racks.

GLAZE • Combine powdered sugar and lemon juice in a small bowl. The consistency will be thin. Pour glaze over cooled gingerbread and let dry completely. Cut gingerbread in 1-inch squares with a sharp knife. Store in tightly covered tins.

STORAGE TIPS

Carol advised us to keep a small piece of apple or orange in each tin of German cookies to maintain the correct moisture, changing the fruit every few days for freshness.

Nürnberger Lebkuchen

Carol explained to us that every German family has its own recipe for gingerbread. This is the Raff family's almond gingerbread. Martin, a German exchange student who visited Pat and Sofia, presented them with a beautifully designed paper package of traditional gingerbread cookies air-mailed from his hometown of Nürnberg by his mother. They tasted familiar.

Makes 6 dozen

5 large eggs
1 lb. & 2 oz. powdered sugar
    (about 3-⅔ c.)
1 lb. unblanched almonds (4 c.),
    finely ground
Grated rind of 1 lemon
5 oz. candied orange peel (1 c.),
    chopped finely
1 T. cinnamon
1 t. nutmeg
½ t. cloves
¼ c. Zwieback or fine bread crumbs
2 T. all-purpose white flour

<u>Powdered sugar icing</u>:
2 egg whites
Juice of ½ lemon
½ to 1 c. powdered sugar (about 2-½
    to 5 oz.)

<u>Traditional decoration</u>:
Multi-colored sugar sprinkles

    Begin the day before or early on the day you plan to bake. In a mixing bowl, beat eggs well and gradually add powdered sugar, continuing to beat until mixture is pale yellow and light. Add remaining ingredients and mix gently to make a soft batter. Cover and refrigerate for 5 hours or overnight.

    Pre-heat oven to 325°. Line cookie sheets with brown paper or cooking parchment. Form dough into walnut-sized balls and place on cookie sheets about 2-inches apart. Bake until lightly browned, about 25 minutes. Remove cookie sheets from oven and set on racks to cool thoroughly. Then lift or peel gingerbread off paper. Depending on the moisture content of the flour, these cookies sometimes turn out with a lacier appearance.

    Although this gingerbread is delicious plain, icing is traditional. For icing, whisk together egg whites, lemon juice and ½ cup of powdered sugar, adding more sugar as needed to make a thin consistency. Spread icing on each cookie with a spatula and then shake multi-colored sugar sprinkles over wet icing. Let icing dry completely and then store in tightly covered tins. (See note about storage on previous page.)

ALMONDS

Almonds are not nuts but stone fruits like peaches and plums. We eat the pits.

Gram Manz' Bräune Kuchen

Catherine found the recipe for these "brown cookies" or molasses gingerbread in her mother's green metal recipe box with a notation in Gram's handwriting, "These are the cookies they are so crazy over." Who can resist such praise? • Attributed to Mrs. Gohlmann, all we know of her is this recipe. • Once when baking this gingerbread, we didn't have enough molasses, so we substituted a mixture of honey, golden syrup and sorghum. We also substituted pecans for almonds, all with excellent results.

Makes 6 dozen

1-½ c. almonds (6 oz.)
¾ c. citron (about 3-½ oz.)
1 qt. molasses (3 lbs.)
1 c. butter (2 cubes)
2 t. cinnamon
1 t. cloves
1 t. cardamom
2-½ lbs. all-purpose white flour, sifted
  (about 8-¾ c.)

2 t. baking soda & 1 t. warm water
¾ c. sour cream
2 oz. rose water
1-½ c. brown sugar

Powdered sugar icing or glaze
  (See pages 256-7.)
72 whole almonds

One or two days before you want to bake these cookies, chop almonds and citron together in a food processor or blender.

In a soup pot, warm together molasses, butter and spices. Gradually add 4 cups of flour. Stir well

In a small bowl or measuring cup, dissolve soda in warm water and add to sour cream. Add rose water and combine with molasses mixture. Then add brown sugar, chopped almonds and citron and remaining flour, about 4-¾ cups. Mix until flour disappears. Dough will be stiff. Cover and let dough sit in a cool place for 1 to 2 days.

Pre-heat oven to 325°. Divide dough in thirds. On a lightly floured board, roll each piece into a large rectangle about ½ inch thick. Fold dough in half, lift gently, place on cookie sheet and unfold. With a paring knife, score the top of the dough lightly in 2-inch squares to be cut **after** baking.

Bake until lightly browned, 20 to 30 minutes. Remove from oven. Cool briefly and cut in squares while still warm. Cool thoroughly and then frost with powdered sugar icing. Top with whole almonds. These cookies keep well in tightly covered tins. (See note about storage on page 256.)

To lie about a far country is easy.

—An Ethiopian proverb

Barbara's Meaty Thighs Gingerbread Cookies

From her Peace Corps posting in Guatemala, Barbara wrote of things she missed at home, "Butter, walls that go to the ceiling, ceilings, the symphony, National Public Radio, croissants, chocolate with flavor, potlucks, Red Hook Ale, hamburgers from the local store . . ." • Barbara used her magic with animals as a veterinarian. At home she had a remarkable bond with a sheep named Granny, who had separated herself from the flock to befriend Barbara. Granny died at 16, survived by many beautiful daughters. • "He's got meaty thighs," observed Barbara of healthy lambs as well as certain two-legged males. • These are the gingerbread cookies you remember from childhood, cut in shapes and decorated with raisins and red hots.

Makes 3-4 dozen

1 c. dark molasses (12 oz.)
1 c butter (2 cubes)
4-¾ c. all-purpose white flour
1 t. baking powder
1 t. salt
1 t. baking soda
1 T. cinnamon
1 T. ginger

2 t. nutmeg
½ c. brown sugar, firmly packed
1 large egg

<u>Optional:</u>
Raisins & red hots
Powdered sugar icing (See pages 256-7.)
Colored sugar sprinkles

Begin several hours or the night before you want to bake these cookies. In a 3 or 4-quart saucepan or a soup pot large enough for mixing cookie dough, warm molasses slowly over low heat. Remove from heat. Add butter and stir until it melts. Cool.

Sift together flour, baking powder, salt, soda and spices into a mixing bowl. Add brown sugar and mix.

In a small bowl or measuring cup, beat egg lightly and stir into molasses. Add flour mixture and combine thoroughly, stirring until flour disappears. Divide dough in half, place each half on a piece of wax paper and press into a 6-inch circle. Wrap tightly in plastic and chill at least 1 hour or overnight.

Pre-heat oven to 350°. Roll out dough ¼ to ½ inch thick on wax paper or a lightly floured board. Cut into shapes with cookie cutters. Place on un-greased cookie sheets about 1-inch apart. To decorate, press raisins and red hots into place.

Bake until puffy and lightly browned, 12 to 15 minutes. Remove from oven and cool on racks. If desired, frost with powdered sugar icing and top with colored sugar sprinkles. Store in covered tins. These freeze well.

After the hyena passes, the dog barks.

—An Ethiopian proverb

Hazelnut Macaroons

Also known as filbert macaroons, this is another recipe from the Raff family.

Makes 6 dozen

1-¼ lbs. hazelnuts/filberts
   (4 c. nuts roasted & finely ground &
   1 c. whole hazelnuts = about 72 nuts,
   roasted & skinned)
½ lb. almonds with skins (2 c. whole),
   finely ground

4 whole eggs
1-¾ c. sugar
1 t. vanilla

Pre-heat oven to 350°. Roast hazelnuts on a cookie sheet until lightly browned, about 7 to 10 minutes. Remove from oven and cool slightly. Lower temperature to 325°.

Skin 72 roasted hazelnuts while still warm by rubbing gently in a dishtowel. Grind remaining 4 cups of hazelnuts finely in a food processor or blender and set aside. Grind almonds finely and set aside.

In a mixing bowl, combine ground hazelnuts, ground almonds, eggs, sugar and vanilla. Mix thoroughly. Spoon batter teaspoon by teaspoon onto un-greased cookie sheets, allowing about 1-inch between cookies. Decorate cookies by pressing a whole skinned hazelnut into the center of each one before baking.

Bake until lightly browned, 15 to 20 minutes. Remove from oven and let sit for several minutes. Then remove from cookie sheets and cool thoroughly on racks. Store in tightly covered tins. (See note about storage on page 256.)

SAVOIR FAIRE

We once took our border collie Ivy to Paris — that's Paris, Kentucky, the capital of Bourbon County — to meet John's childhood friend, Norton, and his wife, Cissy. Norton was famous for loving dogs and he called them all "diggers" with the greatest affection. His own dogs Oatis and Buck worshipped him.

So did Ivy in her own puppy way by sneaking up to the master bedroom during dinner and leaving a tiny dog log. When we discovered Ivy's treasure on a tour of the house an hour or so later, Norton and Cissy burst out laughing. Now that epitomizes style among dog people.

Dutch Butter Cookies

For the holidays, Carol bakes these hazelnut cookies and the hazelnut macaroons on the previous page, plus the two German gingerbreads on pages 256-57.

Makes 8 dozen

¾ lb. hazelnuts/filberts (3 c. whole),
    coarsely chopped
1 c. butter (2 cubes), at room
    temperature
1 c. sugar
1 egg yolk

1 t. vanilla
½ t. cinnamon
½ t. ginger
¼ t. salt
½ c. poppy seeds (about 2-½ oz.)
2 to 2-½ c. all-purpose white flour

Begin several hours or the day before your want to bake Dutch butter cookies. Chop hazelnuts coarsely with a sharp chef's knife, food processor or blender.

Cream butter and sugar in a mixing bowl until light and fluffy. Add egg yolk, vanilla, spices and salt. Mix well and then add chopped nuts and poppy seeds. Mix thoroughly. Add 2 cups of flour gradually and mix until flour disappears. Add as much of the additional ½ cup of flour as needed to make a soft dough which can be handled easily.

Divide dough into quarters. With your hands, form each piece into a roll about 1-½ inches in diameter and 7 inches long. Wrap each roll tightly in plastic and chill for several hours or overnight.

Pre-heat oven to 325°. Slice rolls in rounds about ¼ inch thick and place on un-greased cookie sheets about 1-inch apart. Bake until lightly browned, 12 to 14 minutes. Remove from oven, let sit for several minutes and then remove from cookie sheets to cool on racks. Store in tightly covered tins in the refrigerator or freezer. (See note about butter cookies on page 93.)

ON A COOKIE ROLL

Home from college, Ruby called, "When are we going to bake, Catherine?" "Thursday." Ruby arrived with honey and recipes. Nearly eight hours later we admired our handiwork, covering nearly every surface in the kitchen and laundry room. Ruby was finishing the cleanup. Catherine pulled the last tray from the oven.

Spritz, chocolate-orange pinwheels, honey Lebkuchen gingerbread, Danish pepper snaps, Dutch butter cookies, Scotch shortbread, Pfeffernuesse, Springerle and Mum's chocolate peanut "bickies." "Can you believe it?" asked Catherine. "No," said Ruby, "the total is 58 dozen."

Lene's Danish Pepper Snaps

Here is a cookie you can eat by the dozen. Like a ginger snap but with a pepper bite, these small coin-sized cookies are a traditional Danish Christmas treat. • Lene, her Swiss husband and their son lived up the street from Catherine in Lausanne in the mid-1970's. Lene kept a green glass jar filled with these during the holidays.

Makes 10-12 dozen

**¾ c. butter (1-½ cubes),
  at room temperature
1 c. brown sugar**

**1-⅔ c. all-purpose white flour
2 t. freshly ground black pepper
1 t. cinnamon**

Pre-heat oven to 350°. In a mixing bowl, cream butter and sugar until light and fluffy. Add flour, pepper and cinnamon. Mix until flour disappears.

Turn dough out onto a lightly floured surface and divide in quarters. With your hands, form each piece into a "rope" about 12 to 14 inches long and ½ inch in diameter. With a sharp knife, slice the "ropes" into rounds about ¼ inch thick and place on ungreased cookie sheets about ½ inch apart.

Bake until very lightly browned, 10 to 12 minutes. Remove from oven, let rest on cookie sheets for 2 to 3 minutes and then remove to racks. Cool thoroughly and store in a covered tin or glass jar. These freeze well.

SNOWBOUND

We had that cozy feeling of being trapped in our house by a snowstorm. We talked to Richard Sewall who gave us a quote from an Emerson poem called "The Snowstorm" in which he speaks of "the tumultuous privacy of a storm." The tumult was outside, and the private warm friendship of old burned warm with the fire inside. We had quiet, working and reading times apart, and good talks together at meals, tea time and here and there.

—Jim Ottaway

From a letter written to John's father describing the blizzard that kept us housebound at Jim and Mary's home in New Paltz, N.Y. (March 16, 1993) We returned to New York City for Jim and Mary's 60th birthday celebration in 1998 and it snowed on the second day of spring, the only snow of that winter season.

Darnell's Great Communicator Pfeffernuesse

Darnell gave us a basket of these German pfeffernuesse ("pepper nuts") for Christmas, and we've never stopped talking about them. She began making them to send to relatives because they have almonds in them, and her last name — Mandelblatt — translates from German as "almond leaf." These cookies need to be stored for at least a week before eating, so time in the mail counts. • Darnell advised making lots because gearing up for the grinding and chopping might as well produce a big result. • Darnell comes as close as anyone we know to communicating perfectly — tone of voice, choice of words, respect for others. It's a rare magic. Maybe if we eat enough of her cookies we'll become better communicators, too.

Makes 8 dozen

2-¼ c. raisins (one 15 oz. box)
1 c. almonds (4 oz.)
½ c. citron (about 2-½ oz.), chopped
2-½ to 3 c. all-purpose white flour
2-½ t. cinnamon
1-½ t. cloves
½ t. each: baking powder, baking soda
   & salt

1 t. freshly ground pepper
3 eggs
2 c. brown sugar, firmly packed

Sugar coating:
1 c. powdered sugar (about 5 oz.)
   in a brown paper bag

Several hours or the day before you plan to bake these cookies, chop raisins, almonds and citron finely by hand with a chef's knife or in a food processor. (Darnell uses the fine blade of a food grinder. See page 88 for food processor method.) Set aside in a mixing bowl.

Sift 2 cups of flour with cinnamon, cloves, baking powder, soda, salt and pepper on top of the chopped raisin-almond-citron mixture. Mix together with your hands.

In another bowl, beat eggs and sugar until light and fluffy. Pour into raisin mixture and stir well with a wooden spoon until flour disappears. Dough will be very soft. Add as much of the additional cup of flour as needed in to handle the dough easily.

Divide dough in quarters. With your hands, form each piece into a roll about 1-inch in diameter. Wrap tightly in plastic and chill thoroughly for several hours or overnight.

Pre-heat oven to 350°. Slice rolls into rounds about ¼ inch thick and place about 2-inches apart on un-greased cookie sheets. Bake until cookies are brown on the bottom but still soft on top, about 10 minutes. Remove from oven and cool on racks.

While cookies are still warm, remove from cookie sheet about a dozen at a time and put them in the brown paper bag with powdered sugar. Shake gently. Return to racks and cool completely. Store in tightly covered tins for at least a week before eating. (See note about storage on page 256.)

5,000 Year-Old Springerle Cookies

Heidi explained that these cookies date back to 3,000 B.C., giving them the longest pedigree in the book. Springerle, a Swabian word meaning "little jumper," describes how these cookies come out of their traditional molds. (Swabian is a dialect of German from the Stuttgart region.) • The molds themselves — made of hand-carved wood but also stone and clay — featured designs that were "funny and erotic" from the early Middle Ages until the Victorian era when they became more staid with "pensive, romantic and burlesque interpretations of fairy tales or heroic images," according to the German reference book from which Heidi translated. Alas, our carved wooden springerle rolling pin has a flag, a cross, an owl, a leaf, a fish, a cat and a bird. Springerle molds have also been used to make decorative objects from salt dough that was baked hard, painted and hung on walls or Christmas trees. • Not overly sweet, these hard, long-storing cookies are perfect for dipping in tea, coffee or cocoa. They were a Christmas-time favorite of the Manz family.

Makes 5 dozen

4 eggs, separated
1 lb. powdered sugar (about 3-¼ c.),
  sifted
3 to 3-¾ c. all-purpose white flour

1 t. baking powder
¼ t. salt
¼ t. anise oil

Begin 1 or 2 days before you want to bake these cookies. In the bowl of a mixer, beat egg yolks at high speed until light and fluffy. Gradually add 1 cup of powdered sugar, beating at medium speed.

In a separate bowl, beat egg whites until stiff, and then gradually add 1 cup of powdered sugar, beating gently until it disappears. Fold egg whites into egg yolks and beat gently at low speed. Add remaining powdered sugar and continue beating at low speed until bubbles begin to form, 3 to 4 minutes.

Sift baking powder and salt with 1 cup of flour and add with anise oil, beating at low speed. Add 2 cups of the remaining flour and mix until flour disappears. Then add enough of the last ¾ cup of flour to make a stiff dough. Cover and chill for several hours or overnight.

Turn dough onto a lightly floured surface and roll out about ½ inch thick. Dust the surface of dough lightly with flour. Roll springerle rolling pin across the dough firmly so that the images "print," and then cut into rectangles as indicated by the imprints. If you don't have a springerle rolling pin, roll out the dough thinner, omit dusting the surface with flour, and cut rolled dough into 1x2 inch rectangles. Place cookies on un-greased cookie sheets about 1-inch apart. Cover with a tea towel and let sit for 12 to 24 hours to dry out before baking. (This is an important step because springerle puff-up unattractively during baking without this "rest.")

Pre-heat oven to 300°. Bake until very lightly browned, 25 to 30 minutes. Remove from cookie sheets immediately, lifting carefully with a spatula. (Springerle will have nicely browned bottoms.) Cool thoroughly on racks. Store in covered tins.

Odds & Ends

Win as though you were used to it
and lose as though you liked it.

—Anonymous

Message inscribed on a tile in the ladies' room of the
Isabella Stewart Gardner Museum in Boston.

Nothing-Like-It Homemade Mayonnaise

There's a world of difference between this mayonnaise and store bought varieties. We used to make it with our own hens' beautiful brown eggs. Now that we no longer have chickens, we are careful about eggs because of salmonella. We buy local ones from our good grocery store. • Sometimes Lisa brings us a box of duck eggs with rich yellow yolks and shells hard enough to let you know there's big treasure inside. We prize these.

Makes 1-½ cups

1 whole egg & 1 yolk
1 T. wine vinegar or lemon juice

1-½ c. unflavored vegetable oil
Salt & pepper to taste

In a blender or food processor, combine whole egg and yolk with vinegar or lemon juice. (See recipe for coddled egg on page 203.) With the blender or food processor turned on, slowly add oil in a fine stream. This is the crucial step. If oil is added too quickly, mayonnaise becomes a big, un-congealed oily mess. Season mayonnaise to taste with salt and pepper. Store in a covered jar in the refrigerator.

EASY SAUCES
BEGINNING WITH MAYONNAISE

MUSTARD SAUCE • Add 2 to 3 tablespoons of Dijon mustard to finished mayonnaise and process thoroughly.

MUSTARD-CAPER SAUCE • Add 1-½ tablespoon of Dijon mustard, 3 tablespoons capers, 1 tablespoon caper juice and 3 tablespoons of finely chopped parsley to finished mayonnaise. Mix gently by hand.

The classic Spanish AIOLI • Substitute ½ cup of good olive oil for an equal amount of unflavored vegetable oil. Add 10 to 15 peeled cloves of garlic to finished mayonnaise and process briefly until garlic is well chopped.

BASIL-GARLIC SAUCE • Add 1 cup of fresh basil leaves and 4 peeled cloves of garlic to finished mayonnaise and process thoroughly.

TARTAR SAUCE • Add 2 tablespoons of capers, 2 tablespoons of caper liquid, ⅓ cup of pitted and coarsely chopped olives and 2 tablespoons of parsley to finished mayonnaise. Mix gently by hand.

Marsha's Emergency Salsa

Lisa's sister, Marsha, is an excellent cook as well as a computer wizard. Her salsa got Dean and Lisa through several Edinburgh winters.

Makes 2 cups

16 oz. can "ready cut" tomatoes
1 or more cloves garlic, peeled
   & minced
1 small onion, chopped coarsely
Pinch of salt
1 to 2 T. canned, diced jalapeño
   peppers
Pinch of oregano

<u>Optional</u>:
1 green pepper, chopped coarsely

    In a small bowl, combine all ingredients. That's it. Use salsa immediately or store in a glass jar in the refrigerator.

    If you can't find canned "ready cut" tomatoes, then use canned whole peeled ones, drained. Although it's messy, you can chop them by hand or combine all of the ingredients in a blender or food processor. Process briefly to chop ingredients to a chunky consistency.

HOT TIP

Cissy reminded us to avoid using metal spoons with salsa because its high acid content causes a chemical reaction with metal.

THE SPIRIT MOVES US

Got to keep reaching for the spiritual or the spirit won't find us.

—Dean Livelybrooks

Philosopher & Geophysicist

Tom's Barbecue Sauce

This easy sauce is delicious for chicken or pork chops.

Makes ¾ cup

¼ c. teriyaki sauce
¼ c. light soy sauce
¼ c. or more Dijon mustard

Several splashes of hot sauce
(Tabasco or other)

In a small bowl, whisk together all ingredients. This sauce will be the consistency of half and half. Baste chicken pieces or pork chops with sauce and turn frequently on the grill, basting with more sauce every few minutes.

If you don't have teriyaki sauce, increase soy sauce to ½ cup and add 1 teaspoon of powdered ginger or 1 tablespoon of chopped fresh ginger.

FRANKLY FRANK

Well, Toots, you are about to have an unforgettable experience during your AFS trip, but it will take a great deal of work, tact, and patience on your part to make it successful. Always remember that people have different customs and ways of doing things in various parts of the world. This is even true in the good old U.S.A. So while some things may seem odd to you, be adaptable or like they say — "When in Rome do as the Romans do" whenever possible, but not to the point that you will completely lose your identity as an American.

Now that you are to become a temporary Kumnick, you will undoubtedly find that they have certain rules which must be followed. I know you will cooperate; however, do not forget the various things that your Mother & I have bugged you about over the years, always followed with the old cliché "It is for your own good." I believe that you will find that the Kumnick and Manz Rules will be quite similar.

—Frank Manz

From a letter to his 16-year-old daughter who was heading to the Kumnick family in Australia on the American Field Service exchange program. (January 1964)

Last-Minute Chutney

Keep the ingredients for this easy chutney on hand in your pantry. It takes about half an hour to make and perks up a curry, roast meat, chicken or rice dishes. We also like chutney on top of grilled cheese sandwiches.

Makes about 2-½ cups

Fruit:
17 oz. can of fruit, including syrup
 (peaches, pears, apricots, pineapple
 or fruit cocktail)
              or
3 apples, peeled, cored & cubed
              or
2 c. dried fruit, chopped (mangoes,
 apricots, crystallized ginger, apples,
 pears, blueberries or pineapple,
 a mixture is nice)

½ to ¾ c. vinegar, cider or balsamic
⅓ to ½ c. brown sugar
1 onion, chopped coarsely
½ c. raisins (about 3-⅓ oz.)
2 t. chili powder
2 t. cumin
1 t. turmeric
1 t. dried ginger or 1 T. fresh ginger,
 peeled & minced
1 t. dried mint or 1 T. fresh mint,
 chopped

In a saucepan, combine all ingredients. For **canned fruit**, use syrup the fruit was packed in, ½ cup vinegar and ⅓ cup brown sugar. For **dried and fresh fruit**, use ¾ cup vinegar and ½ cup brown sugar. Bring to a boil over medium heat, lower heat, cover and simmer 30 minutes, stirring occasionally. Remove from heat. Cool and serve. This chutney keeps well in the refrigerator for a week or so in a tightly sealed glass jar.

He had come to the belief that all things were so ordered, from the steps a man took in time, to the tracks of a storm, the like of which came with the season, exchanging their energies with that of a frigid and turbulent sea, and thereby raising waves as if they were themselves some variation on God's erring Wisdom and so able to labor their passion into matter.

—Kem Nunn

From his fascinating book *The Dogs of Winter*

Dora's Swedish Marmalade

On a visit to Scotland, we learned that marmalade originated there as a remedy prepared for an ailing Mary Queen of Scots by her French chef who referred to her affectionately as **ma malade** *or "my sick one."* • *This recipe comes from Emmy's dear Swedish friend Dora.*

Makes as much as you want

Oranges
Lemons
Grapefruit
Water

Sugar
Ginger, chopped fresh, crystallized
 or powdered

Marmalade-making requires steps on each of three days. Use any combination of oranges, lemons and grapefruit. Some of each is nice.

DAY 1 • Wash fruit. Sharpen a large knife and keep it sharp. (Cutting citrus rind seems to dull a knife blade quickly.) Cut fruit into thin slices. We cut fruit on a board with a well around the edge to capture the juice. Remove seeds from fruit and set aside. Place fruit and juice in a soup pot. Tie seeds in a piece of cheesecloth and drop into pot. Cover fruit with boiling water and let sit overnight.

DAY 2 • Bring fruit mixture to a boil over medium heat, lower heat and simmer until tender, 2 to 3 hours, stirring occasionally. (Cooked fruit may be frozen at this point.)

DAY 3 • Measure fruit mixture. Add sugar equal or somewhat less than the volume of the fruit. As little as half works fine. Stir in sugar, making sure your pot is no more than ⅔ full. Add ginger. Emmy uses a "great pinch" of powdered ginger; we prefer finely chopped fresh or crystallized ginger, up to a ¼ cup for a big pot.

Bring fruit-sugar mixture to a boil over medium-high heat. Stir frequently. The fruit mixture passes through several stages while cooking, including an initial foamy one. To get to the jelly stage may take from a ½ hour to 1 hour or more, depending on the size of the pot and character of the fruit.

When marmalade is nearing the jelly stage, it thickens and bubbles become larger, fewer in number and splash vigorously. The color also changes to the deeper orange of finished marmalade. At this time, begin checking jell by placing several drops of marmalade on a cold plate. (Put a plate in the freezer for this purpose.) Emmy explained that marmalade is ready when "the juice wrinkles on a cold plate." Lower heat and fill your jars or other clean containers.

Emmy never bothers to can marmalade because she gives it away immediately. Marmalade keeps for several weeks in the refrigerator. Canned jars of marmalade keep for a year or so stored in a cool, dark place.

ECONOMY MARMALADE • Emmy developed this version to take advantage of discarded citrus skins after the fruit had been eaten or used for juice. We think it's easier to make because the dry skins are less messy to work with than the whole fruit.

Collect skins in a plastic bag in the refrigerator. When you have a suitable quantity, slice them up and cover with boiling water. Follow the directions on the previous page beginning with Day 2. Before cooking, add a **can of frozen orange juice**, a big can of juice for a big pot, a small can for a small pot.

WELL HANDLED

*It's so beautifully arranged on the plate —
you know someone's fingers have been all over it.*

—Julia Child

AN A-1 HITCHHIKER

Although our second border collie was a princess, she came to us as a hitchhiker. We first caught sight of her cavorting with another pup along the side of the interstate out of sight of any exit or house. John stopped the car and backed up to investigate.

The other dog ran off, but the black and white puppy ran straight to John, leaping into his arms. Lively, then a one-year old pup sitting on the back seat, went crazy with pleasure. The puppy went crazy with pleasure, too, cementing her place in the family by peeing on Catherine's lap.

John's father, the Judge, named her. He started with "I-5" after the interstate where we found her, then modified it to "I-V," using the Roman numeral for five. That quickly became "Ivy."

When our new puppy was about 10 months old, we took her to Kentucky to meet the man who had been so intensely interested in her from the moment she arrived. Ivy loved sitting at the Judge's feet, next to his wheelchair, having her ears massaged in a way that takes 88 years of loving dogs to perfect.

Story's Santa Barbara Dried Black Olives

There's nothing more succulent than a good olive. To our surprise and delight, it is easy to make good ones. We started with beautiful, home-grown olives picked by Day Rose and her sister, Natty, one January afternoon at their home in Santa Barbara. We carried our treasure back to Oregon and got started, following Story's simple directions.

Makes as many as you wish

Ripe olives
Rock salt
Burlap bag

Olive oil
Whole cloves of garlic

Combine olives with a greater volume of rock salt and put in a burlap bag in a warm, dry place. Because we live in a moist, cool winter climate, we used our upstairs office with its constant heat. We placed the bag of olives in a large mixing bowl, turning it whenever we thought about it, several times a day. After about 6 weeks, the olives looked "done," suitably dried and wrinkled.

Wash olives thoroughly in cold water to remove salt. Drain them in a colander and lay them in a single layer on top of dishtowels on cookie sheets. Return them to a warm place for several days to dry thoroughly.

In a large frying pan, sauté several whole peeled cloves of garlic in olive oil over medium-low heat for several minutes. Remove frying pan from heat, discard garlic and toss olives with olive oil, lightly coating each one.

Put olives in clean jars, cool them completely, put the lids on and store in the refrigerator. Eat these olives with relish, and give them to important people.

HANDS ON

Catherine's father had a way with animals. It was evident in early photos of Frank as a toddler in a sailor suit with his first dog, Glory, a Boston terrier. There was something about the touch of his hand and the look in his eye.

We also have a photo of Pop at age 13 with Sheik, the prize-winning fox terrier from Gramp's kennel. He was famous in our household from Pop's stories about his high intelligence and voracious appetite for plums.

Odds & Ends

Manz-Best-Friend Dog Biscuits

Both our families have loved dogs. It was difficult to get into John's father's car because the passenger seat was always piled high with dog biscuit boxes, napkin-wrapped pieces of bacon, toast and other treats for his favorite friends. • At the Manzanita Kennel in San Gabriel, Catherine's grandfather raised Scotties and wire-haired terriers. If there was a dog in sight, Catherine's father was petting it, or the dog was sitting on his lap. • This recipe is dedicated to all our four-footers, our first line dish washers, best tasters and truly our best friends, most especially to Bert, Fritzi, Talley, Walt Whitman, Hansie, Crystal, Ajax, Doggus, Lil' Bit, Lively, Ivy, Harper, Daley, Jackson, Tuli and Phoebe.

Makes 10 dozen

2-¼ t. baker's yeast (¼ oz. pkg.)
¼ c. warm water (about 75°)
3-½ c. all-purpose white flour
2 c. wheat flour
2 c. rye flour
1 c. bulgur wheat
1 c. cornmeal

½ c. bran
½ c. nutritional yeast
½ c. non-fat dry milk
2 t. salt
4 c. stock or water from cooking
  vegetables or leftover gravy

Pre-heat oven to 300°. Add baker's yeast to warm water in a measuring cup. Stir to dissolve yeast. In a large mixing bowl, combine dry ingredients. Add yeast mixture and stock to dry ingredients. Mix until flour disappears. Dough will be stiff.

Turn dough onto a lightly floured surface and knead for 3 minutes, adding more flour as needed. Roll out ¼ inch thick and cut into desired shapes. We use a small dog bone-shaped cookie cutter. Place on un-greased cookie sheets about 1 inch apart.

Bake 45 minutes, turn off oven and leave dog biscuits overnight to dry out and harden thoroughly. Store in a tin or tightly covered jar. Lavish these on your best four-footers.

TOP DOG

Bert, a black and tan stray dog, captivated everyone he met. Befriended by John's great-grandfather, John T. Macauley, Bert had the run of The Macauley Theatre, including a box seat next to Colonel Macauley's.

In his lifetime Bert became the mascot of the theatre and chaplain of the Chili con Carne Club in Louisville. When he died, Bert was honored with a tombstone that read, "He was a dog who in his life gave lessons to men."

Emmy's Elixir: The Champagne Cocktail

A well-made champagne cocktail is a drink for celebration. Many years ago in San Francisco, Catherine began looking for the perfect champagne cocktail. She didn't find it until she found John who is fortunate to have a mother who made a perfect one. • Use good, not great, champagne, and don't forget the lemon peel. It's the secret ingredient.

For 1 serving

1 sugar cube
Angostura bitters
1 oz. brandy

Champagne, chilled
Lemon peel

Place sugar cube in a champagne flute or wine glass. Soak with a few drops of bitters. Add one jigger of brandy and fill glass with chilled champagne. Garnish with lemon peel. Serve immediately. Cheers!

---

*There comes a time in every woman's life
when the only thing that helps
is a glass of champagne.*

—Bette Davis
In the film "Old Acquaintances"

A RECIPE FOR ENDURANCE

Emmy and the Judge were visiting Crow Farm on their 55th wedding anniversary. We asked them the secret of their long, successful marriage and the Judge replied swiftly, "She never made me do anything I didn't want to do." Emmy added, "He always let me do whatever I wanted."

We looked at photos of Emmy and the Judge's wedding at Christmas Cove, Maine on September 8, 1930, an event Emmy cited as the first hippie wedding. Emmy wore a simple, yellow organdy dress that the Judge described as "cheese cloth." Her mother made sandwiches for a picnic, a Norwegian friend hand-cranked Brahms First Symphony on the old Victrola, and Papa Strong, Emmy's father, performed the ceremony for family and close friends in the woods behind their summer cottage.

John's Chigger-Chasin' Mint Juleps

Once a year on Derby Day, John gets out the bourbon and makes a batch of these mint juleps to ward off the chiggers of late spring. It works beautifully. • The mint julep is a deceptively powerful drink. We once served our guests more than one, and no one remembered eating dinner or even cared. • In Kentucky julep cups made from silver or pewter are given as prizes. Paul has a fine set from years of golf success with his father at the country club in Louisville. • Caroline's new dictionary was helpful with the derivation of **julep** *from the Persian* **julab,** *literally rose water. A julep has come to mean a sweet drink made from spirits and flavored water.*

For 1 serving

Sugar syrup:
2 c. sugar
2 c. water
Lots of fresh mint

For each mint julep:
2 T. sugar syrup
2 oz. Kentucky bourbon
   (We're fond of a brand called Old Crow.)
Crushed ice
Mint for garnish

Make sugar syrup the day before or at least several hours before you need your mint juleps. For the syrup, combine sugar and water in a small saucepan and bring to a boil over medium heat, stirring well until sugar dissolves. Reduce heat and boil uncovered for 5 minutes. Remove from heat and cool to room temperature.

Fill a jar with sprigs of fresh mint. Pour cooled syrup over mint and refrigerate for several hours or overnight.

To make a mint julep, combine sugar syrup and bourbon in an 8 oz. glass. Fill glass with crushed ice. Top with a sprig of fresh mint and serve immediately with caution.

AN UN-MINT JULEP

Soon after she moved from Mississippi to San Francisco, Caroline was invited to a Kentucky Derby party in neighboring Marin County. In the 1970's Marin County had become famous for its alternative life styles and thus a Derby party in such an environment qualified as an adventure.

As she walked in the door, the host handed Caroline an icy julep, the required drink for Derby Day. She lifted the glass to her lips, but something didn't seem quite right. There was the scent of . . . Let's see, what was that familiar aroma? . . . No, it couldn't be . . . But, yes . . . It was basil . . . A basil julep. The host, generous with his bourbon but sorely confused about herbs, had mistaken basil for mint.

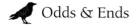

Odds & Ends

Mrs. Kelly's Cold "Cure"

Mrs. Kelly was Irish, of course, and her daughter Kathy O'Day gave Catherine this family remedy many years ago at a party in San Francisco.

One serving

2 oz. bourbon   **Boiling water**
Juice of 1 lemon   **Honey to taste**

Pour bourbon and lemon juice into a mug. Add boiling water and honey to taste. Take to bed and drink slowly. You don't have to be ailing to enjoy this "cure." It also works nicely as a hot toddy on a cold evening.

POWERFUL MEDICINE

Last evening I cured pneumonia and/or tuberculosis with vodka. Amazing.

—Emmy Smith
From a note on pink paper

A SRI LANKAN COUGH REMEDY

1-½ T. whole coriander seeds
1 knuckle fresh ginger, peeled & minced

In a small saucepan, cover coriander seeds and ginger with cold water. Bring to a boil over medium heat. Cover and simmer for 1 hour. Strain and drink as needed.

EMMY'S COUGH REMEDY

1 thermos of hot water

Before going to bed, fill a thermos with boiling water to keep at your bedside. When you cough during the night, drink a few sips of the hot water as needed to still the paroxysms in your throat.

Fife's Arthritis "Cure"

Fife attributed her "cure" to Mrs. Jessie Miller of Magnolia, Kentucky. Mrs. Miller said that it had been handed down for generations in her family, but no one knew its origin. • In the fascinating fact department, Fife explained that gin sales took a dip about 1894, and she wondered if the Bombay Gin Company hadn't promoted this cure to help their sales. Surely, there is a PhD thesis here.

Optional servings

Golden raisins
Bombay gin, enough to cover raisins

Cover raisins with gin. Take 1 heaping spoonful of raisins and gin each night at bedtime.

AND SPEAKING OF CURES . . . .

You'd have to be out of your mind to give a psychiatrist money when you could go out and buy a new pair of shoes.

—Alison Rose

Quoting a friend's mother on the subject of mental health ("Tales of a Beauty" from *The New Yorker*, May 26, 1997)

SCOT MACBETH'S OFFICIAL REMEDY FOR SAHIB'S KNEE
60 mg, codeine
2 to 4 shots of whiskey, preferably Scotch whiskey
Take as needed, not to exceed three times a day.

This remedy, developed by an old mountaineering buddy of Bruce Klepinger's, has a long and fabled history of success. Beargrass MacFiend, also known as Scot Macbeth, was the founder of the Alpine Stomach Club, a prestigious but loosely organized group that specialized in tasting old Scotch whiskeys and telling outrageous tales.

SEEING THINGS

Sherpa much chang drink, many yeti see.

—Dawa Dorje

Our Sherpa sirdar explained sightings of yeti, also known as the Abominable Snowman; chang is local moonshine.

Guillermo's Sangría

Bill White, also known as Guillermo, sent this recipe as a summer tip for "keeping cool and carefree" while porching.

Makes 1 pitcher

Equal parts: Red wine
     Freshly squeezed orange juice
     Sparkling mineral water or club soda
1 or more peaches, sliced to float on top
1 or more jiggers of brandy ("for a true Spanish Sangria," according to Bill)
Sugar to taste, if wine is especially dry
Ice

Combine the above ingredients in a pitcher and drink all day. "Good for you, and friends love it," Guillermo advised.

REFLECTIONS

Listen, instead of bailing your hay this year, why don't you put it in haystacks? Would it mould? They must have had some way to deal with that. What glorious shapes our fields were once host to, with the art of pitching to be mastered. A part of an older, more graceful and subtle America. A place where one could lose a needle, write a poem, a subject for Monet or Van Gogh. A place from which shadows leak . . . .

There is, I firmly believe, a part of the male that can't be satisfied with domestic life and having everything in place. We have to have an outlet for wild ideas and feelings, or we will shut down even more, like our dads. So, I think that one way is a sort of un-willful channeling of creativity through some kind of art form. When deeply felt, it gives us a dialog with our demons and all that multi-level 360° vision that we had when we were kids. That stuff that was shamed out of us, so we would be nice and sit still. That's what I think for now . . . .

We are here doing what we do and being stunned by people's reaction to Bush's War on Peace. They just can't deal with it. There are going to be a lot of resource wars as we try to continue using 40% of them for our 5% of population. But anyone who gets in our way will have a contract out on them. It's a huge global racketeering operation and the population is all set up through their numbed out t.v. lives to give consent without asking questions. T.V. coverage is horrible, adding to confusion. People don't know whether they are at a sporting event, a weapons' trade show or what. God help us. We have to live our history over again . . . .

—Bill White

Odds & Ends

Camp Cooking

THE ART OF NAVIGATION

They were a match made in heaven, Bruce Klepinger at the oars and Ivy, our border collie, at the bow of the raft wearing her yellow life vest, herding every wave, ripple and rock. Bruce called her his navigator on our annual white water rafting trips.

Ivy was first in the boat and first out, always packed and ready to go. In camp she collapsed, worn out by the exertion of navigating and vigorous games of stick.

No morning on these trips would have been complete without one of her speedy raids into the tent for a quick lick, the kamikaze kisser who signaled the new day with canine style.

Reflections on Camp Cooking

We like to take the heat off the kitchen by keeping proficient at camp cooking. It is not only a welcome challenge to cook over an open fire, but it is also practical. We all know that someday the power is going to shut down and leave us all in the dark. But never fear, the camp cooks of the world will be waiting in the wings, having honed their skills for just such an occasion.

When weather permits, we cook on a portable Tuscan grill in Bathtub Barbie. (This grill, sold at one time through the Smith & Hawken catalog, has a folding stand with two elevations and wooden handles on the grill itself for easy positioning.) We double-wrap potatoes and onions in heavy duty aluminum foil and bake them in hot coals while we grill corn, peppers, fish, meat or poultry on top. During the winter or in bad weather, we bring the grill inside and cook in the dining-room fireplace.

We also use a Dutch oven for cornbread, stews, casseroles, pies, cakes and biscuits. Dutch ovens, a versatile and time-honored cooking utensil, were the primary cooking tools for the Lewis and Clark Expedition and travelers on the Oregon Trial. These cast iron pots have tight-fitting lids and become an oven when covered and heated with charcoal. Smooth bottomed Dutch ovens are designed for conventional stoves. Our three-legged camping model perches directly over the coals and the lid has a lip that holds coals to heat the oven from above. A lightweight version made of aluminum is good for camping, but we prefer our heavy cast iron one. Although slow to heat, it heats evenly and stays hot longer.

Dutch ovens can be purchased from specialty kitchen stores, outdoor stores or river-running outfitters. River guides are often masters of this method of cooking. We suggest looking for books about Dutch oven cooking and then experiment for yourself. Remember that adequate ventilation is needed when burning charcoal because it emits poisonous carbon monoxide. Also, avoid canned charcoal starter fluid. It sabotages flavor.

We find that open fire cooking is a treat for visitors, too. There seems to be more room for involvement around a fire than in front of a stove as guests dig for hidden potatoes, run for a container of water to extinguish flare-ups, try to guess if the cornbread in the Dutch oven is done or rescue the peppers before they are blackened. For an outdoor cooking extravaganza, nothing beats making paella over a wood fire. There are enough tasks to keep everyone busy. (See pages 176-84.)

The Key to Camp Cooking

When we headed off on a river trip with Bruce Klepinger, we packed his 15-foot Hy-Side raft with plenty of food, wine, basic cooking equipment and firewood. The load was impressive, a challenge for Bruce's expert packing skills. One year while we were on the river, Bruce dreamed that he had to load a horse onto the raft, too, but the horse trailer proved impossible. Later we bought our own 13-foot Maravia "Spider" inflatable raft and practiced boat skills learned from Bruce on more river explorations.

HERE'S OUR LIST OF ESSENTIALS FOR CAMP COOKING:

Tuscan grill (See previous page.)
2 Dutch ovens (1 with legs)
1 large cast iron skillet
Charcoal briquettes
Old newspaper (in a heavy plastic bag)
Matches (in a waterproof container)
Small butane lighter
3 feed sacks of wood, including kindling
Tongs
Heavy leather gloves (welder's gloves)
Vise grips
Chinese wok spatula
Wooden spoon
Kitchen knife
1 medium-mixing bowl
Long handled fork
Small plastic cutting board
Heavy aluminum foil
Paper towels
Kitchen towels
Sponge
Pot scrubber
Bio-degradable dish washing soap
Plates & silverware
5-gallon plastic water container

Camp Breakfasts with John & Bruce

We have floated Oregon's John Day, Grande Ronde, Owyhee and Rogue Rivers on spring outings with Bruce Klepinger. Breakfast is the most important meal of the day on these trips. John and Bruce take turns preparing their favorites.

Serves 4 & 1 dog

John's Breakfast:
4 medium potatoes
1 large onion
¾ lb. spicy Italian bulk sausage
1 red pepper, chopped
1 green pepper, chopped

Bruce's Breakfast:
4 medium potatoes, baked
1 large onion, baked
1 lb. bacon
½ bunch celery, chopped coarsely
1 bunch green onions, chopped

For John's breakfast, begin the night before by wrapping each potato and onion separately in a double layer of heavy-duty aluminum foil. Place foil-wrapped packages among well burning coals and bake 30 minutes to 1 hour, turning frequently and piercing with a long handled fork occasionally to test if done. When cooked, potatoes and onion will be soft and easy to pierce.

The next morning, unwrap potatoes and onion and chop coarsely. In a Dutch oven or cast iron skillet, sauté sausage until nicely browned. Add chopped peppers and continue cooking for several minutes until peppers are soft. Add potatoes and onion and cook a few minutes more until nicely hot. Remove from heat and serve immediately with toasted bagels or cornbread. (See recipe for cornbread on page 224.)

BRUCE'S BREAKFAST • Follow directions above for baking potatoes and onions the night before. The next morning, unwrap potatoes and onion and chop coarsely. In a Dutch oven or large cast iron skillet, sauté bacon until nicely browned. Remove from pan with tongs, drain on paper towels and crumble nicely.

Pour excess bacon grease from pan. Sauté celery in 3 tablespoons of bacon grease until soft, about 5 minutes. Add crumbled bacon, coarsely chopped potatoes and onion and cook until nicely hot. Remove from heat and top with chopped green onions. Serve immediately with toasted bagels or cornbread.

ELEMENTAL UNDERSTANDING

Every rock's a rock.

—Tom Mains

Philosopher & mason

Tortilla Casserole & Other Camp Food

Cooking is one of the pleasures in camp each evening. We set up Bruce Klepinger's ingenious, waist-high plywood table with four removable pipe legs. On that good work surface, we begin chopping, grating or whatever else is required for our evening meal.

Serves 6 to 8

10 burning charcoal briquettes

1-½ c. minute brown rice
2-¼ c. water
2 T. vegetable or olive oil
1 medium onion, chopped
17 oz. can whole kernel corn
17 oz. can "ready cut" tomatoes

4 oz. can diced Anaheim chiles
11 oz. can cream of chicken, celery or
  mushroom soup
12 corn tortillas, cut in ½ inch strips
½ lb. cheddar cheese, grated (2 cups)

<u>Optional:</u> 2 chicken breasts, grilled &
  shredded

Build a fire and as soon as it is going well, place charcoal briquettes in the flames to get them started. (See page 280.)

Set up a grill over the coals. Bring water to a boil in a kettle or small pot. Pour minute rice into a Dutch oven with legs, add boiling water, cover and let sit. In a second Dutch oven or a cast iron skillet, sauté chopped onion in oil until soft, about 5 minutes. Add onions to rice, then canned corn (undrained), tomatoes (undrained), chiles, chopped tortillas and soup. (Add optional shredded chicken.) Mix gently. Top with grated cheese. Cover.

Set Dutch oven next to the fire with 6 burning charcoal briquettes underneath and 4 more on top of the cover. Turn Dutch oven a quarter turn every 10 minutes so that it heats evenly. Cook the casserole until nicely bubbly, about 40 minutes.

OTHER CAMP MEALS

On our first night in camp we often grill a piece of fresh fish or sausages. In the next day or two, we make a stew from ground beef that has been thawing in the cooler. Tandoori chicken prepared at home using a commercial spice mix can be frozen and then thawed in the cooler in time for dinner on the third or fourth night. We freeze marinated chicken, too, and then grill it the second or third night. We save burritos for the end of the trip, using canned chicken, large flour tortillas, canned refried beans, chopped fresh tomatoes, lettuce and grated cheese. We also make several other recipes found elsewhere in the cookbook:

Cornbread on page 224

Gingerbread on page 102

Enchilada pie on page 154

Risotto on page 197

Brown rice casserole on page 196

Pineapple Upside-Down Cake

We look forward to making John's favorite cake on camping trips.

Serves 6-8 (or 4 hungry campers)

10 burning charcoal briquettes
  (See previous page.)
1 yellow cake mix (18.25 oz.)
1 egg
⅓ c. unflavored vegetable oil
1 c. liquid, pineapple juice & water

¼ lb. butter (1 cube)
1 c. brown sugar
8 oz. can pineapple rounds, drained
8 oz. can crushed pineapple

In a mixing bowl, combine cake mix, egg, oil, pineapple juice and water. Stir together gently until ingredients are well combined.

Melt butter in a Dutch oven with legs. Add brown sugar and spread evenly over the bottom of the Dutch oven. Arrange pineapple circles nicely and top with crushed pineapple. Pour batter gently over pineapple. Cover and position burning charcoal briquettes as directed on previous page. (See also page 280.) Bake until the cake is done, rotating the Dutch oven a ¼ turn every 10 minutes for even heating, 20 to 30 minutes.

We belong so intimately and joyously and tragically to this physical world, and by its own laws we soon must leave it. Yet during these moments one knows, too, with humility and certainty, that each human spirit is immortal — for time cannot destroy whatever element within us reverences the glory of a dawn in the mountains.

—Dervla Murphy

From her book, *In Ethiopia with a Mule*

THE KLEPINGER KNOT

In the world of trekking, keeping your feet in good shape is essential. Bruce Klepinger explained that you can save your feet from a lot of abuse over steep, rocky terrain by tying an overhand knot halfway up your hiking boot. Adjust for an uphill gradient by tightening your boot-laces below the Klepinger knot and loosening them above the knot. For downhill, reverse it by tying the boot loosely below the knot and tightly above the knot to keep your feet from banging uncomfortably into the toes of your boots. This can make a big difference to your comfort on the trail.

The Manual

If time didn't exist, then everything would happen at once.

—Graffiti

Recorded from a bathroom wall by John Smith.

Hospitality

An open door is all it takes. Plus a willingness to put another plate on the table at the last minute or find a sleeping bag for a late night guest. Hospitality is the secret ingredient of entertaining. It is a friendly and gracious way of receiving friends, family and strangers into our homes and making them feel welcome. Its greatest moments are often spontaneous.

We both grew up in families where hospitality was integral to daily life. Our homes in Kentucky and California were filled with friends, strangers, good food and good conversation. Our childhood friends felt so welcome that they adopted our homes and our mothers, Emmy and Marjorie, who provided great meals for everyone.

Emmy brought musicians home to stay and fed them exceptional meals before and after their performances. Frank, Catherine's father, brought students from nearby Caltech home for good food and family life. In both households, there was always room for one more at the table, a "one more" which could swell to a sizable number. Everyone always ate and talked with relish, the conversation every bit as important as the food.

In addition to Christmas, Thanksgiving and birthdays, the Manz family had one big party each year at New Year's. The party began on New Year's Eve with a houseful of guests, awaiting Frank's early morning bugle call to rise and shine. We ate donuts and then headed up the street in the pre-dawn darkness to claim our places for the Rose Parade. On New Year's Eve, Marjorie prepared her traditional goulash in a baby-bathtub-sized roaster to feed the next day's guests who often numbered more than 30. On New Year's Day, everyone crowded the buffet table in the dining-room and spilled outside onto the front porch and lawn to enjoy the warm sunshine and watch the post-parade gridlock on our normally placid street. It was always a hearty good time.

The Fall Frolic was an important tradition for Kentucky's Smith family. Emmy and Macauley's city friends gathered for a weekend of hard labor at their old farm. It was an old fashioned house party memorable for sore muscles and high spirits fueled by Emmy's sumptuous meals and the Judge's peerless martinis. In the midst of great gaiety, this jolly group cut and split enough wood for the winter. They used cross-cut saws (no power saw then) and trimmed nasty buckberries from the pasture with clippers (no bush hog then). John remembers how much everyone ate and how much they laughed.

These good times continue in our own traditions and practices here at Crow Farm, but they began in each of our family homes.

Basic Party-Giving

We've learned over the years that planning and organization make it easier to give a party, but timing and group chemistry are a roll of the dice. There's no way to plan for the magic which transforms an ordinary evening into an extraordinary one. We just thank our lucky stars when it happens. • It shouldn't be an ordeal to have a party. The whole point of a party is to orchestrate a framework in which people you care about come together to enjoy themselves. You should be able to have a good time, too. For those who are getting started entertaining, these are our hints.

PLAN AHEAD

Write down a guest list, the menu and a shopping list. Catherine sometime loses her mind before a big event and it helps to make lists. It can be a problem to set the table for too few guests or discover mid-recipe that you don't have the secret ingredient for your main course.

PREPARE IN ADVANCE

The freezer is a great ally, allowing food preparation to be done at one's convenience rather than at the last minute. Catherine also likes to set the table and arrange flowers ahead of time because it is a pleasure done at her own pace. • Shop ahead during the holidays. Buy staples in advance and then, if possible, avoid the grocery store madhouse on the day or two before Thanksgiving and Christmas. The craziness can be contagious.

ACCEPT HELP

People like to participate. Let them. It will help you and give them pleasure. Plan a *potluck* and ask your friends to bring their favorite foods. Potluck gatherings are always great fun and the food invariably wonderful. • Invite someone comfortable to come early and help with last minute tasks. Once at Thanksgiving, friends lifted the kitchen table into the living-room and got it set for dinner. (We could not fit all 21 guests around our dining-room table, so we combined two tables.) Then they went out to the workshop to round up two boards to convert the enormous dog kennel from our visiting grand-dog into a kitchen table for hors d'oeuvres. We covered it with a tablecloth and no one noticed our improvisation. We couldn't have done it without helpful friends. • Delegate. You get to be the general, so enjoy asking for help — filling water glasses, opening wine bottles, pouring juice, entertaining children, cutting bread, locating serving spoons, putting out the butter, making gravy, carving the turkey or being d.j. If need be, make a list of possible tasks for your guests.

BE FLEXIBLE

Invite someone spontaneously, change your mind at the last minute, decide to skip a course or leave something out to simplify. No one cares if you follow your original plan.

AVOID FRETTING

Try not to worry about non-essentials. So what if the dogs just walked all over the clean floor with muddy feet? The floor will be even dirtier after 21 people walk in out of the rainstorm for dinner. Concentrate on what's important: first, everyone's comfort and then the food.

TRY SWITCH-SITTING

This is a technique developed by John's Aunt Betsy after she married Air Force General E. E. Partridge later in life. She always followed strict military protocol in her seating arrangements at the beginning of dinner parties, but mid-way through she would invite everyone to change places. The purpose was to liven things up, to allow people to sit next to someone different, to pep-up conversation. We have no doubt this created havoc for the kitchen staff but it made for a livelier party — and she got away with it.

CLEAN UP

Good guests help clean-up. This is John's cardinal rule and because of it, he is the most famous guest-dishwasher we know. After dinner he always heads for the sink, knowing full well that every host and hostess can always use this kind of help. We know that it lifts the spirits of the host and hostess to wake up to a clean kitchen the morning after a big party.

MANAGE LEFTOVERS

Send leftovers home with guests. They may be delighted to have an extra lunch or dinner instead of you having food containers falling out of your own refrigerator.

SOME TRIP

Well, after we left the farm, we were held up by bandits at Crow, witnessed a train robbery in Drain, and caught a 400-ton whale in Coos Bay. Then Robert Redford invited us for dinner and we partied with Robert and Steven Spielberg that night!

—Cherie Hiser

From a thank you note written with an eye to its future resting place in our reading basket of letters and cards; Cherie, a photographer, created Aspen's Center of the Eye.

The Manual

Dancing with Dishes

The big secret of dish washing and general clean-up is music, loud music. It's important to create a cheery atmosphere when you have cleaning tasks and music helps a lot. We have pair of small speakers in the kitchen, up high so that sound fills the room. Our favorite choices for cleaning are Basia's first recording, *Time and Tide*, Bonnie Raitt's *Nick of Time*, *Phantom of the Opera* and *South Pacific* with Kiri Te Kanawa. Our preference for dinner music is Gregorian chant or other early music. John believes strongly that music with English vocals is too distracting to be good dinner music.

The second secret of dish washing is rinsing everything right away. As soon as you've finished using it, rinse it off or fill it with soapy water or drop it in a sink filled with soapy water. This is a good habit.

When planning our new kitchen, we initially dismissed the idea of a dishwasher. After all, we already had John. Our friends insisted that we would be foolish to miss the opportunity to install a dishwasher easily during our remodeling. So we did. It's lucky we listened because we use it with great frequency and pleasure. It helps tremendously, particularly when we've had a crowd for dinner. Of course, there are still dishes, pots and pans which can't go in the dishwasher — copper and cast iron, wooden spoons, knives, old china, etc. We keep the dishwasher set on the economy setting that has a shorter cycle and lower heat. It's so quiet thanks to Ryan's soundproofing that we often turn it on during dinner. Very convenient.

PARTY TRICKS

The new days of the dishwasher are a far cry from the old days of Catherine's party dish washing. Catherine was known to pile all the dishes in the bathtub, fill it with soapy water and leave them to soak. She would then wash a few each day over the next several days, speeding up the process if she wanted a bath. (Yes, the shower was a separate unit.) You can imagine the surprise of more than one friend who unwittingly visited the bathroom while the dishes were soaking.

The Importance of Tables

God bless all those associated with us by friendship, consanguinity and grace. —Our favorite blessing

"Soup's on," my father used to call, letting us know that it was time to come to the table for dinner. The ritual of being called to the dinner table, then sitting down to eat and talk about our day at school was an important part of my childhood. Looking back on it now, I realize that it shaped my views about food and eating. The table is as essential to nutrition as the food pyramid and the recommended daily allowance of vitamins and minerals.

You can eat anywhere in your house and it is great fun to put a small table in a different room, in front of your fireplace, on your front porch or in front of a window with an especially fine view. You'll enjoy discovering new eating areas. We like candles on the table at dinner because their soft, pleasant light creates a different atmosphere from other meals and other times of day.

We are deeply grateful that we are able to eat so well and share so many meals with family and friends around a table. Let's always hope for more tables and better use of the ones we have.

REFLECTIONS

Although I passed muster in other fields, I was a failure as cannon fodder, uniformed. Accepting a lst Lieutenant commission (USAF) in 1942 when I was 37, I was sent to Officer's Training School in Miami Beach in August 1942. Not as rough as Officer's Candidate School — same intentional discomforts. They asked me why I threaded my belt through the belt buckle the wrong way? My father died before I was 4 years old. I was raised by two widows.

Sent to drill troops at Rome Air Force Base near Syracuse, N.Y. I had to seek help from a Private on how to pirouette an "about face"!

I was Acting Legal Officer for 18 months at the Air Force Procurement Office at 67 Broad Street, N.Y. I never knew the Air Force rules for contracts that I was approving every day!

Some 10 months in the Pentagon, March '45 to January '46. Plowing up the long steps to the Pentagon one morning, I failed to salute General George Catlett Marshall! Another day, I had my usual feet on the desk posture when four star General "Hap" Arnold popped open the door and genially? cynically? asked, "What are you boys doing here?" I was too taken aback to respond, but a local Captain George answered for us.

—Macauley Smith

Reminiscing about his military career in World War II.

What about Dinner?

If you are new to the world of cooking and entertaining, then this section is intended to help you figure out dinner, to plan pantry supplies so that you can pull something out of a hat when needed and to give you a hand when preparing for a major event.

Easy-to-Prepare Dinners from Supplies on Hand (Basic supplies listed on page 294.)

Brown rice, p. 196
Cheese *soufflé*, p. 170
Easy *soufflé*, p. 171
Grits pudding, p. 173

Pasta with *pesto*, p. 162
Potato *omelette*, p. 62
Risotto, p. 197
Quick soup, p. 69

Clam *spaghetti*, p. 160
Pasta nada, p. 164
German lentils, p. 169
Chile relleno casserole, p. 171

Prepare-Ahead Dinners

Baked tomatoes, p. 189
Beef burgundy, p. 144
Black beans, p. 167
Borscht, p. 78

Chili, p. 151
Lasagna, p. 165
Red cabbage casserole, p. 191
Soups, pp. 68-83

Chicken curry, pp. 138-9
Stew, p. 145
Yogurt chicken, p. 136

Easy-to-Prepare Dinners Requiring Certain Ingredients (Consult recipes for shopping list.)

Enchilada pie, p. 152
Leek & potato soup, p. 75
Squash soup, pp. 76-7
Chowder, clam, corn or fish, p. 79
Crab vermouth, p. 130
Crab with tomatoes & rice, p. 129

Chicken with black bean sauce, p. 134
Roast chicken with lemons & garlic, p. 133
Chicken with rice & broccoli, p. 132
Baked chicken with yogurt & lime juice marinade, p. 136

Hungarian goulash, p. 156
Lamb meatballs, p. 153
Meat loaf, p. 149
Pasta with leeks & bacon in cream sauce, p. 161
Pasta with pesto, p. 162
Turkey *piccata*, p. 141

State Dinners Suitable for the Queen or a Quarterback (Consult recipes for shopping list.)

Appetizers
Olivada, p. 109
Artichoke dip, p. 114
Caviar pie, p. 117

Main Dishes
Baked salmon, p. 125
Beef burgundy, p. 144
Bouillabaisse, p. 120
Chicken curry, pp. 138-9
Indonesian noodles with pork & shrimp, p. 157
Leg of lamb, p. 154
Paella, seafood or vegetarian, pp. 176-85
Tenderloin of beef with pasta, p. 147

Desserts
Belgian torte, p. 101
Chocolate *mousse*, p. 49
Brandied fruitcake, p. 96-7
German carrot torte, p. 48
Hazelnut torte, p. 100
Orange peel cake, p. 98

Eating Outside: Porches & Picnics

There's nothing nicer than a leisurely dinner on the porch to enjoy the warm, summer air. We like these easy picnic-style meals that can be prepared ahead and then enjoyed in the out-of-doors. • In addition to the salads listed below, we also like to make big Greek salads with garden-fresh tomatoes and peppers, Walla Walla sweet or red torpedo (a variety named because of its shape) onions, Kalamata or other olives, feta cheese and artichoke hearts dressed lightly with lemon juice or balsamic vinegar and olive oil. (See also **The Porch** *on pages 14-15.)*

PORCH DINNERS

Avocado & mango salad, p. 206

Beet salad, p. 209

Broccoli salad, p. 210

Caesar salad, p. 203

Chinese chicken salad, p. 213

Curried chicken salad, p. 212

Greens with baked chèvre, p. 205

Pizza, p. 222

Potato salad, p. 208

Shrimp salad, p. 214

Greens with yellow peppers, feta, mushrooms
    & caramelized almonds, p. 204

PICNIC FOODS

Applesauce, p. 65

Apricot loaf, p. 106

Baklava, p. 239

Biscotti, pp. 90-1

Broccoli salad, p. 210

Chicken salad with pesto, p. 162

Chinese chicken salad, p. 213

Eggplant "caviar," p. 116

Focaccia, pp. 220-1

Frittata/baked eggs, p. 60

Gazpacho/cold tomato soup, p. 83

Olivada/tapenade appetizer, p. 109

Onion sandwiches, p. 84

Meatloaf sandwiches, p. 149

Pasta with pesto, p. 162

Potato *omelette*, p. 62

Potato-tuna roll, p. 200

Red pepper salad, p. 188

Sardine dip, p. 108

Shortbread, p. 89

Tuna sandwiches with cottage
    cheese on muffins, p. 85

Yogurt cheese, p. 111

Whole wheat spice bread, p. 103

Zucchini bread, p. 105

Brownies, p. 42

Easy Does It: Eating Out of the Pantry

We like to be prepared. We get home late and want to eat right away. Someone drops in unexpectedly. These are easy dinners that we can pull out of a hat.

IMPROMPTU DINNERS from SUPPLIES on HAND

(See following page for a list of supplies.)

Tortillas with beans, cheese, salsa & yogurt or sour cream

Scrambled eggs with sautéed onions & peppers, cheese & salsa

Black beans with rice, cheese & salsa

Corned beef hash with sautéed onions & peppers, sour cream
& French fried onion rings (Emmy's favorite)

Baked potatoes with sautéed vegetables, cheese & salsa

Pasta with whatever is on hand (garlic, olive oil, Parmesan, etc.)

An ordinary *omelette* or a fried egg on toast

Supplies to Have on Hand for Easy Dinners

*With some basic supplies on hand in your pantry and refrigerator, you can come up with half a dozen different meals at the last minute. See also the list of **Easy-to-Prepare Dinners from Supplies on Hand** on page 291 and the list of **Impromptu Dinners from Supplies on Hand** on the previous page.*

In the 'FRIG
Butter

Sharp cheddar cheese

Eggs

Milk

Parmesan cheese

Salsa

Tortillas

Sour cream or yogurt

PRODUCE
Garlic

Green onions

Yellow & red onions

Potatoes

Peppers

In the FREEZER
Bread

Chicken stock

Peas

Pesto

Pine nuts

Walnuts

PANTRY
Arborio rice

Basmati rice

Brown rice

Cream of tartar

Grits, instant

Lentils

Olive oil

Oil cured olives

Pasta

Red pepper flakes

Salt & pepper

Vegetable oil

Vinegar

CANNED GOODS
Black beans

Chicken stock

Chiles

Clams

French fried onions

Corned beef hash

Re-fried beans

Tomato sauce

Food for Kids

MEALS

Breakfast
Corncakes, p. 54
Baked grits with cheddar cheese, p. 173
Cinnamon rolls, p. 58
Cinnamon toast, p. 59
Poached eggs, p. 61
Fried green apples, p. 66
Blueberry muffins, p. 53
Cornbread, p. 224
Rice pudding, p. 64

Dinners
Roast chicken, p. 133
Mashed potatoes, p. 247
Risotto, p. 197
Pasta with pesto, p. 162
Chicken soup, pp. 69, 74
Poached eggs, p. 61
Meatloaf, p. 149
Enchilada casserole, p. 152
Spaghetti, p. 166

Dinners continued
Brown rice with cheese, p. 196
Potato-tuna roll, p. 200
Chicken/broccoli & rice, p. 132
Baked grits with cheese, p. 173
Green beans, p. 192
Meatballs/tomato soup, p. 150
Easy *soufflé* with bread cubes & cheddar cheese, p. 171

SNACKS & SIDES

Snacks
Banana bread, p. 104
Ricotta & yogurt cheese, p. 111
Tuna sandwiches with cottage cheese, p. 85

Salads
Coleslaw, p. 207
Carrot & raisin, p. 207

Breads
Oatmeal, p. 217
Banana, p. 104
Cinnamon rolls, p. 58
Cornbread, p. 224
Soufflé bread, p. 86
Swiss egg bread, p. 219
Focaccia, pp. 220-1
Pizza, p. 222
Biscuits, pp. 223, 229
Cinnamon toast, p. 59

COUGH SYRUP
Mary Ottaway told of her successful substitute for cough syrup for her three children: 1 teaspoon of Crème de Menthe plus a shot for mom.

SWEETS & TREATS

Cakes
Pound, p. 94
Yellow, p. 95
Gingerbread, p. 102
Chocolate, p. 46
Carrot, p. 99
Cheesecake, p. 231

Cookies
Chocolate-peanut, p. 45
Oatmeal-raisin, p. 88
Chocolate chip, p. 43
Shortbread, p. 89
Gingerbread, p. 259
Brownies, p. 41

Desserts
Apple crisp, p. 228
Applesauce, p. 65
Custard, p. 234-5
Strawberry shortcake, p. 229
Zucchini bread, p. 105
Fruit-cake, pp. 96-7 (Kids love it!)
Rice pudding, pp. 64, 233
Brownies, p. 41
Chocolate mousse, p. 49
Ice cream, p. 236
"Hedgehogs" with pears, p. 40
Chocolate sauce, p. 40
Sour cream sauce, p. 228

Food Trivia

APPLES & ORANGES

Marjorie reminded us never to buy an apple without a stem. Having lived in orange-growing country her entire life, she also advised that a navel orange must always have a good, big navel.

FOOD STORAGE

TOMATOES • Bruce LeFavour taught us to avoid keeping tomatoes in the refrigerator. They ripen better and store more successfully at room temperature or in a cool but not cold place. Emma showed how to ripen green tomatoes by putting them in a brown paper bag with an apple. Lisa explained that apples give off lots of ethylene gas, nature's ripening agent. Barbara taught us that the same principle works to produce a bloom on a bromeliad. We've also discovered that drying garlic in the sun room near our bromeliad causes it to bloom each year.

BASIL • Fresh-cut basil keeps for nearly a week at cool room temperature (about 65°) with the stems in water. It wilts quickly in the refrigerator. As a bonus, basil makes an attractive bouquet.

NUTS • To keep nuts from getting rancid, store them in tightly covered jars in your freezer, Pat advised.

HERBS & SPICES • Faith reminded us to put stickers with dates on all our herbs and spices so we can throw them out after a year. In a perfect world, we might remember to do this.

CHEESE • Wrap cheese in new plastic wrap or foil before putting it back in the refrigerator. Fresh wrapping prolongs the life of cheese.

BROWN SUGAR • When brown sugar gets rocklike, soften it by putting a piece of bread in the container. Ann wrote that a piece of apple will do the same.

RICE & SALT • To keep rice dry, put several crackers in the container and to keep salt dry, put several grains of rice in your salt shaker.

FOOD TRICKS

COFFEE • Joseph explained that you can improve bitter coffee in a restaurant by adding several grains of salt to it.

The Manual

SPICY FOOD • In further advice on food repair, Joseph advised us to add honey or grated unsweetened baking chocolate to salsa or chile if it's too spicy. The amount depends on volume and taste and, of course, the honey would make it sweeter.

LEFTOVERS • Edie suggested adding leftover salad to a pot of soup. Norma Gene keeps a container in the freezer for leftover "soup things," including vegetables and salad that eventually go into a pot of soup.

FOOD PREPARATION

MANGOES • Max taught us to slice each mango parallel to the pit, one slice on each side of it, making two oval sections of fruit. Then score the flesh of each oval in a grid to make bite-sized pieces. Be careful not to pierce the skin. Peel the skin back and drop the pieces into a serving bowl. The real reward is leaning over the sink and chewing on the pit.

FROSTING • Bruce LeFavour taught us to add a few grains of salt to a frosting or icing to enhance a subtle flavor, such as lemon or rum, which may be overwhelmed by the sugar.

ONIONS • Mary gets the prize for a most creative household hint. To keep from crying when she was peeling onions, she once donned a snorkeling mask. It worked perfectly. Then her young son and two friends walked unexpectedly through the back door. Her son's acute embarrassment at his mother's unconventional behavior weighed heavily against the success of this technique. Anne's solution is easier but not much better in the Embarrassment Department. Peel onions while holding a piece of bread in your mouth.

CINNAMON • For really good cinnamon, grind your own in a clean coffee grinder or with a mortar and pestle. Use fragile-looking cinnamon sticks for easier grinding, suggested Victoria.

Random Household Hints

CLEANING

CANDLE WAX • Many years ago Sally Harper demonstrated how to remove candle wax easily from a wooden table top by scraping gently with an old credit card. They now make a small plastic scraper suitable for this as well as its intended purpose of scraping food preparation surfaces. For sheer style, an old Saks Fifth Avenue credit card is hard to beat for this purpose.

GREASE • Our shoemaker taught us to remove grease from leather by coating the grease spot with a thin layer of rubber cement. Let the rubber cement dry for 30 minutes and then rub it off. Repeat several times until grease disappears.

LINENS • Susan explained that the old fashioned practice of boiling linens and lace to remove stains is much easier on the natural fibers than washing, even on the gentle cycle.

DISHWASHER • Victoria surprised us with the suggestion that we could clean the interior of our dishwasher by running it empty with Tang in place of dish detergent, allowing the citric acid to work on built-up deposits.

And speaking of cleaning, our cousins Cauley, Olga and Ann have the cleaning gene in a big way. So, we listen when they advise us about cleaning strategies. Cousin Ann wanted to make sure that we knew the following:

VASES • You can clean vases and other narrow-necked vessels by adding one tablespoon of rice, a big splash of white vinegar and some water. Shake and watch the rice act as a mild abrasive.

TEA STAINS • To clean tea, coffee and other stains from delicate china, including tea cups or even sturdy pottery mugs, sprinkle baking soda on a damp rag or sponge and rub gently.

KNIVES • To clean carbon steel or other non-stainless steel knife blades, dip a wet cork in cleanser and scrub.

WOOD

FURNITURE POLISH • Make your own furniture polish by combining 2 parts white vinegar with 1 part boiled linseed oil and 1 part turpentine.

FINISHING • We finished our Douglas fir kitchen cupboards with four coats of John Jones' traditional recipe for wood finish made of 3 parts boiled linseed oil, 2 parts turpentine and 1 part varathane. It makes a beautiful surface.

SCRATCHES • For Ann's walnut trick, break apart a fresh walnut half and use it to rub out scratches on wood furniture.

HUMMINGBIRD FOOD

Our heaven-sent veterinarian Devon gave us her recipe for hummingbird food: 9 parts water & 1 part white sugar. Heat in a small saucepan until the sugar dissolves, stirring occasionally. Remove from the heat and cool before filling the hummingbird feeder. No coloring needed.

FIRST AID

Lisa explained that you should put ice, not butter on burns. Ice not only relieves pain but also prevents scarring by allowing much needed oxygen to get to the burn. Butter, on the other hand, prevents oxygen from reaching the tissue.

MISCELLANEOUS

WINE CORKS • Faith observed old wine corks used as kindling at a French country inn.

CARE of SILVER • In the dishwasher, keep **silver & stainless steel** separated from each other to avoid **electrolysis**. Don't put flatware knives in the dishwasher because heat destroys the glue that holds blades and handles together.

CARE of KNIVES • High heat takes the edge off sharp knives so we wash them by hand.

EMMY'S QUESTIONS FOR A NEW YEAR

John's mother Emmy created the following questionnaire for the New Year of 1996 when Barry and Edie, Emmy's "adopted" children, were visiting Crow Farm:

*Of the new material items added to your life,
what are you expecting to be the most helpful or valuable?*

Of the old items in your life, what do you treasure most?

What are you most grateful to heaven for?

What are you most grateful to an individual for?

In the past year, did you make a new friend?

What was your best success in the past year? What was your worst failure?

In the last calendar year, what was the best spell you had?

What do you look forward to most in the new year?

Tell something you learned in the past year.

Bad Manners

Thrice blessed are we to our friends:
We come,
We stay,
And presently we go away.

Emmy suggested we write a book called *The Painless Visitor*. Instead we decided to write one chapter on manners for this cookbook and slap an irresistible title on it to reel you in.

Although this incorporates the collective wisdom of our own experiences as well as those of our family and friends, we realize that its major value may be as a page which you can tear out and give to your grandchildren so they may, hopefully, profit from the previous transgressions of ourselves and others.

The quote above is from our great friend Harper Brown who, as a careful student of life, had much to say about visiting. "Guests should always add more than they take away" was his golden rule. Of course, there are endless ways to manifest this. If your hosts lead busy lives, you can carry food to their house and cook it. Or one can pitch in and work side by side with your hosts to get their work done sooner. Or one can simply pitch in and help with the usual chores and be self-contained so that your presence doesn't interrupt the daily tasks of your hosts.

A few particulars about visiting. It is extremely important to your hosts that you discuss your arrival time and your departure with them. Both ends of the visit are significant. Arrival times are important because of meal planning and preparation as well as transportation. Departure times are crucial because open-ended arrangements can be awkward or worse.   Over-staying your welcome is a real hazard even when visiting your nearest and dearest. A hymn that Emmy is fond of quoting goes like this: *Peace, perfect peace, with loved ones far away*. It took us years to grasp the real meaning of this little gem.

Some people have particular dietary requirements for various reasons: religious, medical, preferential or simply fickle. If you are not willing or able to eat what the household might present for you, it is important that you either bring your own foods or inform your hosts in advance about your requirements.

It is essential for visitors to follow the house rules, if there are any. We once had a visitor who was very careful to follow our wishes by smoking outside — when we were home. The guest had no idea that we could tell with one sniff on our return that the sacred leaves had been burning in the house while we were away. We said nothing, but thereafter we took our friend with us when we left the house.

If you intend to take a dog along with you, be sure to clear it with your hosts. One of our transgressions was to take our sweet tempered Lil' Bit on a visit to Eastern Oregon. During the visit our virtuous small dog positively nailed the host dog to the carpet, causing lifelong trauma to the little hostette and lifelong embarrassment to ourselves. We were bad guests. Dogs are often unwelcome on farms because descendants of wolves frequently don't mingle well with livestock. Gardens and flowerbeds also suffer from energetic pups who don't know the local boundaries.

If you are sick, stay home. Guests can leave a houseful of nasty germs behind them after a visit.

Being a guest or having guests is too important not to do it well. How else can we see where our loved ones live, meet their friends, take their walks and hear their stories in person? How else can we have loved ones in our home, show them how much they mean to us, spoil them a little, be inspired by their ideas and interested in their lives? This guest business enriches our lives.

GOOD MANNERS

Our neighbors, the Kelloggs, were staunch Methodists and strict teetotalers. Mrs. Kellogg was a lifelong member of the Women's Christian Temperance Union. They loved my non-church-going father who practiced his religion in good deeds for the Kelloggs and everyone else in our neighborhood. When we would visit the Kelloggs at their beach house in Balboa, there would be a few cans of beer tucked in the back of the refrigerator for Pop, their way of making him feel at home.

EVER READY

Emmy called it her "poltergeist," the crafty spirit who sneaked off with important papers, hid her glasses, ate pens and probably consumed all those lost socks. At age 89, she took special precautions for Halloween. Opening her freezer, we discovered her clown mask stored tidily on top of her supply of Halloween candy.

Emmy on Guests

Over the years, Emmy has sent us assorted notes and advisories as she reflected on many decades of entertaining.

THE WHY OF VISITING

Can you can learn what a visitor hopes to get out of his or her visit:

- Rest?

- A chance to work in peace?

- Knowledge of the area?

- Perspective on his or her own life?

- The chance to know you better?

- An adventure in gardening or cooking?

What other lines of hope may he or she have?

SUGGESTIONS TO EASE THE STRAIN OF A SIZABLE HOUSE PARTY

- Maintain a clear schedule so that your own life (meetings, appointments, desk work, meditating or whatever) is not eroded.

- If you are clear about your schedule, then this also gives your guests time-off they may need.

THE BEAUTY OF SACK LUNCHES

Make lunch as they do at Colorado's Redstone Inn or on Sierra Club trips:

- Set out all lunch items at breakfast: peanut butter, ham, tuna, hard boiled eggs, bread, cookies & fruit plus paper bags.

- Have each guest makes his/her own lunch.

This creates independence for all because you can eat when you want & where you wish. You can go off on an expedition together or in opposite directions.

BREAKFAST IS NOT ALWAYS A SOCIAL MEAL

Breakfast need NOT be a social meal and this can free the kitchen.

• Make breakfast flexible.

• Set-up food & drink on a table or porch or wherever for whenever your guests want to eat. This is easy & convenient for your guests & you are not left dangling.

• Use a thermos for coffee or boiling water for tea. Equipment for this & a toaster are a good investment.

• Put out cans of V-8, good Melba toast & good jams. (See page 59 for Emmy's baked toast.)

• Don't forget prunes or other dried or stewed or fresh fruit & yogurt & good cold cereals.

• Go Dutch with a European breakfast of cheese, ham & dark bread.

Remember that late sleepers allow you to eat on your own schedule.

NOTE: Emmy gave Catherine extra credit for sleeping late on visits to Kentucky because it gave her easy, undivided time with John

---

AN END-RUN ON DIRTY GLASSES

• Endless dirty glasses to wash can be the killer, so make a house rule:
NO GLASSES EXCEPT AT DINNER.

• Use the Sierra Club technique with Sierra Club cups. Each person is responsible for his own cup for every use & knife & fork & spoon.

• Put out a pail of soapy water for washing.

MISSING PERSONS

Isn't it too bad that those other people couldn't show up for drinks?

—Betsy Strong Cowles Partridge

Favorite saying after having a particularly good time in small company.

The Gift of Flowers

It all started in childhood when Mama had us celebrate May Day by making paper baskets, filling them with flowers from our garden and delivering them to our neighbors on South Holliston. My sister and I hung the baskets on door handles, rang doorbells and ran. It was exhilarating: the phantom gift with all pleasure in the doing and giving.

Flowers are essential for the pleasure their beauty brings both in the garden and on the table. In the garden they are joyful splashes of color, grown for their beauty alone. An arrangement on the table adds something substantial to the feeling of a meal.

Here at Crow Farm, we have our own flowers most of the year, beginning with hellebores in January; primroses, violets, snow drops, crocus, early daffodils and forsythia in February; daffodils and violas in March; tulips, hyacinth, azaleas, bleeding hearts, lilacs, quince, cherry, crabapple, pear and apple blossoms in April; peonies, rhododendron, *geum*, clematis, day lilies and California poppies in May; lupine, oriental poppies and *alstromeria* in June; lilies and calendulas in July; nasturtium, dahlias, cone flowers, black-eyed Susans and zinnias in August; fall crocus and asters in September. The faithful varieties of iris — bearded, Dutch, dwarf, Japanese, Siberian and Gladwin — from March through July and roses from April through November. One year we scrounged a last bouquet of calendulas for Thanksgiving and geraniums from the sun room on New Year's Eve.

We have favorite old vases and some new ones, plus a half-dozen different-sized and shaped frogs for flower arranging. One of the best vases is still the Mason jar.

Flower arranging is a great pleasure perhaps because it represents bringing the outdoors inside. I've tossed out narrow ideas about combining flowers, trying to match up certain colors and avoid others. The oddest combinations can work — crimson roses with orange calendulas, softened by gray-green leaves, for example. There is some quality of color in flowers that makes them compatible through nature's own harmony. There are exceptions to this, as Lisa pointed out recently, after observing some badly mis-matched rhododendrons in a local garden.

It always feels like a triumph to put together what you have, however odd or paltry the assortment. By Thanksgiving we usually do not have much in the garden but dead plants. Even those have possibilities. Dried pods with scarlet berries from a Gladwin iris combined with the dried tops of a sedum (Indian Chief) plus rose hips make an interesting arrangement.

A highlight of our floral year is the late spring bloom of an orchid cactus (*Epiphyllum*) that originally came from my mother's garden in California. We have two of these in our sun room and their spectacular eight inch phosphorescent coral blossoms are show stoppers for a brief 24 hours.

Eating on the Road

On driving trips, we always take at least one water bottle and usually two. Having a water bottle nearby makes it easy to drink along the way which we often forget to do when traveling. We also take a thermos of tea or coffee or hot water. We believe in picnic lunches when traveling because a picnic breaks up a long drive and refreshes by giving you the possibility of stopping at a beautiful spot for lunch instead of a fast food parking lot. We pack a small cooler with lunch fixings and a frozen bottle of water to keep it cool. Our favorite bread is a moist whole grain one which will keep for days. (The best ever was Stella's oatmeal bread that kept a full ten days.) We may pack a whole roast chicken, feta cheese, oil-cured olives and nuts. When the garden is in high gear, we don't leave home without a bag of tomatoes and cucumbers. Apples travel nicely, too, plus a brownie or two and an old yogurt container filled with carrot sticks. We also recommend Emmy's 2,000 Mile Sandwiches and AnnaDay's Apricot Loaf. (See recipes on pages 85 & 106.)

Our "Waitress/Waiter of the Year Award" started on our wedding anniversary one year. On a driving trip, we'll find ourselves in a roadside restaurant where we get exceptional service from a good, cheery soul. We reward this person by writing a note indicating that he or she has been designated "Waitress/Waiter of the Year" and enclose a $20 tip when $1.50 would have sufficed. Then we sneak out and invent for ourselves the scene when the big winner discovers the reward.

We walk out of restaurants that don't suit us. We've gone as far as sitting down, opening our napkins, drinking our water and reading the menu before realizing that the place is not right for us. Sometimes we know as soon as we walk into a restaurant that something is very wrong — bad management, hostilities, a personal or personnel crisis. When we do figure it out, we get up and leave. It makes us feel much better not to be captives of someone else's bad karma.

THE RIGHT ATTITUDE

Anyone who has some good will
can find good will everywhere.

—An Irish Traveler

From Amos Oz' novel, *Don't Call It Night*

Canning

We preserve pears, apples, blackberries, oranges, lemons, grapefruit, tomatoes, beans, plums, red peppers, strawberries, raspberries, grapes, cherries, quince, apricots and peaches. We make sauce, syrup, catsup, jelly, jam, chutney, preserves, vinegar, fruit butter and more. We like to use our own produce, but we also buy flats of fruit from local farms or roadside stands.

The Bible for canning is *Ball's Blue Book*, an inexpensive guide published by the same company which makes canning jars. We refer to this frequently for information about canning times and other technical details. We also call Karen for her custom canning advice. She has tried everything, including such delicious inventions as banana marmalade and kippered cherries.

We sterilize canning jars in the oven by placing clean jars on a cookie sheet in a pre-heated 250° oven for 20 minutes. We have found that hot jam or marmalade ladled into these hot jars provides enough heat to seal the lids. We also use the convection oven for some canning instead of the traditional pot of boiling water on the cook top. It's much easier, although it is not a method approved by the U.S. Department of Agriculture.

We like to name our canned goods after events going on at the time we are canning them. *Siberian Express Marmalade*, for example, was canned during the big winter storm of that name. *Last Posthole Chutney* went into its jars the day we finished replacing an old fence between our hayfield and our neighbor's.

Our large chest freezer is another asset. We freeze pesto, string beans, fresh tomato purée, tomato paste, dried tomatoes, blackberries, blueberries, apple juice and other vegetables as well as beef from our latest calf. Karen freezes pesto in heavy plastic freezer bags pressed into thin sheets so she can break off the amount she needs easily. Bill and Max freeze their pesto in ice cube trays to make easy individual servings. We often freeze fruit with some sugar in heavy plastic freezer bags, waiting for a more convenient time to preserve it. Karen freezes puréed strawberries in ice cube trays and then makes smoothies during the winter, combining the strawberries with fresh bananas. She also purées herbs such as cilantro or dill with water and then freezes it. Salsa can also be successfully frozen.

It's important to keep track of what you have in your freezer. We label food as we put it into the freezer, writing the contents and date on a piece of freezer tape or a small white office label with a pencil or permanent marker and then sticking it on top of the container or package. (Spills and moisture in the freezer can "erase" non-indelible pens.) We also know extremely organized people who keep a master list of the contents of their freezers. An admirable idea.

Our Harvest Maid food dehydrator is excellent for drying apples, pears, tomatoes, sunflower seeds, strawberries, bananas and more. We use our flea market Champion juicer for grape and other juices. We also have an old apple press that we bring out in the fall, inviting friends to help make the world's best apple juice. Kids love to turn the crank, adults do, too.

We store canned goods, canning supplies such as jars and lids, the food dehydrator, apple press, garlic, wine, dog food and a good deal of miscellany in the fruit room. It is one of the farm's many outbuildings located just a few steps from the laundry room door, our main entrance to the kitchen and the house. Formerly a small milk house, this cool, dark 8x10 foot space has walls filled with sawdust for insulation as well as a concrete floor, one small window and shelves on three walls.

WHAT GOES AROUND COMES AROUND

One night when Bruce Klepinger was eating polenta with us, he recalled that his great aunt used to make corn meal mush to sell. She filled tin cans with it, making cylinders for easy slicing so that it could be fried up and served with butter and maple syrup.

Now the old, familiar corn meal mush has become polenta and it's a gourmet item available at our grocery store in an 18 oz. plastic-wrapped cylinder for $2.79. We think that Aunt Beenie would be very surprised.

Bruce described his Aunt Beenie — a nickname given by his sisters and him— as a "tall, elegant old German lady" whose real name was Caroline Beck. She and her husband, Uncle Charles, were home-farmers in Indiana. They raised pigs and chickens. They also made a special scrubbing soap from rendered fat and oak wood ash as well as wreathes of "weeds," as Bruce described them, which they would collect each fall. On Saturdays Aunt Beenie would bake rolls and breakfast breads, including hot cross buns at Easter, to sell in town. Perhaps their most enterprising business was renting palm trees to local churches at Christmas and Easter. Bruce recalled that the palm trees summered outside at their farm. It must have been quite a sight. Life was good for the Becks and they each lived to be about 100 years old.

The Munching Band

It's dark outside and we've just finished dinner. Everyone gathers in the soft light of the living room. One by one we reach into the large basket to select our instruments. The choices are difficult. Will it be the old hubcaps or the musical lobster? The harmonica or the ocarina? The rainmaker or the musical spoons? The yogurt containers of rice or the hollow wooden box? The bugle or the xylophone? The bongos or the baby gong? The triangle or the tambourine? The cow bell or the tin flute? The crow call or the whistle? The drum or the sandpaper blocks? The Javanese guitar or the Balinese violin? The castanets or the ukulele?

Someone taps out a rhythm on the drum, the flute trills, the hubcaps clang, there are whistles, bangs, shakes, rattles and rolls. It's another rousing performance of the Crow Farm Munching Band. (The conductor of the Eugene Symphony Orchestra once visited during a Munching Band performance, and quickly fled, horrified at the sound.)

Everyone has the required skills for our band and the average kitchen or garage has more than enough "instruments." No rehearsals, only performances. No wrong notes, only fascinating sounds. The point is participation and a spirit of play. The feeling of connection can be breathtaking.

We have one more musical device to share with you. Our nephew Macauley taught us the **BLACK KEY TRICK** for playing the piano. If you stick to the black keys — any combination of black keys — you cannot hit a wrong note. You can make original music whenever you want. It's a delicious thrill to sit down at a piano and, with no prior experience, be an immediate success. Duets are fun, too.

KEEP ON DANCING

Her who dances and runs away
Lives to dance another day.
—Warrick Anderson

Inspired by Oliver Goldsmith's verse from
The Art of Poetry on a New Plan (1761):

For he who fights and runs away
May live to fight another day;
But he who is in battle slain
Can never rise and fight again.

The Manual

Stories & Entertainment

We hope you'll sit in a comfortable chair with a cup
of tea and read this section while you are waiting for
a cake to bake or bread to rise. We will be honored
if you take our book to bed and fall asleep with it.
This is designed to be entertainment or relaxation,
not work.

The Ultimate Dog Story

On Tuesday, February 21, 1995, I took Lively and Ivy, our border collies, for a hike up an unknown logging road. Owned by Seneca, a local logging company, it was closed off by a gate marked "No Trespassing." I had heard about it from the family who owns the store where we get our dog food. (When you write a check for feed, their dog takes it out of your hand and delivers it to Mrs. Diess, the bookkeeper. I also learned that if you borrow a pen to write a check, their dog also makes sure that the pen gets back to its owner.)

There were several rock quarries just off the logging road with resulting steep cliffs, some of them 100 feet high. On the way back from our walk, about 4 p.m., Lively suddenly took off like a shot after a deer. Ivy stayed close at hand. I didn't see Lively at all after that although I called and backtracked. Then I returned Ivy to the truck and walked back up the mountain searching one more time. Finally at wit's end, I returned to the farm just as Catherine came back from town. We went out again. I walked the logging road once more before returning to the truck after dark. No Lively.

At Catherine's marvelous suggestion, I called Bruce Klepinger, our friend, mountaineer and trekking guide and asked if he could help us search for Lively the next morning at first light, 7 a.m. He agreed.

Catherine and I didn't sleep much that night. We knew that Lively was out there somewhere, either dead or wounded or simply lost. There are cougars and coyotes in the area and I had been warned by the Diesses that a trapper had set traps or laid out poisoned meat to kill the predators and protect the neighborhood farm animals.

The next morning Bruce showed up and we drove over to the gate just off Doane Road. We followed my original trail but went further, watching for dog tracks. On the way back, we started climbing behind the cliffs to see if Lively could have fallen over a cliff in pursuit of a deer. When we got close to the top of a hill, we looked over the edge and below us we could see a small black head. It was Lively, nearly invisible against the rocky backdrop. He was 20-feet down a steep chute and had been standing and sitting on a tiny ledge no bigger than his 50-pound body. Immediately below him was a 60-foot drop. Above him it was too steep for him to climb back out. He had been staying quietly in that position for the past 17 hours, not making a sound, even when we passed within sight.

I stood on the rim above and reminded Lively to sit and stay still, hoping that my familiar voice would make him calmer than I felt, while Bruce returned to the truck to pick up the climbing rope we had brought along. Lively knew that help was near and he once began groaning with impatience and probably fear. He was inches from a fatal fall.

When Bruce returned 25 minutes later, he expertly rigged up a system so I could be his anchor and belay him over the side. Before he disappeared from my view, I reminded Bruce that if push came to shove, he was more important than our precious dog. He nodded grudgingly.

Bruce dropped out of my sight for about five minutes as he worked his way down, kicking powerfully to make each step in the steep, muddy slope. It was not easy going. Bruce said that small rocks and sand began to rain down the chute and finally Lively covered his head with his paws, glued to the interior wall of his shelf. When Bruce got within reach, he had to instruct Lively firmly to sit and stay. After he had secured his own footing as much as possible on Lively's precariously small ledge, Bruce then rigged Lively up in an elaborate double crotch knot sling using what he described as a "squash knot." That rope was attached to a second one that he had me haul up as Lively assisted by clawing his own way up the steep slope. Bruce then hauled himself up the climbing rope. Reunited at the top, Lively wagged his tail extravagantly and headed immediately to a private place to do his business. He had not fouled his small nest. Then we three romped on the ground together with joy and relief.

It's nice to have a one person Animal Rescue Unit for a friend because Catherine and I couldn't possibly have saved Lively by ourselves.

BEST FRIENDS

It seems to me that the good lord in his infinite wisdom gave us three things to make life bearable — hope, jokes and dogs, but the greatest of these was dogs.

—Robyn Davidson

From her book, *Tracks*

THE EYES HAVE IT

Our last gift to John's father was a dog, a life-sized, sand-cast, painted beagle lying down with a dog biscuit in its paws and a strikingly alert expression on its face. The Judge named her Phoebe and she was a trouble-free companion during his last months. Later Emmy would take Phoebe on house calls, including to young Chelsea's bedside following surgery. Phoebe proved to be a most satisfactory pet.

Before she traveled to Kentucky, Phoebe spent a short time here at Crow Farm. When we took her out of the box, our border collie Lively took one sniff and ignored her. Clearly she wasn't "real" for him.

Ivy, our other border collie, sniffed, too, but what her nose failed to communicate her eyes did clearly. There was a new dog in our midst and Ivy had no intention of letting this creature out of her sight. She appointed herself guardian of the motionless dog. Ivy's vigilance persisted even after we returned Phoebe to her box. No, Ivy was not going to be fooled by a box. She had her mind's eye on its contents, still a threat to the canine order of our home. We presume it was a great relief for Ivy when the interloper was packed and mailed to Kentucky.

Barnyard Boatworks

Odd as it may seem, boats are a very important part of our life at Crow Farm. Our work here is determined mostly by the length of the day. During the longest days of the year, near the end of June, the sun rises about 5:30 a.m. and last light is close to 10 p.m. You can imagine what effect those long, hot days have on the garden, the corn patch, the fruit trees, the fields and the lawn. We rise early and are usually at work as long as the light lasts, often having dinner at 9:30 in the evening. In the late summer the days shorten somewhat, but the heat intensifies, sometimes into the 90°s, occasionally higher. How does one escape the tyranny of the sun or find relief from the daily routine of the farm? We have found our answer in boats.

When we need a respite from farm work we pack up sandwiches and cool drinks near the end of the day and drive about eight miles to the local lake where we keep a 12-foot wooden sailboat. We ease up the sail and shove off, whether there is any wind or not. We explore the marshes and bird sanctuaries, anchor in a cove for a picnic, slip into the water if we're too hot, and use the last light breezes or the paddles to work our way back to the slip before total darkness. The water world has a way of washing away the day, transporting us to another realm, giving us renewed energy for tomorrow's chores.

There also comes a time when we just need to get away, to rest up, to detach from the phone and the mail and our everyday life. That is when we retreat to the coast and spend a night or two on our sturdy old pocket cruiser, a home-made, 24-foot wooden sailboat. In the winter we stay tied up at the dock and use shore power to heat the small cabin. We read, sleep, sip tea and listen to the cold rain beat on the cabin top. In warmer months we head out into the ocean, or sail on the river, sometimes lying at anchor and pulling up crabs for a seafood dinner.

Boats are our refuge from being overcome by the demands of the land.

It was like driving a loaf of bread.

—Tenold Peterson

Describing how it felt to pilot a 45 foot houseboat
through the canals of Sweden.

A Fish Story

This is John's story of a sailing adventure featuring an esteemed fisherman and a memorable fish.

When sailing down the coast of Washington and Oregon, it is not necessary to look at a chart to know when you pass the mouth of the Columbia River. Clear coastal salt water that travels southward in a one knot current is suddenly hit by muddy drainage from a 250,000 square mile area that gushes out the mouth of the continent's second largest river. It was close to twilight. We had been sailing since dawn from Grays Harbor. Even though our stout, wooden sailboat was almost ten miles off shore, the swirling currents from the river's discharge were twisting us around like a stick in a storm gutter. The terrain is flat around the mouth of the Columbia and no land would be in sight until we approached the headland where Lewis and Clark's party, with Sacajawea, examined the carcass of a whale in January, 1806, during their historic trek across the continent.

The disturbed waters off the mouth of the Columbia River are not a pleasant place to be. The sea is confused and one has to continually work the tiller to keep on course. Traffic is often heavy with large vessels from around the world heading into the river to Portland and beyond. Darkness was approaching and we were in for another night at sea and then most of the next day before we would pass Yaquina Head and dock at Newport, Oregon, our destination.

Catherine was standing in the companionway, wondering how to keep our spirits up with a good meal. "Nicholas, we need a salmon," she told him. Nicholas got out the stubby fishing rod and lure. Catherine started heating some potatoes and onions on the camp stove. Just as dark was approaching, Nicholas hauled in a beautiful silver salmon just the right size to feed the three of us. We cleaned it on the deck, sliced it into chunks and popped them into the pot with the potatoes and onions. In ten minutes, we had the best meal of our lives. The best fisherman, we decided, was one who can deliver a meal when you need it most.

Who feeds the father feeds the son.

—Adapted from an Ethiopian proverb

Holy Cow

"Let me read your palm, good madam," offered the kindly old gentleman shortly after my elephant ride around the fortress of Jaipur. His face was earnest. I had been transported by more than an elephant that morning, falling under India's exotic spell, some combination of powerful smells, opulent sights, unbelievable stories and awesome reality.

"Yes, of course, please read my palm," I replied as if agreeing to an ordinary request.

He took my right hand in his own, studied it carefully and reported, "You will marry happily, live a long time and feed a red cow on Thursdays."

"Well, that's very interesting," I noted, disappointed by the Chinese fortune-cookie-style reading. The part about the cow made it comical, immediately dismissed as harmless Indian entertainment. I never gave it another thought.

Then some years later, I was going through old papers, including letters and journals that recount my trip around the world when I met both the palm reader and, later, John. Suddenly the part about the cow made brilliant sense. The old man was right, I was feeding a red cow on Thursdays and others days as well. We had been feeding her since John and I got married years before. I also realized that John had never heard the story although he was the central figure in it.

On our wedding day, John had led me into the barnyard to find my wedding gift. He guided a thorough search and finally directed my gaze toward the cow standing 20-feet in front of us.

"That's it," said John.

"What do you mean?" I asked, not understanding.

"The cow, she's your wedding gift," explained the expectant groom.

Too surprised to speak, I contemplated the most substantial present I had ever received: a 14-month old red cow weighing nearly half a ton.

"She's beautiful," I finally got out, finding my voice.

"Yes," agreed John, "look at that straight back. She's part white face Hereford and part Charolais. She's a beauty all right."

"We'll call her Dhole," I suggested, "after Dawa's *zupchuk* on our trek. You remember that sweet creature he was taking to his farm, don't you?"

"Yes, of course," replied John, smiling. He had not forgotten a moment of our enchanted time in Nepal, nor his interest in Dawa's farm animal, a cross between a yak and a cow, who had shared our camp for several nights, following us along the trail to Namche Bazaar.

We laughed. Several hours later, John and I officially began our fairy tale marriage, surrounded by Bruce Klepinger, Jim Ottaway and other friends from our Nepal trek, Jim's wife Mary, Dean and Lisa Livelybrooks. The red cow completed the wedding party, fulfilling the old man's prophecy and my wildest dreams. We are working hard on our long life together.

In the Long Run

John's father, Macauley Letchworth Smith, went to the IX Olympiad in Amsterdam in 1928 as one of the top runners of his day. His mother, Mary Margaret Macauley Smith, collected newspaper clippings about his races and photos of his teams that his wife, Emilie Strong Smith, assembled into a scrapbook during the summer of 1933 just before John was born. We have referred to this scrapbook as well as Emmy and John's recollections to tell Macauley's story.

Emmy said that Macauley's remarkable night vision helped launch her husband's running career. He lived at Ann's Acres in a household of women with his Aunt Rachel Bigelow, his mother and "my beautiful sister Ann," as he always referred to his younger sibling. (His father and uncle had died years earlier.) Macauley loved to tell of his escape, homework finished, running in the dark across the Country Club golf course, into the next valley, across the Muddy Fork of Bear Grass Creek, up and across the Waters' corn field to the farmhouse at Locust Grove. He would then sleep there in one of the big beds under a pile of quilts. Mrs. Waters counted Macauley as her sixth son, even the favorite. Up early Macauley would run home again and catch the trolley to school. Emmy is still puzzling over whether or not he would have eaten a big farm breakfast with the Waters family before heading home.

Macauley's running career began at Phillips Andover Academy in the fall of 1921. At that time, he would have reached his full height of 5'8" and his lifelong 135 lbs. Everyone was expected to participate in sports at Andover. Years later Emmy imagined a teacher steering him toward running, an authoritative shove in a direction that would shape his life.

In June 1922, Macauley ran to victory in the 1-mile, helping Andover beat Exeter for the first time since 1915. Of that race, a reporter wrote, "Smith, who appeared to have run on his nerve alone, showed the courage of a Trojan and all sympathized with him in his heart-breaking race with the Exeter favorite. Smith came through in to a roar of applause in one of the bitterest fights ever witnessed on a school track." He won by 12 yards in a time of 4:37 and was elected the captain of the cross-country team for his senior year.

At Yale in the fall of 1923, Macauley broke the three mile record with a time of 20:04-⅗. Two weeks later he set a freshman intercollegiate record of 16:22 on the new 3-mile course at Van Cortlandt Park, an extension of New York City's Central Park. After that "the bespectacled 19 year old Yale harrier" set a new record for the big 6-mile cross country race at Van Cortlandt Park with a time of 31:24, bettering the old record by 46 seconds and finishing 175 yards ahead of his nearest competitor in a field of 250." A reporter noted, "Smith was not a bit tired after the race." He was elected captain of the Yale track team for the 1925 season and re-elected captain for the 1926 season.

Macauley ran "on the boards" during the winter of 1924-25, including a 2-mile race at the N.Y. Athletic Club in which he competed against the greatest runner of the era — Paavo Nurmi — the "Flying Finn" who had taken the previous Olympic Games by storm. Macauley was probably a shoe-in for the 1-mile race, but when no one would register against Nurmi in the 2-miles, the management looked to Smith. Nurmi held several world records for this distance and set a new one of 8:58, so fast that one sportswriter speculated it would probably never be equaled.

In May Macauley broke another meet record by winning the 2-mile race at Princeton in 9:41, although his best time that year was 9:38-3/5. He was slowed in the fall season by injuries from a motorcycle accident after he swerved to avoid a dog and fell, breaking his collarbone. Somehow he still managed to finish eleventh in Van Cordlandt Park in November. A year later in the last race of his intercollegiate cross country career, he set a final record of 27:53-3/5 on Yale's 6-mile Woodbridge Hills course. His mother was on hand for that victory.

Shortly after graduation from Yale, Macauley competed at Stamford Bridge, England on July 9, 1927 in a meet matching Harvard and Yale with Oxford and Cambridge. He topped Oxford's star by 120 yards in the 3-mile race, leading from start to finish. The *London Times* waxed poetic, "The three miles was, in my opinion, the finest performance of the afternoon. For a man to beat 14:45 on a wet track, making the pace the whole way, is a truly great performance . . . Smith ran a wonderful race with perfect judgment and sound knowledge of pace. I commend this beautiful knowledge of pace to all would-be 3-milers." His times were 4:46 for the first mile, 9:54-4/5 at the second and 14:44-1/5 at the finish.

In the summer of 1928 Macauley was selected to compete in the 5,000 and 10,000-meter events at the IX Olympiad in Amsterdam. On July 31 he beat Paavo Nurmi in the 5,000-meter trials in a "great sprint on the last lap" for a time of 15:04. (The world record of 14:28-1/5 was held by Nurmi, but Macauley's own best time of 14:57-2/5 in the pre-Olympic try-outs was one of the best performances since the American record of 14:45 had been set in 1920.)
In the 5,000-meter race on August 3, 1928 Macauley stuck to the heels of Nurmi and then Nurmi's teammate Willie Rittola for 8 of 13 laps, but he faded in the backstretch of the ninth lap and withdrew. His American teammate Leo Lermond kept the pressure on for another three laps, but then he, too, could not maintain the pace and finished 50 yards behind Sweden's Edvin Wide who finished third. Surprisingly Rittola won in 14:38 with Nurmi in second place. There was speculation that Nurmi, having already won the 10,000 meters — his seventh Olympic victory — in a fierce battle with Rittola, ceded the win in the 5,000 meters to his fellow Finn.

Macauley ran his final race a week later in the Empire Games at Stamford Bridge, England. He won the 3-mile contest by a yard in the last quarter mile in 14:37-2/5.

For 60 years Macauley refused to speak about his running career. He finally confided that he was angry with his coach for sending him out as a "rabbit" to pace the formidable Nurmi and thus denying him the opportunity to run his own best race at the Olympics. A few years before his death, we sent him an article reporting that Nurmi had used performance-enhancing drugs during his running career. In his last years, Macauley was still pacing himself, lapping the dining room table with his walker to maintain his strength and mobility. He died at age 89 in 1993 after a lifetime spent running his own race.

Letters from Afar

From letters written by our nephew, Macauley Lord, while he and his wife, Carol Lestock, were living in Siberia for six months during 1990-91, both working for an exhibit sponsored by the USIA:

It is an 18 million dollar display designed to educate Soviets about the importance of design (architectural, graphic, product and automotive) in the daily lives of Americans. It is currently set up in an athletic field house in Khabarovsk. It is open to the public free of charge, six days/week for the month of December. We have between 2,000 and 12,000 visitors per day.

I am sitting at my library monitor post at the Exhibit. I am to make sure that only people with special invitations enter the library. I like this post because (a) I have time to write letters when things aren't busy and (b) I speak lots of Russian here explaining to people what the library is. Our conversations go something like this: "Excuse me, please. May I &*^%$ library. I *&^%$ medical student who &*^%$#@# exhibit." I say, "I'm sorry. I don't understand Russian very well. This is a technical library for Soviets who are specialists in architectural, graphic, product and automotive design. Are you a specialist in one of these fields?" "Yes, I am interested in graphic *&^%$. But *&^%^&&*." I usually manage to get the gist of what is said to me in Russian. Also, I seem to be learning a lot by osmosis . . . .

Our day so far: Up at 8 am (first light). Breakfast in the hotel restaurant of blini (quite good) and "omelette" which is a weightless beige mass made, we think, of powdered eggs. [A gent stops at my desk where I am now working to point at our Washington, D.C. metro map and say that "it's little" that "the Moscow Metro is BIG."] We leave on foot for the public market at 9:00. We walk past the massive concrete apartment blocks that seem to have been creatively designed to deaden the collective aestheticism of the masses. After 25 min. of walking on the icy sidewalks (there is no snow removal here of any significance) we arrive at the rinok or public market.

The rinok is a bustling place of commerce in food, fur hats, blue jeans, tropical fish and birds, etc. It is a place where we see state and private enterprises side-by-side. The failure of this economy is plain. In one five-second visual sweep, we see long lines for state items and no lines for private ones. Today, the Sovs will find here no cheese, eggs, milk, sugar, tea. (We saw our first bread for sale in four days this morning during our walk. But, we get plenty through the hotel.) They will find private meat but at exorbitant prices. Honestly, though, I really doubt that anyone will go hungry here. The food stores are well stocked compared to Moscow, Leningrad et al.

Outside the rinok, we see beautiful fur hats for 400 rubles ($80.00 at the official exchange rate), terrible knock-offs of Nike basketball shoes (you would pay $10.00 for these at K-Mart's bargain basement) for 350 rubles, shoddy blue jeans for 200 rubles.

Carol leaves at 10:15 to walk back to work while I actually shop. I buy raw peanuts, apples, dried apricots, cooked squid, spicy soybean sprouts, mandarin oranges, and fresh pasta! On the way back to the hotel, I walk past the Central Universal Magazine (store) where anything one wants is nowhere to be seen.

Midnight back at the hotel. Wonderful dinner tonight with Luda, Sasha, Vanya, Galya, Slava and Yura. The conversation touched on atrocities in nearby labor camps, the food crisis and (in the minds of some) the imminent civil war. Vanya thinks we should return to the good old days of Stalin. Galya says only the intelligentsia should be permitted to have political authority. Slava says that Gorbachev is the No. 1 enemy of the people. Luda serves us vodka milkshakes.

Becoming Part of History

This is Catherine's story of her first trip to Europe as a 19-year old student.

In the summer of 1968 I traveled to Eastern Europe and the former Soviet Union with a group of students led by a brilliant, eccentric professor from Harvard named Alex Lipson. We traveled in VW vans rented in Paris and camped, including along the Maginot Line in northern France and just off the Mozhaysk Road outside Moscow where Napoleon was stopped in 1812. We saw photographs in Minsk, Smolensk and other Russian cities taken before World War II and after, the post-war skylines dominated by the shells of bombed-out buildings and piles of rubble. In what was then called Leningrad, we heard stories about the nearly three-year siege that isolated that city from the rest of Russia and the world. We saw bullet holes in the walls of buildings in downtown Warsaw. The shocking reality of man's inhumanity to man was nowhere more evident than at Auschwitz. I was standing next to Lucien, a graduate student at the City College of New York, when he caught sight of his family name, Weisbrod, on a suitcase in an enormous pile of baggage.

In Poland, we met an English teacher when asking directions on the road after dark and he invited us home. He was thrilled to be able to welcome us. We stayed up much of the night talking with him, his son and daughter-in-law. They were relieved by the thaw in their local politics mirroring what was called the Prague Spring in neighboring Czechoslovakia. The next morning our host pointed out a local Communist Party official who looked like he would have preferred to lock us up as we walked through town to buy bread and milk. I have worried that our host may have paid dearly in months to come for his open-hearted hospitality.

Lucien bribed the guards at the Polish-Soviet border with old copies of Playboy so that we wouldn't be searched. Throughout the former Soviet Union we had to stand in long lines to buy delicious black bread but not much other food worth mentioning, except the superb ice cream. We were not allowed to photograph gas stations or railroad stations, a prohibition enforced by the Intourist Guide who traveled with us at all times once we arrived in Moscow. We met agent provocateurs in campgrounds with their ears to the ground for signs of inappropriate political discussion. We met hustlers who wanted to change our dollars at exorbitant black market rates and buy our blue jeans. We met fearsome old ladies who critiqued our behavior and clothing in rapid fire Russian. We met extraordinarily kind people who spoke English and were starved for contact with Westerners. They invited us home and fed us tea and vodka.

One member of our group, a student from Princeton who seemed to be following in the steps of that university's famous *bons vivants*, drove his new Jaguar XKE. Needless to say, he was the hero wherever he parked. Crowds gathered immediately for a first look at that beautiful car. He generously spent time opening the hood and discussing the features of his car in rudimentary Russian. He single-handedly contributed more to the reputation of the Good American than many foreign aid programs.

En route to Moscow in late June, we were pulled off the main road and made to wait on a side road for several hours. We were puzzled at the time but later understood that the Soviet Army had been moving tanks and troops westward in preparation for their invasion of Czechoslovakia in August.

When we left the Soviet Union after six weeks, our van was partly disassembled at the border as guards made sure we were not exporting works of literature or other contraband. From the Soviet border we drove across a no-man's land and were warmly greeted by a Romanian border guard pointedly speaking to us in French. A second guard dressed in a white lab coat sprayed our tires with a bilious green disinfectant, a clear message that we had left dangerous territory.

JAMES BOND RE-VISITED

On the same trip described above, we had an accident late one Saturday afternoon on a rain-slick road outside Moscow. There had just been another accident in the same location but the vehicle and a motorcycle had not been removed from the two lane road because the authorities had not yet arrived. The driver of our van, Bruce, had swerved to avoid hitting the other vehicles and somehow we flipped over. Fortunately, no one was hurt seriously although Kathy had to spend a harrowing night in the hospital under observation for a concussion. I escaped with broken frames on my glasses and a bruise the size of a watermelon and the color of an eggplant on my thigh.

Remarkably, after some repairs our van still ran in spite of the fact that it looked like a crushed can. We found that people were now much more interested in our vehicle, joking about it and probably about us, too. Someone dubbed it Fantobus and the name stuck. We taped Fantobus in Cyrillic letters on the front end and became instant celebrities in town after town.

That was the era of James Bond. Not to be outdone by the Western hero, the Russians in collaboration with an Italian film company had produced a series of films starring a James Bond-type character named *Fantomas*.

Fantomas was the pop hero of the Soviet Union that summer and our Fantobus was the perfect foil for his celebrity. We finally did see one of these hilariously bad films, "*Fantomas* versus Scotland Yard," in an outdoor theater in the Caucasus. The enthusiasm of the crowd was infectious, making up for the conspicuous cinematic defects of the film itself, a truly bad imitation of the original Bond.

Food Literacy: The No Taste Test

What is the main ingredient in *"sonofabitch stew"*?
- a. A politician of your choice.
- b. A media personality with whom you disagree.
- c. *"Marrow gut,"* the perennial favorite of cowboys.
- d. Roadkill.

What is the difference between *"spotted dick"* **and** *"spotted dog"*?
- a. The difference is cosmetic: both are suet puddings.
- b. Raisins count as *"spots,"* even when my dog Spot growls.
- c. In literature, Dick and Jane usually walked the dog.
- d. One gets rolled, the other is a cylinder.

What is *"toast water"*?
- a. A form of compost tea.
- b. A mistake involving a breakfast staple.
- c. A substitute for champagne in hard times.
- d. A folk remedy for healing that led to our custom of *"toasting"* to health.

What does *"Teheroa"* **mean?**
- a. A suburb of Teheran with no underground facilities.
- b. An invitation to go rowing in a Maori dialect.
- c. An algorithm involving predictions for flooding, *"The Teheroa Function"*
- d. A famous New Zealand clam.

How would you use *"portable soup"*?
- a. It would be handy on long flights.
- b. As a good substitute for Elmer's glue.
- c. To avoid using *"veal glue,"* its first cousin.
- d. As a down-load to a hungry iPod.

What is *"yarg"*?
- a. An expression of extreme disdain: *"He behaved like a yarg."*
- b. A cheese made by the Gray family in the Cotswalds; "yarg" is "gray" backwards.
- c. A nautical epithet for missing the boat, *"Oh, yarg!"*
- d. The sound heard before administering the Heimlich maneuver.

What is *"tutmaç?*
- a. A longer skirt for ballerinas.
- b. The Turkish word for noodles.
- c. An explosion following over-consumption of macaroni.
- d. Literally, *"Do not cause hunger."*

What is *"spitchcock"*?
- a. The rooster in Harry Potter.
- b. The surname of Alfred Hitchcock's spiteful cousin.
- c. Method for grilling eel.
- d. A butterflied bird.

Source of Terms: *The Oxford Companion to Food* by Alan Davidson (1999) • Answers on page 348

Stories & Entertainment

The Spectacular Appendix

> *May you have a long life and a quick death.*
>
> —Old Gaelic toast
>
> Quoted by Mike Smith
> (Inverness, Scotland, 1997)

The Museum

Displayed in a small cabinet, our collection consists of several dozen objects that have been unearthed around the farm in the course of gardening, digging, remodeling and other daily activities.

Department	Item/Description	Size	Site
Antiquities & Mummies	2 arrowheads of gray flint	Assorted	Garden
	5 rodent mummies with tails (2 with skin & 1 with fur)	Assorted	House
	Frog mummy, flattened	1-⅝" x 1-¾"	House
	Mummified pancake: embossed designs	4" diameter	Kitchen
Household Artifacts	2 porcelain doorknobs, brown & white	1-⅞" diameter	Garden
	2 pottery shards of glazed ceramic	Assorted	Garden
	Glass stopper	2" x 1"	Garden
	Wallpaper fragments	Assorted	House
	Glass duck head, blue & white	2" x 1-⅜"	Garden
Games & Toys	4 marbles (orange, blue marbled with orange & white, beige marbled with brown, & dark red)	⅝" diameter	Garden
	Softball, stuffed with John & Dean's hair; created by Lisa Livelybrooks	¾" diameter	House
	Gun fragment, rusted; Harrington & Richardson automatic ejecting revolver; manufactured from 1891-1941; probably used as target shooting firearm	4" diameter 5-½" across	Barn
	Ceramic arm, probably from doll	1-⅝" long	Garden
Miscella-neous	Stiff leather glove thumb	3-¾" x 1-⅞"	Garden
	Cage of wood & screen for queen bee	3" x 1-⅛" x ¾"	U.S. Mail
	Bone kneecap of calf	3-½" x 2-¼"	California
	Connector of lead, wood & copper	6-½" long	Garden
	3 square-headed nails, rusted	Assorted	Garden

Denture Dog: An Original Word Game

There is something called *literary license* where authors sneak whatever they want into an otherwise earnest endeavor. In case you had any doubts, this is it — our only chance to rescue this home grown Crow Farm game from total obscurity. We hereby introduce it to you.

Complete instructions follow. But first, here are some of the practical uses of this feisty game. Denture Dog will instantly drive cobwebs from your brain. If we get sleepy on a driving trip, Denture Dog comes to the rescue. Safer than coffee, more stimulating than FM, this is one of our regular bag of tricks on trips. In public places, Denture Dog guards against unwanted lip reading and can even permit undetected communication when talking is frowned upon. We could go on and on. Only mercy restrains us.

The Denture Dog practice session takes a mere 10 seconds. All that is required is a serious attitude and the one-time use of a mirror. The instructions are these: stand in front of the mirror, lock your teeth together, make a big smile and, without moving your lips, repeat these words as loudly as possible: [DENTURE DOG SAYS . . .]. Good. The game, of course, is to express yourself using words that do not disturb the tranquility of your grimace. The brain searches for words to express your thoughts while bypassing your facial muscles. Phrases like *Yipes, there's a worm in my baby romaine* are out, [Eek, I ascertain a slug in this junior lettuce] is in. A simple declarative sentence can become a real mind-bender under the watchful eye of Denture Dog. We also use Denture Dog in letters, signified by brackets [thus]. [Good luck.] [Easy does it.]

SETTING IT STRAIGHT

[All errors in this text are kitty-cat-created.]

—Denture Dog

An After Dinner Tail

This is a true story that we were told after dinner by our friend Mark, a fine young environmental lawyer who is also a surfer. If you have a sensitive stomach, please close the book now.

One evening Mark and several friends were sitting around a cabin in a ruggedly beautiful, isolated coastal area. Everyone was despondent because a national surfing magazine was going to expose their secret surfing preserve to thousands of readers. Their long gloomy silence was suddenly broken by a snap.

Mark got up, opened the cupboard, picked-up a mousetrap bearing a wiggling creature. He walked back to the group and to everyone's discomfort, he set the full trap in the middle of the table. The surfers watched as the mouse quivered its last.

"One hundred dollars," said Mark. The group sat in stunned silence. "You would really eat that mouse for a hundred bucks?," asked one of them in disbelief. "You bet." Mark, with a spontaneous burst of bold inspiration, had discovered the ultimate distraction. Gloom was now on the run.

The place was turned upside down. Pockets, tackle boxes, the cookie jar, old socks, under the mattress, between the cushions. $103 in bills and small change found its way onto the table next to the motionless mouse.

An hour of strenuous negotiation followed to hammer out the final conditions of the wager. Only one lemon wedge permitted. Tartar sauce limited to one tablespoon. Mouse to be consumed in three parts, as is. No cooking. No gutting. No de-furring or skinning. Chewing required on each part. No spitting allowed. Parts must be swallowed and retained for at least one hour. The tail would be affixed in the cabin guest book where the meal would be recorded and signed by all witnesses.

Mark went to work. He got on the radio-phone and called a friend who is a doctor. He asked about the consequences of his proposed meal. "Negligible risk," the doctor concluded.

A place was set, the lemon and tartar sauce fetched. The knife was sharpened and the furry creature was cut into three parts with the tail set aside as evidence. Mark first took the head, chewed and swallowed. Then the upper body, chewed . . . swallowed. Finally, the lower body, chewed . . . . swallowed. Now the 60 minutes. Mark kept the mouse down 62 minutes. He got the money and his friends got their money's worth. The blues had been blown away by imaginative consumption.

> *One who proposes an exchange knows which is the better.*
>
> —An Ethiopian proverb

Mark's Mouse Tartare

Buried at the back of the appendix, this is the <u>only</u> recipe in the cookbook that we do not recommend. It is a variation on steak tartare and so named as a tribute to the Mongol influence on western cuisine.

Serves 1

1 fresh mouse
1 lemon wedge
1 T. tartar sauce

Remove tail. Divide mouse in thirds, using a sharp knife or cleaver. Arrange attractively on a plate. Garnish with lemon. Serve immediately with tartar sauce.

HARD NEWS

You may have seen her as you entered if you had to pass by the barn, but if not, it is the most grievous message imaginable that I have to tell.

Rosie slipped into the creek up above the barn and, in trying to get out, dug a hole almost her size. When I found her, she was unmovable. Thank goodness George and Lorna were home. They and two grandsons and, later, a daughter and son-in-law came to help. We got Rosie to the barn with George's tractor and covered her with hay and curtains from the shop. I dried her off with dog towels and gave her some electrolytes to drink. We massaged her until 10 p.m.

Rosie is unable to stand and needs to be hung up to allow her legs to function again, but George questions the barn poles' integrity. For now, she is feeling better, trying unsuccessfully to stand, groaning, but less bloaty.

The decision hangs as to whether she lives or dies. You may choose to put her out of her misery or to construct a framework to hang her or try the tractor bucket. She's too heavy for us all to heft and too stiff to support herself if we did lift her up. It's a very difficult predicament.

I am so sorry that this happened while you were away. It's awful to come home to, I know. Please call when you arrive and we can decide what's next. I can take tomorrow off if need be. I feel Rosie has made progress and I'd hate to abandon her now.

--Barbara Rattenborg

We got home late Sunday and conferred with Barbara immediately. Rosie seemed better the next morning. The vet was encouraging but concerned about her ragged breathing. He gave her a Vitamin B shot. Later we gave her electrolytes with the help of our loyal neighbors George and Lorna. When we went to turn her in the afternoon, she had just breathed her last. (January 1996)

Water Sports

When I was growing up, we had numerous pets, an aged daschund, a Siamese kitten who disappeared before her first year was out, two alley cats who lived to ripe old ages, an eccentric canary captured in my sister's second grade classroom, two hamsters who mercifully died before their midnight antics drove us all crazy, a few tadpoles which I carried home from first grade in my thermos, the infamous mice for my eighth grade science project on "intelligence," and, last but not least, our beloved goldfish, Cleo.

Cleo began life in that nether world from which carnivals supply themselves with fish. We won her in the ping-pong ball toss at the Pike in Long Beach, California and carried her home in a plastic bag of water.

Cleo's food of choice — pellets in a small blue tin that featured a goldfish on the front — came from Kress' dime store on Colorado Boulevard. We also learned to buy sea grass there which we carried home in those nifty waxed cardboard boxes with metal handles, more frequently associated with Chinese takeout food. Cleo passed through a series of increasingly large glass bowls until my father declared that she had reached her limit in a bowl that held about a gallon of water.

Cleo would let Pop know when it was time to change her water by blowing bubbles which we could hear as they broke the surface of the water. Perched at eye level on top of bookshelves between our living and dining rooms, Cleo had a fish eye view of the central part of our house. Once her bowl was moved to a lower, more protected location and Cleo made an immediate fuss by blowing bubbles. Pop quickly recognized her distress and moved Cleo back to her preferred vantage point.

I still don't know what conclusion to draw from the fact that Cleo grew horns the year before she died more than 10 years after becoming part of our family.

I own every rock.

—Emmy Smith

Describing her love of Christmas Cove, Maine where she spent many happy summers as a child, married John's father, spent summers with her own children, and returned often for visits with her favorite cousin.

Credits

*To Mama and Pop for encouraging me to enjoy the kitchen. • To my sister Connie for her support of my cooking through tireless dishwashing and enthusiastic eating. • To Linnie Doyle Savage Trumble from Texas, a fine cook, who took my interest in cooking seriously and gave me my first cookbook, **River Road Recipes** by the Junior League of Baton Rouge, Louisiana. • To Mum for her inspired cooking and generous hospitality, and for being mum. • To Howard and Edith French for friendship and food with great style. • To Ron Rick for his beautiful watercolor and years of design advice. • To Dean and Lisa Livelybrooks for their computer consultations. • To Faith Echtermeyer for inspiration that helped shape this book and her photograph on the back cover. • To Liz Johnson for her enthusiastic support and advice. • To Carol Bryan, Bill Cadbury, Lisa Livelybrooks, Barbara Rattenborg and Maxine Scates for reading the manuscript. • To Ryan Collay for Mac "style" lessons on a Saturday afternoon. • To Sharon Ottolia for her photograph on the back cover. • To Joey Blum for guiding the second edition of this cookbook.*

Credit and our gratitude for these recipes go to Alexandra's grandmother (who preferred not to be named), Emily Smith Baker, Shirley Eyler Baker, Andrea Barry Smith, Mary Jean Elizabeth Kumnick Bartlett, Maxwell Bartlett, Tom Beer, Gladys Biram Belden, Joy Post Bennett, Betty Higgins Benton, Barry Bingham, Edith Stenhouse Bingham, Laura Howell Smith Bissel, Joey Emil Blum, Nancy Connolly Blum, Ruby Emilia Blum, Samuel Emil Blum, Barbara Smith Brooks, Frances Rowins Bruce, Carol Weber Bryan, Mary Lou Bryant, Sally Gulsvig Cairnes-Wurster, Helen McCormick Church, Cissy Clay, Dora Donaldson Ekelund, Ruth Draheim, Faith Echtermeyer, Andy Erickson, Peg Spies Erickson, Anuncia Escala, Maya Escudero, Alan Etes, Anne Fisher, Angela Freeman Foster, Lee Ella "Leedy" Tipping Garrison, Ariadna Gil, Maribel Giner, Sally Harper, Pat Shaw Harris, AnnaDay Hiser, Elaine "Laney" Johnson House, Lynn Howell, Susan Elswick Howell, John Jones, Mrs. Kelly, Olga Monks Kimball, Bruce Klepinger, Lene Kolly, Story Bissel Kornbluth, Lorna Mabel Turpin Cram Kumnick, Bruce LeFavour, Pat Saaf LeFavour, Maureen Bender Levandowski, Marsha Lynn Lively, Norma Gene Garrison Lively, Solange Lively, Dean William Brooks Livelybrooks, Lisa Katheryn Lively Livelybrooks, Andy Loebelson, Ruth Kammerer Lord, Myrtle "Tee" Jones Luvisi, Scot MacBeth, Sofia Galson McManus, Henrietta Griffin McNeilly, Darnell Rudd Mandelblatt, Franklin Allen Manz, Marjorie Rowins Manz, Mrs. Jessie Miller, Mae Neal Manz, Elida Griffin Ogden, Mary Hyde Ottaway, Emma Ellis Owens, Kathryn "Kate" Frances Paisley, Elizabeth Strong Cowles Partridge, Caroline Morgan Passerotti, Karen Clingman Peterson, Lew & Cathy Phelps, Frances Le Forge Pfister, Maria Christina Raff Poetzinger, Ilse Strauch Rothschild Raff, Barbara Ana Rattenborg, Violet Ray, Betsy Green Rick, Margot Stewart, Lucille Stookesberry Rowins, Marian Bertina Loberg Rowins, Heidi Sachet, Maxine Scates, Paul Semonin, Emilie Strong Smith, Nicholas Smith, Alexandra Stepanian, Mardy Stonebeck, Susanna, Devon Trottier, Christian Leigh Watchie, Emily Miller Wells, Bill White & Fife Skobie Wickes. Also Shelley Canter, Edna Bielefeld, Loretta Eckert Mingram, Margaret Mackenzie, Liz Hawke Titus, Kathleen Comstock, Annie Fulkerson, Lin Cook Harpster, Bonnie Brown Hartley, Julie Hauck, Jacqueline Kaufman and Julia Carol Poetzinger.

> *The wonders keep piling up.*
>
> —Marjorie Manz
>
> A comment to her daughter, Catherine, several days before she "tipped over" in 1999.

Technical Notes & Update

A quick word about computers. They are not easy-to-operate machines, although some are easier than others. But computers accomplish an astounding amount of work very quickly. This cookbook is our first effort at "desktop publishing," using an Apple Macintosh in the home. This replaces the old system that required a string of specialists, including a layout artist, copy editor, typesetter and paste-up person. Our project soon overwhelmed our original computer, a Mac Plus, so we graduated to several times to the infinitely faster iMac G5 with large amounts of additional memory.

To join the computer world takes some dollars, some nerve and, most important, at least one or more computer pals — people who have similar hardware (computers, etc.) and software (programs) and are just a phone call away so they can answer your questions and keep you from the strait jacket.

If you are wondering how we chose our computer, here is the answer. Most machines can be divided into two categories, the Apple and IBM types. When I asked my friend Bill which was best for us, he said, "The Macintosh is for icon-oriented people; the IBM is for code-type people. You two are icon-types." We got a Macintosh and produced the cookbook, ready for the printers, on Microsoft Word 5.1 using Berkeley as a typeface.

It was Catherine who really made this book possible by learning the complexities of formatting, indexing, sizing and pagination — skills that require more patience and ability than her partner could muster.

Our computer pals were Ron Rick, graphics; Dean and Lisa Livelybrooks for many things and Robert Hewlett of MacTonic for everything else. Dean was on call for delivery of all 786,811 characters of the text of the first edition to the printer. The new edition has 706,194 characters. Chrissy Richards was the design and technical shepherd of the second edition.

SINCE 1998: Nicholas married Suzanne with her three "ready-mades," Jordan, Alex and Katya. • Tavi is working on a PhD in environmental physics at Colorado University. • Day Rose graduated from Yale and married Max. • Ruby is a junior at Seattle University. • Zoë is valedictorian of her class at Crow High School. • Madeline will row at the University of Wisconsin. • Emily and John Baker divorced carefully with their children in mind. • Mac, a joker and a good student, plays soccer and La Crosse. • Cole, also a good student, plays football. • Emmy is 101 years old and she sometimes feels like 1000. • Mum celebrated her 95th birthday. • The roof got replaced. • The porch rotted and got rebuilt. • There were three presidential elections, 9/11 and two wars. • Our cottonwood tree invaded the vegetable garden, then got roughed up by a storm and taken down. • Our new garden is a work in progress. • We lost Marjorie, Henrietta, Barry, Sally, Gladys, Margot, Dave, Rick, Milt, Harry, Susan, Lively, Ivy and Eve. • We gained Julia, Wilson, Tom, Lilli, Joel, Martin, Anna, Brad, Julie, Harper and Chrissy's new son Beckett • We created Bathtub Barbie and the Annex. • We shared lots of good meals, laughed, shed tears, learned some new lessons and re-learned some old ones. • We are grateful for every minute of every day. (December 2009)

Index

THE END?

*What bothers me though is that
none of it is ever final;
you can't ever finish anything.*

—Margaret Atwood

Index

Index

ANSWERS to Food Test on page 320:
1c; 2a, d; 3d; 4d; 5c; 6b; 7b, d; 8c.

Thank you for this happy ending.

LaVergne, TN USA
21 December 2010
209577LV00003B/2/P

9 781450 513722